THEATRE CLOSURE AND THE PARADOXICAL RISE OF ENGLISH RENAISSANCE DRAMA IN THE CIVIL WARS

Focusing on the production and reception of drama during the theatre closures of 1642 to 1660, Heidi Craig shows how the "death" of contemporary theatre in fact gave birth to English Renaissance drama as a critical field. While the prohibition on playing in many respects killed the English stage, drama thrived in print, with stationers publishing unprecedented numbers of previously unprinted professional plays. Stationers also anatomized the whole corpus of English drama, printing the first anthologies and comprehensive catalogues of drama. Craig captures this crucial turning-point in English theatre history with chapters on royalist nostalgia, clandestine theatrical revivals, Interregnum Shakespearean publication and a new reading of Beaumont and Fletcher's *A King and No King*.

HEIDI CRAIG is Assistant Professor of English at Texas A&M University, editor of the *World Shakespeare Bibliography*, and co-editor of *Early Modern Dramatic Paratexts*. She is the recipient of fellowships from the Huntington Library, Newberry Library, and Folger Shakespeare Library.

THEATRE CLOSURE AND THE PARADOXICAL RISE OF ENGLISH RENAISSANCE DRAMA IN THE CIVIL WARS

HEIDI CRAIG

Texas A&M University

CAMBRIDGE
UNIVERSITY PRESS

Shaftesbury Road, Cambridge CB2 8EA, United Kingdom

One Liberty Plaza, 20th Floor, New York, NY 10006, USA

477 Williamstown Road, Port Melbourne, VIC 3207, Australia

314–321, 3rd Floor, Plot 3, Splendor Forum, Jasola District Centre, New Delhi – 110025, India

103 Penang Road, #05–06/07, Visioncrest Commercial, Singapore 238467

Cambridge University Press is part of Cambridge University Press & Assessment, a department of the University of Cambridge.

We share the University's mission to contribute to society through the pursuit of education, learning and research at the highest international levels of excellence.

www.cambridge.org
Information on this title: www.cambridge.org/9781009224031

DOI: 10.1017/9781009224017

First published 2023

A catalogue record for this publication is available from the British Library.

Library of Congress Cataloging-in-Publication Data
NAMES: Craig, Heidi, author.
TITLE: Theatre closure and the paradoxical rise of English Renaissance drama / Heidi Craig.
DESCRIPTION: Cambridge ; New York, NY : Cambridge University Press, [2023] | Includes bibliographical references and index.
IDENTIFIERS: LCCN 2022034397 (print) | LCCN 2022034398 (ebook) | ISBN 9781009224031 (hardback) | ISBN 9781009224055 (paperback) | ISBN 9781009224017 (epub)
SUBJECTS: LCSH: Theater and society–England–History–17th century. | English drama–17th century–History and criticism. | Theater audiences–England–History–17th century. | Authors and readers–England–History–17th century.
CLASSIFICATION: LCC PN2592 .C73 2023 (print) | LCC PN2592 (ebook) | DDC 792.0942–dc23/eng/ 20220913
LC record available at https://lccn.loc.gov/2022034397
LC ebook record available at https://lccn.loc.gov/2022034398

ISBN 978-1-009-22403-1 Hardback

Contents

v

Figures

Acknowledgements

I have had the remarkable good fortune to know brilliant, generous people who have supported my work and me. It's a pleasure to acknowledge them here, even while knowing that these thanks are inadequate, incommensurate with all I have received. I am sure to forget someone important: if that's you, please excuse my omission and know that I am grateful for all you have done for me.

This book emerges from a dissertation completed at the University of Toronto, where Jeremy Lopez was a superlative dissertation supervisor and mentor. This book and my career would not have been possible without his intellectual exuberance, boundless energy, supreme generosity and astonishing support. Thank you.

My dissertation committee at the University of Toronto was roundly wonderful: I benefited from Marjorie Rubright's theoretical perspicacity and Holger Schott Syme's deep knowledge of early modern theatre. During my defense, Alan Galey, Lynne Magnusson, and external reader Marta Straznicky offered crucial, careful insights. My teachers, mentors, and friends at the University of Toronto enriched my graduate journey: John Astington, Arlynda Boyer, Stephen Coughlin, Cristina D'Amico, Jeff Espie, John Estabillo, David Galbraith, Jillian Harkness, Paul Harrison, Alex Hernandez, Deni Kasa, Jonathan Kerr, Katherine Vitale Lopez, Heather Murray, Anthony Oliveira, Julie Prior, Matt Riesling, Katherine Shwetz, Sarah Star, Paul Stevens, Adie Todd, Audrey Walton, Christopher Warley and Dan White. My teachers at the University of St Andrews and Concordia University's Liberal Arts College established an intellectual foundation which continues to bolster me: Andrew Murphy, the late Barbara A. Murray, Neil Rhodes, Lorna Hutson, Alex Davis, Philip Parry, Ariela Freedman, Katharine Streip, Frederick Krantz, Mark Russell, Eric Buzzetti, the late Virginia Nixon, and Geoffrey Fidler.

Early on in my academic career, I lucked into a Folger year-long dissertation seminar led by Jean E. Howard and Pamela H. Smith, from whom I learned alongside a smart and collegial cohort: Charlotte Buechler, Joseph Bowling, Alexis Butzner, Dean Clement, Rachel Dunn, Jonathan Holmes, Andrew Miller, Victoria Muñoz and Aaron Pratt. The book project was supported by generous short- and long-term fellowships from the Huntington Library in 2015 and Folger Shakespeare Library in 2018-19, respectively, where the wealth of their holdings are rivalled only by the extraordinary community of scholars, librarians and staff members I had the pleasure of knowing: Faith D. Acker, Patricia Akhimie, Betul Basaran, Anna Riehl Bertolet, Liza Blake, Claire M. L. Bourne, Claire Bowditch, Heidi Brayman, Meaghan J. Brown, Sophie Byvik, Urvashi Chakravarty, Thomas Cogswell, Bradin Cormack, Rachel Dankert, LuEllen DeHaven, Carla Della Gatta, Adhaar Noor Desai, Ross Duffin, Holly Dugan, Raffaella Fabiani Giannetto, Alan B. Farmer, Andy Fleck, Jessica Frazier, Amanda Herbert, Steve Hindle, Elaine Hobby, Penelope Geng, David Goldstein, Musa Gurnis, Heather James, Eric Johnson, Laurie Johnson, Paulina Kewes, Nancy Klein Maguire, Roslyn Knutson, Douglas Lanier, Rebecca Laroche, Victor Lenthe, Zachary Lesser, Kathleen Lynch, Jack Lynch, Dianne Mitchell, Erin McCarthy, Jason McElligott, Bénédicte Miyamoto, Lucy Munro, Simon Newman, Sarah Neville, Deborah Payne, Sara Pennell, Chelsea Philips, Peter Radford, Stacey Redick, Camille Seerattan, Diana Solomon, Mihoko Suzuki, Marjorie Swann, Elisa Tersigni, Scott Trudell, Stacie Vos, Kathryn Vomero Santos, Abbie Weinberg, Sarah Werner, Owen Williams, Heather Wolfe, Jennifer Wood and Georgianna Ziegler. This comically long list conveys what a great time I had with you in LA and DC: thank you for your friendship, erudition, and encouragement, which sustained me during my time as a peripatetic scholar.

I'm grateful for the opportunities and invitations to try out this book's various ideas at conferences and in edited collections over the years: thanks in particular to Mark Bayer, Cat Clifford, Jeffrey Doty, Lukas Erne, Rory Loughnane, Ivan Lupić, Tara L. Lyons, Christopher Matusiak, Joshua McEvilla, Joseph Navisky, Harry Newman, Richard Priess, Eoin Price, Devani Singh, Tiffany Stern, Jitka Štollová, Jacqueline Vanhoutte, and Mary Erica Zimmer. David McInnis generously shared his work with me prior to publication; Marissa Nicosia and Misha Teramura pointed me in the right direction, showing me materials I would have otherwise missed. Covering all of these above categories are Emma Depledge and Rachel Willie, from whose work on mid-seventeenth century drama I have learned so much, and whose encouragement has meant the world. Laura Estill, Jonathan Goldberg, Sonia Massai, and Valerie Wayne have gone out of their way to support me in many ways, for many years now, and I am so grateful to them.

Thanks are due to Joseph Gamble, Megan Heffernan, Megan Herrold, Adam G. Hooks, Alexander Paulsson Lash, Emily Shortslef, Katherine Walker and Benjamin VanWagoner, for both reading portions of the manuscript and for providing consistently excellent company. Late in the writing process, the universe blessed me with Molly G. Yarn as editor, copy-editor, and indexer. She helped me finally get this book out the door. I'm grateful to two anonymous readers at Cambridge University Press for their incisive comments and suggestions. Thank you to Emily Hockley, who was a patient, kind, smart editor. Thanks also to Cambridge University Press's Anand Gurusamy and Marijasintha Jacob Srinivasan and the rest of the editorial team who worked on the manuscript. Any mistakes that remain are mine alone. An early version of Chapter 2 was published as "Missing Shakespeare, 1642–1660" in *English Literary Renaissance* and is reproduced here with permission.

I began this project in my graduate salad days, when I was green in judgement, but I finished it in maroon, as an assistant professor at Texas A&M University. I could not ask for better colleagues than Joshua DiCaglio, Sara DiCaglio, Ira Dworkin, Amy Earhart, Marcela Fuentes, Emily Johansen, Lauren Liebe, Regina Mills, Britt Mize, Anne Morey, Mary Ann O'Farrell, Kevin O'Sullivan, Andrew Pilsch, Sarah Potvin, Sally Robinson, Shawna Ross, Bryan Tarpley, Apostolos Vasilakis and David McWhirter. Susan Egenolf recommended the Faculty Success Program and served as a program mentor. Maura Ives was a wonderfully supportive and edifying department head. Working alongside Margaret Ezell and Laura Mandell has been a true pleasure; each is a titan of their respective fields whose intellect is rivalled only by their conviviality. At the *World Shakespeare Bibliography*, it's an honour to work with Kris L. May and Katayoun Torabi, and with Dorothy Todd, who has been a dear friend for several years now. I'm grateful to the Melbern G. Glasscock Center for Humanities Research for a Glasscock Publication Support Grant, to the ADVANCE NCFDD Faculty Success Program for my FSP fellowship, to the Department of English for imaging costs and other research support, and to Dalaiah Eiland and Leah Speelman for administrative support.

Finally, I owe my deepest gratitude to my family. My parents, Sue and Ian Craig, and my sisters, Nadia and Julie Craig, have unstintingly loved, supported, and humoured me from the very beginning. The addition of Ben, Josephine, and Harrison Waldman and Dave and Roger Bourdon to the immediate family has been a wonderful thing. My jovial and generous extended Craig family sustained me before, during and after the writing process: Sheila and Tim Casgrain, Judy and John Groves, Alynn Casgrain and David Upper, Andrew and Lindsey Groves, Sean and Melanie Casgrain took good care of me in Toronto. Uncle "Eh" Andrew Craig encouraged me in my poetic pursuits; Jeff and Christine Groves and Stuart Casgrain and Élodie Champoux provided good times in NY and Montreal. My Winder aunts, uncles and cousins – Christy Winder and Tim, Dave, Jessica, Ryan and Emma Henry, Barb Winder and Norm, Andrew, Taylor, Brooke and Nicole Rathie, Michelle Winder and Mike Sims, and the late, dearly missed Jennifer Winder – all cheered me on, and I dearly appreciate it. My family extends beyond bloodties: Julie and the late, dearly missed Paul Grech supported me from day one. I met Erin O'Donnell in Montreal, lived with her in LA, and am so glad to know her still. Isaac Stephens and Kathleen McGuire were great friends in DC, in the US South, and in Zoomland during the pandemic. Already blessed with a big, beautiful, boisterous family, I happily married into another one: thank you to the Howards, Bartletts and Listers, all of awesome aunts, uncles, cousins and kids, especially to Amy and Leah Bartlett and Abe Greenspoon, who ensured I had fun even in the depths of writing, and to Katharine Howard and Nate Charlow, and Veronica Howard and Daniel Bernhardt, my splendid new cousins in Toronto. I completed a crucial period of the writing process in COVID lockdown living with my in-laws, Francie and Lance Howard, who were extraordinarily generous with their home, thoughts, and love. Typical of Howard conscientiousness, their granddaughter and our daughter, Pascale Susan, considerately arrived the day after I submitted my manuscript to the press; she is a miracle and a marvel. Last and most of all, my husband Nathan Howard has been an unwavering source of love, kindness, support, and utter brilliance. He is so good, and really just the best. This book is for him.

Introduction
Survivors of the Stage

In *Pleasant Notes upon Don Quixot* (1654), printed twelve years after a Parliamentary ordinance outlawed the public performance of plays, Edmund Gayton mourns the loss of "our late stage" and celebrates the endurance of printed playbooks, which

> [s]tand firme, and are read with as much satisfaction as when presented on the stage, they were with applause and honour. Indeed, their names now may be very wel chang'd & call'd the works not playes of *Iohnson, Beaumont and Fletcher, Cartwright*, and the rest, which are survivers of the stage.[1]

The closure of the theatres finally settled an old aesthetic controversy. Four decades prior, Ben Jonson was mocked for naming his play collection *Works* (1616); by 1640, his presumption was still a target for derision: "Pray tell me *Ben*, where doth the mistery lurke, / What others call a play you call a work."[2] In 1654, Gayton affirms the "works" label and its claims for the drama's enduring value, not only for Jonson but also for Francis Beaumont and John Fletcher, and William Cartwright (all of whom had been recently published in posthumous dramatic collections), as well as "the rest," a locution that consolidates a wide range of unnamed dramatists into a coherent group. Gayton does not say that the "works" label for plays was always valid. Rather, he locates English drama's transformation in the present moment, that plays' "names *now* may be . . . *chang'd*" into works. The catalyst of this transformation is the theatrical prohibition itself, which spurred theatrical nostalgia, print publication, and play-reading, all crucial factors in English drama's cultural ascendancy. From the perspective of 1654, the recalled theatre is not morally dubious, but is associated with "applause and honour," able to both entertain and edify. Gayton pronounces the theatre dead, but the dramatic work has escaped

---

[1] Edmund Gayton, *Pleasant Notes upon Don Quixot* (London: William Hunt, 1654), p. 273.
[2] *Wit's Recreation* (London: Humphry Blunden, 1640), sig. G3v.

alive, "standing firm" in print and supplying similar satisfactions to the reader as it once did to the playgoer. Playbooks are what remain of an idealized theatrical culture, now extinct: the treasured "survivors" of the "late stage."

On 2 September 1642, English Parliament banned public performance with an ordinance stating that "[p]ublic Stage-plays ... being Spectacles of Pleasure, too commonly expressing lascivious Mirth and Levity," do not agree "with the Seasons of Humiliation" and ordering that "[p]ublic Stage Plays shall cease, and be forborn."[3] This order was issued shortly after the outbreak of the first English Civil War, which had started two weeks earlier, on 24 August 1642. Criticism traditionally regarded the theatrical ordinance as the culmination of a long-standing anti-theatrical grudge borne by the Puritans who dominated Parliament in the mid seventeenth century. Later critics described the ordinance as a pragmatic attempt to establish public safety in a volatile moment by discouraging large gatherings of people.[4] Even more recently, these revisionist accounts have themselves been revised. N. W. Bawcutt notes that, although characterizing the theatrical prohibition as a "Puritan ban" on theatre oversimplifies things, ideology did motivate the 1642 closures.[5] The architect of the ordinance was Francis Rous, a committed Calvinist who characterized playhouses as "Churches of Satan" and advocated the replacement of "lascivious" stage plays with fasting.[6]

No matter Parliament's intention, however, the ordinance of 1642 immediately and lastingly devastated the English theatre industry. Initially framed as a temporary measure, active "while these sad causes and set Times of Humiliation do continue," public performance was banned in England for eighteen years, throughout the English Civil Wars (1642–51) and Interregnum (1649–60), until both English theatre and the monarchy were restored in 1660. It is true that the public stage was never fully silenced; illegal performances continued in London and in the provinces across this period. Yet illegal performance, undertaken in reduced

---

[3] "Order for Stage-Playes to Cease," in *Acts and Ordinances of the Interregnum, 1642–1660*, ed. C. H. Firth and R. S. Rait (London: His Majesty's Stationery Office, 1911), pp. 26–7.

[4] Martin Butler, *Theatre and Crisis 1632–1642* (Cambridge: Cambridge University Press, 1984), pp. 1–24.

[5] N. W. Bawcutt, "Puritanism and the Closing of the Theaters in 1642," *Medieval and Renaissance Drama in England*, 22 (2009), 179–200 (p. 200).

[6] Christopher Matusiak, "Elizabeth Beeston, Sir Lewis Kirke, and the Cockpit's Management during the English Civil Wars," *Medieval and Renaissance Drama in England*, 27 (2014), 161–91.

theatrical circumstances and subject to punishing raids, could not compare with the economically and creatively vibrant theatrical tradition prior to 1642. The theatrical prohibition effectively eliminated acting and play-writing as viable professions. Gayton's remarks exemplify how the closure of the theatres was described as a form of cultural death in the mid seventeenth century. For eighteen years, the dramatic text was the only legitimate way to consume professional plays, that is, plays produced for the commercial theatres and staged by professional actors starting around 1567, when the first purpose-built theatre was constructed. English playbooks printed after 1642 simultaneously gestured to the death of theatre and enabled the drama to survive.

Theatre Closure and the Paradoxical Rise of English Renaissance Drama in the Civil Wars offers a posthumous history of early modern professional drama during the eighteen-year theatrical prohibition. Despite the pervasive metaphor about the death of theatre, English drama did not disappear during the Interregnum. Nor did the prohibition cause people to simply forget about the professional theatrical tradition of the late sixteenth and early seventeenth centuries. Indeed, the opposite occurred. Far from being a dramatic dead zone, the era of the theatre ban was a time of intense dramatic production, innovation, and reflection – on the stage, on the page, and in the cultural imagination. Newly rare and illicit, theatrical activity was increasingly prized among theatre practitioners and aficionados; actors and spectators risked imprisonment and steep fines to stage and attend clandestine performances. The decline of theatrical infrastructure and threat of raids led to the advent of a new theatrical form, the "droll": short playlets extracted from professional plays that could be staged cheaply and quickly. In the book market, English drama thrived. There was a surge in first editions of professional plays, reversing the publication trends of the previous four decades. The period witnessed the invention of several new English dramatic forms in print – the first serialized play collection, the first dramatic anthology, the first comprehensive bibliography of English plays in print – and the proliferation of dramatic commentary in paratexts. Yet even as it appeared in novel forms, English professional drama was associated with a quickly receding cultural past. That 1642 was seen to mark the death of English theatre provided contemporaries with critical distance and a sense of historical otherness that enabled them to take stock of their own theatrical past. This led to pre-1642 drama – what we now call "Renaissance" or "early modern" drama – being viewed as a distinct genre and critical field.

"Old Plays" from "The Last Age"

The year 1642 was regarded as a historical breach. Critics have noted that "the last age" was a phrase consistently used after 1660 to describe the political and cultural life of the pre-1642 period.[7] In *Historia Histrionica* (1699), James Wright's nostalgic dialogue on theatre history, the speaker Lovewit wishes that "they had Printed in the last Age (so I call the times before the Rebellion) the Actors names over the Parts they Acted, as they have done since the Restauration. And thus one might have guest at the Action of the men, by the Parts which we now read in the Old plays."[8] The "last age" is here defined politically (the moment "before the Rebellion") but also in terms of dramatic culture, as a theatrical moment not adequately materialized by print culture: Wright wishes that playbooks printed before 1642 included cast lists (as Restoration playbooks tended to do), to give insights into the performances of long-gone actors. That playbooks printed "before the Rebellion" usually omitted lists of actors' names alongside their parts represents a lost opportunity, a missing historical artefact that cannot be retrieved. Most importantly, Wright's dialogue reveals a conception of a dramatic category linked to a particular period: "old plays" from the "last age." We see similar references across the post-1660 period: as their titles hint, John Dryden's *Essay on the Dramatic Poetry of the Last Age* (1672), appended to his *Conquest of Grenada*, and Thomas Rymer's *Tragedies of the Last Age* (1678) each present the drama of Shakespeare, Fletcher, Jonson, and their dramatic contemporaries as a distinct category of plays from a bygone era. Dryden elsewhere refers to pre-1642 dramatists as an antediluvian breed sundered by a historical cataclysm: "the Gyant Race, before the Flood."[9] When the public theatre resumed in 1660, the pre-1642 plays divided between Thomas Killigrew's King's Company and William Davenant's Duke's Company were called

---

[7] See "The Last Age," in David Haley, *Dryden and the Problem of Freedom: The Republican Aftermath, 1649–1680* (New Haven: Yale University Press, 1997), pp. 140–72; Jack Lynch, *The Age of Elizabeth in the Age of Johnson* (Cambridge: Cambridge University Press, 2003), pp. 7–8, pp. 143–64; Paul Hammond, "The Restoration Poetic and Dramatic Canon," in *The Cambridge History of the Book in Britain: Volume IV, 1557–1695*, ed. John Barnard and D. F. McKenzie with Maureen Bell (Cambridge: Cambridge University Press, 2002), pp. 388–409 (pp. 390–1).

[8] James Wright, Historia Histrionica: An Historical Account of the English Stage, *Shewing the Ancient Use, Improvement and Perfection of Dramatick Representations in This Nation in a Dialogue of Plays and Players* (London: William Haws, 1699), p. 3.

[9] John Dryden, "To My Dear Friend Mr. Congreve on His Comedy Call'd the *Double Dealer*," in William Congreve, *The Double Dealer* (London: Jacob Tonson, 1694), sig. a2r–v. See Gunnar Sorelius, *'The Giant Race before the Flood': Pre-Restoration Drama on the Stage and in the Criticism of the Restoration* (Uppsala: Almqvist & Wiksell, 1966).

"Principal Old Stock Plays."[10] The designation of "old plays" was not only a critical term deployed by drama critics like Dryden and Rymer, or a means for theatre managers to organize their offerings. The wider public also conceived of pre-1642 plays as a distinct category, as we see from John Evelyn's diary entry of 1661 in reference to *Hamlet*: "Now the old plays begin to disgust this refined age."[11]

References to "old plays" from the "last age" as a way to conceptualize pre-1642 drama were pervasive after 1660. Yet the notion (if not the specific language) of the pre-1642 period as the "last age" was also apparent during the 1640s and 1650s. The perception of historical distance is plastic; once a critical rupture is perceived, even temporally recent moments can seem distant.[12] Critics observe how the violent political, social, and cultural upheaval of the English Reformation produced a sense of historical discontinuity and contrast that came to be seen as the divide between the medieval and early modern periods. Tim Harris observes that historical periods "reflect patterns that have become discernible only from the vantage of hindsight."[13] It is suggested by the etymology of "period," meaning "to terminate": crucial to periodization is the sense of a clearly demarcated end.[14] The first decades of the 1500s came to be regarded by contemporaries as a physical and institutional break with the past; the moment immediately prior came to be seen as "something distant and sharply *different*" as James Simpson explains.[15] As commentators both then and now have noted, the early 1640s effected changes comparable to the Reformation. Thanks to the palpable destruction wreaked by the English Revolution, individuals in the

---

[10] John Downes, *Roscius Anglicanus* (London: H. Playford, 1708), p. 9.

[11] John Evelyn, *The Diary of John Evelyn*, ed. E. S. de Beer, 6 vols. (Oxford: Clarendon Press, 1955), III, p. 304 (26 November 1661).

[12] Angus Vine, *In Defiance of Time: Antiquarian Writing in Early Modern England* (Oxford: Oxford University Press, 2013), p. 17. See also Lucien Febvre's notion of the "passé imprecis" in *Le Problem de l'incroyance au XVIe siècle: La religion de Rabelais* (Paris: Editions Alain Michel, 1948), pp. 432–3.

[13] Tim Harris, "Periodizing the Early Modern: The Historian's View," in *Early Modern Histories of Time*, ed. Owen Williams and Kristen Poole (Philadelphia: University of Pennsylvania Press, 2019), pp. 21–35 (p. 22).

[14] Nigel Smith, "Time Boundaries and Time Shifts in Early Modern Literary Studies," in *Early Modern Histories of Time*, ed. Owen Williams and Kirsten Poole, pp. 36–53 (p. 37).

[15] James Simpson, "Ageism: Leland, Bale and the Laborious Start of English Literary History, 1350–1550," *New Medieval Literatures* 1 (1997), 213–35 (p. 221). On creation of divide between the medieval and early modern periods, see Margreta de Grazia, "The Modern Divide: From Either Side," *Journal of Medieval and Early Modern Studies*, 37.7 (2007), 453–67; Brian Cummings and James Simpson, eds., *Cultural Reformations: Medieval and Renaissance in Literary History* (Oxford: Oxford University Press, 2010); Alexandra Walsham, "History, Memory, and the English Reformation," *The Historical Journal*, 55.4 (2012), 899–938. On periodization, see Ted Underwood, *Why Literary Periods Mattered: Historical Contrast and the Prestige of English Studies* (Stanford: Stanford University Press, 2013).

1640s and 1650s had a sense of living through a moment of abrupt historical change, and of the fundamental alterity of the preceding period, which was chronologically close but culturally distant. Contemporaries conceived of a difference between their present and the past conceived as such, as a moment existing on the other side of a historical watershed.

While references to the "last age" are limited between 1642 and 1660, the period offers many references to "old plays." A report of an illegal performance of Beaumont and Fletcher's *A King and No King* in 1647 states that the players were "playing the old play."[16] The Puritan John Rowe describes a disastrous provincial performance of *Mucedorus* in 1653 by stating, "This Play was an old Play, and had been Acted by some of Santon-Har-court men many years since."[17] The first edition of the pre-1642 professional play titled *The Queen* (1653) is called an "Excellent old play" on its title page. Even though *A King and No King*, *Mucedorus*, and *The Queen* were in active circulation on stage and in print in the Interregnum, they were classified as "old plays" because the moment in which they were created was seen to be over. The sense of a dramatic watershed helped create the impression of broader historical watershed: that is, part of the formulation of the "last age" as a general term for pre-1642 England was the fact that it was the cultural home to "old plays."

The closure of the theatres prematurely aged English professional drama as a class of texts, rendering the drama newly venerable and consolidating the wide variety of plays from the previous seven decades into a select grouping. "Old plays from the last age" turned out to be an enduring dramatic category – at least, the plays embraced by that label continue to be thought of as a coherent group, now called "Renaissance" or "early modern" drama, or plays from "Shakespeare's time."[18] In this book, the label "pre-1642 drama" is mostly used for clarity, but "early modern" and "Renaissance" are also used; while these specific labels are anachronistic

---

[16] *Mercurius Pragmaticus*, 5–12 October 1647.

[17] John Rowe, *Tragicomoedia, or a Relation of the Wonderful Hand of God at Witney* (Oxford: Henry Cripps, 1653), sig. ¶4v.

[18] Tracing the rise of these later designations for English drama is beyond the scope of this book. But Jakob Burckhardt's *The Civilization of the Renaissance in Italy* (1860) conceived of the "Renaissance" as the rebirth of individuality and subjectivity in line with the cultures of classical antiquity. Referring to Shakespeare as a "renaissance dramatist" emphasized his use of classical dramatic genres, tragedy and comedy and classical sources like Plutarch. The critical term "early modern" gained traction in the 1980s with the advent of New Historicism, which sought to incorporate literary study into a wider account of politics, economics, and history as part of understanding modernity. See David Wiles, "Medieval, Renaissance and Early Modern Theatre," in *The Cambridge Companion to Theatre History*, ed. David Wiles and Christine Dymkowski (Cambridge: Cambridge University Press, 2012), pp. 55–72 (pp. 63–4).

insofar as they were not used in the 1640s and 1650s, they are useful as current critical terms that correspond to a category of drama emerging in the mid seventeenth century. No matter what we call it, the dramatic category and field of study bound by the theatre closures in 1642 has remained remarkably consistent since the 1640s. As Ellen MacKay notes, "the terminus of the English stage's 'golden age' is uncommonly absolute – no date serves the turn of dramatic periodization better than 1642."[19] Martin Wiggins argues that the year 1642 "sliced" dramatic culture like a "guillotine," connecting the stark finality of the theatre closures with the execution of King Charles I, seven years later.[20] As we shall see, contemporaries made the same connection between theatrical and political life in the 1640s and 1650s. Conceiving of a distinct dramatic category defined by 1642 as a terminal boundary is a legacy of mid seventeenth-century discourse.

If the pre-1642 period is the "last age," what about the period from 1642 to 60? Partly because 1642 has served as a reliable period boundary for so long, drama scholars often ignore the subsequent eighteen years, regarding this period as a cultural vacuum.[21] Susan Wiseman observes that, for drama scholars, discussion of the theatrical ordinance of 1642 often replaces study of the next eighteen years.[22] In fact, dramatic publication and performance continued throughout the period, and dramatic criticism flourished like never before. In the 1640s and 1650s, we see the first sustained body of inquiry of the English theatrical and dramatic "past" conceived as the past. The notion that the pre-1642 period represented a distinct cultural moment – the "last age" – with a discrete collection of plays ("old plays") paved the way for a coherent system of critical study and disciplinary analysis.

Crucial to this development was the pervasive sense of cultural loss: a sense of decline spurs an urge to preserve the past. The historiographical impulse gains particular urgency in moments of perceived widespread destruction: "ruins may make historians," as Margaret Aston pithily puts it.[23] This monograph draws on theories about the relationships between

---

[19] Ellen MacKay, *Persecution, Plague and Fire: Fugitive Histories of the Stage in Early Modern England* (Chicago: University of Chicago Press, 2011), p. 196.
[20] Martin Wiggins, "Where to Find Lost Plays," in *Lost Plays in Shakespeare's England*, ed. David McInnis and Matthew Steggle (Basingstoke: Palgrave Macmillan, 2014), pp. 255–78 (p. 264).
[21] Susan Wiseman, *Drama and Politics in the English Civil War* (Cambridge: Cambridge University Press, 1998), pp. 1–16; Margaret J. M. Ezell, *The Oxford English Literary History, Volume V: 1645–1714: The Later Seventeenth Century* (Oxford: Oxford University Press, 2017), p. xviii.
[22] Wiseman, *Drama and Politics*, pp. 1–2.
[23] Margaret Aston, "English Ruins and English History: The Dissolution and the Sense of the Past," *Journal of the Warburg and Courtauld Institutes*, 36 (1973), 231–55 (pp. 231–2).

loss, death, desire, and historiography.[24] Censorship inevitably calls more
attention to that which is suppressed; people are powerfully motivated to
seek out that which is denied to them.[25] Susan Stewart notes that "nostalgia cannot be sustained without loss," suggesting how absence prompts
idealization.[26] Jonathan Kramnick notes nostalgia's role in any emerging
sense of periodization, arguing that "the present understands itself in terms
of a past from which it has broken and toward which it casts a longing
glance."[27] Adriana Cavarero argues that biography only becomes complete
at the moment of death,[28] recognizing that some measure of closure is
necessary before one can generate historical narratives. Mark Salber
Phillips notes that a perception of "critical distance" is necessary for the
practice of historiography,[29] while Lucy Munro notes the importance of
historical "otherness" and contrast to establish cultural archaism.[30] The
pervasive impression of the death of theatre after 1642 spurred dramatic
and theatrical historiography. The allied processes of recollection (in
incipient forms of theatre history and dramatic criticism) and collection
(the frenetic publication of full-length plays and creation of dramatic
compendia) were material substitutes for the lost theatrical past. As theatrical traditions, practitioners, and buildings were swept away, they entered
the realm of the idealized historical imagination.

[24] Jacques Lacan, "La Direction de la Cure," in *Ecrits* (Paris: Editions du Seuil, 1966), p. 642; Richard
 Boothby, *Death and Desire (RLE: Lacan): Psychoanalytic Theory in Lacan's Return to Freud* (New
 York: Routledge, 1991); Michel Foucault, *Les mots et les choses* (Paris: Editions Gallimard, 1966),
 pp. 376, 387; Jonathan Dollimore, *Death, Desire and Loss in Western Culture* (London: Taylor &
 Francis, 1998); Graham Holderness, "'I Covet your Skull': Death and Desire in *Hamlet*," in
 Shakespeare Survey, vol. 60, ed. Peter Holland (Cambridge: Cambridge University Press, 2017),
 pp. 224–37; Douglas Beecher, "Nostalgia and the Renaissance Romance," *Philosophy and
 Literature*, 34.2 (2010), 281–301 (pp. 285–6); Harriet Philips, *Nostalgia in Print and
 Performance, 1510–1613* (Cambridge: Cambridge University Press, 2019); Svetlana Boym, *The
 Future of Nostalgia* (New York: Basic Books, 2002).
[25] Michael Holquist, "Corrupt Originals: The Paradox of Censorship," *Papers of the Modern Language
 Association*, 109.1 (1994), 14–25 (p. 14).
[26] Susan Stewart, *On Longing: Narratives of the Miniature, the Gigantic, the Souvenir, the Collection*
 (Durham: Duke University Press, 1992), p. 145.
[27] Jonathan Brody Kramnick, *Making the English Canon: Print-Capitalism and the Cultural Past*
 (Cambridge: Cambridge University Press, 1998), p. 53.
[28] Adriana Cavarero, *Relating Narratives: Storytelling and Selfhood* (New York: Routledge, 2000),
 pp. 12–13. See also Andrew Griffin's *Untimely Deaths in Renaissance Drama: Biography, History,
 Catastrophe* (Toronto: University of Toronto Press, 2019); Michael Neill, *Issues of Death: Mortality
 and Identity in English Renaissance Tragedy* (Oxford: Oxford University Press, 1997); Frank
 Kermode, *Sense of an Ending: Studies in Theory of Fiction* (Oxford: Oxford University
 Press, 1967).
[29] Mark Salber Phillips, *On Historical Distance* (New Haven: Yale University Press, 2013).
[30] Lucy Munro, *Archaic Style in English Literature, 1590–1674* (Cambridge: Cambridge University
 Press, 2013).

Theatre Closure posits a conceptual overlap between the play as a "corpse" (or "body," "relic," or "remnant") and the emergence of a corpus of "old" or "dead" plays.[31] Memorial dramatic editions printed before 1642 gathered the "remnants" of stage plays into published collections, and provide an important analogue for printed drama after the closure of the theatres. In the First Shakespeare Folio of 1623, Ben Jonson elegized the "Memory of My Beloved the Author," the late Shakespeare, and characterized his textual corpus as "what he hath left us." Just as the death of the individual dramatist established the conditions of his canonization and the collection of his corpus, so too was the literary elevation and corporatization of English professional drama a posthumous phenomenon. After 1642, an entire theatrical tradition was memorialized, with printed drama regarded as its priceless bequest. In his commendatory poem to Beaumont and Fletcher's first folio (1647), Roger L'Estrange suggests how the closure disrupted the *topos* of literary immortality that is a conventional feature of memorial volumes: "Beaumont and Fletcher: Return'd? Methinks it should not be / No, not in's works: plays are as dead as he."[32] Beaumont and Fletcher are dead, but so too is the stage. Without the vitality of embodied performance, the playbook is simply a corpse. But the Beaumont and Fletcher folio of 1647 is offered as a handsome volume that largely completes the Beaumont and Fletcher authorial corpus (Figure I.1). From the corpse of English professional theatre, the corpus of English Renaissance drama sprouted and bloomed.

Theatre Closure and Theatrical Decline

The closure of the theatres immediately compromised the livelihoods of theatre professionals. In *The Actors Remonstrance or Complaint, for the Silencing of Their Profession, and Banishment from Their Severall Play Houses* (1643), the anonymous author complains of the economic fallout following the theatrical ordinance. Having lost the "Profession which had before maintained us in comely and convenient Equipage," actors are now "left to live upon our shifts, or the expence of our former gettings, to the

---

[31] On analogy between "corpse" and "corpus", see Susan Zimmerman in *The Early Modern Corpse and Shakespeare's Theatre* (Edinburgh: Edinburgh University Press, 2005); Thea Cervone, "The Corpse as Text: The Polemics of Memory and the Deaths of Charles I and Oliver Cromwell," *Preternature: Critical and Historical Studies on the Preternatural*, 2.1 (2013), 47–72 (pp. 48–9).

[32] Roger L'Estrange, "On the Edition of Mr Francis Beaumonts, and Mr John Fletchers PLAYES Never Printed Before," in Francis Beaumont and John Fletcher, *Comedies and Tragedies* (London: Humphrey Moseley and Humphrey Robinson, 1647), sig. c1r.

Figure I.1   Frontispiece and title page from Francis Beaumont and John Fletcher,
Comedies and Tragedies (Humphrey Moseley and Humphrey Robinson, 1647).
Courtesy of the Folger Shakespeare Library.

great impoverishment and utter undoing of ourselves, wives, children, and dependents."[33] The economic damage extended beyond actors and their families, to playwrights, doorkeepers, and musicians, to the "tiremen" and others who worked behind the scenes on costumes, wigs, and props,[34] to the "tobacco-men" and others who sold items and services to spectators. The author fears that the industry will never recover, noting that "such a terrible distresse and dissolution hath befallen us, and all those that had dependance on the stage that it hath quite unmade our hopes of future recoverie."[35] Such pessimism, however, is belied by the intended function of the petition, which requests permission to resume playing. Had the

---

[33] *The Actors Remonstrance or Complaint, for the Silencing of Their Profession, and Banishment from Their Severall Play Houses* (London: Edward Nickson, 1643), p. 4.

[34] On theatrical labours, see Natasha Korda, *Labour's Lost: Women's Work and the Early Modern English Stage* (Philadelphia: University of Pennsylvania Press, 2011).

[35] *The Actors Remonstrance*, p. 4.

request of 1643 been quickly granted, parts of the theatre industry could probably have picked up more or less where it left off.

Worries about permanent theatre closure or the industry's inability to recover would have seemed hyperbolic in 1643. The 1642 closure was initially understood as a temporary response to an immediate crisis, akin to the familiar plague closures. Across its seven-decade history, the English theatre industry frequently endured months-long closures that sometimes extended into years. As recently as 1636–7, the playhouses had remained shuttered for eighteen months. After a plague outbreak closed the London playhouses in 1641, *The Stage Players Complaint* (1641) expresses the same sort of worries that would be uttered two years later in *The Actors Remonstrance*. The stage player reminisces about happier days "when my heeles have capoured over the stage," and concludes that "(alas) we must looke for no more of these times I feare."[36] In 1641, this fear proved to be unfounded, as the theatres eventually reopened. To be sure, extended plague closures were extremely disruptive to theatre companies: some folded altogether, and personnel and practices were shuffled. Yet, prior to 1642, even if individual companies perished, the theatre industry as a whole had always rebounded. In the mid-1640s, no one could have anticipated how long the playhouses would remain closed. *The Actors Remonstrance*'s ostensibly exaggerated fear that English theatre was "con-demned to a perpetuall, at least a very long temporary silence" turned out to be true.

Already compromised in 1643, the theatre industry sank still further in the years that followed, due both to deliberate governmental attacks on theatre and the inevitable decline that attended an industry with no reliable producers or consumers. Although playing "virtually ceased" dur-ing the first English Civil War (1642–6),[37] illegal performance seems to have become a frequent occurrence in London in 1647 and 1648, as evidenced partly by the fact that Parliament felt compelled to renew the ordinance against playing four times, on 16 July 1647, 11 August 1647, 22 October 1647, and 9 February 1648. The last renewal, "An Ordinance for the utter suppression and abolishing of all Stage-Plays and Interludes," made plain its intention to shutter the theatres permanently on the grounds of immorality, warning that stage plays attract "the high provo-cation of Gods wrath and displeasure" and are not to be "tolerated

---

[36] *The Stage Players Complaint* (London: Thomas Bates, 1641), sig. A3r.
[37] Judith Milhous and Robert D. Hume, "New Light on English Acting Companies in 1646, 1648, and 1660," *Review of English Studies*, 42 (1991), 487–509.

amongst Professors of the Christian Religion."[38] While the original order of 1642 represented a "rapid response to a dangerous situation," rather than the culmination of Parliament's campaign against theatre, as Susan Wiseman notes, the evidence suggests that "the edict of 1642 *turned into* a campaign as the wars went on."[39] In 1652, Richard Brome characterized the prohibition as an "epidemical ruin of the scene," capturing the long-standing affinity between the plague closures and mid-century ones (indeed, the plague was also understood by some as evidence of God's wrath for England's immorality), but also revealing that the damage to the scene was not temporary, but ruinous.[40]

The raids of illicit performances highlight the incredible risks people took to satisfy their desire for theatrical entertainment and to practice their chosen profession. The Sheriffs of London or the Parliamentary army ambushed performances, seizing costumes and profits from ticket sales, fining and jailing players and spectators, and, in some cases, pressing them into the army.[41] The extent to which the newsbooks dwell upon the seizure of costumes suggests how vexing this particular loss was for the players.[42] The threat that raids posed to actors' livelihoods led to the emergence of drolls, which could be staged quickly, lessening the chance that performances would be raided and costumes confiscated. As Francis Kirkman relates, drolls were "the fittest for the actors to represent," "there being little cost in cloaths, which often were in great danger to be seized by the then souldiers, who as the poet says, *Enter the Red Coat, Exit Hat and Cloak*."[43]

A large raid on theatrical activity occurred on 1 January 1649, the same day that the House of Commons ordered the establishment of a special

---

[38] "February 1648: An Ordinance for the Utter Suppression and Abolishing of All Stage-Plays and Interludes, within the Penalties to be Inflicted on the Actors and Spectators Therein Expressed," in *Acts and Ordinances of the Interregnum*, pp. 1070–2.

[39] Wiseman, *Drama and Politics*, pp. 3, 5.

[40] Richard Brome, "To the Right Noble, Ingenious, and Judicious Gentleman, THOMAS STANLEY, Esq," in Richard Brome, *A Jovial Crew, Or The Merry Beggars* (London: J. Y. for Edward Dod. and Nathaniel Ekins, 1652), sig. A2r. On plague closures, see Leeds Barroll, *Politics, Plague and Shakespeare's Theatre: The Stuart Years* (Ithaca: Cornell University Press, 1991).

[41] Leslie Hotson describes a parliamentary raid on a fencing match at the Fortune as "a means of drafting men into the Parliament army." *Commonwealth and Restoration Stage* (Cambridge, MA: Harvard University Press, 1928), p. 17.

[42] *The Weekly Account*, 4 October 1643; *A Perfect Diurnal*, 17–24 December 1649; *The Man in the Moon*, 23–31 January 1650; *Weekly Intelligencer*, 26 December 1654/5; *A Perfect Account of the Daily Intelligence*, 27 December–3 January 1654/5; *The Weekly Intelligencer*, 11–18 September 1655.

[43] Francis Kirkman, "Preface," in *The Wits, or, Sport upon Sport, Part I* (London: Francis Kirkman, 1672), sig. A3r.

court to try King Charles I for treason (he was executed publicly twenty-nine days later). The authorities carried out a coordinated crackdown on Drury Lane, Salisbury Court, and the Fortune (forewarned, the Red Bull players escaped). The newsbook *The Kingdom's Weekly Intelligencer* for 2–9 January 1649 reported that after the players at Salisbury Court were arrested near the end of their performance, "they were carried to White-Hall with their Players cloathes on their backs. In the way they [i.e. the soldiers] oftentimes tooke the Crown from his head who acted the King, and in sport would oftentimes put it on again."[44] The player king's uncrowning by Parliamentary soldiers foreshadowed England's real-life drama – within a month, King Charles would face his executioner on the scaffold. Given the pervasive rhetoric surrounding the "murder" of the English theatre, the regicide by the same government who shuttered the theatres made the royalist association between plays and the English monarchy almost inevitable.

The "death" of theatre was also literalized by the visible collapse of the theatre industry. The second Globe Theatre appears to have been demolished in 1644 or 1645; tenements were in its place by 1655.[45] On 16 July 1645 the Commons ordered that "[t]he Boarded Masque House at Whitehall, the Masque house at St James, and the Courts of Guard, be forthwith pulled down, and sold away." Apparently, the timber was not immediately disposed of, but lay in piles for two years at Scotland Yard, prompting one commentator to speculate ominously that "timber of the late erected playhouse in White Hall" "lye in the posture of a very large Bonfire ready to welcome the King and his Nobles."[46] The renewed theatrical ordinance of February 1648 ordered that the remaining playhouses be "pulled down" (a contemporary expression that can mean both "dismantled on the interior" and "levelled to the ground"). On 24 March 1649 Parliamentary soldiers pulled down Salisbury Court, the Phoenix (also known as the Cockpit), and the Fortune Theatre. The February 1648 ordinance's classification of all actors as "rogues" abolished their previous legitimacy derived from Royal Patents, adding still more barriers to the acting profession.[47] Although as late as 1647, theatre professionals could

[44] *The Kingdom's Weekly Intelligencer*, 2–9 January 1648/9.
[45] See Herbert Berry, "Folger MS V.b.275 and the Deaths of Shakespearean Playhouses," *Medieval and Renaissance Drama in England*, 10 (1998), 262–93.
[46] Qtd. in Hotson, *Commonwealth and Restoration Stage*, p. 13.
[47] *English Professional Theatre, 1530–1660. Theatre in Europe: A Documentary History*, ed. Glynne Wickham, Herbert Berry, and William Ingram (Cambridge: Cambridge University Press, 2000), pp. 134–5.

hope for a resumption of theatre, the changes in the late 1640s banished any hope of meaningful return. Political and cultural changes were irrevocable: the king was dead, the monarchy abolished, and the English theatres would not return as they once were.

Walking around London in the early 1650s, one would witness evidence of theatre's irreparable decline. A decade after the theatres closed, the English dramatist Richard Flecknoe wrote, "A whimzey written from beyond the seas, about the end of the year, [16]52, to a Friend lately returned into England," printed in Flecknoe's *Miscellania* (1653). The "Whimzey" is an imaginary walking tour of England, written from abroad: the royalist Flecknoe exiled himself to the Continent and South America during late 1640s and early 1650s to escape England's civil strife. Flecknoe takes note of changes to the cultural and political landscape wrought since the war and revolution, and wistfully describes happier days. Flecknoe imagines arriving at the vacant Blackfriars Theatre. He bewails the desertion of the formerly bustling indoor commercial theatre: "Passing on to Blackfriars and seeing never a play bill on the gate, no coaches on the place, nor doorkeeper at the playhouse door with a box like a churchwarden desiring you to remember the poor players."[48] The once-vibrant area is drained of activity and atmosphere: no more playbills advertising plays, no clattering of horses' hooves as they whisk spectators to and from performances, no more wheedling from the doorkeeper, whose box no longer jangles with coins. Confronting the desolate Blackfriars, Flecknoe offers an "epilogue to all the plays were ever acted there," repurposing the dramatic form that concludes individual plays and applying it to an entire theatrical tradition:

> Poor House that in days of our Grand-sires,
> Belongst unto the mendicant fryars,
> Where so oft in our father's days,
> We have seen so many of Shakespeare's plays,
> So many of Johnson's, Beaumont's and Fletcher's
> Until I know not what Puritan teachers
> (Who for their tone, their language, and action
> Might 'gainst the stage, make bedlam a faction),
> Have made with their Rayleighs, the players as poor
> As were the Fryers, and poets before.[49]

[48] Richard Flecknoe, *Miscellania* (London: Thomas Roycroft for J. Martin and J. Allestrye, 1653), p. 141.
[49] Ibid.

Flecknoe invokes Blackfriars' medieval history as a priory, shuttered in the Dissolution by zealous Protestant reformers. Reincarnated as a theatre, Blackfriars has once again been rendered silent by the reformers' Puritan descendants. The players are impoverished and rendered obsolete much like the friars were a century before. Through his comparison between the Dissolution (a symbol of widespread devastation) and the closure of the theatres, Flecknoe insists on the magnitude of the latter. Gazing at the vacant Blackfriars in his mind's eye, Flecknoe blames the Puritans for their opposition "gainst the stage." Flecknoe's biased characterization of the Puritans does not necessarily reflect reality – recent scholarship has challenged the familiar association between Puritanism and anti-theatrical attitudes.[50] But no matter the actual attitudes or activities of Puritans, Royalists like Flecknoe who dominated dramatic discourse in the 1640s and 1650s perpetuated the stereotype of theatre-hating Puritans, as well as the trope of Royalists being sympathetic to English professional drama. It is no coincidence that some of our field's most persistent critical clichés date to the moment of the theatre ban, for it is in this period that the critical field of English Renaissance drama was born. Flecknoe's prejudice represents one of the founding myths of early modern drama studies.

Flecknoe nostalgically recalls the theatrical abundance of the playhouse that formerly showcased "so many" plays of Shakespeare, Jonson, Beaumont, and Fletcher, contrasting it with the current moment of theatrical scarcity that deprives spectators of pleasure and reduces players to penury. Playgoing is an evanescent pleasure lost to posterity, but the activity is not yet fully consigned to yesteryear. After ascribing it to "our Fathers days," Flecknoe qualifies that "we have seen so many" plays, the inclusive "we" incorporating Flecknoe into a dwindling group of early modern spectators. In 1652, playgoing is still a living memory, but one receding into the past. Flecknoe is part of a dying breed; future generations would have no first-hand experience of pre-1642 theatre. This generational shift was already becoming apparent in the early 1650s. Martin Butler notes that, in the copious prefatory material to William Cartwright's posthumous dramatic collection printed in 1651, several authors of commendatory poems "can be shown to have been too young to have known the theatres before they closed in 1642, and they speak of 'reading'

---

[50] Margot Heinemann, *Puritanism and Theatre* (Cambridge: Cambridge University Press, 1980); David Scott Kastan, "Performances and Playbooks: The Closing of the Theatres and the Politics of Drama," in *Reading, Society and Politics in Early Modern England*, ed. Kevin Sharpe and Steven N. Zwicker (Cambridge: Cambridge University Press, 2003), pp. 167–84 (p. 168).

rather than 'seeing' the plays."[51] After 1642, early modern theatre could be accessed through successive levels of historical memory: memories of direct experience, reports from those who had direct experience of the theatre, and, as time went on, increasingly from second- and third-hand accounts and textual records. The closure of theatres, then, essentially established the modern conditions of early modern theatre history, not accessed first-hand but rather mediated by texts and reports. Though Flecknoe's walking tour is imaginary, a material encounter with Blackfriars was still possible in 1652. Yet Blackfriars was demolished in August 1655 to make room for tenements, disappearing along with the performances it had staged. Tiffany Stern argues that by the Restoration, "the long-demolished" Blackfriars playhouse was "a locus for all-purpose nostalgia," one that folded together longing for the politics and culture of pre-war England.[52] Yet, as the "Whimzey" indicates, Blackfriars nostalgia was present in the 1650s, even before the building came down.

More dramatic losses were endured in the 1650s. The popular dramatist Richard Brome fell on hard times after the theatres closed. In the prefatory matter to his *Jovial Crew* (1652), Brome described himself as "poor and proud":[53] a year prior he had applied for quarterly pension payments for washing, "beverage," and gown money; by September 1652 he was dead.[54] More theatrical venues and their denizens were destroyed. The Hope Theatre, a dual-purpose venue "for stage-plays on Mondays, Wednesdays, Fridays, and Saturdays, and for the baiting of Bears on Tuesdays and Thursdays," was demolished in 1656. Handwritten marginalia in a copy of John Stow's *Annals* (1631) notes the unceremonious end of a lively, long-standing entertainment venue, which "was built in the year 1610, and now pulled down to make tenements."[55] The report adds the gruesome detail that, after the demolition, seven of the Hope's bears "were then shot to death on Saturday the 9 day of February, 1655 [i.e. 1656], by a company of soldiers" under the command of Thomas

---

[51] Butler, *Theatre and Crisis*, p. 9.

[52] Tiffany Stern, "'A Ruinous Monastery': The Second Blackfriars Playhouse as a Place of Nostalgia," in *Moving Shakespeare Indoors*, ed. Andrew Gurr and Farah Karim-Cooper (Cambridge: Cambridge University Press, 2014), pp. 97–114.

[53] Brome, "To Thomas Stanley, Esq," in Brome, *A Jovial Crew*, sig. A2r.

[54] Martin Butler, "Brome, Richard," in the *Oxford Dictionary of National Biography* (Oxford: Oxford University Press, 2004), http://doi.org/10.1093/ref:odnb/3503.

[55] Anonymous, handwritten note appended to a 1631 edition; see John Stow, *Annales, or a generall chronicle of England* (London: Richard Meighen, 1631), Folger MS V.b.275. See also Berry, "Folger MS V.b.275."

Pride, the Parliamentarian commander who had instigated Pride's Purge and participated in the regicide.[56]

As Pride's involvement suggests, the suppression of the theatres was just one facet of a broad agenda of political and cultural reform. The Long Parliament was elected in autumn of 1640 after eleven years of King Charles I's Personal Rule (1629–40). Parliament quickly set out to reverse what it regarded as the popish excesses, cultural licentiousness, and political oppression of King Charles I, William Laud, Archbishop of Canterbury, and the louche Royalists who backed them.[57] Parliament reoriented the ecclesiastical calendar around the Sabbath and religious fasts. They condemned Christmas, Easter, and Whitsuntide as superstitions and in June 1647 attempted to ban the holy days outright. Sunday markets and summer fairs were outlawed or severely curtailed; commerce, sports, and travel on the Sabbath were outlawed, as were maypoles and Morris dances.[58] Reforms wrought changes to the city's edifices, in addition to theatrical demolition. In 1642, Parliament halted the much-needed restoration work on St Paul's Cathedral, which Charles I had initiated in the 1630s.[59] St Paul's nave was used as an army barracks during the Civil Wars, and at one point stabled 800 horses. Parliament dissolved cathedral chapters; the unauthorized iconoclastic destruction of altars, altar-rails, images, and stained glass in 1641–2 gave way to state-sanctioned acts of religious vandalism after 1643.[60]

At the same time, the brutal English Civil Wars were exacting a shocking death toll. Out of England's estimated pre-war population of five million people, the total dead from direct and indirect causes during the three wars amounted to 3.7 per cent of the population; the estimated population losses were 6 per cent in Scotland, and perhaps as high as 40 per cent in Ireland.[61] Cultural reforms caused their own carnage. On 3 June 1649, following an injunction banning all commercial activity on the Sabbath, soldiers under the command of Thomas Pride opened fire on watermen who flouted the prohibition, killing and wounding several watermen and bystanders, including a small child walking along the

---

[56] Folger MS V.b.275.
[57] Bernard Capp, *England's Culture Wars* (Oxford: Oxford University Press, 2012), p. 7.
[58] Ibid., pp. 8–9, 203.
[59] Stuart Mottram, *Ruin and Reformation in Spenser, Shakespeare and Marvell* (Cambridge: Cambridge University Press, 2019), p. 149.
[60] Capp, *England's Culture Wars*, pp. 7–8; Mottram, *Ruin and Reformation*, p. 132.
[61] Charles Carlton, *Going to the Wars: The Experience of the British Civil Wars, 1638–1651* (New York: Routledge, 1994), pp. 212–14.

Thames with her father who was killed by a stray bullet.[62] The long-standing tradition of "swan upping" – where young swans were counted and assigned to the monarch and trade guilds – ended abruptly when Parliamentary soldiers killed the king's swans; according to legend, the swans only returned to the Thames with the Restoration of the monarchy.[63] The River Thames itself reeked of death. The water poet John Taylor, appointed London's water bailiff during the wars, recalled how "Dead hogs, dogs, cats and well flayed carrion horses / Their noisome corpses soiled the water courses."[64] War and reform led to economic depression, death, disease, ruined edifices, and smashed images. For civilians not killed by war or disease, poverty and starvation were constant threats. The ranks of the ill and injured, widows, orphans, and abandoned children swelled. Local church chapters struggled to cope with indigent parishioners; children were found dead in the street, others were left freezing, starving, and clothed in rags.

Much of this widespread devastation is registered in Flecknoe's "Whimzey." Wandering through London, Flecknoe muses, "I shall admire at the wondrous change I find there, with the marks of Reformation almost upon every sign-post." In the aftermath of Pride's firing on the watermen in 1649, Flecknoe notes their muted bellows: "the Watermen bawle nothing nigh so loud now, as they were wont to do."[65] Passing by the dilapidated St Paul's Cathedral, Flecknoe imagines that he shall find it "cruelly sick of the Stone, voiding every day some, and quite Apoplectique with all its faculties and organs suspended"; his anatomical puns on kidney stones and failing organs gesture to the cathedral's ruined masonry and its inactivity as a house of worship.[66]

Flecknoe recalls the sensual pleasures that could once be had at Bartholomew Fair. He populates the real-life summer fair in Smithfield (now defunct) with characters from Ben Jonson's eponymous play: "O Smithfield, thou that in Times of yore, / With thy Ballets didst make all England roar, / Whilst Goodwife Ursuly look'd so bigg / At the roasting of a Bartholomew Pig / And so many Enormities everywhere / Were observed by Justice Overdoe there."[67] Flecknoe rehearses Jonson's notion of the

---

[62] *Perfect Occurrences*, 8 June 1649, 1–8; *The Moderate*, 29 May–5 June 1649.

[63] Helen MacDonald, "In Search of Post-Brexit England, and Swans," *New York Times Magazine*, 5 January 2017.

[64] Qtd. in Carlton, *Going to the Wars*, p. 208   [65] Flecknoe, *Miscellania*, p. 139.   [66] Ibid.

[67] Ibid.

Puritans as iconoclastic, anti-sensual, anti-theatrical, hypocritical zealots.[68] In Jonson's *Bartholomew Fair*, the Puritans Justice Overdo and Zeal-of-the-Land Busy are ultimately humiliated, while the pig-woman and bawd Ursula, and other peddlers of down-market pleasures, triumph. By Flecknoe's time, real-life events had overturned the outcome of Jonson's play, and brought Smithfield's revelry to an abrupt and unexpected end: "Full little (I muse) didst thou thinke then / Thy mirth should be spoiled by the Banbury man."[69] In Flecknoe's telling, thanks to the Puritans (traditionally associated with the Oxfordshire town of Banbury), the heady excesses of the Bartholomew Fair are mere memories, firmly consigned to the "times of yore." In Flecknoe's "Whimzey," the nostalgic recollection of theatre is part of a broader process of cultural remembrance. The vacant Blackfriars Theatre is embedded within a landscape of widespread loss and ruin, of forbidden summer fairs and ruined cathedrals. Flecknoe's polychronic consideration of cultural reform equates the causes and effects of the English Reformation with those of the Revolution. Written by a self-exiled Royalist envisioning the destruction of traditions and monuments, Flecknoe's reverie contains both geographical and temporal nostalgia, encompassing nostalgia's original meaning of homesickness, and its later connotation of yearning for an absent, idealized past.

Eventually, however, Flecknoe's nostalgic historical attention narrowed to the theatre alone. His *A Short Discourse on the English Stage* (1664) is the first recognized work of English theatre history. But if theatre history proper is not yet fully formed, the theatre historiographical impulse is clearly visible in Flecknoe's "Whimzey" from 1652. In both the "Whimzey" and *A Short Discourse*, theatrical silence prompts remembrance of the glorious days of theatre. The latter begins with the reflection that "our Stage ha's stood at a stand this many years"; in the former, a contemplation of the vacant Blackfriars prompts a reflection on staged

---

[68] On Jonson's "invention" of the Puritan, see Patrick Collinson, *The Puritan Character: Polemics and Polarities in Early Seventeenth-Century English Culture* (Los Angeles: William Andrews Clark Memorial Library, University of California, 1989); Patrick Collinson, "Ben Johnson's *Bartholomew Fair*: The Theatre Constructs Puritanism," in *The Theatrical City: Culture, Theatre and Politics in London, 1576–1649*, ed. David L. Smith, Richard Strier, and David Bevington (Cambridge: Cambridge University Press, 1995), pp. 157–69; Patrick Collinson, "Ecclesiastical Vitriol: Religious Satire in the 1590s and the Invention of Puritanism," in *The Reign of Elizabeth I: Court and Culture in the Last Decade*, ed. John Guy (Cambridge: Cambridge University Press, 1995), pp. 150–70.

[69] Flecknoe, *Miscellania*, p. 139.

performances of Jonson, Shakespeare, and Beaumont and Fletcher. Theatre history literally starts with the theatrical prohibition.[70]

Theatre Closure and the Paradoxical Rise of English Renaissance Drama in the Civil Wars

By the late 1650s, someone strolling around in Southwark or Drury Lane would find vestiges of the ruined English professional theatre: vacant or demolished playhouses, illicit or raided performances. But one would get a different impression of English drama in the mid seventeenth century if one strolled into St Paul's Churchyard, the centre of the English book trade. To be sure, walking in the shadow of the dilapidated St Paul's Cathedral, the publications one would find for sale in the nearby bookstalls would bear witness to a troubled cultural and political moment. Playbooks' title pages continued to reproduce theatrical attributions; title page claims that a text was "lately played" would be belied by the stark reality of contemporary theatrical conditions. For younger readers who had no experience of legal public performance at all, such attributions to pre-1642 performance took on a cultural life and meaning of their own, beyond the level of the individual performances (now long silent), playing companies (now disbanded), and venues (now pulled down). The page was still tenaciously tied to the stage, even if, for many, performance had shifted from the actual to the imagined. Other paratexts gestured explicitly to specific losses: the first edition of James Shirley's *The Court Secret* (published as part of Shirley's *Six New Plays*, 1653) (Figure I.2), declares the tragicomedy was "Never Acted, But prepared for the Scene at BLACK-FRIERS." Slated for performance in September 1642, *The Court Secret*'s theatrical premiere was thwarted by the 2 September 1642 theatrical ordinance. The title page of Beaumont and Fletcher's *The Wild Goose Chase* (1652) declares that the play was printed for the "private Benefit of John Lowin and Joseph Taylor," the unemployed veteran co-leaders of the King's Servants, who were cast out of work by the prohibition. Philip Massinger's *Three New Plays* (1655) (Figure I.3), invokes the recent political and theatrical turmoil when it characterizes texts performed by his "Late Majesties Servants," "late" referring both to the dead Charles I and the disbanded King's Servants.

---

[70] Richard Flecknoe, "A Short Discourse on the English Stage," in *Love's Kingdom* (London: R. Wood, 1664), sig. G3r.

Figure I.2   Authorial frontispiece portrait and title page from James Shirley, *Six New Plays* (Humphrey Robinson and Humphrey Moseley, 1653).
Courtesy of the Huntington Library.

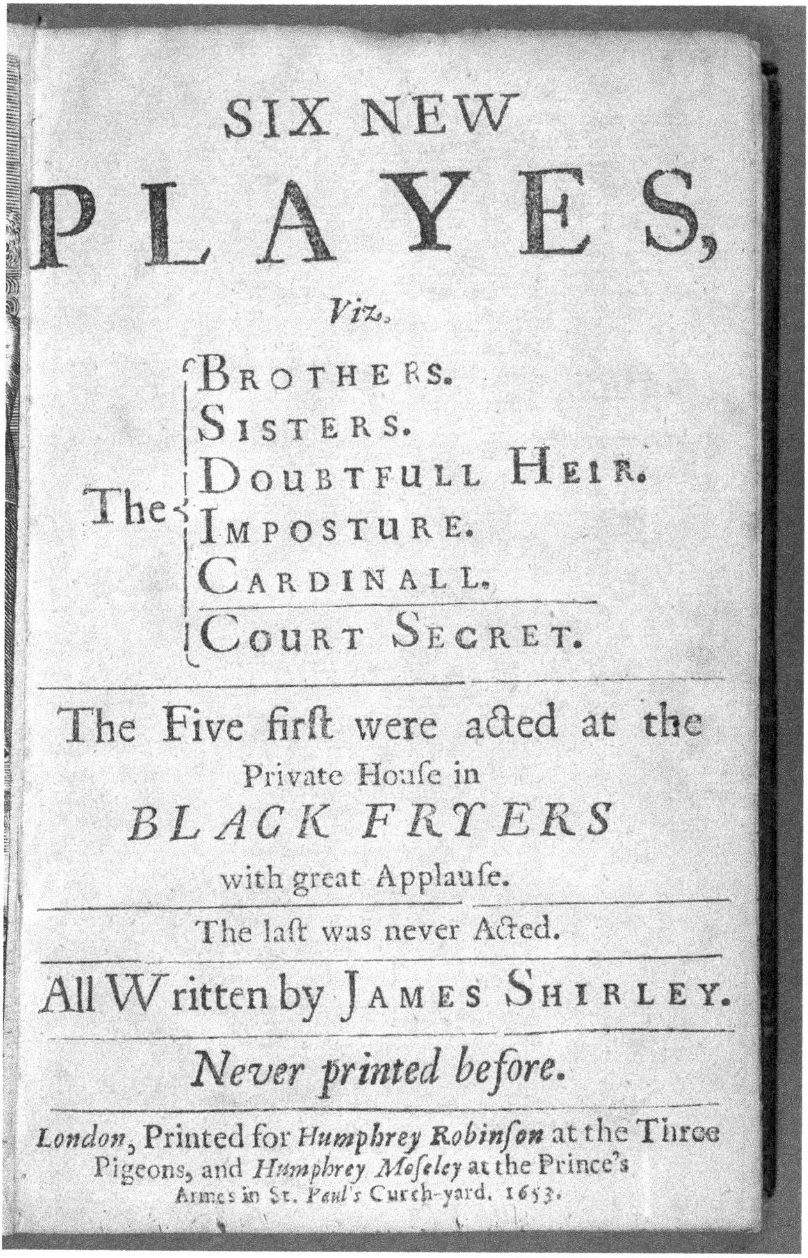

SIX NEW
PLAYES,

Viz.

The
- BROTHERS.
- SISTERS.
- DOUBTFULL HEIR.
- IMPOSTURE.
- CARDINALL.
- COURT SECRET.

The Five firſt were acted at the
Private Houſe in
BLACK FRYERS
with great Applauſe.

The laſt was never Acted.

All Written by JAMES SHIRLEY.

Never printed before.

London, Printed for *Humphrey Robinſon* at the Three
Pigeons, and *Humphrey Moſeley* at the Prince's
Armes in St. *Paul's* Curch-yard. 1653.

Figure I.2 (*cont.*)

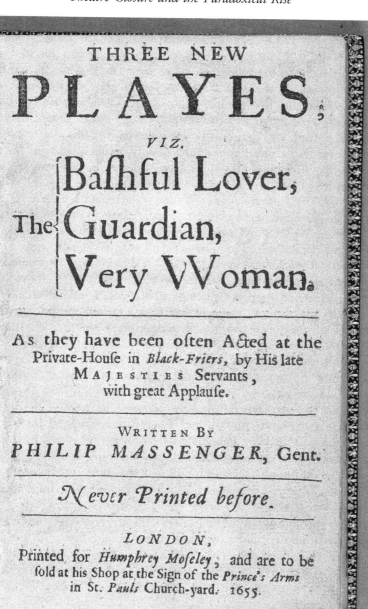

THREE NEW
PLAYES;

VIZ.

The { Bashful Lover,
Guardian,
Very VVoman.

As they have been often Acted at the
Private-House in *Black-Friers*, by His late
MAJESTIES Servants,
with great Applause.

WRITTEN BY
PHILIP MASSENGER, Gent.

Never Printed before.

LONDON,
Printed for *Humphrey Moseley*; and are to be
sold at his Shop at the Sign of the *Prince's Arms*
in St. *Pauls* Church-yard. 1655.

Figure I.3   Title page from Philip Massinger, *Three New Plays* (Humphrey
Moseley, 1655).
Courtesy of the Huntington Library.

And yet, alongside these poignant reminders of abortive theatrical efforts, unemployed theatre professionals, and political upheaval, London bookstalls in the mid seventeenth century would also reveal English drama's resilience. Despite, or rather, because of the decline of commercial theatre, English professional drama thrived in print. The closure of the theatres worked "to the stationers' gains," Richard Brome noted in 1647, as dramatic production and consumption migrated to print.[71] The predominance of printed drama after 1642 was neither immediate nor inevitable, however. Publication of drama sharply declined between 1642 and 1645: while fifty-nine playbooks were printed in the two-year span between 1640 and 1642, only one single-text playbook, William Davenant's *The Unfortunate Lovers* (1643), appeared between 1643 and 1645. The playbook market began to recover after 1645, thanks largely to the concerted efforts of Interregnum stationers, who transformed the absence of theatre into a commercial and cultural opportunity. For the first time, stationers dominated dramatic production, and they seized upon the practical opportunities and rhetorical possibilities of drama's near-exclusive existence in print. Creating and responding to audience demand whetted by live theatre's absence, stationers acquired and published large numbers of previously unprinted scripts shed by the ailing theatre companies, producing dramatic abundance in a time of theatrical dearth. As a result, the 1650s was the third-most productive decade for printed drama since the 1570s. Many of these playbooks featured paratexts that emphasized the authority and value of the dramatic medium of print.

Leading the way was Humphrey Moseley (c. 1603–61), the most important and prolific publisher of English drama in the Interregnum. The wealth of Moseley's dramatic publication output would be displayed at his bookshop in Paul's Churchyard, the Prince's Arms. With his partner Humphrey Robinson, Moseley published the most significant dramatic publication of the Interregnum, Francis Beaumont and John Fletcher's collected works in folio, *Comedies and Tragedies* (1647), which included thirty-five previously unprinted plays and thirty-seven commendatory poems by prominent poets, dramatists, and public figures. Moseley also published the afore-referenced Massinger's *Three New Plays* (1655) as part of an innovative series of small, single-author dramatic collections printed in octavo, launched with James Shirley's *Six New Plays* (1653,

---

[71] Richard Brome, "To the Memory of the Deceased but Ever-Living Author in These Poems Master John Fletcher," in Beaumont and Fletcher, *Comedies and Tragedies*, sig. g1r.

co-published with Robinson) and Richard Brome's *Five New Plays* (1653). Evidently successful, Moseley extended the *New Plays* series with Massinger's *Three New Plays* (1655), *Two New Plays* by Lodowick Carlell (1657), and *Two New Plays* by Thomas Middleton (1657). The stationer Andrew Crooke imitated Moseley, publishing his own edition of Richard Brome's *Five New Plays* (featuring five different plays) in 1659. These plays were "new" only in terms of their publication history – many were composed and staged decades earlier – but such publications revealed the continued vitality of English drama in print.

The *New Plays* editions were new not only in terms of content, but also in terms of format: they represent the first serialized collection of English drama. Each of the *New Plays* editions was bibliographically uniform: printed in octavo, with a formulaic title ("New Plays" preceded by the particular number of plays), featuring commendatory poems and an engraved portrait of the author. Paulina Kewes notes Moseley's innovation, arguing that each individual *New Plays* author "emerges as a central unifying presence which binds together and confers value upon a corpus of disparate and hitherto dispersed texts."[72] The binding of dispersed texts under a single author was not new, however; this was also the logic behind the collected works of Jonson, Shakespeare, Beaumont and Fletcher, and Cartwright. Moseley's real innovation was to collect the collections.

To paraphrase Kewes, Moseley's *New Plays* serial collection binds together disparate and dispersed collections from multiple dramatists into a single generic corpus. The central, unifying presence in *New Plays* is indicated by its title: novelty and genre. On the title pages of these editions, "PLAYS" is given top-billing, printed above and in larger type than the individual dramatist's name or theatrical company, and larger than their claims of "newness." The emphasis on genre speaks to the fact that the *New Plays* authors were generally not from the upper-ranks of the English dramatic corpus, nor do the modest octavo editions attempt to "monumentalize their texts, nor do they insist on the laureate status of their authors."[73] Instead of dubiously asserting dramatic value, Moseley ingeniously added value to each lesser dramatist by bundling their individual authorial corpora together and marketing them as part of a larger, multi-author dramatic corpus. Each individual collection of the *New Plays* asserts the value of its respective dramatist, not to elevate him specifically

---

[72] Paulina Kewes, "'Give Me the Sociable Pocket-Books . . .': Humphrey Moseley's Serial Publication of Octavo Collections," *Publishing History*, 38 (1995), 5–21 (p. 11).

[73] Benedict Scott Robinson, "Thomas Heywood and the Cultural Politics of the Play Collections," *Studies in English Literature, 1500–1900*, 42.9 (2002), 361–80 (p. 372).

but to confer value upon a particular class of texts: "plays." If individual collections effect the canonization of their particular authors, we might say that series collections effect the canonization of "plays," a term that (recalling Gayton's distinction) evokes theatrical entertainment as opposed to the more obviously literary "work" or "dramatic poem."

Browsing the inventory at Moseley's bookshop, one would find another new printed dramatic form: the first printed commonplace book composed exclusively of English dramatic extracts and, therefore, "the first English drama anthology,"[74] John Cotgrave's *English Treasury of Wit and Language* (1655). *The English Treasury* belongs to a hybrid genre, positioned between the commonplace book and dramatic anthology.[75] Plays are digested into didactic and lyrical chestnuts as well as longer extracts that seem to offer little practical application yet evoke the source play's narrative. *The English Treasury*'s exclusive reliance on English drama powerfully asserts the genre's value as a source of moral wisdom and rhetorical exempla. Historically, the commonplace tradition suggests that early modern readers regarded plays not as "unified artistic wholes, but as sources to be dismantled, changed, and mined for wit, wisdom and song."[76] This form of reading is "far removed from the tacit assumptions of our modern critical practice which . . . privileges the larger narrative over the excerpt, the coherent whole over the fragmented piece."[77] In his preface, however, Cotgrave betrays misgivings about his method of reading, apologizing for the losses that attend his extractions: "if [extracts] seem to lose ought of their native vigour or beauty in the transplanting, I would hope it is reasonably recompensed in the more usefulnesse of the method they are now in."[78] His apology reveals an appreciation of coherent narrative wholes, a form of reading that lends itself to the anthology. Jeremy Lopez observes *The English Treasury*'s "structural and rhetorical attempt to represent the whole through the part," and argues that the edition "seems to assume that its reader had a good sense of the whole dramatic corpus that lies just

---

[74] Jeremy Lopez, *Constructing the Canon of Early Modern Drama* (Cambridge: Cambridge University Press, 2014), p. 45.

[75] Emma Depledge, *Shakespeare's Rise to Cultural Prominence* (Cambridge: Cambridge University Press, 2018), p. 27. Thank you to Emma for sharing a copy of her manuscript with me prior to publication.

[76] Laura Estill, *Dramatic Extracts in Seventeenth-Century English Manuscripts: Watching, Reading, Changing Plays* (Lanham: University of Delaware Press, 2015), p. xxii.

[77] Sasha Roberts, *Reading Shakespeare's Poems in Early Modern England* (Basingstoke: Palgrave Macmillan, 2002), p. 100.

[78] John Cotgrave, "To the Courteous Reader," in *The English Treasury of Wit and Language* (London: Humphrey Moseley, 1655), sig. A2v.

behind the excerpts."[79] Cotgrave explains that his extracts are "collected out of the most and best of our English dramatic poems," thus offering a quantitative and qualitative ("most and best") corpus of English drama.[80] As a commonplacer, Cotgrave nominates the "English dramatic poem" as a worthy supplier of *sententiae*. As an anthologist, Cotgrave offers an historical and aesthetic precis of English drama as a genre.

From Moseley's Prince's Arms in St Paul's Churchyard, one could wend one's way to Thread-Needle Street to find Ben Jonson's Head, a bookshop that Robert Pollard was operating by 1655. This was the first known instance of a playwright's likeness being used as a shop sign, and Jonson's Head speaks of his high level of celebrity: to be legible as a sign, a portrait has to be immediately recognizable. At first glance, a playwright's visage used as a bookshop sign seems to speak to Interregnum dramatic culture's reorientation around print culture and individual authors. Jeffrey Masten observes, "[I]t seems that the idea of a playwright's head as a sign arrives on the scene only after the closing of the theaters," noting the possibility that "a playwright's head is not thinkable under the sign of the working theater."[81] And yet, counterintuitively, Pollard never actually published any of Jonson's plays. In fact, Jonson was notably absent from the increase in playbook publication after the theatres closed: the Jonson folio publications of 1640 and 1641 marked the last time Jonson's plays would be printed for two decades. Jonson's authorial persona was divorced from his actual texts: this suggests how dramatic culture by the Interregnum had a life independent from actual theatrical or textual production or consumption. Well-known dramatists and plays permeated part of the cultural tradition as free-standing cultural icons.

At Ben Jonson's Head, one would find yet another innovation in printed drama: the first comprehensive catalogues of English printed plays. Edward Archer's "An Exact and perfect CATALOGUE of all the PLAIES that were ever printed," an alphabetical list of 651 play titles in print appended to the first edition of Thomas Middleton, William Rowley, and Thomas Heywood's comedy *The Old Law* (1656, first performed 1618) (Figure I.4),[82] sold at Jonson's Head. Archer's catalogue expanded on

---

[79] Lopez, *Constructing the Canon*, p. 45.   [80] Cotgrave, *The English Treasury*, title page.
[81] Jeffrey Masten, "Ben Jonson's Head," *Shakespeare Studies*, 28 (2000), 160–8 (p. 160).
[82] The title page to the 1656 edition of *The Old Law* attributes the play to Philip Massinger, Thomas Middleton, and William Rowley. *DEEP: Database of Early English Playbooks*, ed. Alan B. Farmer and Zachary Lesser, http://deep.sas.upenn.edu. and *Thomas Middleton and Early Modern Textual Culture* attribute the play to Middleton, Rowley, and Thomas Heywood; I follow the modern attribution.

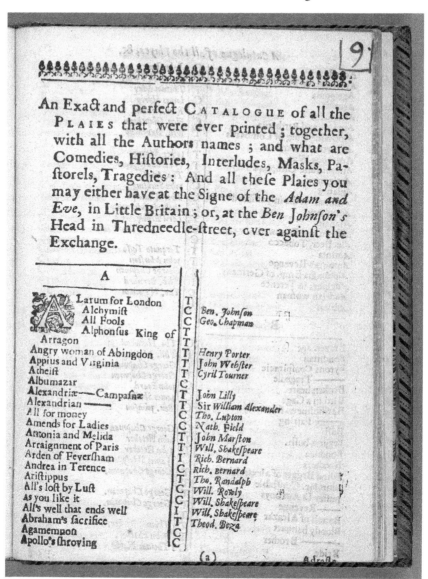

Figure I.4 "An Exact and perfect CATALOGUE of all the PLAIES that were ever printed," dramatic catalogue appended to Thomas Middleton, William Rowley, and Thomas Heywood, *The Old Law* (Edward Archer, 1656). Courtesy of the Huntington Library.

Richard Rogers and William Ley's "An exact and perfect Catologue of all Playes that are Printed" (1656), an alphabetical list of 502 printed plays that had been produced a few months earlier, attached to Thomas Goffe's pastoral drama *The Careless Shepherdess* (1656).[83] These two comprehensive catalogues represent the first efforts to gather and make legible the entire corpus of English plays in print; they are the first enumerative bibliographies of English drama.

The two comprehensive catalogues of 1656 have much in common with the shorter commercial book list advertisements that stationers included in their editions starting in the 1650s, which Adam Hooks argues "transformed printed drama into a distinct generic field."[84] Yet the comprehensive catalogues offer a different picture of genre from the commercial book lists, which focus on professional drama and on newer or best-selling titles.[85] In their quest for comprehensiveness, Rogers and Ley's and Archer's catalogues feature texts that rarely appear in other book lists, placing old titles, such as the anonymous *Interlude of Youth* (written c. 1513, first printed 1530), for which demand must have been low, alongside newer titles like Goffe's *The Courageous Turk* (1656). In the comprehensive catalogues, play titles are listed alphabetically, not the best way to advertise the newest or most popular titles. Although the comprehensive catalogues of 1656 fail as commercial texts, they excel as informational ones. The catalogues' inclusivity and non-hierarchical alphabetical arrangement by play title reveals that their main purpose is not to sell or rank plays. Instead, they aim to inform, functioning as encyclopaedias of English printed drama. The comprehensive catalogues include pre- and post-professional amateur plays (*Damon and Pithias* [1571] and Robert Cox's *Acteon and Diana* [1656]), university drama (*Gammer Gurton's Needle* [1575]), pre- and post-1642 closet drama (*The Tragedy of Mariam* [1616] and Cosmo Manuche's *The Just General* [1652]), the royalist *The Famous Tragedy of King Charles I, Basely Butchered* (1649), and the republican *Marcus Tullius Cicero* (1651). The catalogues offer a wide array of texts, with diverse theatrical, linguistic, and political backgrounds, gathered under the single heading of "English plays," united through their shared characteristic of existing in print. English drama is positioned as a

---

[83] In a related development, John Playford's comprehensive music catalogue, "A Catalogue of All the Musick-Bookes That Have Been Printed in England, Either for Voyce or Instruments," appeared in 1653.

[84] Adam G. Hooks, "Booksellers' Catalogues and the Classification of Printed Drama in Seventeenth-Century England," *Papers of the Bibliographical Society of America*, 102.4 (2008), 445–64 (p. 464).

[85] Ibid., p. 462.

voluminous, flexible category that embraces a vast corpus of printed plays from the last century and a half.

The inclusion of each comprehensive catalogue is advertised on the title pages of the respective playbooks to which they are appended, *The Careless Shepherdess* and *The Old Law*, which announce that the play text appears "with an Alphabetical catalogue of all such Plays that ever were Printed" and "with an exact and perfect catalogue of all the plays, with the Authors Names" (Figure I.5).[86] A title page is meant to attract buyers; as a rule, commercial book list advertisements are not themselves advertised on title pages. The comprehensive catalogues' claims of exactness and perfection also distinguish them from other book list advertisements: these adjectives praise the list itself, not its individual entries. Other "exact and perfect" catalogues were available in the seventeenth century; for instance, one could buy "AN exact and perfect List of their Majesties Royal Fleet, now actually at Sea" (1688):[87] exactness and perfection are meant to make the list itself, rather than the items, appealing for purchase. Exactness, perfection, completeness, and alphabetical organization are selling points for reference works designed to amass, record, organize, and convey large amounts of information: stationers envisioned that people would be interested in these catalogues as references of printed drama. As Derrick R. Spires has recently noted, the twentieth-century bibliographer Dorothy Porter taught us that bibliographical lists, catalogues, and organizational principles "are all arguments about what matters, how they matter, and ways of knowing."[88] That Interregnum stationers bothered to compile the titles of English playbooks in alphabetized printed catalogues, with an expectation that consumers would be interested in these kinds of texts, suggests English drama's value, as something worthy of knowing.

In the comprehensive catalogues of 1656, only printed plays are listed, rather than plays performed but not printed. Obviously, the choice to include only printed plays in a catalogue has a commercial dimension: print is an enabling condition of selling plays. Nevertheless, the catalogues

[86] Thomas Goffe, *The Careless Shepherdess* (London: William Ley and Richard Rogers, 1656), sig. A1r; Thomas Middleton, Thomas Rowley, and Philip Massinger, *The Old Law* (London: Edward Archer, 1656), sig. A1r.
[87] "AN exact and perfect List of their Majesties Royal Fleet, now actually at Sea ... Printed for John Amery ... to be sold by Randal Taylor, near Stationers-Hall," in Joseph Bennet, *A True and Impartial Account of the Most Material Passages in Ireland since December, 1688* (London: John Amery, 1689).
[88] Derrick R. Spires, "On Liberation Bibliography: The 2021 BSA Annual Meeting Keynote," *Papers of the Bibliographical Society of America*, 116.1 (2022), 1–20 (p. 19).

THE

Excellent Comedy, called

THE OLD LAW:

OR

A new way to pleaſe you.

By ⎰ *Phil. Maſſinger.*
   ⎱ *Tho. Middleton.*
   ⎰ *William Rowley.*

Acted before the King and Queene at *Salisbury Houſe,*
and at ſeverall other places, with great Applauſe.

Together with an exact and perfect Catalogue of all
the Playes, with the Authors Names, and what are
Comedies, Tragedies, Hiſtories, Paſtoralls,
Masks, Interludes, more exactly Printed
then ever before.

LONDON,
Printed for *Edward Archer*, at the ſigne of the *Adam*
and *Eve*, in *Little Britaine.* 1656.

Figure I.5   Title page from Middleton, William Rowley, and Thomas Heywood, *The (
Law* (Edward Archer, 1656).
Courtesy of the Huntington Library.

resist the commodification of plays. Omitting (commercially enticing) collected editions, the comprehensive catalogues instead list individual plays-in-collection, like *Antony and Cleopatra*, *Macbeth*, and *Measure for Measure*, although in 1656 these plays were only available in print in Shakespeare's First or Second Folios. One could not, properly speaking, possess a "playbook" called *Measure for Measure* in 1656. One could, however, know that the play text belonged to a corpus of English drama in print. The contents of "exact and perfect" catalogues represent not so much a bookseller's entire inventory of commodified playbooks to buy, but rather an authoritative corpus of all English plays in print. Because they excluded performed yet unprinted plays, the catalogues are not a guide to the entire history of English drama.[89] Rather, they reflect a fundamental reorientation of English drama's identity around print, partly as a result of the prolonged theatre closures. In an era without the opportunity for theatrical performance, print superseded performance as the crucial element of a play's cultural currency: the catalogues record a conception of dramatic identity that is no longer chiefly performance-specific. As the theatrical prohibition progressed, plays increasingly relied on possessing some kind of textual iteration to meaningfully "exist" for producers and consumers alike; this text-centric definition of drama endures in modern critics' reliance on textual remnants to study early modern plays.

The three new printed dramatic forms that first appeared in the 1650s – ⸱ *New Plays* series, the first all-drama printed commonplace book and ᠊᠊atic anthology, and the first comprehensive catalogues of printed ᠈ – speak to the intense productivity and innovation in printed drama ᠈ theatres closed. All follow the same structural logic of the compen-᠊᠊ly to unite parts of drama to present a broader view of English whole. These three compendia are sites where the genre, texts, ᠈eld of Renaissance drama begin to be visible: each consolidates ⸱s into a coherent dramatic category ("plays," "English dra-᠊᠊rinted drama), and materialize an aspect of the English ᠈full-length play, dramatic extract, title).

ᴉm responds to the moment's pressures and opportuni-᠈e theatre industry creating new professional plays, found fresh ways of repackaging old material, in ᠈ all-drama commonplace book, or an innovative

ᴉd

᠊᠊e *History of the British Stage: 1660–1900* (Cambridge: Cambridge

drama series of older texts that audaciously called itself *New Plays*. The *English Treasury*'s appearance is explicitly tied to English drama's recent decline: Cotgrave explains that his publication is meant to defend the "dramatic poem" at a time when it has been "lately too much slighted."[90] The title's metaphor of the "treasury," meanwhile, spotlights the volume's conservatory function in a moment of dramatic loss. From the outset, book catalogues were designed partly to preserve the cultural past. In *The Catalogue of English Printed Books* (1595), the first printed catalogue of English books, Andrew Maunsell characterized himself as a "remembrancer," declaring that his catalogue was designed to "draw to your memories Books that you coulde not remember."[91] In this context, remembrance has a commercial dimension (one can only purchase plays one is aware of) but is also a crucial step in preserving England's cultural and intellectual inheritance. Displaying the same impulse, the first instances of bibliographical cataloguing were prompted by the widespread destruction of texts during the Dissolution. Trevor Ross explains that "[t]he very act of recording ... presumed the need for such a register. Were it not for the catalogues, it seemed, all of these long-dead authors would have been left to oblivion."[92] Analogously, the theatre closures provoked a desire to exhaustively compile and preserve an earlier generation of artistic output that was quickly receding into the mists of memory. Indeed, the theatrical prohibition not only motivated, but also enabled the conditions for the "exact and perfect" catalogues' creation. Although the catalogues include material written after 1642, rhetorically, the complete lists gesture to a mood of dramatic conclusion. A definitive, ostensibly fixed list of something is only possible once one can be sure there are no new examples.

2 September 1642 has been called the best-known date in English theatre history.[93] Dramatic criticism, however, has mostly neglected the next eighteen years, called the "obscurest chapter in the history of English literature" and perceived as a "gap" between the two "national" dramatic traditions of the Renaissance and Restoration.[94] Earlier studies that attend

[90] Cotgrave, *The English Treasury*, sig. A3r.
[91] Andrew Maunsell, "To the Worshipful the Master, Wardens, and Assistants of the Company of Stationers," in *Catalogue of English Printed Books* (London: Andrew Maunsell, 1595), sig. A4r.
[92] Trevor Ross, *The Making of the English Literary Canon: From the Middle Ages to the Late Eighteenth Century* (Montreal and Kingston: McGill-Queen's University Press, 1998), p. 61.
[93] Kastan, "Performances and Playbooks," p. 167.
[94] Hyder E. Rollins, "A Contribution to the History of the English Commonwealth Drama," *Studies in Philology*, XVIII (1921), 267–333 (p. 267); Wiseman, *Drama and Politics*, p. 1.

to English theatre and drama during the Civil Wars and Interregnum tend to frame dramatic activities chiefly in terms of the era's major political and military conflicts. They either advance the persistent identification between Royalist politics and English drama on the one hand and Puritanism and anti-theatricalism on the other, or challenge this familiar binary to instead demonstrate the complex and varied co-option of individual plays from across the political spectrum, from Royalist to Republican. *Theatre Closure and the Paradoxical Rise of English Renaissance Drama in the Civil Wars* builds on the politically inflected scholarship of Interregnum dramatic and literary culture by Dale Randall, Nancy Klein Maguire, Susan Wiseman, Janet Clare, Rachel Willie, Emma Depledge, Lois Potter, Nigel Smith, and Steven Zwicker, as well as early twentieth-century work by T. S. Graves, Leslie Hotson, and Hyder Rollins.[95] But the book also modulates notions about Interregnum dramatic culture as encapsulated by Zwicker's statement that after 1649 there was "no distinction between politics and aesthetics," and that "all of this era's work of the literary imagination is embedded in polemic and contest."[96] To be sure, in this moment of acute civil strife, English theatre and drama – both individual plays and those institutions more generally – were produced and interpreted with politics in mind. But dramatic producers and consumers in this period also made a concerted effort to transform English drama into a realm *apart* from politics, presenting plays in ways that sometimes seem to wilfully neglect contemporary crises, and revel in a more bellelettrist appreciation of drama. Ironically, those who were perhaps the most committed to this strategy were Royalists themselves, who saw themselves as guardians of English high culture, as opposed to philistine Puritans. Attempts to cast theatre and drama apolitically, then, could themselves be politically motivated. In this way, *Theatre Closure and the Paradoxical Rise of English Renaissance Drama in the Civil Wars* differs from earlier studies that unpack the politics of the individual plays composed, staged, printed, or alluded to in the Interregnum, and focuses instead on

---

[95] Dale Randall, *Winter Fruit: English Drama, 1642–1660* (Lexington: University Press of Kentucky, 1995); Wiseman, *Drama and Politics*; Rachel Willie, *Staging the Revolution: Drama, Reinvention and History, 1647–72* (Manchester: Manchester University Press, 2015); Janet Clare, *Drama of the English Republic, 1649–60* (Manchester: Manchester University Press, 2002); Depledge, *Shakespeare's Rise*; Nancy Klein Maguire, *Regicide and Restoration: English Tragicomedy, 1660–1671* (Cambridge: Cambridge University Press, 1992); Hotson, *Commonwealth and Restoration Stage*; Rollins, "A Contribution"; Hyder E. Rollins, "The Commonwealth Drama: Miscellaneous Notes," *Studies in Philology*, 20.1 (1923), 52–69.

[96] Steven N. Zwicker, *Lines of Authority: Politics and English Literary Culture, 1649–1689* (Ithaca: Cornell University Press, 1993), pp. 1–2.

the political dimensions accorded in this moment to theatre and drama more generally, as concepts. Given that Royalist commentators sometimes deliberately strove to downplay the drama's political aspects, the latter can be difficult to discern, but the phenomenon indeed represents one of the critical "paradoxes" at the heart of this study. The Interregnum's self-consciously depoliticized dramatic discourse paved the way for more straightforwardly aesthetic criticism in later centuries.

While previous studies have illuminated this obscure period of literary history, this book is the first to argue that this period is not only worthy of consideration, but central to understanding the critical practice of early modern drama. The major strands of the field – theatre history, dramatic criticism, bibliography – began in the middle decades of the seventeenth century partly in response to the theatrical prohibition. Strikingly, many approaches to and key documents of English drama and theatre history are said to emerge in the mid seventeenth century. David Scott Kastan credits Humphrey Moseley with "inventing" English literature in the 1640s.[97] Peter Holland, Ellen MacKay, and Richard Schoch argue that theatre history starts with Flecknoe's *A Short Discourse* (1664).[98] Adam Hooks claims that dramatic enumerative bibliography begins with Francis Kirkman's 1661 comprehensive catalogue.[99] As noted above, Jeremy Lopez calls Cotgrave's *English Treasury* the first dramatic anthology,[100] while Michael Gavin argues that English literary criticism was born in the 1650s.[101] Several of these branches of dramatic criticism, anthologization, bibliography, and theatre history flourished most fully after the Restoration. But their earliest instances actually occurred during the 1640s and 1650s, and were driven by changes effected by the theatrical prohibition. Flecknoe's "Whimzey" of 1652 anticipates many of the strategies, sentiments, and examples of *A Short Discourse*; one can trace a

---

[97] David Scott Kastan, "Humphrey Moseley and the Invention of English Literature," in *Agent of Change: Print Culture Studies after Elizabeth L. Eisenstein*, ed. Sabrina Alcorn Baron, Eric N. Lindquist, and Eleanor F. Shevlin (Boston: University of Massachusetts Press, 2007), pp. 105–24 (pp. 113–14).

[98] Peter Holland, "A History of Histories, from Flecknoe to Nicoll," in *Theorizing Practice: Redefining Theatre History*, ed. W. B. Worthen with Peter Holland (Basingstoke: Palgrave Macmillan, 2003), pp. 8–29; MacKay, *Persecution, Plague and Fire*, pp. 3–4; Schoch, *Writing the History of the British Stage*, pp. 76–7.

[99] Adam G. Hooks, *Selling Shakespeare: Biography, Bibliography and the Book Trade* (Cambridge: Cambridge University Press, 2016), p. 148.

[100] Lopez, *Constructing the Canon*, p. 45.

[101] Michael Gavin, *The Invention of English Criticism: 1650–1760* (Cambridge: Cambridge University Press), 2015.

direct line from Kirkman's Restoration dramatic bibliographies to the comprehensive catalogues of 1656.

This book demonstrates the prolonged theatrical prohibition's influence on dramatic commentary. The closure of the playhouses contributed to the first sustained body of literary, specifically dramatic, criticism, as dispersed dramatic coteries reproduced their communities in the printed pages of dramatic paratexts, which swelled in this period. The collapse of theatre brought new attention to and appreciation of the entire field of English plays. Kastan's author-centric model of literature's origins overlooks Moseley's prioritization of "plays" above individual authors. This book instead offers a "post-authorship" account of dramatic canonization and corpus-formation, demonstrating how after the theatres closed in 1642, the set of plays produced up to that year were seen to cohere as a distinct group, what we now call "early modern" or "Renaissance" drama. During and thanks to the theatrical prohibition, pre-1642 drama was for the first time viewed as a distinct genre and critical field.

Scholars of disciplinary periods, fields of cultural production, and canon formation help me theorize the Interregnum as a moment when the related but distinct terms "field," "period," and "corpus" of English Renaissance drama were created, and its canonization occurred. Pierre Bourdieu's sociology of canon formation describes the material, commercial, and social forces that create value, arguing that "the producer of the value of the work of art is not the artist but the field of [cultural] production."[102] Bourdieu's displacement of the artist as the primary agent of his or her own canonization and emphasis instead on the canonizing powers of a "field of production" that includes publishers, critics, and adapters helps me clarify how the era of the theatrical prohibition – when dramatic commentary and innovative forms of adaptation joined dramatic publication practices already entrenched by 1642 – must be understood as a key moment of field creation and canonization. In terms of individual plays, the Interregnum was chiefly a period of dramatic corporatization – that is, the establishment of an inclusive dramatic corpus (evidenced, for instance, in the comprehensive printed dramatic catalogues of 1656) – rather than of canonization. Canonization is important in the Interregnum, however, insofar as canonization was occurring across the entire genre of English drama: that is, pre-1642 plays *as a group* acquired a higher cultural standing. The common canonization of pre-1642 drama as a whole might seem to contradict the process of exclusion on which

---

[102] Pierre Bourdieu, *Sociology in Question* (London: Sage, 1993), p. 141.

canonization relies. Exclusion is still at work even here, however, not in terms of individual plays, but rather in terms of the kinds of genres accorded literary status. The genre of English drama was elevated above other kinds of printed ephemera: whereas plays and pamphlets were treated similarly in the late sixteenth and early seventeenth centuries, by the mid seventeenth century, plays acquired a status apart and above that of printed ephemera. Certainly, the mid seventeenth century in many ways continued processes visible in the earlier part of the seventeenth century, but the Interregnum accelerated these processes, and cemented plays' status, due partly to the powerful effect of theatrical nostalgia and its attendant effects on the perception of plays' cultural value.

These views were expressed in dramatic paratexts and other works that represent the first sustained body of inquiry of the English theatrical and dramatic "past." As early as the mid-1640s, the year 1642 was taken as the kind of fissure producing historical contrast which theorists of periodization note is crucial for period formation. When a conception of this discrete "period" of dramatic style ("the last age") was subjected to critical study or disciplinary analysis, the result was an emerging sense of a "field."[103] Usually, critics locate the first systematic dramatic studies in the Restoration, but *Theatre Closure* demonstrates their earlier origins in the era of the theatrical prohibition. Frank Kermode's notion that canon formation relies on the "continuity of attention and interpretation," bestowed by prominent institutions, transforming mere "opinion" into cultural "knowledge,"[104] likewise points to the middle decades of the seventeenth century as central to English drama's canonization. Although the academic institutions on which Kermode dwells had yet to embrace the field of English dramatic study, the increasingly prominent printed paratextual discourse in the Interregnum made conventional and pervasive the activity of dramatic criticism itself.

***

Theatre Closure and the Paradoxical Rise of English Renaissance Drama in the Civil Wars explores how the decline of theatre between 1642 and 1660 lastingly transformed the production, consumption, and conception of English professional drama on the stage, in print, and in the public consciousness. *Theatre Closure* reconciles theatre history and book history, two

---

[103] On the emergence of the pre-1642 moment as a distinct period, see Chapter 5.
[104] Frank Kermode, *Forms of Attention* (Chicago: University of Chicago Press, 1985), pp. 74, 67.

approaches usually treated in isolation, to posit the reciprocal influence of drama's two media – the absent (or illegal) stage and the printed page.[105] Chapter 1 ("Dead Theatre, Printed Relics") argues that a pervasive sense of English theatre's demise during the 1640s and 1650s drove the cultural ascendancy of English plays. Kermode defines literary classics as "old books that people still read."[106] The theatre ban transformed English plays into textual objects from another era – that is, it made them seem both older and more bookish – facilitating their widespread acceptance as literature. While individual authors like Shakespeare and Jonson were canonized by the 1630s, this chapter demonstrates that English drama as a whole acquired a comparable literary status only after the theatres closed. An important precursor for this process was the marketing of stage flops as literature: unfavoured plays were deemed to exceed the capacities of vulgar theatrical audiences, and therefore, must be sophisticated. Because failed stage plays were less likely to be revived onstage, they needed to be preserved in print or else sink into oblivion. In the early years after the theatres closed, dramatic discourse followed the older rhetorical example of downplaying printed plays' theatrical origins to assert their cultural value. As the theatre ban dragged on, however, thanks to theatrical nostalgia, a play's theatrical origins contributed to, rather than detracted from, its "literary" respectability. Plays were described as printed "relics" of the dead theatre, a metaphor that anticipated and acquired weight from the execution and martyrdom of Charles I in 1649. In short, the genre of English drama was canonized posthumously.

At Ben Jonson's Head, the stationer Robert Pollard advertised his inventory with Jonson's recognizable and esteemed likeness, and published

---

[105] Important article-length interventions in theatre history in this period include Milhous and Hume's "New Light on English Acting Companies in 1646, 1648 and 1660," which traces the plights of various underemployed actors during the theatrical hiatus. Christopher Matusiak's "Elizabeth Beeston, Sir Lewis Kirke, and the Cockpit's Management during the English Civil Wars" explores the continued (and ultimately abortive) investment in the Phoenix/Cockpit theatre during the ban. Book-historical approaches to this period include Paulina Kewes's scholarship on serial publication of octavo collections (Kewes, "Sociable Pocket-Books," pp. 5–21); Adam Hooks's work on booksellers catalogues (Hooks, "Booksellers' Catalogues"); Laura Estill's work on dramatic commonplacing (Estill, *Dramatic Extracts*; Laura Estill, "The Urge to Organize Early Modern Miscellanies," *Papers of the Bibliographical Society of America*, 11.2 (2018), 27–73); and Jitka Štollová's and Marissa Nicosia's work on dramatic paratexts (Jitka Štollová, "'This Silence of the Stage': The Play of Format and Paratext in the Beaumont and Fletcher Folio," *Review of English Studies*, 68.1 (2017), 507–23; Marissa Nicosia, "Printing as Revival: Making Playbooks in the 1650s," *Papers of the Bibliographical Society of America*, 111.4 (2017), 469–89), which highlight the innovations of the dramatic book trade during the Interregnum.

[106] Frank Kermode, *The Classic: Literary Images of Permanence and Change* (Cambridge, MA: Harvard University Press, 1975), p. 43.

a wide range of dramatic and non-dramatic material, but no Jonson plays. A similar separation between authorial persona and printed texts is visible in the Interregnum circulation of Shakespeare. Chapter 2 ("Old Shakespeare") considers the decline of Shakespearean play publication during the 1640s and 1650s, even as the authorial figure of Shakespeare was celebrated as a standard of dramatic value. While dramatic publishing flourished in the middle decades of the seventeenth century, only two new editions of Shakespeare plays (*Othello* and *King Lear*), one new edition of a poem (*Lucrece*), and one new title page for a reissued edition (*The Merchant of Venice*) appeared. I ascribe this relative Shakespearean shortfall to stationers capitalizing on the availability of and demand for "new" (i.e. previously unprinted) professional plays in a moment without an active theatre. This emphasis on dramatic novelty neglected Shakespeare's oft-printed plays, but ensured the survival of many other plays in the early modern English dramatic corpus. This chapter also considers the limited Shakespearean publications in the Interregnum, texts that bear witness to "old" Shakespeare's established yet imprecise respectability, a quality that led to a range of textual appropriations.

The third chapter ("Canonizing Beaumont and Fletcher") considers the reception and production of the most popular dramatists on the illegal stage and on the printed page during the Civil Wars and Interregnum: Beaumont and Fletcher. Surveying the considerable body of dramatic paratexts from and commentary on illegal performances of their plays, this chapter offers reasons for Beaumont and Fletcher's particular popularity. Reading against the grain of politicized criticism that has characterized (and inhibited) approaches to Beaumont and Fletcher for the last four centuries, I offer an alternative reading of *A King and No King* that argues that this paradoxical play is simultaneously political and not political: audiences were drawn to the play's aesthetic qualities, but for reasons that often reflected their political investments. While *A King and No King*'s provocative title undoubtedly speaks to the crises in monarchical succession and identity of the 1640s and 1650s – Charles II's status as a king was in question after execution of his father Charles I, while many saw Lord Protector Oliver Cromwell as a king in everything but name – the deliberately puzzling quality of the title also speaks to the play's preoccupation with crises of personal identity, familial relations, and verbal and ontological paradoxes, which are often displaced in criticism in favour of more overtly politicized readings. But while *A King and No King*'s paradoxes need not be read in the context of Interregnum politics, in practice, Beaumont and Fletcher's topsy-turvy sensibilities spoke to the vertiginous moment of the mid seventeenth century as well as to Royalists' bellelettrist sensibilities.

The last two chapters consider how the theatrical prohibition lastingly transformed dramatic attitudes and practices. The restoration of the theatres in 1660 is typically conceived as a "fresh start" in English theatrical culture. Chapter 4 ("Chronic Conditions") demonstrates that the 1660s marked not simply a change but also a continuation of many of the conditions of the 1640s and 1650s. It focuses on the theatrical professionals who continued to be marginalized from the industry, and the consequent effects on theatre, print publication, and dramatic discourse. The effects of the theatrical prohibition continued to shape dramatic activities and discourse even after the theatres reopened. Chapter 4 is paired with Chapter 5 ("Morbid Symptoms"), which challenges critical commonplaces that locate the origins of dramatic criticism and theatre historiography in the Restoration, and traces these instead to the Interregnum. This chapter articulates the role of the theatrical prohibition in the emergence of different strands of early modern dramatic studies: theatre history, dramatic criticism, and bibliography. Theatre history begins after 1642 because that is when theatre became history. "Exact and perfect" lists of playbooks were interesting in their own right, as encyclopedic repositories of information. Comprehensive enumerative bibliography was a means to shore up the ruins of the dramatic past; as Angus Vine notes, "encyclopedism is the name of the antiquarian game."[107] Prefatory dramatic criticism recreated in print the conversations that had otherwise taken place in person at the playhouse, among people now dispersed due to war and economic collapse. Due to the restrictions on theatre, English drama was repackaged and reconceived in ways that still inform our engagements with early modern drama. Together, these final two chapters argue that both the "fresh start" theory of Restoration theatre and the "new" Restoration dramatic studies must actually be understood in terms of the continuation of the Interregnum's dramatic attitudes and practices after 1660.

"Literary history is a morgue where one seeks out the friend one most loved," claims the nineteenth-century German literary critic Heinrich Heine, suggesting that the primary concern of literary history is to engage with the literary past from which one is irremediably estranged.[108] Heine's

---

[107] Vine, *In Defiance of Time*, p. 18.
[108] Qtd. in Seth Lerer, "Literary Histories," in *Cultural Reformations*, ed. Cummings and Simpson, pp. 75–94 (p. 75).

formulation helps us understand what happened to English professional drama during the theatrical prohibition. The decisive conclusion of professional theatre in 1642 made both possible and necessary a coherent conception of the lost genre. The perception that early modern professional drama died after 1642 prompted efforts to elegize and anatomize the genre. In fact, the drama neither died nor disappeared between 1642 and 1660; the attempt to silence plays was only partially successful and, ultimately, temporary. Yet during the theatre's prolonged pause, contemporaries lived with the fear that it might never return. For two long decades, the fear of drama's irrecoverable loss prompted efforts of recovery that lastingly shaped the category of English Renaissance drama as a genre and critical field.

CHAPTER I

Dead Theatre, Printed Relics

Introduction: Last Remains and Sprightly Posthumes

Texts provided the only legitimate life for plays between 1642 and 1660. The playbook market enjoyed its status as the primary supplier of dramatic novelty, printing "new" playbooks that countered the sterility of the stage. Yet this could not last: Without an active theatre industry, eventually, at least in theory, the stock of previously unprinted professional scripts would run out. In his all-new folio collection of Beaumont and Fletcher (1647), the stationer Humphrey Moseley describes his novel offerings as "all you must ever expect."[1] Moseley creates pre-emptive nostalgia for the excitement of new plays. He could easily give voice to the theatrical nostalgia expressed by the other contributors to the folio; his unexpected emphasis on novelty reveals a longing not only for stage plays, but also for the process of theatrical creation – the regular generation of new plays. After declaring that the present collection has "no omissions," however, Moseley admits, "One only play I must except (for I mean to deal openly), tis a comedy called the *Wild Goose Chase*, which hath been long lost, and, I fear, irrecoverable."[2] Moseley tantalizes readers with a single missing play from an otherwise complete authorial corpus: This lacuna pulses with potential energy, deferring any sense of finitude. Moseley describes the circumstances of the manuscript's loss, and appeals for its return: "a person of quality borrowed it from the actors many years since, and (by the negligence of a servant) it was never returned; therefore now I put up this *si quis*, that whosoever hereafter happily meets with it, shall be thankfully satisfied if he please to send it home."[3] The request partakes of a well-established early modern paratextual convention that refers to the loss (or near loss) of manuscripts prior to publication. Kara J. Northway

---

[1] Humphrey Moseley, "The Stationer to the Readers," in Beaumont and Fletcher, *Comedies and Tragedies*, sig. A4r.
[2] Ibid.   [3] Ibid.

evocatively calls this convention the "lost-sheep paratext," evoking the Parable of the Shepherd who loses and then recovers a single sheep, where "hee reioyceth more of that sheepe, then of the ninetie and nine which went not astray."[4] The lost-sheep paratext conveys the yearning for lost items, and the high value accorded to things lost and found, over and above things that are consistently, reliably available. For readers of the 1647 folio, the "one only . . . long lost" play, teasingly out of reach, is more desirable than the thirty-five others to which they have immediate access.

Remarkably, someone apparently heeded Moseley's plea and returned *The Wild Goose Chase* manuscript, which Moseley printed in 1652 in a single-text folio edition, enabling owners of the larger folio collection of 1647 to bind the two publications together, thus reuniting the lost play with its fellows.[5] By filling a gap left conspicuously open in the 1647 folio, *The Wild Goose Chase* replaces the previous feeling of expectation with one of closure and completeness. On its title page, *The Wild Goose Chase* is called the "noble, last, only remains" of Beaumont and Fletcher. The edition is significant both as the "last new play" of Beaumont and Fletcher and as one that miraculously escaped loss. Its dramatic paratexts conflate life and death: The familiar metaphors of publishing as childbirth are fused with those of memorial publication. James Ramsey's commendatory poem, "On Mr. Fletcher's Wild-Goose Chase Recovered," calls the play a "sprightly posthume, whom our pious fear / Bewailed as if it an abortive were" but that does "more glorious by burial grow."[6] The "sprightly posthume" evokes its dead parent even as it assumes a vibrant, independent life of its own. The image of the near "abortive" indicates the reorientation of dramatic identity around print after the closure of the theatres: In a context without theatre, composed and staged plays must be printed to exist. Instead of representing the miscarriage of dramatic efforts, however, the missing *Wild Goose Chase* manuscript was merely "buried." The recovered text is "more glorious" after its flirtation with oblivion.

The Wild Goose Chase is a post-posthumous publication, the last gasp of Fletcherian drama, appearing after the author's death, his 1647 memorial

---

[4] Kara J. Northway, "'I haue lost it': Apologies, Appeals, and Justifications for Misplacing *The Wild-Goose Chase* and Other Plays," in *Loss and the Literary Culture of Shakespeare's Time*, ed. Roslyn L. Knutson, David McInnis, and Matthew Steggle (Basingstoke: Palgrave Macmillan, 2020), pp. 75–93 (p. 86). Thank you to Misha Teramura for drawing this essay to my attention.

[5] Some early copies are bound this way. For instance, see the digitized microfiche reproduction of the original in Harvard University Libraries, on *Early English Books Online*.

[6] James Ramsey, "On Mr. Fletcher's Wild-Goose Chase Recovered," in Francis Beaumont and [John Fletcher], *The Wild-Goose Chase* (London: Humphrey Moseley, 1652), sig. A4r.

collection, and the collapse of an entire theatrical tradition, as elegized in the edition's paratextual matter. *The Wild Goose Chase*'s title page (Figure 1.1) declares that the play was printed for the "private benefit" of John Lowin and Joseph Taylor, the veteran co-leaders of the King's Servants, London's most prominent acting company and the house company of Fletcher and Shakespeare. Lowin and Taylor provide a poignant dedication bewailing the "cruell Destinie" that has rendered them "Mutes and Bound." Acknowledging their irrelevance in this new era of textual drama, Lowin and Taylor wish the reader "the same kind joy in perusing of it, as we had in the Acting." They bid adieu to the stage: "And now Farewell our Glory! Farewell your Choice Delight! . . . Farewell the Pride and Life o'th' Stage . . . so exeunt."[7] The letter ends with a sad echo of theatrical activity, with the actors taking their leave not from a scene in a play, but from a theatrical tradition that had drawn to a close.[8] By the 1650s, the pre-war theatrical tradition was hollowed out.

Northway demonstrates that the "lost-sheep paratext" pervaded sixteenth- and seventeenth-century literary culture, across different genres. But the psychology underlying the lost-sheep paratext – in which that which is lost (and potentially recovered) is more treasured than that which was always present – took on new significance in mid seventeenth-century dramatic culture, when losses were endured across the entire English dramatic tradition, both page and stage. The fact and threat of destruction accorded new status to both dramatic texts and the absent theatre: The playbook staved off further loss and acquired new respectability through its ties with a longed-for medium.

Moseley's story of the loss and recovery of *The Wild Goose Chase* manuscript has been accepted by some critics and regarded sceptically by others.[9] But, whether Moseley was lucky or lying, his story and the

---

[7] John Lowin and Joseph Taylor, "The Dedication: To the Honour'd, Few, Lovers of Drammatick Poesie," in Beaumont and Fletcher, *The Wild-Goose Chase*, sig. A2r.

[8] On John Lowin's career, see Barbara Wooding, *John Lowin and the English Theatre, 1603–1647: Acting and Cultural Politics on the Jacobean and Caroline Stage* (Surrey: Ashgate, 2013).

[9] John Fletcher, *A Critical Edition of John Fletcher's Comedy, The Wild-goose Chase*, ed. Rota Herzberg Lister (New York: Garland Publishing, 1980), p. xxxix; Kastan, "Performances and Playbooks," pp. 173–4; Grace Ioppolo, *Dramatists and Their Manuscripts in the Age of Shakespeare* (London: Routledge, 2013), p. 146. Northway studies the story and suggests Moseley was telling the truth. She notes that, while early modern stationers were accused of deliberately withholding books from publication to generate sales at a later date, the five years between the folio collection of 1647 and the appearance of the 1652 edition "would seem a long time to pull off an astrologer's scam" ("'I haue lost it'," p. 87). But Moseley was accustomed to playing the long game, sometimes waiting five years between entering texts into the Stationers' Register and publishing them. Moseley would have a clear economic incentive to withhold a play from an otherwise complete collection, the belated

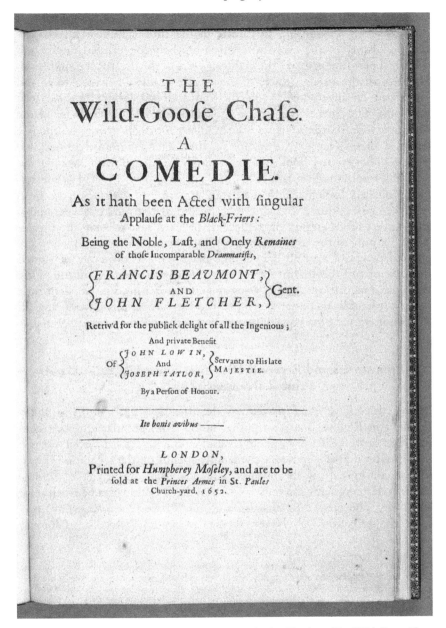

THE
Wild-Goofe Chafe.
A
COMEDIE.

As it hath been Acted with fingular
Applaufe at the *Black-Friers*:

Being the Noble, Laft, and Onely *Remaines*
of thofe Incomparable *Drammatifts,*

FRANCIS BEAUMONT,
AND }Gent.
JOHN FLETCHER,

Retriv'd for the publick delight of all the Ingenious ;

And private Benefit

Of {*JOHN LOWIN,*
And {Servants to His late
JOSEPH TAYLOR, {MAJESTIE.

By a Perfon of Honour.

Ite bonis avibus ——

LONDON,
Printed for *Humpherey Mofeley,* and are to be
fold at the *Princes Armes* in St. *Paules*
Church-yard. 1 6 5 2.

Figure 1.1   Title page from Francis Beaumont and John Fletcher, *The Wild Goose Chase*
(Humphrey Moseley, 1652).
Courtesy of the Huntington Library.

resultant edition of *The Wild Goose Chase* illuminate ideas about printed drama and its relationship to theatre in the Interregnum. This chapter offers a history of the evolving relationship between printed drama and theatrical performance over the eighteen years of the theatrical prohibition. I argue that the steady decline of the theatre industry between 1642 and 1660 had an inverse effect on the status of the printed professional playbook: The further the theatre's fortunes fell, the higher those of the playbook rose. As the years without public performance wore on, people resigned themselves to the reality of an England without professional theatre. The printed book was increasingly burdened with keeping the dramatic tradition alive. But even "new" printed plays smelled of mortality: Publishers brought forth dramatic "remains" or "relics" of the dead theatrical past. Printed dramatic relics served as both material mementos and objects of veneration of the lost tradition, a way to keep the theatre "alive," if only in the cultural imagination. Theatre's absence added to the cultural cachet of English drama: The playbook was physically separated from the absent theatre but drew ever closer to the idealized theatre of the nostalgic imagination. As the living fragments of a dead practice, printed relics perpetuate the essence of the theatre for eternity, producing an English literary drama equally rooted in the theatrical and the material.

Prehistories and Received Histories: Theatrical Failure and Printed Drama, c.1567–1642

Many critics have cited the era of the theatrical prohibition as a key moment in English drama's transformation from popular entertainment into literature. Usually, these arguments perpetuate the broader precept that English drama's literary ascendancy depends on the separation (physical or conceptual) of the printed playbook from performance.[10] Some early modern dramatic discourse erects sanitizing boundaries between stage and page. The preface to Shakespeare's *Troilus and Cressida* (1609) presents the text from "A Never Writer, to an Ever Reader," famously

---

publication squeezing one more purchase out of the completist buyers of the Beaumont and Fletcher folio, while also reigniting interest in the folio collection. That the title of the play involves a seemingly futile hunt for a "wild goose" aligns suspiciously well with Moseley's account: In the play, Oriana gets the seemingly unattainable object of her affections, just as the reader of the 1647 folio eventually receives the long-lost play.

[10] For an overview and interrogation of this theory, see Zachary Lesser and Peter Stallybrass, "The First Literary *Hamlet* and the Commonplacing of Professional Plays," *Shakespeare Quarterly*, 59.4 (2008), 371–420 (p. 409).

claiming that the play was "never staled with the stage, never clapper-clawed with the palms of the vulgar ... [nor] sullied with the smoky breath of the multitude."[11] David Scott Kastan notes that in Shakespeare's First Folio of 1623, the actors John Heminge and Henry Condell establish Shakespeare "as a single (and singular) author rather than a playwright working collaboratively within the economies of the theatre." Kastan continues, "If Heminges and Condell unexpectedly slight the theatre, the reasons are not hard to guess. The volume is aimed at readers or, more exactly, buyers, who may very well be put off by a more overt theatrical claim. Plays were still subliterary ... thus the book presents itself as literary."[12] Ben Jonson's ambivalence about the theatre is well known; he routinely disparaged the stage to bolster his authorial status and the literary status of his plays.[13] Similar strategies seem to inform the production and consumption of printed drama in the Interregnum. Louis B. Wright observes that "the focusing of attention upon the reading of plays, a natural result of the prohibition on acting, tended to increase the prestige of drama as literature."[14] Wright focuses on play-reading as the engine driving English drama's rising status; Kastan emphasizes dramatic publication's new dominance, remarking that "paradoxically, the closing of the theatres helped to preserve the plays that made up the dramatic repertoire (and arguably even ensured the successful transformation of drama into a literary form) by intensifying the market for published playbooks."[15] Ann Baynes Coiro observes that "the combination of print's dominance and the concomitant stage ban finally accelerated theatre's alchemical change into dramatic poetry,"[16] while Paulina Kewes similarly argues that during the theatrical prohibition, "removed from the undignified sphere of performance, plays began to acquire a new cultural respectability."[17]

---

[11] "A Never Writer to an Ever Reader," in William Shakespeare, *Troilus and Cressida* (London: Richard Bonian and Henry Walley, 1609), sig. ¶2r.

[12] David Scott Kastan, *Shakespeare and the Book* (Cambridge: Cambridge University Press, 2002), pp. 31, 72.

[13] Julie Sanders, *Ben Jonson in Context* (Cambridge: Cambridge University Press, 2010), p. 197; Jonas Barish, *The Antitheatrical Prejudice* (Berkeley: University of California Press, 1981), pp. 133–9; Alan B. Farmer and Zachary Lesser, "Vile Arts: The Marketing of English Printed Drama, 1512–1660," *Research Opportunities in Renaissance Drama*, 39 (2000), 77–165.

[14] Louis B. Wright, "The Reading of Plays during the Puritan Revolution," *The Huntington Library Bulletin*, 6 (1934), 73–108 (pp. 107–8).

[15] Kastan, "Performances and Playbooks," p. 176.

[16] Ann Baynes Coiro, "Reading," in *Early Modern Theatricality*, ed. Henry Turner (Oxford: Oxford University Press, 2015), pp. 534–55 (p. 535).

[17] Paulina Kewes, *Authorship and Appropriation: Writing for the Stage in England, 1660–1710* (Cambridge: Cambridge University Press, 1998), p. 27.

None of these arguments quite accounts for English drama's shifting status in this moment. While play-reading and play publishing undoubtedly dominated dramatic consumption and production in the Interregnum, these practices date back to the earliest days of theatre.[18] And yet, in addition to representing a larger portion of dramatic activity, play printing and play-reading seem to have been qualitatively different in the Interregnum. Why? Kewes observes that the removal of playbooks from the stigmatized spaces of the theatre allowed them to assume new levels of respectability. Even after the playhouses had been closed for nearly two decades, however, plays were never entirely "removed from the sphere of performance," at least not in the minds of readers and stationers. Even if plays were physically separated from the theatre, they were conceptually tethered to it: Title page theatrical attributions, cast lists, and other dramatic paratexts announced a play's connections to the theatre. *The Wild Goose Chase* includes a cast list that is unprecedentedly elaborate, acknowledging the performances of "MIRABELL . . . Incomparably Acted by Mr. Ioseph Taylor," "BELLEUR . . . Most naturally Acted by Mr. Iohn Lowin," and "PINAC . . . Admirably well Acted by Mr. Thomas Pollard," among others.[19] The adverbs are unusual; G. E. Bentley calls *The Wild Goose Chase* cast list "the most descriptive of the printed casts for plays of the King's company."[20] But the list is not exactly "descriptive" – compare the vague praise of "incomparable" and "natural" with the vivid description of Edward Alleyn "stalking" the Elizabethan stage[21] – but it is celebratory, and distinctly retrospective. The list exemplifies how Interregnum playbooks took even greater pains to assert a connection to the theatre. The memory – or, increasingly, the *idea*, distinct from actual events – of the theatre continued to shape readers' impressions of playbooks long after the physical playhouses closed. At the time that *The Wild Goose Chase* was printed, the playhouses had been closed for a decade, and would remain closed for another eight years. With many deprived of the theatrical pleasures they had previously enjoyed, and with growing numbers of people without first-hand experience of theatre, the pre-1642 tradition was increasingly idealized – the lost object of memory and longing.

[18] Julie Stone Peters, *Theatre of the Book, 1480–1880: Print, Text, and Performance in Europe* (Oxford: Oxford University Press, 2000), p. 8.

[19] "Drammatis Personæ," in Beaumont and Fletcher, *The Wild-Goose Chase*, sig. [a2v].

[20] G. E. Bentley, *The Professional Player of Shakespeare's Time, 1590–1642* (Princeton: Princeton University Press, 1984), p. 257.

[21] On Alleyn's "stalking" see Jeremy Lopez, "Alleyn Resurrected," *Marlowe Studies*, 1 (2011), 167–80.

The stigma of the stage, then, did not simply disappear along with the physical playhouses. Thanks to theatrical nostalgia, it actually transformed into prestige, likewise attached to the playbook. The *Wild Goose Chase* paratexts assert the beauty and dignity of the declining theatrical profession, a legacy that contributes to the beauty and dignity of the "dramatic poesie" of the printed text. A theatrical provenance became an asset, not a liability, adding to, rather than detracting from, a play's cultural status. Critics have questioned whether "literature" was a pre-existing category into which English drama could be classified in the seventeenth century. Kastan notes that "scholarly overemphasis on early modern drama in its accounts of the literary achievement in England has distracted us from seeing that English literature had not yet even formed as a category of collection and organization."[22] Kastan characterizes Moseley's poetic and dramatic output as the "invention" of English literature. This "invention" should not be credited to Moseley alone, but rather to the publication activity of the 1640s and 1650s more generally. The retrospective idealization of English professional theatre after its prohibition, combined with the material and cultural endurance of playbooks after 1642, accorded playbooks an unprecedented cultural value, enabling the invention of English vernacular literature, a category of which English drama was an essential part.

The theatre ban reconfigured the relationship between stage and page, as critics have observed. Rachel Willie describes the emergence of the "paper stage" in the mid seventeenth century as "an arena that simultaneously allows dramatic representation to hibernate until it can be reawakened in performative form and offers a platform where drama is staged in print."[23] Marta Straznicky argues that play-reading in the Interregnum is often "imagined as a substitute for playgoing rather than an extension of it."[24] John Barnard, Kastan, Kewes, Randall Ingram, and Jitka Štollová focus their attention on Moseley and his creation of "serious literary drama" in the Interregnum.[25] Štollová notes that Moseley's 1647 Beaumont and Fletcher

---

[22] Kastan, "Humphrey Moseley," p. 110. See also Adam G. Hooks, *Selling Shakespeare*, p. 157.

[23] Willie, *Staging the Revolution*, pp. 28–9.

[24] Marta Straznicky, *Privacy, Playreading, and Women's Closet Drama, 1550–1700* (Cambridge: Cambridge University Press, 2004), p. 68.

[25] John Barnard, "London Publishing, 1640–1660: Crisis, Continuity, and Innovation," *Book History*, 4 (2001), 1–16 (pp. 8–9); Kastan, "Humphrey Moseley"; Kewes, "Sociable Pocket-Books"; Randall Ingram, "First Words and Second Thoughts: Margaret Cavendish, Humphrey Moseley, and 'the Book'," *Journal of Medieval and Early Modern Studies*, 30.1 (Winter 2000), 101–24 (p. 105); Štollová, "This Silence of the Stage."

folio offers itself as "a literary supplement for silenced theatres."[26] As I demonstrate in the following sections, Moseley's mid-1640s strategies, while innovative, also recalled earlier sales techniques, particularly those used to market theatrical failures.

Moseley is undoubtedly the most productive and important of the period's dramatic stationers, but he is far from the only stationer or commentator to contribute significantly to contemporary dramatic discourse. Marissa Nicosia contrasts Moseley's dramatic publishing strategies, "fundamentally oriented around selling plays as reading material," with those of the players-turned-stationers who imagined dramatic publication as a kind of theatrical "revival." Nicosia argues that "while many publishers considered that print metamorphosed drama into poetry, player-publishers instead reverted to the language and imagery of acting and the stage to reiterate the performative nature of their printed works."[27] Nicosia usefully expands the conversation out from Moseley, offering a broader view of the discourse that surrounded dramatic publishing in the shadow of the vacant theatres. But Moseley's own attitudes changed over time, eventually focusing on plays' performativity, as we see in *The Wild Goose Chase* prefatory matter. Moreover, Nicosia perpetuates the opposition between dramatic "poetry" on one hand and plays' "performative nature" on the other. This binary was active when the theatres were open, and even in the first years after the 1642 prohibition, when theatre could still dampen the cultural cachet of the printed book. But by the late 1640s, "poetry" and "performance," far from being mutually exclusive, came to be mutually reinforcing.

The argument that the "literary" printed playbook needed to downplay its theatrical origins has been rightly questioned. Zachary Lesser notes that while some early seventeenth-century playbooks included paratextual material "explicitly to distance their plays from the theatre," most publishers "appealed to a play's performance onstage and expected their customers to be theatregoers themselves."[28] An important subset of texts indeed deliberately detached plays from the theatrical tradition, however: printed plays that flopped onstage. Marta Straznicky notes that "enterprising publishers and playwrights" turned theatrical failure "into a selling point, distinguishing discerning readers from the vulgar uncomprehending

---

[26] Štollová, "This Silence of the Stage," p. 516.   [27] Nicosia, "Printing as Revival," pp. 471, 489.
[28] Zachary Lesser, "Playbooks," in *The Oxford History of Popular Print Culture*, vol. 1, ed. Joad Raymond (Oxford: Oxford University Press, 2011), pp. 521–35 (p. 527).

audiences."[29] Walter Burre's edition of Ben Jonson's *Catiline* (1611), a notorious stage flop, included a Latin epigraph by Horace on the title page: "*His non Plebecula gaudet. | Verum Equitis quoq[ue], iam migrauit ab aure voluptas, | Omnis, ad incertos oculos, & gaudia vana.* [The rabble do not delight in this. Indeed, all satisfaction of the knights as well has now migrated from the ear to uncertain eyes and vain joys]."[30] The motto transforms stage failure into a sign of cultural merit – the theatrical mob is demarcated from a smaller, more discerning reading audience.[31] Francis Beaumont's *The Knight of the Burning Pestle*, John Webster's *The White Devil*, and John Fletcher's *The Faithful Shepherdess* all also failed onstage and were subsequently printed in editions that staked claims for their respective plays' literary status with some kind of dismissal of the "uncapable multitude" who failed to appreciate the play onstage.[32] Ann Baynes Coiro argues that the publication of *The Faithful Shepherdess* (1608) following its failure onstage is a "defining moment in the story of early modern theatricality's transformation into dramatic poetry."[33]

The stationer Walter Burre (active between 1597 and 1622) made a career out of publishing stage flops. Zachary Lesser argues that "for Burre, nothing succeeded like failure: the publisher created something of a specialty in plays that had been scorned by theatre audiences."[34] Burre published Beaumont's *Knight of the Burning Pestle* (1613) six years after its disastrous premiere by the Children of the Queen's Revels in 1607. In his dedication to the company's theatre manager Robert Keysar, Burre blames the play's failure on undiscerning spectators' "want of iudgement": "not vnderstanding the priuy marke of Ironie about it," the spectators "vtterly reiected it." In contrast, Keysar, with his "iudgement, vnderstanding, and singular loue to good wits," recognized the play's merits, which led him to keep a copy of *Knight*'s manuscript for four years after its failed run. Keysar eventually sent the manuscript, "an infant and somewhat ragged," to Burre, who "fost[e]red it priuately in [his] bosome these two yeares," eventually printing *The Knight of the Burning Pestle*'s first quarto in 1613. Burre emphasizes that his efforts and those of Keysar, to preserve the vulnerable, child-like manuscript for six years, rescued *The Knight of*

[29] Straznicky, *Privacy*, p. 69.   [30] Ben Jonson, *Catiline* (London: Walter Burre, 1611), title page.
[31] Zachary Lesser, *Renaissance Drama and the Politics of Publication* (Cambridge: Cambridge University Press, 2004), pp. 54–65.
[32] On marketing of *The White Devil*, see Straznicky, *Privacy*, pp. 68–70; on the marketing of *The Faithful Shepherdess*, see Coiro, "Reading," p. 543.
[33] Coiro, "Reading," p. 543.   [34] Lesser, *Politics of Publication*, p. 52.

the Burning Pestle from "perpetuall obliuion."[35] Recalling the rhetorical strategies of lost-sheep paratexts, it is not only the exclusion of the theatrical rabble that elevated stage failures: the threat of oblivion made their texts more highly valued.

"Oblivion" does not simply mean physical non-existence; to fall into oblivion is to disappear from cultural memory. Prior to the prohibition, even if they were not printed, popular stage plays could be kept in the public consciousness through theatrical revival (at least in theory). Popular stage plays like *Bold Beauchamp* and *The Jew of Malta* were not considered "lost" in the early modern period, even though they were, respectively, never printed and belatedly printed. For plays that failed on stage, however, the threat of oblivion was more acute: they were less likely to circulate on stage, and their unused manuscripts were more liable to be displaced and lost forever. For stage failures, a printed iteration was needed for a play to "exist"; stage failures, then, reoriented the play's identity and existence around print. And, when they finally were printed, plays recovered from "perpetual oblivion" were marketed as especially valuable due to their brush with death.

Stage flops printed before 1642 reveal the relationship between theatrical failure, the risk of oblivion, and printed literary drama: a play fails onstage, risks physical and cultural disappearance, but is recovered and printed in a text that is valued more for its near loss. The same relationship holds after 1642, but now the cause and scope of theatrical failure is altered. Failure is not due to unpopularity, but to governmental prohibition; failure was not limited to individual plays but encompassed an entire industry. Critics have noted in passing the affinity between the marketing of pre-1642 printed stage flops and post-1642 playbooks. Marta Straznicky points out that "until the 1640s, printed plays rarely address their readers (if they address readers at all) as an audience markedly different from the play's spectators. The occasional exception is a play that failed in performance and is therefore marketed in print to a readership that is distinct from the original audience."[36] Coiro notes that, in the prefatory matter to *The Faithful Shepherdess*, "Jonson makes an eerily prescient prediction, calling the stage failure of *The Faithful Shepherdess* a 'Martirdome' that 'crown[s]' 'thy murdred Poëme: which shall rise / A glorified worke to Time, when Fire / Or moathes shall eate, what all these Fooles admire.'"[37]

---

[35] Walter Burre, "The Epistle Dedicatory," in [Francis Beaumont], *The Knight of the Burning Pestle* (London: Walter Burre, 1613), sig. A2r.
[36] Straznicky, *Privacy*, p. 63   [37] Coiro, "Reading," p. 544.

The "murdered" poem is "martyred," made more glorious through its recovery from the threat of moths, time, and fire. In this case, unpopularity "killed" the play; the metaphor of dramatic "martyrdom" acquired more power when the theatres were shuttered, and still more after the regicide.

During the first few years after the theatrical prohibition in particular, the rhetoric of print publication recalls that of pre-1642 stage flops. This strategy is exemplified in Thomas May's commendatory verse, "To my Honoured Friend M. Ja. Shirley, Upon the Printing of his Elegant POEMS," printed in James Shirley's *Poems &c*, published by Humphrey Moseley in 1646. May reassures Shirley that the removal of his plays from the stage will lead to a longer, more rarefied life in print:

> Although thou want the theatre's applause,
> Which now is fitly silenc'd by the laws,
> [. . .]   it was not fit
> We should lose such monuments of wit
> As flow'd from thy terse pen: the press alone
> Can vindicate from dark oblivion
> Thy POEMS, friend: those that with skill can read
> Shall by thy judges now, and shall, instead
> Of ignorant spectators, grace thy name
> Though with a narrower, yet a truer fame,
> And crown with longe life thy worthy pains.[38]

May's poem rehearses many of the marketing strategies of stage flops printed before 1642: deprived of a life onstage, the play is threatened with "dark oblivion," from which it can be rescued by "the press alone." "Ignorant spectators" are distinguished from "[t]hose that with skill can read," who grant Shirley "narrower, yet truer fame," granting his dramatic "POEMS" the "long life" of literary immortality which is the obverse of oblivion. Certainly, as critics have noted, the closure of the theatres transformed dramatic audiences into an exclusively literate group, excluding illiterate spectators. Plays and playreaders no longer risked being associated with the vulgar mob who previously enjoyed stage plays, so it would make sense if the status of both playbooks and their readers rose as a consequence. But these are essentially the same arguments made about pre-1642 printed stage flops. One might argue that the mechanics of stage failure and printed literary drama visible before 1642 was simply enacted over an entire dramatic field after the theatres closed. This is partly true,

---

[38] Thomas May, "To My Honoured Friend M. Ja. Shirley, Upon the Printing of His Elegant Poems," in James Shirley, *Poems &c*. (London: Humphrey Moseley, 1646), sig. A5r.

but it is wrong to simply consider English drama's post-1642 status as a magnified version of the process experienced by pre-1642 printed stage flops. May follows well-trodden paths, but his misplaced scorn hints at the different circumstances: it is not the "ignorant spectators" who misjudged the play and threatened it with oblivion, but "the laws" that deprived Shirley's plays of "applause."

Anxiety about dramatic "oblivion" existed prior to 1642, and not only for stage flops. In *The English Traveller* (1633), Thomas Heywood complains that negligent or jealous actors lost or withheld his manuscripts: "my Playes are not exposed vnto the world in Volumes, to beare the title of Workes, (as others) one reason is, That many of them by shifting and change of Companies, haue beene negligently lost, Others of them are still retained in the hands of some Actors, who thinke it against their peculiar profit to haue them come in Print."[39] As we shall see in the next chapter, the closure of the theatres solved the problem of actors jealously guarding scripts from play publishers, who could be considered rivals for audience attention: hard-up theatre companies sold off unused scripts to stationers, making available a new supply of manuscripts.[40] While the theatre ban solved one of Heywood's problems, his complaint about the menace that "the shifting and change of Companies" posed to dramatic manuscripts amplified after 1642, once the manuscripts were not of immediate use, the companies who safeguarded them dispersed, and the venues in which the manuscripts were kept were vacated, demolished, or put to different uses. The English Civil War posed its own threat to dramatic manuscripts. William Proctor Williams argues that the war and the "attendant pillaging of the houses of people of importance including their libraries by combatants from both sides would also have caused the loss, almost certainly permanent loss, of some dramatic manuscripts."[41] The closure of the theatres, then, was a double-edged sword for dramatic manuscripts, making them more likely to be printed, but also more likely to be lost altogether.

[39] Thomas Heywood, "To the Reader," in Thomas Heywood, *The English Traveller* (London: Robert Raworth, 1633), sig. A3r.

[40] Recent critics have posited a less antagonistic relationship between the book trade and the theatre industry. Rather than theatre companies jealously withholding scripts from stationers, perhaps a more plausible idea is that companies kept scripts of plays that continued in repertory, which meant that they wouldn't have been available for publication until after the theatres closed. Nevertheless, we can take Heywood's comments as evidence of anxiety about the rivalry between the playhouse and book trade, even if this rivalry is overstated.

[41] William Proctor Williams, "What's a Lost Play?: Toward a Taxonomy of Lost Plays," in *Lost Plays in Shakespeare's England*, ed. David McInnis and Matthew Steggle, pp. 17–30 (p. 18).

In dramatic paratexts after 1642, we see an urgency to find and preserve dramatic manuscripts to prevent further loss. In James Shirley's "Postscript to the Reader" to his own *Poems &c.* (1646), the author claims that he had no intention of printing his poems, "But when I observed most of these Copies corrupted in their transcripts, and the rest fleeting from me," he changed his mind.[42] Shirley's statement partakes of the routine modesty topos of the author's prefatory letter, but his concern about the proliferation of corrupt copies and the loss of fugitive manuscripts seems to have been particularly problematic in the Interregnum. In another Shirley paratext, this one penned for his *Gentleman of Venice*, first performed in 1639 and first printed by Moseley in 1655, Shirley describes his dramatic manuscript as a baby who grows up and wanders off: "I must acknowledge many years have past, since it did *vagare in cunis* [wail in the cradle] and when it had gotten strength, and legs to walk, traveling without direction, it lost it self, till it was recovered after much inquisition, and now upon the first return home, hath made this fortunate addresse, and application to your Patronage."[43] In lost-sheep paratexts, the metaphor of the manuscript as a baby often recurs, conveying the manuscript's vulnerability and value to its creator. Shirley's characterization of his text recalls Burre's reference to the "infant and ragged" manuscript of *The Knight of the Burning Pestle*, and the nearly "abortive" text of *The Wild Goose Chase*. Even the basic threat of time increased in the 1640s and 1650s: in 1613, Burre praised Keysar for holding on to *The Knight of the Burning Pestle* manuscript for four years, and himself for preserving it "in his bosom" for another two before the play could be safely printed. When *The Gentleman of Venice* (1655) appeared, its unused, arguably useless (from a theatrical perspective), and ostensibly misplaced manuscript had managed to survive for sixteen years before it could reach publication.

Seeking out "vindication" to recover his lost and corrupted manuscripts, James Shirley turned to Humphrey Moseley, with whom he began a long-standing collaboration in the 1640s.[44] Moseley dominated dramatic publishing in the Interregnum partly thanks to his voracious acquisition of manuscripts. In his stationer's address to the 1647 Beaumont and Fletcher folio, Moseley justifies the volume's expense by noting the difficulty of acquiring authorial manuscripts:

---

[42] James Shirley, "Postscript to the Reader," in Shirley, *Poems &c.*, sig. F8r.
[43] James Shirley, "The Epistle Dedicatory," in James Shirley, *The Gentleman of Venice* (London: Humphrey Moseley, 1655), sig. A2r.
[44] On the Shirley and Moseley collaboration, see Štollová, "This Silence of the Stage," pp. 507–23.

Twere vaine to mention the Chargeablenesse of this VVork; for those who own'd the Manuscripts, too well knew their value to make a cheap estimate of any of these Pieces, and though another joyn'd with me in the Purchase and Printing, yet the Care & Pains was wholly mine, which I found to be more than you'l easily imagine, unless you knew into how many hands the Originalls were dispersed.[45]

Moseley's comments affirm Shirley's concerns about the dispersal of dramatists' "fair" copies. Obviously designed partly as a selling point, Moseley's story is corroborated by the dramatist Aston Cockayne. In his "Apology to the Reader" for his collection *Small Poems of Diverse Sorts* (1658), Cockayne notes how he was given the manuscript of Beaumont and Fletcher's *The Mad Lover*, which spurred him to write a commendatory poem about that play, which was later included in the 1647 folio's prefatory matter. "My noble friend and kinsman Mr. Charles Cotton," Cockayne explains, "sent me that single play [i.e. *The Mad Lover*] in a manuscript, which I had divers years in my hands; therefore when I found the players prohibited to act, I writ those poor verses with an intention to have had the Mad Lover printed single." Cockayne's comments suggest how the closure of the theatres prompted both dramatic commentary and textual preservation. He possessed the manuscript for "divers years," but it was only when the players were "prohibited to act" that he was motivated to write a commendatory poem with an eye to publish *The Mad Lover* in a single-text edition. Cockayne did not, in the event, print the play. He relates how, when Moseley's "large volume came forth," his cousin Cotton "commanded from me" the text (either *The Mad Lover* manuscript, the commendatory poem, or both) "and gave the printers,"[46] hinting, perhaps, at Moseley's influence in the book market.

In that same Apology, Cockayne describes the dispersal and unauthorized publication of his own manuscripts, illustrating the trials faced by manuscripts during the upheaval of the English Civil Wars. Cockayne fought on the Royalist side, was arrested and was held in the Marshalsea Prison for several years. Before he left home, Cockayne entrusted his dramatic and poetic manuscripts to a friend for safekeeping, an attempt that seems to have failed. He relates, "at my going once out of London, I left them with a friend of mine, who dying, they were dispersed into

---

[45] Moseley, "The Stationer to the Readers," in Beaumont and Fletcher, *Comedies and Tragedies*, sig. A4r.

[46] Aston Cockayne, "The Author's Apology to the Reader," in Aston Cockayne, *Small Poems of Diverse Sorts* (London: William Godbid, 1658), sig. A3r.

divers hands."[47] The stationer William Godbid obtained a damaged manuscript of Cockayne's play *The Obstinate Lady*, hired someone else to rewrite the missing conclusion and epilogue, and published the play, again revealing the great licence taken by Interregnum stationers. Worried that his other texts would undergo the same fate as *The Obstinate Lady*, Cockayne made a "diligent inquiry" after his manuscripts but found that he "cannot get them delivered without parting with some money." Cockayne enlisted Godbid's help in obtaining the manuscripts, acknowledging that "without his assistance I should not have recovered them out of a Gentlemans hands whom I will forbear to name."[48] Though Cockayne refrains from naming him, Catherine Shaw demonstrates that the "Gentleman" was none other than Humphrey Moseley.[49]

Moseley was determined to corner the market on dramatic manuscripts; as I will discuss in Chapter 2, his efforts substantially altered the corpus of early modern commercial drama in print. Moseley's investment, commitment, and major contributions to the creation and preservation of the English dramatic canon are well known. What is discussed less often is that Moseley's interest in publishing drama began in earnest only after the closure of the theatres.[50] In the first two decades of his career in the book trade, which began with his apprenticeship to Matthew Lownes in 1619, Moseley published or played a role in publishing canonical English poets, English translations of foreign vernacular and classical texts, and English lyric poetry.[51] But he only printed one play. In 1639, Moseley published the first quarto of Richard Zouche's *The Sophister* (*Fallacy, or the Troubles of Great Hermenia*); his next dramatic publications were hybrid poetry and drama collections by John Milton (1645), John Suckling (1646), and James Shirley (1646), followed by the momentous Beaumont and

---

[47] Ibid.   [48] Ibid.

[49] Aston Cockayne, *The Obstinate Lady*, ed. Catherine Shaw (New York: Garland Publishing, 1986), pp. l–li.

[50] John Curtis Reed offers a chronological overview of Moseley's production in "Humphrey Moseley, Publisher" in *Oxford Bibliographical Society: Proceedings and Papers*, vol. 2 (Oxford: Oxford University Press, 1930), pp. 57–144; see especially pp. 104–5.

[51] Prior to Moseley joining him, Matthew Lownes published plays by John Marston and Ben Jonson in the first two decades of the 1600s, and an edition of Spenser's *Faerie Queene* in 1617. By the time Moseley joined him in 1619, Lownes had turned away from drama and was focused on reprints of well-respected vernacular poetry, including the seventh folio of Philip Sidney's *Arcadia* (1622, which Lownes reissued five times), a translation of Boccaccio's *Decameron* (1625), as well as English and ancient histories and many sermons. Between 1629 and 1634 Moseley ran a flourishing bookselling business with Nicholas Fussell: they printed Donne's *Six Sermons upon Several Occasions*, but no drama. By 1638, Moseley was established independently at the Prince's Arms, where he would spend the rest of his career; between 1638 and 1642 he published three or four books a year, including verse miscellanies and conduct manuals.

Fletcher dramatic collection (1647).[52] For some reason, Moseley shifted his publishing focus in the mid-1640s, turning his considerable energies towards English drama. Practical reasons probably played a role: noting the increased supply of dramatic manuscripts sold off by actors and companies who could no longer use them, combined with the fact that the audience's appetite for drama was whetted by live theatre's absence, Moseley perhaps sensed an opportunity to capitalize on supply and satisfy demand.

Moseley's edition of *The Sophister* (1639) also hints at less practical reasons for pivoting to drama. This first foray into dramatic publishing reveals Moseley's lofty vision for what printed drama could be: he relied on tested strategies to frame his plays as "literary" drama by distancing the texts from the stage. *The Sophister*'s title page includes a Latin tag from Horace: "*His non Plebecula gaudet* [The plebeians do not delight in this]."[53] This is an abbreviated version of the epigraph included on Walter Burre's first edition of Jonson's *Catiline* (1611), which as we have seen was designed to turn stage unpopularity into evidence of the play's cultural value. Although we do not know how *The Sophister* was received on stage, it is a dense, allegorical university play written for an academic audience and printed almost thirty years after it was first staged. Moseley's recycling of *Catiline*'s Horace epigraph for *The Sophister* is unlikely to have been a coincidence. Around 1640, Humphrey Moseley was selling copies of *Catiline*'s third quarto (1635), which featured the same Latin tag.[54] Later, Moseley also published commonplace books that drew heavily from *Catiline*.[55] The reused tag reveals Moseley's awareness not only of the literary dramatic tradition exemplified by Jonson, but also of the classicized version of the author that Burre created through paratextual framing that recast theatrical failures as literary drama. From Burre, Moseley learned that theatrical failures could be good business, and indeed, Moseley ultimately made a career of printing theatrical failures as literature. After 1642, of course, theatrical failure became industry-wide, giving Moseley an entire dramatic field to draw on.

[52] Štollová, "This Silence of the Stage," p. 509 n.8.
[53] Richard Zouche, *The Sophister* (London: Humphrey Moseley, 1639), sig. A1r.
[54] *British Drama 1533–1642: A Catalogue, Vol. 6: 1609–1616*, ed. Martin Wiggins and Catherine Richardson (Oxford: Oxford University Press: 2015), p. 170.
[55] G. E. Bentley, "John Cotgrave's *English Treasury of Wit and Language* and the Elizabethan Drama," *Studies in Philology*, 40 (April 1943), 186–203 (pp. 199–200). See also Joshua J. McEvilla, with contributions from Sean M. Winslow, *Cotgrave Online*, created 2014, revised August 2020, *The Shakespeare Authorship Page*, ed. Terry Ross and David Kathman, https://shakespeareauthorship.com/cotgrave/.

Contemporary commentators relished the central irony of the theatrical prohibition: far from obliterating plays, the prohibition drove plays into a more enduring format. In his dedication to the Beaumont and Fletcher folio, Richard Brome remarks: "You that are worthy, may by intercession / Find entertainment at the next impression."[56] Dramatic activity is light "entertainment"; although the playhouses are closed, dramatic diversion is provided by the "impression" of the printing press. In his commendatory poem to the same volume, Thomas Stanley also describes the playbook as a substitute for the absent theatre, but rather than mere "entertainment," the printed play offers immortal literature: "They that silenc'd Wit / Are now the Authors to Eternize it; / Thus Poets are in sight of Fate reviv'd / And Plays by Intermission longer liv'd."[57] Stanley equates the playbook's material endurance with its cultural longevity; the press transforms plays into eternal poetry. Though they differ in their characterization of the playbook's cultural status, either as pleasant recreation or serious literature, Brome and Stanley share the belief that the prohibition will be a temporary "intercession" or "intermission." Even by 1647, five years into the prohibition, people expected the public theatre to return.

The belief that the playhouses would reopen was connected to the widespread notion, still prevalent in 1647, that Charles I and Parliament would arrive at a consensus.[58] In his commendatory poem to the Beaumont and Fletcher first folio, Richard Brome suggests that Charles I would soon return and that the playhouses would reopen thereafter:

> In the first year, our famous Fletcher fell,
> Of good King Charles who graced these poems well,
> Being then in life of action, but they died,
> Since the King's absence or were laid aside,
> As is their poet. Now at the report,
> Of the King's second coming to his court
> The books creep from the press to life not action;
> Crying onto the world, that no protraction
> May hinder Sacred Majesty to give
> Fletcher, in them, leave on the stage to live.[59]

---

[56] Brome, "To the Memory," in Beaumont and Fletcher, *Comedies and Tragedies*, sig. g1r.

[57] Thomas Stanley, "On the Edition," in Beaumont and Fletcher, *Comedies and Tragedies*, sig. b4v.

[58] Ann Hughes, "The Scots, the Parliament and the People: The Rise of the New Model Army Revisited," in *Revolutionising Politics: Culture and Conflict in England, 1620–60*, ed. Paul D. Halliday, Eleanor Hubbard, and Scott Sowerby (Manchester: Manchester University Press, 2021), pp. 180–99; Mark Kishlansky, "Mission Impossible: Charles I, Oliver Cromwell and the Regicide," *The English Historical Review*, 125.515 (2010), 844–74.

[59] Brome, "To the Memory," in Beaumont and Fletcher, *Comedies and Tragedies*, sig. g1r.

Brome here asserts the parallel fates of Fletcherian theatre (and theatre more generally) and royalist politics. John Fletcher died in 1625, the same year Charles I ascended to the throne. Though Fletcher was gone, Charles I's patronage of theatre enabled the "life of action" of Fletcher's plays onstage. Now, with the King's political troubles, the poems have "died": deprived of the lifeblood of performance, the manuscripts are set aside to moulder in obscurity like the corpse of their "poet." But in 1647, the "King's second coming to his court" heralded the potential reconciliation of King and Parliament and promised the recovery of yet another of England's pre-1642 institutions, the theatre. The return of his "Sacred Majesty" would resurrect Fletcher's dead dramatic poems, giving them "leave on the stage to live." Playbooks function as the harbinger of what Brome sees as the inevitable return of both Charles I and public performance.

In the interim, the printing press keeps English plays alive, but in a diminished form: the unperformed printed playbook offers "life not action," a middle ground between the "life of action" of theatrical performance, and the total annihilation of that tradition. Brome is ambivalent about print's ability to recapture the vitality of embodied performance. The books *creep* from the press – a slow, weakened movement, a far cry from the robust movements of actors. Publication ensures a modicum of survival: the "creeping" playbook at once asserts the endurance of English drama and gestures to all that had been lost.

In their dedicatory epistle to Philip Herbert, Earl of Pembroke and Montgomery, in the Beaumont and Fletcher folio of 1647, ten actors from the King's Servants are pessimistic about their prospects but stop short of characterizing the prohibition as permanent. They acknowledge their patron's continued support, "from which wee did for many calme years derive a subsistence to ourselves, and protection to the scene (now withered, and condemn'd, as we fear, to a long Winter and Sterilitie)."[60] Although they bewail the closure of the theatres, the description of the hiatus as a "long Winter" maintains hope and anticipation for a spring-like return of theatrical abundance. Moreover, even though the theatre scene was doubtless "withered," the fact that ten principal actors of a major playing company were able to unite and contribute to the folio belies such pessimism. Even by 1647, many theatrical personnel could still eke out a living. In 1646, the King's Servants successfully petitioned Parliament for

---

[60] John Lowin, Joseph Taylor, Richard Robinson, et al., "The Epistle Dedicatorie," in Beaumont and Fletcher, *Comedies and Tragedies*, sig. A2r.

the back salary that was owed to them. They continued to stage plays illegally, and between 1647 and 1648 seem to have done so quite frequently.[61] Five years into the prohibition, it appeared that at least a significant portion of the King's Servants could resume playing if the prohibition was suddenly lifted.

The belief that the playhouses would eventually reopen informed rhetoric about the status of the playbook. Moseley and Shirley's prefatory addresses to the Beaumont and Fletcher folio of 1647 provide the *loci classici* for the critical commonplace that commentators marketed Interregnum playbooks as literary texts for reading by dismissing the theatre. In his stationer's address "To the Readers," after describing the difficulty of gathering dispersed Beaumont and Fletcher manuscripts, Moseley traces his "original" copy texts directly to "the Authors themselves," eliding the theatrical tradition that "mutilated" the authors' text (albeit with their "consent"):

> VVhen these Comedies and Tragedies were presented on the Stage, the Actours omitted some Scenes and Passions (with the Author's consent) as occasion led them; and when private friends desir'd a Copy, they then (and justly too) transcribed what they Acted. But now you have both All that was Acted, and all that was not; even the perfect full Originalls without the least mutilation.[62]

In Moseley's telling, print undoes the "mutilations" and "omissions" of the stage and restores the "perfect, full, original" text of the "authors'" intention. The playbook is the plays' true realization, an improvement over flawed theatrical iterations. As Marta Straznicky explains, in Moseley's address, "there is no longing glance back at an earlier age in which the plays could be fulfilled in their intended medium, nor at any future performance imagined ... The book in effect supersedes performance."[63] Far from being an object of nostalgia, theatrical performance is an inferior condition to be overcome through print.

Likewise, in his oft-quoted preface to the Beaumont and Fletcher folio, James Shirley asserts the superiority of reading plays over watching them. He reflects on the loss of the stage, but instead of lamenting its loss or anticipating its return, he advocates for the printed text as a worthy

[61] Milhous and Hume, "New Light on English Acting Companies."
[62] Moseley, "The Stationer to the Readers," in Beaumont and Fletcher, *Comedies and Tragedies*, sig. A4r.
[63] Straznicky, *Privacy*, p. 73.

substitute, and suggests that the "silence of the stage" actually improves dramatic reading:

> And now Reader in this Tragicall Age where the Theater hath been so much out-acted, congratulate thy owne happinesse that in this silence of the Stage, thou hast a liberty to reade these inimitable Playes, to dwell and converse in these immortall Groves, which were only shewd our Fathers in a conjuring glasse, as suddenly removed as represented, the Landscrap is now brought home by this optick.[64]

Shirley proposes that the transition from stage to page, though forced, is nevertheless fortuitous. The playbook grants readers unprecedented control and "liberty" over the play text, usually the purview of the actors. Claire M. L. Bourne notes that "Shirley's metaphor of dwelling suggests" that, unlike watching a performance, "reading can move in BOTH directions – readers always have ready, material access to what has come before, whether for reference, reflection, interpretation or some other use."[65] "Dwelling" in the text that is "brought home" also captures the domestication of the play, its movement away from the public spaces of the theatre to the private closets of the reader.

But again, reading and owning professional playbooks date back nearly to the advent of professional theatre. Why should these experiences differ after the theatres closed? In Shirley's telling, estrangement from performance facilitates a different, more serious sort of dramatic reading, independent from the sensual distractions of the stage. Ann Baynes Coiro notes Shirley's evaluative contrast between the mistrustful "conjuring glass" of the stage play and the "optick" of the playbook, a "scientific instrument for the educated."[66] Performance is an obstacle to dramatic immersion and comprehension; its absence better allows readers to both immerse themselves in the text and analyze it critically. Shirley explains that the reader will find "yourself at last grown insensibly the very same person you read, and then stand admiring the subtle Tracks of your engagement."[67] Reading produces intense self-identification with dramatic character, but also allows for the critical distance required for careful study of the text. The theatrical prohibition suddenly casts the press and its products in a new light; as Shirley explains, "thought too pregnant before, [the press] shall be now look'd upon as greatest Benefactor to Englishmen."[68] In this

---

[64] James Shirley, "To the Reader," in Beaumont and Fletcher, *Comedies and Tragedies*, sig. A3r.
[65] Claire M. L. Bourne, "'High Designe': Beaumont and Fletcher Illustrated," *English Literary Renaissance*, 44.2 (2014), 275–327 (p. 291).
[66] Coiro, "Reading," p. 547.
[67] Shirley, "To the Reader," in Beaumont and Fletcher, *Comedies and Tragedies*, sig. A3r.   [68] Ibid.

formulation, the closure of theatres is presented as a long-awaited event that finally allows playbooks to come into their own.

Moseley and Shirley's prefatory matter recalls pre-1642 strategies to downplay a stage flop's theatrical origins to elevate the playbook: reframing theatrical failure as an opportunity to create literary drama, demarcating spectators from playbook readers. Moseley's denigration of the actors and elevation of the author recall Heminge and Condell slighting the theatre and elevating Shakespeare in F1. Shirley's separation of spectators from readers recalls similar tactics by Walter Burre. But while Shirley describes the reader's new-found control over the playbook in terms of immersion, ownership, and study (arguably experiences that were available when reading a wide range of genres), in the same volume, John Webb describes it in distinctly theatrical terms: "The Presse shall give to ev'ry man his part / And we will all be Actors; learne by heart."[69] The absence of live theatre offers new agency, allowing the reader not only to inhabit dramatic character, but also to step into roles vacated by actors. Printed alongside paratexts that insist upon the playbook's "readerly" status, Webb's suggestion that readers will co-opt the role of actors suggests how the theatre continued to positively inform understandings of the playbook. The reader is not compared to the spectator (as they so often are), but rather to the actor; play-reading is not comparable to passive spectatorship, but to active playing. The reader is expected to pay serious attention to the text, "learn by heart" and memorize the lines just as an actor would. The reader's agency is defined in a theatrical-literary way: both print and the theatre contribute to the playbook's status as worthy of serious study.

Most notably, even Shirley's famous valorization of play-reading does not totally insult theatre. The spectators from which readers are distinguished are no longer "vulgar," or "ignorant," but rather "our fathers." Shirley doubtless posits the superiority of his experience compared to the previous generation's, but even as he gently mocks "our fathers" for their theatrical puzzlement, they are still figures of respect and intimacy for the current readership. It was no longer necessary to erect class- and education-based boundaries between readers and spectators: chronology and the law achieved them more reliably. If a separation between stage and page is a common strategy to assert the playbook's status, after 1642, this did not

---

[69] John Webb, "To the Manes of the Celebrated Poets and Fellow-Writers Frances Beaumont and John Fletcher upon the Printing of Their Excellent Dramatick Poems," in Beaumont and Fletcher, *Comedies and Tragedies*, sig. c2v.

require forswearing theatre: playgoing became the purview of the prior generation, a part of the quickly receding, wistfully recalled past.

In 1647, as we have seen, to some the return of King Charles I and the theatre appeared imminent. The year 1648 represents a turning point, both theatrically and politically.[70] The King's Servants, the most successful of English theatre companies, began to feel the full effects of the lengthy interdiction in war time England. Four of the principal actors who had signed the dedicatory epistle to the Beaumont and Fletcher folio died within the next two years: Stephen Hammerton (1614–c.1648), Richard Robinson (d. 1648), Thomas Pollard (d. 1649), and Richard Benfield (d. 1649). Contemporary reports of Hammerton – a young actor who had grown up in the company, who was famed for playing romantic leads, and who was evidently identifiable by first name only – confirm his popularity. Shirley's Epilogue to Suckling's *The Goblins* announces, "Oh if Stephen should be killed, / Or miss the lady, how the plot is spilled!" while prefatory matter to Thomas Killigrew's *The Parson's Wedding* (performed 1641, printed in collection in 1664) similarly laments, if "Stephen misses the Wench ... that alone is enough to spoil the Play."[71] If audiences were so highly invested in "Stephen's" success in life and love on stage, his early death must have struck a blow. In 1652, a commendatory poem in *The Wild Goose Chase* observes the cultural and economic catastrophe of the theatrical prohibition, expressed by the theatrical famine and actual hunger of well-known veteran actors Joseph Taylor and John Lowin: "In this late dearth of wit, when Jose and Jack / Were hunger-bit for want of fowl and sack." The playbook serves as a replacement for theatre, both symbolically and practically: "His nobleness found out this happy means / To mend their diet with these Wild-Goose scenes / By which he has revived in a day. / Two poets and two actors with one play."[72] The optimism was misplaced, however: both Taylor (d. 1652) and Lowin (d. 1653) would be dead within a year. Of the ten signatories of the Beaumont and Fletcher folio dedication, only one, Theophilus Bird, survived into the Restoration. As the theatre ban dragged on, and actors

[70] Kishlansky, "Mission Impossible," p. 845; Sean Kelsey, "Politics and Procedure in the Trial of Charles I," *Law and History Review*, 22.1 (2004), 1–25.

[71] James Shirley, "Epilogue," in John Suckling, *The Goblins* (Humphrey Moseley, 1646), p. 64; Thomas Killigrew, *The Parson's Wedding*, in *Comedies and Tragedies Written by Thomas Killigrew* (Henry Herringman, 1664), p. 140. See also John H. Astington, *Actors and Acting in Shakespeare's Time: The Art of Stage Playing* (Cambridge: Cambridge University Press, 2010), p. 200.

[72] W. E., "An Epigram upon the Long Lost and Fortunately Recovered WILD-GOOSE CHASE," in Beaumont and Fletcher, *The Wild-Goose Chase*, sig. A2v.

died off or left the trade, it became clear in retrospect that English theatre, which in the early 1640s had seemed merely ailing, had actually been dying. The hope that theatre would resume was increasingly replaced with the realization that the pre-1642 tradition was permanently lost. This transformed attitudes towards the playbook.

Postponing Oblivion: Playbooks Post-1649

Royalist politics and English theatre reached a point of no return in 1648, when it became clear to Parliament that cooperation with Charles I was impossible. Charles I was imprisoned in late 1648, and executed publicly on 30 January 1649. The regicide transformed Charles I into a martyr among his supporters and mitigated critique among his opponents. Relics became an important focus for royalist energies in the aftermath. Capitalizing on the public's affection for the martyred king, people sold items marketed as Charles's hair, pieces of his clothing, and sand and cloth soaked in the king's spilled blood.[73] Caroline relics were put to varied uses, some to preserve Charles's memory, others to miraculously cure disease and disability through contact with the "King's touch."[74] They were politically fraught. Religious relics were associated with Roman Catholic and Orthodox Christian traditions, and were among the ritual objects Reformed Protestants had tried to eliminate during the last century. Relics informally remained an important element of devotional practice in post-Reformation England. Archbishop William Laud's reinstatement of religious objects in the liturgy of the Caroline Church of England in the 1630s drew objections from the Reformed Protestants who dominated Parliament.[75]

The term "relic" is elastic and expansive: it can be an object of remembrance or veneration, which recalls or perpetuates a particular absent person, place, thing, or practice. Critics define the relic as a "material manifestation of the act of remembrance,"[76] and a "mnemonic bridge,"[77]

---

[73] Rachel Willie, "Sacrificial Kings and Martyred Rebels: Charles and Rainborowe Beatified," *Etudes Episteme (Special Issue on Regicide)*, 20 (2011), https://doi.org/10.4000/episteme.428; Joad Raymond, "Popular Representations of Charles I," in *The Royal Image: Representations of Charles I*, ed. Thomas Corns (Cambridge: Cambridge University Press, 1999), pp. 47–73

[74] William Fulman and Richard Perrinchief, *Basilika the Workes of King Charles the Martyr* (London: Miles Flesher, 1662), p. 59.

[75] Kenneth Fincham and Nicholas Tyacke, *Altars Restored: The Changing Face of English Religious Worship, 1547–c.1700* (Oxford: Oxford University Press, 2007), pp. 227–305.

[76] Alexandra Walsham, "Introduction: Relics and Remains," *Past & Present*, 206 (2010), 9–36 (p. 13).

[77] Eviator Zerubavel, *Time Maps* (Chicago: University of Chicago Press, 2003), pp. 43–4.

"linking the past and present in a concrete and palpable way."[78] Of course, relics are not merely mementos: Alexandra Walsham explains that a distinguishing feature of relics is "their capacity to operate as a locus and conduit of power." She continues that the relic "is not a mere symbol or indicator of divine presence" but "is an actual physical embodiment of it, each particle encapsulating the essence of the departed."[79]

Apart from traditional "relics," Charles's posthumous power circulated physically through images, icons, and texts. Among the printed texts that propagated the power of the martyred king, the most important was *Eikon Basilike* (1649), purported to be Charles's final meditations as he awaited his execution. This book, probably already in circulation on the day of Charles's execution, was among the best-selling books of the seventeenth century, and led to an outpouring of texts that commemorated Charles as a Christian martyr according to the *Eikon's* model.[80] The *Eikon* functioned as a "printed relic" of Charles I; as Elizabeth Sauer argues, "just as the king's relics were invested with a life-giving power … *Eikon Basilike* had displaced the king's body and yet bore a synecdochic relationship to the author."[81] In the *Eikon*, Kyle Vitale writes, "Charles I shifts from a physical, fleshy presence to a textual, bookish one: flesh realized in text."[82] A highly controversial figure when alive, once Charles was safely in the grave, Andrew Lacey explains, the king's supporters "could elaborate the image of the patient, Anglican martyr safe in the knowledge that he was not going to frustrate their efforts by any precipitate actions of his own."[83] As a printed relic, the *Eikon* presented an idealized vision of Charles and transmitted his power, simultaneously restoring him and emphasizing his absence.

The regicide offered an irresistible analogy for the theatrical prohibition: English monarchy and English theatre were both killed off by the same opponent. The metaphor worked both ways: various tracts called Charles a "performer," his execution a real-life "tragedy," ghoulishly "applauded" by his enemies.[84] Andrew Marvell's "An Horatian Ode upon Cromwell's

[78] Walsham, "Relics and Remains," p. 13.   [79] Ibid.
[80] Elizabeth Sauer, *"Paper-Contestations" and Textual Communities in England, 1640–1675* (Toronto: University of Toronto Press, 2005), p. 63.
[81] Ibid., p. 75.
[82] Kyle Vitale, "A Reverence for Books" (doctoral dissertation, University of Delaware, 2016), p. 224.
[83] Andrew Lacey, *The Cult of King Charles the Martyr* (Woodbridge: Boydell and Brewer, 2003), pp. 50–1.
[84] Scholarship has noted "theatrical" representations of Charles I: see Elizabeth Skerpan-Wheeler, "The First 'Royal': Charles I as Celebrity," *Papers of the Modern Language Association*, 126.4 (2011), 912–34; Richard Helgerson, "Milton Reads the King's Book: Print, Performance, and the Making

Return from Ireland" (1650) describes, "That thence the Royal actor borne / The tragic scaffold might adorn: / While round the armèd bands / Did clap their bloody hands."[85] As if to reinforce the connection between the prohibition and the regicide, Parliament strengthened its campaign against theatre around the time of Charles's trial and execution. On 24 March 1649, Parliamentary soldiers pulled down the Salisbury Court theatre, the Phoenix (also known as the Cockpit), and the Fortune playhouses.

Dramatic paratexts like the prologue to the closet play *The Famous Tragedie of King Charles I, Basely Butchered* (1649) parallel the downward trajectories of the English monarchy and drama: "Their bloody Myrmidons, o'the table round / Project, to raze, our theatres to the ground ... For having killed their king, where will they stay / That through God, and Majesty make way / Throwing the Nobles, and the Gentry down / Levelling all distinctions to the Crown."[86] Although Parliament killed the king and razed the theatres, levelling both playhouses and the social hierarchy, the *Famous Tragedie*'s prologue celebrates the endurance of the printed text in the face of Parliamentarian suppression:

> Though Jonson, Shakespeare, Goffe and Davenant
> Brome, Suckling, Beaumont, Fletcher and Shirley want
> The Life of action, and their learned lines
> Are loathed by the monsters of the times
> Yet your refined souls can penetrate
> Their depth of merit.[87]

Despite the efforts of the "monsters of the times," print allows readers to continually enjoy English plays, albeit in a different form. That plays are deprived of the "life of action" recalls Richard Brome's description of playbooks creeping to "life not action," while the prologue's reference to readers' sustained contemplation, where they "penetrate" the deep "merit" of "learned lines," recalls strategies to present the post-1642 playbook as serious reading. The endurance of the playbook symbolizes royalist resistance, a victory against the murderous "monsters" who executed Charles,

---

of a Bourgeois Idol," *Criticism*, 29 (1987), 1–25; Nancy Klein Maguire, "The Theatrical Mask / Masque of Politics: The Case of Charles I," *Journal of British Studies*, 28 (1989), 1–22.

[85] Andrew Marvell, "An Horatian Ode upon Cromwell's Return from Ireland," in *Andrew Marvell: The Complete Poems*, ed. Elizabeth Story Donno (New York: Penguin, 2005).

[86] "Prologue," in *The Famous Tragedie of King Charles I, Basely Butchered* (1649), sig. A4r.

[87] Ibid.

while the playbook itself also represents the artefacts salvaged from a "razed" theatrical tradition.

The prologue to *The Famous Tragedie of King Charles I* unites the icons of Elizabethan and Jacobean drama (Jonson, Shakespeare, Beaumont, and Fletcher) with the supposedly lesser lights of the Caroline era (Thomas Goffe, William Davenant, Richard Brome, John Suckling, and James Shirley). Alan B. Farmer and Zachary Lesser suggest that the 1630s playbook market split new Caroline dramatists from a canon of "classic" Elizabethan and Jacobean dramatists.[88] But, as I will discuss in more detail in the next chapter, in the late 1640s, far from stratifying older dramatists and newer Caroline ones, the Interregnum poem instead suggests a unified genre of pre-1642 English dramatists across the Elizabethan, Jacobean, and Caroline periods: the living Davenant and Shirley are incorporated into the same tradition as long-dead Shakespeare and Beaumont. These different dramatists are partly united by their shared fate of "want[ing] the Life of action." Tanya Hagen argues that "one of the early distinguishing features of an old play was the expiration of its active career on the stage"[89] (to which I would merely add, its expiration from the stage on which it originally appeared). The dramatists listed by the *Famous Tragedie*'s prologue all belong to a bygone era of English theatre: all their plays are "old plays."

The concept of old plays existed while the theatres were active, but their age was tempered by their ability to be revived onstage. Lucy Munro, focusing on Marlovian revivals in the 1630s, argues that Caroline revivals of older plays were marked "by the contrasting pressures of nostalgia and continuity," and had a "somewhat paradoxical status as works which exemplified an older tradition but nonetheless continued to have life and vitality in performance."[90] The closure of the theatres, however, eliminated this source of life. Sapped of the vitality of performance, old plays were simply old. Theatrical nostalgia supplanted the Caroline era's sense of theatrical continuity: though it was not immediately recognized as such, the year 1642 came to be understood as a distinct break with the past. The

---

[88] Alan B. Farmer and Zachary Lesser, "Canons and Classics," in *Localizing Caroline Drama: Politics and Economics of the Early Modern English Stage, 1625–1642*, ed. Alan B. Farmer and Adam Zucker (Basingstoke: Palgrave Macmillan, 2006), pp. 17–41 (pp. 17–18).

[89] Tanya Hagen, "Thinking outside the Bard: REED, Repertory Canons, and Editing Early English Drama," in *REED in Review: Essays in Celebration of the First Twenty-Five Years*, ed. Audrey W. Douglas and Sally-Beth MacLean (Toronto: University of Toronto, 2006), pp. 216–34 (p. 232, n. 16).

[90] Lucy Munro, "Marlowe on the Caroline Stage," *Shakespeare Bulletin*, 27 (2009), 39–50 (p. 40).

prohibition freed up previously unprinted plays for publication, but once the "last new plays" were published – and paratexts like those from the 1652 edition of *The Wild Goose Chase* indicated that that milestone was soon to come – all English plays became old plays, in terms of composition, performance, and publication. While individual "old plays" existed before 1642, the theatrical prohibition prematurely aged English drama as a genre.

Relics of the Dying Scene

Dramatic paratexts created and capitalized on nostalgia for the concluded theatre, offering up the printed play as consolation. In his commendatory poem to James Shirley's *The Cardinal* (1652), John Hall describes playbooks as printed "reliques" that preserve the memory of and perpetuate the "dying scene":

> So, when our English dramma was at hight,
> And shin'd, and rul'd, with Majesty and might
> A sudden whirlwind threw it from it[s] seat,
> Deflower'd the Groves, and quench'd the Muses['] heat.
> Yet as in Saints, and Martyr'd bodies, when
> They cannot call their blessed souls agen
> To earth, Reliques and ashes men preserve
> And think they do but what, blest they deserve:
> So I, by my devotion led, aspire
> To keep alive your noble Vestal fire,
> Honour this piece, which shews, Sir, you have been
> The last supporter of the dying Scene.[91]

Hall's imagery of "saints and martyred bodies" preserved through treasured relics borrows from the iconography of the cult of "Charles the Martyr." Just as the lack of a living Charles I made it easier to propagate an image of the idealized king in print, analogously, the absence of an actual theatre industry made it easy to view the theatre through rose-tinted glasses. Charles's textual incarnation in the *Eikon* was presented as a "devotional object which, through its narrative of Charles I's unjust death and apotheosis, begs reverence and careful attention from its readers."[92] The paratexts of printed drama tried to evoke a similar effect. In Hall's poem,

---

[91] John Hall, "To the Surviving Honour and Ornament of the English Scene, Iames Shirley," in James Shirley, *The Cardinal* (London: Humphrey Moseley and Humphrey Robinson, 1652), sig. A4v.
[92] Vitale, "A Reverence for Books," p. 209.

the dying scene is sanctified, its destruction comparable to that of the anointed King – the material relics of each serving as objects of memory and devotion. The relic cannot fully resurrect the dead object, which can never again be "called to earth." The material text offers in its place a different kind of dramatic embodiment, one that simultaneously gains power from absence and endurance. Both human life and theatrical performance are inherently transient; after 1642, "English drama" as a whole reached a definite conclusion. Although performance was gone forever, the "relics and ashes" of English drama's material remains were to be preserved and venerated, valued for their ability to disclose the "soul" of theatre.

References to the playbook as a "relic" predate 1642; John Milton refers to Shakespeare's "hallow'd reliques" in his dedicatory poem to Shakespeare's Second Folio (1632).[93] But the metaphor became commonplace after 1642, as theatrical death swept the entire industry, and became even more widespread after the regicide. Annabel Wharton's definition of relics is worth quoting at length as it illuminates this metaphor's particular power and aptness in relation to the Interregnum playbook:

> A relic is the remnant of a history that is threatened by forgetting. It records duration and postpones oblivion. It offers reassurance that the past retains its authority. It collapses time. A relic is a sign of previous power, real or imagined. It promises to put that power back to work. A relic is a fragment that evokes a lost fullness. It is a part that allows the embrace of an absent whole. It is the living piece of a dead object.[94]

In a moment when "oblivion" threatened English dramatic culture, the printed playbook promised the perpetuation of the past – in material, and sometimes mystical ways. The relic was a less vital, fragmentary version of embodied theatrical performance, but it allowed the "essence" of theatre to live on.

Hall's description of the downfall of English drama which once "ruled" with "majesty and might" obviously equates drama with the monarchy, noting their common end in the face of a "sudden whirlwind." As we have seen in the *Famous Tragedie's* prologue, contemporaries read political dimensions into the playbook's ability to perpetuate theatre in a moment of governmental prohibition. So too have modern critics: Jitka Štollová

---

[93] J[ohn] M[ilton], "An Epitaph on the Admirable Dramatic Poet, W. Shakespeare," in William Shakespeare, *Comedies, Histories, and Tragedies* (London: Robert Allott, 1632), sig. ᵖA6r.

[94] Annabel Jane Wharton, *Selling Jerusalem: Relics, Replicas, Theme Parks* (Chicago: University of Chicago Press, 2006), p. 1.

characterizes the 1647 folio as "a bibliographical act of defiance against the closure of theatres" and "a symbol of royalist commitment."[95] The prefatory matter of *The Wild Goose Chase* can also be read in this light. Richard Lovelace's commendatory poem offers the printed Fletcher play as an alternative to the late Charles I: "Unhappy murmerers, that still repine / After th' eclipse our sun does brighter shine. / Recant your grief and your true joys know: / Your bliss is endless, as you feared your woe!"[96] Sophie Tomlinson argues that "these lines conflate the political dissatisfaction of Royalist supporters at the death of Charles I with the dissatisfaction of would-be theatregoers, who will be cheered by the reappearance of Fletcher ('our sun') in print."[97] While the authorities can suppress the theatre and the king, the playbook flourishes defiantly. For early readers and modern critics alike, political and theatrical nostalgia are deeply intertwined.

And yet, although Hall's poem asserts the value of English drama through comparison with the martyred Charles, the elevation of drama is not merely a by-product of royalist nostalgia. The ordinance against theatre is not simply a consequence of attacks on the crown, but a comparable loss, which is to be mourned in the same way. Hall compares the theatre to Charles, yet he employs the language of monarchy and regicide to emphasize the significance of the *theatre's* demise, not the other way around. The primary loss to be mourned here is the "dying scene," not Charles. The playbook was not only a royalist symbol, or a relic of pre-1642 culture in general, but a relic of the stage in particular. The theatrical prohibition was its own cultural catastrophe, aligned with the regicide but also separate from it. As I will discuss in Chapter 3, when we examine contemporary responses to dramatic production in this period, what we often see is an interest in drama *as* drama, not simply as a vehicle for political nostalgia. Or more precisely, contemporaries (at least Royalist contemporaries) did not simply study individual plays for their ideology, but strove to elevate the broader concepts of English theatre and drama as a realm apart from politics. As we shall see, however, this entails a paradox, since the elevation itself is political.

The metaphor of the "relic" was sometimes used without explicit reference to the martyred Charles I. A commendatory poem by R. C. for

[95] Štollová, "This Silence of the Stage," p. 507; see also Randall, *Winter Fruit*.
[96] Richard Lovelace, "On the Best, Last, and Only Remaining Comedy of Mr. FLETCHER," in Beaumont and Fletcher, *The Wild-Goose Chase*, sig. A2v.
[97] Francis Beaumont and John Fletcher, *The Wild Goose Chase*, ed. Sophie Tomlinson, in *Three Seventeenth-Century Plays on Women and Performance*, ed. Hero Chalmers, Julie Sanders, and Sophie Tomlinson (Manchester: Manchester University Press, 2006), p. 320.

the anonymous play *The Queen,* published by Alexander Goughe in 1653, uses the image to defend the play's cultural value. R. C. at first praises the theatre as a "quickening art" that revives "dead examples" and suggests that the press is a source of lively action in the absence of live theatre:

> Is it unlawfull since the stage is down
> To make the press act? [. . .] the guiltles presse
> Weares its own innocent garments: its own dresse.
> Let it come Forth Midwife Goughe, securely; and if some
> Like not the make or beautie of the play
> Bear witnes to't and confidently say
> Such a relict as once the stage did own,
> Ingenuous Reader, merits to be known.[98]

Marissa Nicosia argues that, with its sartorial imagery and references to "quickening," R. C.'s poem utilizes "a language of embodied performance to show that printing a play is a kind of performance," one that can replicate the "vitality" of stage plays. She continues that Goughe's edition of *The Queen* "is figured as an act of revival that will save the play as an embodied artifact."[99] Yet the imagery of the relic troubles any straightforward sense of vitality or revival. R. C. remarks that "the press acts," aided by "Midwife Goughe," to bring play into the world, but his childbirth metaphor takes a macabre turn: the delivered text is not a hale bairn but a "relic" of the stage, or "an Excellent Old Play," as the first edition of *The Queen* is advertised on its title page. Like James Ramsey's characterization of *The Wild Goose Chase* as the "sprightly posthume," the mixed metaphor of the birthed relic expresses the paradox of printed drama in the Interregnum, simultaneously old and new, dead and alive.

The combination of macabre and lively imagery is also visible in the dedication to Thomas Wriothesley, Earl of Southampton, in John Ford and Thomas Dekker's *The Sun's Darling,* printed in 1656 by the King's Servant actor Theophilus Bird and his fellow unemployed actor Andrew Pennycuicke. In their dedication, Bird and Pennycuicke describe how Southampton's patronage and publication resurrects in print a play deprived of life on stage:

> Herodotus Reports that the Ægyptians by Wrapping their Dead in Glasse, presents them lively to all posterity; But your Lordship will do more, by the Vivifying beames of your Acceptation, Revive the parents of this Orphan

---

[98] R. C., "To Mr. Alexander Goughe upon His Publishing the Excellent Play call'd *the Queen*; or *the Excellencie of her Sex,*" in Alexander Goughe, *The Queen* (London: Thomas Heath, 1653), sig. A3r.

[99] Nicosia, "Printing as Revival," p. 489.

Poem, and make them live to Eternity. While the Stage florisht, the POEM liv'd by the breath of Generall Applauses, and the Virtuall Fervor of the Court; but since hath languisht for want of heate, and now neere shrunk up with Cold, creepes (with a shivering feare) to Extend it self at the Flames of your Benignity.[100]

Dramatic publication is not simply mummification, a material preservation of the once-living body of performance; it breathes new life into a play deprived of the playhouse's "breath of the general applause." Nicosia argues that dramatic publication here is akin to theatrical revival, and indeed that the publication could function as a forerunner to actual revival on stage.[101] Yet far from suggesting performance, Pennycuicke and Bird point out the failure of the text to approximate the liveliness of the theatre: the play "creeps" from the press, the same metaphor Richard Brome used in the 1647 folio to describe the emergence of the playbook to "life not action." The playbook is not dead, exactly, but it cannot offer the vibrancy of theatrical performance – the press can only keep plays alive in diminished form. The closure of the theatres was a profound cultural and economic loss, one that was mitigated, but not fully redeemed, by the survival of printed drama. The fact that Andrew Pennycuicke changed professions suggests that any expression of hope for theatrical revival was by the mid-1650s a mere fantasy. By then, even if public performance was suddenly legalized, players could not easily restart the industry.

And yet, though the playbook cannot fully revive performance, it offers something different, and more lasting, in its place. The printed playbook will allow Ford and Dekker to "live to Eternity." The printed playbook, to cite Richard Brome's and Thomas Stanley's descriptions respectively, offers "life after life," and "eternizes" the play after the death of theatre. Theatrical performance is time bound, ephemeral, and performed by mortals with a fixed human lifespan; by definition, therefore, it cannot be eternal. In the place of vital, impermanent performance, the playbook offers neither temporary life on stage nor the faux-life of mummification, but the *essence* of vital performance, preserved for perpetuity in print. Desire for the temporary theatrical "revival" gives way to a celebration that the immortal dramatic poem retains its theatricality.

---

[100] Theophilus Bird and Andrew Pennycuicke, "To the Right Honorable THOMAS WRIATHESLEY," in John Ford and Thomas Dekker, *The Sun's Darling* (London: Andrew Pennycuicke, 1656), sig. A2r.
[101] Nicosia, "Printing as Revival," pp. 488–7.

Theatrical Oblivion

John Earle's prefatory poem to the Beaumont and Fletcher folio of 1647 (written decades earlier) argues that it is just a matter of time before the gatekeepers of canon formation recognize Beaumont's literary value:

> [W]e that better know,
> Will a more serious houre on thee bestow,
> Why should not Beaumont in the Morning please
> As well as Plautus, Aristophanes?
> Who if my Pen may as my thoughts be free,
> Were Scurrill Wits and Buffons both to Thee
> Yet these our Learned of severest brow,
> Will deigne to looke on, and to note them too,
> That will defie our owne, tis English stuffe,
> And th' Author is not rotten long enough.[102]

It is easier to idealize the cultural output of the distant past; even classical authors had a "thriftier fame" in "their own times."[103] Earle looks ahead to the moment when Beaumont will be "rotten long enough" to attain the same markers of cultural respectability that the dramatic ancients have in the seventeenth century: to be encountered chiefly through the text, to be read in the serious scholarly hours of the morning, when one's intellectual faculties are at their sharpest. Earle prophecies that "when thy name is growne / Six ages older, [it] shall be better known."[104] Earle captures the process of literary elevation but overestimates the length of time needed to ensure Beaumont's canonization. The theatre ban sped up the rate of decomposition of English Renaissance dramatists. This "English stuff" could be enshrined in an English literary canon, which was created partly to accommodate it. The theatrical prohibition prematurely aged English professional plays as a group, but thanks to the closure, pre-1642 plays were not rotten, but relics of the theatrical past. The perception that these plays belonged to an absent past was crucial to their continued literary canonization. As noted in the Introduction, even once the theatres were restored, pre-1642 professional plays revived on stage retained their wizened reputation as "old plays" from the "last age."

---

[102] John Earle, "On Mr BEAVMONT. (Written thirty yeares since, presently after his death.)," in Beaumont and Fletcher, *Comedies and Tragedies*, sig. c3v–c4r.
[103] Ibid.   [104] Ibid.

In the 1640s and 1650s, the absent theatrical past became an object of longing. In 1609, *Troilus and Cressida*'s address to the reader proclaimed that the play had never been performed, stating that it was not "clapper clawed" with palms of the "vulgar." The title page to the first edition of James Shirley's *The Court Secret* (1653) likewise states it was "Never acted, but Prepared for the scene at Blackfriars," offering a *Troilus*-like declaration that the play was not acted, but with an opposite view of theatre's merits. Slated to premiere in late summer 1642, *The Court Secret*'s debut was cancelled due to the 2 September 1642 ordinance, the first known casualty of the theatrical prohibition. Shirley's dedication to William Wentworth, Earl of Strafford presents

> a Poem, one, that wearing no Ribbands in the forehead; not so much as warranted by Applause; for it happened to receive birth when the stage was interdicted, and wanted that publique Seal which other Compositions enjoyed; Though it hath been read and honour'd with the Allowance of some men, whose Opinion was as acceptable to mee, as the Vote of a smiling Theater.[105]

Shirley's wistful image of the "smiling theatre" is a far cry from the messy realities of the actual theatre (or at least of pre-1642 descriptions of it) with its seedy patrons, overwhelming sights and smells, and risk of contagion, invoked by anti-theatricalists and theatre devotees alike while the theatres were open.[106] The metaphor of childbirth recurs, but not to describe the dramatic text as a near-abortive, nor as a wandering baby who finds its way home, nor as a relic gruesomely brought into the world by a stationer-midwife. Rather, Shirley's brainchild lacks the "public seal," the formal identity of being a professional stage play, which only a life on the commercial stage could grant. The "abortive" here is not a missing manuscript, but the theatrical work that would never come to fruition on the early modern stage.

England's seven-decade professional theatrical tradition was lost forever; the restored theatre was a wholly different animal. After the theatres closed, the pre-1642 theatre was increasingly equivalent to the classical theatre of Plautus and Aristophanes, insofar as it was distant, accessible only through text, and coloured by the rose-tinted glasses of

---

[105] James Shirley, "The Epistle Dedicatory," in James Shirley, *The Court Secret* (London: Humphrey Moseley and Humphrey Robinson, 1653), sig. A2r.

[106] On the phenomenological and sensual experiences of theatrical performance (both thrilling and off-putting), see *Shakespeare's Theatres and the Effects of Performance*, ed. Farah Karim-Cooper and Tiffany Stern (London: Bloomsbury, 2013), especially Holly Dugan, "'As Dirty as Smithfield and Stinking Every Whit': The Smell of the Hope Theatre," pp. 195–213.

nostalgic memory and imagination. While the plays could be revived under the drastically different conditions of illegal Interregnum or Restoration theatre, theatrical conditions of the period before 1642 – what contemporaries came to call the theatre of the "last age," and we now call the "Renaissance" or "early modern" theatre – were gone.[107] While worrying about manuscript loss and "perpetual oblivion," pre-1642 commentators never thought to worry about the loss of an entire theatrical tradition. In "Where to Find Lost Plays," Martin Wiggins observes that "'lostness' is not, by definition, an inherent characteristic or even a necessarily irrecoverable situation"; manuscripts could always potentially be recovered in libraries, castles, attics.[108] But the tradition of early modern professional theatre began its irreversible decline in 1642 and could never be found in someone's attic. In 1647, Shirley celebrated that "The Landscape is now brought home by this optick," but did not realize that this movement was unidirectional: plays would never again be performed on stage under their original conditions of performance.

---

[107] See Chapter 5 for further discussion on the emergence of a contemporary perception of a period divide in dramatic history, and its relationship to current conceptions.

[108] Wiggins, "Where to Find Lost Plays," p. 258.

CHAPTER 2

Old Shakespeare

Introduction: Shakespeare without Shakespeare

William Shakespeare's likeness decorates the title page of John Cragge's *Wits Interpreter* (1655) (see Figure 2.1), but his contribution ends there.[1] None of Shakespeare's texts are actually included in this miscellany of extracts from poems and plays, home remedies, tricks and ciphers. *Wits Interpreter*'s frontispiece does, however, signal its literary and non-literary contents: Shakespeare's portrait appears alongside the dramatists and poets Ben Jonson (whose texts are likewise absent), Thomas Randolph, Edmund "Spencer," and Philip "Sydney," as well as the political figures "T[homas] More," [The Earl of] "Strafford," [Cardinal] "Richelieu," and "Dubartas." These portraits, Adam Smyth notes, "evoke an imprecise and largely non-literary sense of respectability" that is designed to attract the "wiser Reader," at whom the volume is aimed.[2] Although it omits Shakespeare and Jonson, *Wits Interpreter* does nevertheless include a significant amount of poetic and dramatic material, including a section of English drolleries, or "drolls," which are short playlets or extracts from longer plays. The sources of the fifty-one drolls are unacknowledged, but are drawn from thirty different plays by James Shirley, John Fletcher, Philip Massinger, John Ford, Richard Brome, and others, including closet and university plays.[3] In selecting the extracts, Cragge explains that when looking over "the private papers of the choicest wits . . . I crossed out whatsoever I could hear had been formerly published."[4] The emphasis on novelty (unusual for

---

[1] Traditionally assigned to John Cotgrave, *Wits Interpreter* is now ascribed to John Cragge. See Joshua McEvilla, "John Cragge's *The Wits Interpreter*," *The Library*, 8.3 (2017), 337–44.

[2] Adam Smyth, *"Profit and Delight": Printed Miscellanies in England, 1640–1682* (Detroit: Wayne State University Press, 2004), p. 75; Arthur Marotti, *Manuscript, Print and the English Renaissance Lyric* (Ithaca: Cornell University Press, 1995), p. 273.

[3] John H. Astington, "Dramatic Extracts in the Interregnum," *Review of English Studies*, 54 (2003), 601–14.

[4] John Cragge, *Wits Interpreter* (London: Nathanial Brookes, 1655), sig. A4r.

Figure 2.1   Frontispiece from John Cragge, *Wits Interpreter* (Nathanial Brookes, 1655).
Courtesy of the Huntington Library.

miscellanies, which tend to recirculate existing material) may explain the exclusion of extracts from Shakespeare, the most-printed dramatist and a favourite of anthologists since the late sixteenth century. But Shakespeare's image is enlisted to lend his broad cultural prestige to the extracts of his late-Stuart dramatic successors and to non-literary content. *Wits Interpreter* speaks to a wider trend in the Civil Wars and Interregnum: though his name and image had considerable cachet in this period, the publication of texts by Shakespeare plunged. Shakespeare was more popular in theory than in practice.

This chapter addresses the mysterious decline in full-length publications of Shakespeare's work during the Interregnum, as well as his continued circulation in printed commonplace books, drolls, and book list catalogues. No Shakespeare plays were printed in the 1640s, and they were mostly excluded from the spike in dramatic publication in the 1650s. Only two new editions of Shakespeare's plays appeared between 1642 and 1660: Jane Bell's edition of *King Lear* (Q3 1655) and William Leake's edition of *Othello* (Q3 1655). Leake also reissued *The Merchant of Venice* (Q3 1652, a reissue of Lawrence Hayes's Q3 1637) with a new title page. John Stafford and William Gilbertson published *The Rape of Lucrece* with a continuation of the poem by John Quarles titled *The Banishment of Tarquin* (1655). Until recently, the few critics who comment on Shakespeare's decline in this period have mostly mentioned it in passing, characterizing it as an anomalous dip in his trajectory from the best-selling dramatist of the early seventeenth century to England's "national poet" in the eighteenth century.[5] Emma Depledge has recently demonstrated Shakespeare's ongoing appearance in Interregnum drolls, ballads, and commonplace books, reading them as evidence of Shakespeare's "continued popularity during the Interregnum."[6] But "unpopularity" is an inadequate explanation for Shakespeare's decline in the Interregnum playbook market, while signs of his "popularity" are not quite convincing – or at least depend on an undertheorized notion of popularity.

The first part of this chapter addresses Shakespeare's relative absence from the playbook market, systematically examining the stationers who

---

[5] Gary Taylor, *Reinventing Shakespeare: A Cultural History from the Restoration to the Present* (London: Hogarth Press, 1990), p. 12; Andrew Murphy, *Shakespeare in Print: A History and Chronology of Shakespeare Publishing* (Cambridge: Cambridge University Press, 2003), p. 33; Lukas Erne, *Shakespeare and the Book Trade* (Cambridge: Cambridge University Press, 2013); Michael Dobson, *The Making of the National Poet: Shakespeare, Adaptation and Authorship, 1660–1769* (Cambridge: Cambridge University Press, 1992).
[6] Depledge, *Shakespeare's Rise*, pp. 16–31.

together held the rights to the thirty-eight plays in the modern Shakespeare
canon but who, for various reasons, did not publish them. Legal battles
and the deaths of stationers caused publication projects related to
Shakespeare to be held up or postponed. In other cases, stationers who
held the rights to Shakespeare's plays diverted their attention to political
texts or to previously unprinted plays. As John Cragge's aversion to what
"had been formerly published" suggests, dramatic novelty became especially important in the Interregnum playbook market. Because effectively
all of Shakespeare's texts were printed and reprinted before the
Interregnum, he could never really seem "new."[7] Stationers' interest in
new plays ensured the survival of many plays in the early modern dramatic
corpus, legitimized partly through their association with Shakespeare.

The second part of this chapter focuses on Shakespearean print publication in the Interregnum, in full-length plays and in the abbreviated
forms of commonplace books and printed allusions to Shakespeare's name,
his characters and play titles, the latter especially in book list catalogues.
Rather than "popular," a better term for Shakespeare's cultural status in
the mid seventeenth century is "versatile," as he was appropriated for a
variety of political, cultural, and scholarly purposes. Shakespeare lent
himself to vastly different forms of dramatic consumption and appreciation: in the Interregnum, Shakespeare was variously an emblem of royalism and republicanism, a figure of classical high culture and of working-
class English entertainment. Shakespeare was celebrated as the author of
indelible dramatic characters at the same time that his plays were mined for
decontextualized fragments. Shakespeare's name, his characters, and play
titles were frequently mentioned as obvious standards of cultural value, but
these references do not always suggest familiarity with his works' actual
contents. Various play titles were misassigned to his name because they
sounded "Shakespearean," an increasingly stable category of dramatic
organization. Above all, Shakespeare appeared "old" in the mid seventeenth century. Modern critics have mistaken this oldness for a low point
in Shakespeare's reputation, but Shakespeare was always around, and
familiar from allusions and textual fragments.

Because, as demonstrated in the Introduction, dramatic production and
consumption changed drastically after the theatres closed, for a clearer
picture of a dramatist's mid-century reputation, it is necessary to look
beyond the types of texts that defined pre-1642 dramatic consumption

---

[7] It should be noted that *Macbeth* and *Julius Caesar* went on to receive their first quarto/single-play
editions in 1674 and 1684, respectively.

(i.e. full-length plays) to the dramatic fragments (e.g. extracts, listed play titles) in which professional plays increasingly circulated after 1642. Given Shakespeare's considerable presence in these abbreviated texts, one must be wary of misinterpreting the story they tell about his mid seventeenth-century reputation. John Cotgrave's *English Treasury of Wit and Language* (1655) is the most cited – and the most potentially misleading – evidence of Shakespeare's popularity in Interregnum print culture.[8] Certainly, Shakespeare is the most-quoted dramatist in the volume, but the volume's most-cited plays are Fulke Greville's *Alaham* and *Mustapha*, sententious closet plays whose didacticism, rather than their popular appeal, served Cotgrave's purposes.

Moreover, *The English Treasury* does not attempt to capitalize on the selling power of Shakespeare's name: its extracts omit the names of dramatists, play titles, and contextual clues like character names. It's unlikely that the average seventeenth-century reader would recognize that Shakespeare supplied most of the extracts; Martin Wiggins characterizes the process of recovering Cotgrave's sources as, "in the absence of the modern digital tools I used ... an act of almost unimaginable scholarly heroism."[9] *The English Treasury* is the obverse of *Wits Interpreter*: where Cragge offers the image of "Shakespeare" without his texts, *The English Treasury* offers Shakespeare's texts without "Shakespeare." In the Interregnum, the authorial figure of Shakespeare was increasingly separated from his texts; his strong cultural cachet was sometimes attended by a vague, imprecise familiarity with his works. Despite little new print publication, Shakespeare was a well-known dramatist in this period – but for which plays, exactly, was not always clear.

Missing Shakespeare, 1642–1660

By some accounts, Shakespeare's First Folio (F1) of 1623 was a success. The large, expensive volume sold sufficiently well to warrant a second edition (F2) only nine years later in 1632. By contrast, thirty-one years passed before the Third Folio (F3) appeared in 1663/4. Critics see the longer gap between F2 and F3 as evidence of the reading public's waning interest in Shakespeare in the Civil Wars and Interregnum.[10] But it

---

[8] See Depledge, *Shakespeare's Rise*, p. 27; Bentley, "John Cotgrave's *English Treasury*"; Estill, *Dramatic Extracts*, pp. 90–2.
[9] Wiggins, "Where to Find Lost Plays," p. 277.
[10] Kastan, *Shakespeare and the Book*, pp. 63–4, 79–84.

appears that a legal battle was at least partly responsible for F3's delay. Sixteen of the eighteen Shakespeare plays first printed in F1 – *The Tempest, The Two Gentlemen of Verona, Measure for Measure, The Comedy of Errors, As You Like It, All's Well that Ends Well, Twelfth Night, The Winter's Tale, 1 Henry IV, Henry VIII, Coriolanus, Timon of Athens, Julius Caesar, Macbeth, Antony and Cleopatra,* and *Cymbeline* – were the subject of a bitter Chancery Court dispute that endured from 1637 to 1661.[11]

On the one side were Mary Allot, widow of Robert Allot, publisher of F2, and Philip Chetwind, Mary Allot's second husband and the eventual publisher of F3. On the other side were the stationers Andrew Crooke, Robert Allot's former apprentice, and John Legate. The sixteen titles had been co-owned by Edward Blount and Isaac Jaggard, publishers of F1. In 1630, Robert Allot acquired the rights to Blount's share of the sixteen plays; the brothers Thomas and Richard Cotes held the rights to Jaggard's portion; Robert Allot and Thomas Cotes respectively published and printed Shakespeare's F2 in 1632. When Robert Allot died in 1635, his share of the sixteen Shakespeare plays, as well as forty-five other titles, was transferred to Mary Allot. In 1636, she married Chetwind. Normally upon remarrying, a widow's printing rights would transfer to her new husband, but Chetwind, a cloth-maker, was not a member of the Stationers' Company. As a result, Mary Allot was forced by court order to forfeit her rights to all titles and copies, transferring them to Crooke and Legate on 1 July 1637 according to the following entry in the Stationers' Register:

> Master Legatt and Andrew Crooke Entered for their Copies by Consent of Mistriss Allot and by order of a full Court holden the Seauenth day of Nouember [1636] last All the Estate Right Title and Interest which the said Master Allot hath in these Copies and parts of Copies hereafter following which were Master Roberte Allotts deceased.[12]

The matter did not end there, but rather was the beginning of an acrimonious legal dispute in which Mary Allot and Chetwind attempted to reclaim their printing rights. Complicating matters further, the brothers Thomas (d. 1641) and Richard Cotes still held the rights to Jaggard's share

---

[11] Apart from these sixteen plays, the other two Shakespeare plays first printed in F1, *The Taming of the Shrew* and *King John*, were not entered into the Stationers' Register by Blount and Jaggard in 1623 and their rights therefore were not transmitted to Blount and Jaggard's heirs. John Smethwick held the rights to *The Taming of the Shrew* by virtue of owning *Taming of a Shrew*; as for *King John*, John Dewe might have had a claim to the text, owing to his ownership of the similarly titled *The Troublesome Reign of King John*. See Murphy, *Shakespeare in Print*, p. 44.

[12] *A Transcript of the Registers of the Company of Stationers of London, 1554–1640 A.D.*, ed. Edward Arber, 5 vols. (London: privately printed, 1875–94), IV, pp. 387–9.

of the sixteen plays, as well as five or six titles from Thomas Pavier (*A Midsummer Night's Dream, Henry V, 2 Henry VI, 3 Henry VI, Pericles,* and potentially *Titus Andronicus*) all of which were transferred to Richard Cotes's widow Ellen (or Eleanor) Cotes after his death in 1653.

Henry Farr reconstructs the history of the Allot/Chetwind copyrights, revealing the bitter litigation that plagued the Allot estate for over two decades.[13] In January 1662, Mary Allot and Chetwind petitioned for a restoration of their printing rights, remarking on a "long and expensive twenty years' suit in Chancery, to the utter ruin of the petitioners."[14] Farr comments that "[w]hatever the result of this petition may have been, Chetwynd appears to have attained some measure of success, for he published much more freely afterwards" – including Shakespeare's F3 in 1663. Though she is not mentioned in F3, Ellen Cotes might have been involved in its publication, as she worked as a printer for Chetwind as early as 1653.[15]

The Allot-Chetwind/Crooke-Legate lawsuit and the attendant business troubles of the stationers did not occur in a vacuum, but over a politically tumultuous quarter-century that profoundly affected the English book trade. The fall of the Star Chamber in 1641, the English Civil Wars and Revolution (intermittently from 1642 to 1651), and the Interregnum (1649–60) caused crises in the English book trade that compromised the authority of the Stationers' Company, disrupted distribution networks, and shrank markets.[16] Thanks to these same contemporary conflicts, however, the era's book trade also witnessed innovation and indeed even growth in the areas of printed news and political tracts: the periodical and newspaper press were invented in these decades, and printed pamphlets flooded the market with radical political and religious ideas.[17] John Barnard surveys the book trade's output in the 1640s and 1650s, attending to both frequently discussed genres of periodicals, heterodox pamphlets, and Royalist publications, as well as texts and genres that have received less attention.[18] Although certain kinds of printed drama (especially politically

---

[13] Henry Farr, "Philip Chetwind and the Allott Copyrights," *The Library*, 15 (1934), pp. 129–60. See also Don-John Dugas, "Philip Chetwind and the Shakespeare Third Folio," *Harvard Library Bulletin*, 14.1 (2003), 29–46.

[14] Cited in Farr, "Philip Chetwind," p. 129.

[15] Murphy, *Shakespeare in Print*, p. 53; Farr, "Philip Chetwind," pp. 159–60.

[16] Barnard, "London Publishing"; D. F. McKenzie, "The London Book Trade in 1644," in *Bibliographia*, ed. John Horden (Oxford: Leopard Head Press, 1992), pp. 131–52.

[17] David R. Como, "Print, Censorship, and Ideological Escalation in the English Civil War," *Journal of British Studies*, 51.4 (2012), 820–57; Jason McElligott, *Royalism, Print and Censorship in Revolutionary England* (Woodbridge: Boydell, 2007).

[18] Barnard, "London Publishing," pp. 2–3.

inflected closet drama and semi-dramatic dialogues) have received relatively significant critical attention,[19] it is productive to consider the place
of playbooks in the book trade as a whole, both who printed them and
how popular they were relative to other kinds of texts.

While some stationers (discussed in more detail below) specialized in
playbooks and not much else, playbooks were also published and sold by
the same people who were producing the short political tracts that were
coming out in huge numbers in the early 1640s. Barnard cites D. F.
McKenzie's analysis of a small group of booksellers who dominated the
publication of texts from various religious and political movements
(Quakers, Ranters, Levellers, Radicals, Independents, among others),
namely, the publishing partners Lodowick Lloyd and Henry Cripps,
William Larner, Thomas Simmons, Henry Overton, and Giles Calvert,
and their main printers, James Cottrell, John Maycock, and Matthew
Simmons.[20] Some of these stationers were involved in the playbook trade.
Lloyd and Cripps printed Leonard Willan's Interregnum-era pastoral
tragicomic closet play *Astraea or Love's True Mirror* (1651), adapted from
Honoré D'Urfé's *L'Astrée*, an influential French pastoral novel published
between 1607 and 1627, a play that also served as a source for Fletcher's
Valentinian (1647) and his *Monsieur Thomas* (1639).[21] Although the
notable Quaker publisher Giles Calvert does not appear to have published
any dramatic texts, his younger brother George sold the 1655 edition of
the Sidneys' *The Countess of Pembroke's Arcadia*, a collection of non-
dramatic texts and the occasional royal entertainment *The Entertainment
at Wanstead* (*The Lady of May*). The Sidney collection was printed by
William Dugard, publisher of John Milton's *Pro Populo Anglicano Defensio*
(1651), a polemic in Latin that justified Parliament's execution of Charles
I. Prior to his edition of Milton's polemic, Dugard had been imprisoned
for publishing *Eikon Basilike* (1649); clearly, as John Barnard notes,
Dugard was among those stationers "willing to work for both government
and opposition, radicals and the orthodox."[22] Meanwhile, at the Black
Spread Eagle, where Giles Calvert also worked, the publisher John

[19] For example, in Wiseman, *Drama and Politics* and in Randall, *Winter Fruit*.
[20] Barnard, "London Publishing," p. 3, citing D. F. McKenzie, "The London Book Trade in the Later
    Seventeenth Century," Sandars Lectures 1976, mimeographed copies deposited in British Library,
    Bodleian Library, Brotherton Library (University of Leeds), pp. 12–13.
[21] Sister Mary Catherine McMahon notes that Willan's "masque was an attempt to dramatize certain
    episodes in the *Astrée* and presupposed great familiarity with the novel." "Aesthetics and Art in the
    Astrée of Honoré D'Urfé" (doctoral dissertation, Catholic University of America, 1925), p. 36 n. 50.
[22] Barnard, "London Publishing," p. 4.

Hardesty printed the second edition of Henry Killigrew's professional Caroline-era tragicomedy *Pallantus and Eudora* (1653). Perhaps unsurprisingly, given that printers had incentives to produce a wider range of genres for interested publishers, the radical printers discussed by McKenzie and Barnard also produced notable dramatic texts. James Cottrell, whom Henry Plomer characterizes as a printer responsible for "a good many pamphlets that offended the authorities" during the Commonwealth, also printed Thomas May's Caroline comedy *The Old Couple* (1658), as well as the first edition of *The Witch of Edmonton* (1658).[23] Barnard notes that "[t]he concern of publishers was in the first (and usually the last) place commercial ... the profit motive could create strange alliances."[24] The Catholic Royalist stationer John Playford collaborated with a Parliamentarian and possible Leveller on *King Charls his Tryall*, entering the title into the Stationers' Register in 1649.[25] Playford became known for his musical publications, and was responsible for printing James Shirley's masque *Cupid and Death* (1659).

As all this suggests, commercial interests could lead stationers to diversify their publication agendas to incorporate different genres. Still, it seems that in the book trade, newsbooks and polemical tracts had a significant advantage over other kinds of texts; Barnard notes that while radical authors saw books as a means to spread their views, "for the booksellers it meant sure sales."[26] The *English Short Title Catalogue* lists 29,873 publications printed between 1642 and 1660; playbooks represent a tiny fraction of this total output, with only 315 dramatic editions appearing between these years, 165 of them professional, and the majority of those (126) first editions.[27] How did this differ from the period prior?[28] Alan B. Farmer and Zachary Lesser debated Peter Blayney about the popularity of playbooks before 1642, with Blayney contending that playbooks represented an insignificant portion of the overall book trade and Farmer and

[23] Henry Robert Plomer, *A Dictionary of the Booksellers and Printers Who Were at Work in England, Scotland and Ireland from 1641 to 1667* (London: Printed for the Bibliographical Society, 1907), p. 54.
[24] Barnard, "London Publishing," p. 5.   [25] Ibid., pp. 5, 14 n. 35.   [26] Ibid., p. 5.
[27] My reckoning relies on the *English Short Title Catalogue*, http://estc.bl.uk, and on *DEEP*.
[28] Peter Blayney, "The Publication of Playbooks," in *A New History of Early Modern English Drama*, ed. John D. Cox and David Scott Kastan (New York: Columbia University Press, 1997), pp. 382–422; Alan B. Farmer and Zachary Lesser, "The Popularity of Playbooks Revisited," *Shakespeare Quarterly*, 56.1 (2005), 1–32; Peter W. M. Blayney, "The Alleged Popularity of Playbooks," *Shakespeare Quarterly*, 56.1 (2005), 33–50; and Alan B. Farmer and Zachary Lesser, "Structures of Popularity in the Early Modern Book Trade," *Shakespeare Quarterly*, 56.2 (2005), 206–13.

Lesser arguing for their importance. Blayney states that new plays "never accounted for a very significant fraction of the trade in English books," amounting to between 1.2 per cent and 1.6 per cent of the entries in the *Short-Title Catalogue* from 1583 to 1642.[29] By this measure, the market share of new professional playbooks fell between 1642 and 1660, occupying only 0.42 per cent of entries in the *English Short Title Catalogue* during this period.[30] To determine popularity, like Blayney, Farmer and Lesser attend to criteria including the total number of editions, market share, and profitability. They argue, however, that "the criterion that brings us closest to consumer demand is the rate of reprinting of playbooks, since a publisher's decision to reprint can usually be assumed to indicate both that the previous edition had sold out (or was about to sell out) and that the publisher anticipated continued demand."[31] Focusing on reprint rates, again the 1640s and 1650s represent a decline in the overall popularity of playbooks, especially from the previous decade of the 1630s. As I demonstrate below, during the 1640s and 1650s, dramatic stationers moved away from reprints to focus on newly printed plays. I will offer reasons for this shift; for the time being, however, it is important to emphasize that the era's political and religious conflicts played out in print – scores of newsbooks, periodicals, sermons, pamphlets, tracts, closet plays, and dialogues appeared, in support of both royalist and republican agendas – and that these texts seem to have represented a surer bet for some stationers than dramatic publications.

While some of the era's stationers participated in both political and literary publication, others – including Miles Flesher (or Fletcher) and Richard Cotes, both of whom held rights to Shakespeare's plays – shifted their attention away from literary productions and towards political and religious ones. Flesher, a prosperous printer active in the administration of the Stationers' Company,[32] held the rights to *Hamlet*, *Romeo and Juliet*, *Love's Labour's Lost*, *The Taming of the Shrew*, and *King Lear* from 1642 until his death in 1664, yet he did not reprint any of them.

[29] Blayney, "The Publication of Playbooks," p. 417, n. 8.
[30] The *Short-Title Catalogue*, on which Blayney, Farmer, and Lesser's studies largely rely, ends in 1640. For texts printed after 1640, Blayney relies on *The English Short Title Catalogue*, and I do likewise. A. W. Pollard and G. R. Redgrave, eds., *A Short-Title Catalogue of Books Printed Scotland, & Ireland and of English Books Printed Abroad, 1475–1640*, 2nd ed., 3 vols., rev. W. A Ferguson, and Katharine F. Pantzer (London: Bibliographical Society, 1976–9). Blayney, "The Alleged Popularity of Playbooks," pp. 49–50.
[31] Farmer and Lesser, "The Popularity of Playbooks Revisited," pp. 4–5.
[32] Cyprian Blagden, *The Stationers' Company: A History, 1403–1959* (Stanford: Stanford University Press, 1977), pp. 138–44.

Flesher's neglect of the titles is especially curious given that, unlike the automatic transfer of rights from dead stationers to their heirs, he actively sought the rights to Shakespeare's plays. Flesher was clearly interested in Shakespeare at one point, but for some reason this interest faded. The date Flesher acquired four of his five Shakespeare titles – 14 September 1642, three weeks after the outbreak of the first English Civil War – points towards one explanation. Having secured the rights to *King Lear* (with twenty-five other titles) from Nathaniel Butter on 21 May 1639 in return for a £600 loan, Flesher purchased the four other Shakespeare titles from Francis Smethwick. Smethwick had inherited the four plays (along with fourteen other literary and devotional titles) from his late father John Smethwick. The younger Smethwick entered the eighteen titles into the Stationers' Register on 24 August 1642 and transferred seventeen of them to Flesher three weeks later. The Civil War, however, appears to have caused a radical shift in Flesher's publishing focus.

While scholars of early modern poetry know Flesher as the first printer of Donne's *Poems by J. D.* (1633), historians of the English Civil Wars know him as a "prominent Royalist" who "mainly produced religious and educational pamphlets."[33] Flesher's political and religious publications came at the expense of his literary output. After publishing a modest eight plays in the 1630s, he printed no plays in the 1640s or 1650s, and while he reprinted Donne's *Poems* in 1635, 1639, and 1649, he is not mentioned in the imprints to the 1650 and 1654 editions, the latter published by his son, James Flesher. Amid Flesher's political publications and affiliations, his interest in literature appears to have fallen by the wayside. Flesher's Shakespearean play publication may have been collateral damage of the English Civil Wars.

Contemporary political turmoil might have also sidelined the Shakespearean publications of Richard Cotes. From his late brother Thomas (printer of F2), Richard Cotes inherited the rights to Jaggard's share of the sixteen folio plays after 1641, as well as five or six Shakespeare titles formerly held by Pavier – *A Midsummer Night's Dream, Henry V, 2 Henry VI, 3 Henry VI, Pericles*, and possibly *Titus Andronicus*. These titles also went unprinted during the Civil Wars and Interregnum. Unlike Flesher, Cotes did publish drama in the period, but he focused on non-professional plays, publishing a collection of four Latin university plays in 1648. Notably, Cotes published *The Tragedy of the Famous Orator Marcus*

---

[33] McElligott, *Royalism, Print and Censorship*, p. 133; Amos Tubb, "Independent Presses: The Politics of Print in England during the Late 1640s," *The Seventeenth Century*, 27 (2012), 287–312 (p. 293).

Tullius Cicero (1651), the most significant republican closet play of the period. Of course, one publication does not a staunch (or even sometime) Republican make – Cotes's involvement may simply have been an opportunistic move in the context of the new Commonwealth. But either explanation helps account for his aversion to printing Shakespeare, who exemplified the old-guard cultural productions that the new government was trying to eradicate.

While political upheaval in the 1640s may have turned Flesher and Cotes's attention away from Shakespeare, in the decade before, the stationer John Norton had attempted to capitalize on the political relevance of Shakespeare's history plays. Norton held the rights to *Richard II*, *1 Henry IV*, and *Richard III*, and printed five quartos of the three plays across the late 1620s and 1630s: two editions of *Richard III* (Q7 1629 and Q8 1634), one of *Richard II* (Q6 1634), and two of *1 Henry IV* (Q8 1632 and Q9 1639). Alan B. Farmer argues that Norton's reprints "retained a certain political currency in Caroline England because they dramatized the dangers of civil war" and were ideologically consistent with proto-royalist politics.[34] Given his record, Norton might have continued to exploit the topicality and political leanings of the history plays during the Civil Wars and Interregnum; however, Norton died in 1640, cutting short any further publishing strategies.

Another Shakespeare rights-holder, John Smethwick, also died in the early 1640s. Like Norton, Smethwick was an inveterate reprinter of playbooks, and of Shakespeare quartos in particular. All of Smethwick's dramatic publications were reprints, and in the 1620s and 1630s he did not publish playbooks by dramatists other than Shakespeare. Upon acquiring the rights to *Hamlet, Romeo and Juliet, Love's Labour's Lost,* and *The Taming of the Shrew* as well as several other popular dramatic titles around 1607 from the late Nicholas Ling, he reprinted them frequently over the next three decades, issuing three quartos of *Romeo and Juliet* (Q3 1609, Q4 1623, Q5 1637), three quartos of *Hamlet* (Q3 1611, Q4 1625, Q5 1637), the first quarto of *The Taming of the Shrew* (1631), and the second quarto of *Love's Labour's Lost* (1631). Many of Smethwick's single-text quartos were printed around the same time as F1 (1623) and F2 (1632). Smethwick was a member of the folio syndicate, therefore the single-text quartos issued around the same time as F1 and F2 do not represent an

---

[34] Alan B. Farmer, "John Norton and the Politics of Shakespeare's History Plays in Caroline England," in *Shakespeare's Stationers: Studies in Cultural Bibliography*, ed. Marta Straznicky (Philadelphia: University of Pennsylvania Press, 2013), pp. 147–76 (p. 149).

attempt to compete with the collections; Sonia Massai suggests *Romeo and Juliet* Q4 was meant as "pre-publicity" for F1.[35] The decline in Shakespeare publication in the 1640s and 1650s is therefore unlikely simply to be the result of the publication of F2, which clearly did not stymie further Shakespearean publication in the 1630s. Rather, Smethwick's activities hint at separate markets for expensive folios and for more affordable quartos in the 1630s; it also reveals his belief that the market had not yet reached a Shakespeare saturation point, and perhaps never would. Moreover, as years passed, F2's potential to depress subsequent publications of Shakespeare became increasingly unlikely: two decades after the publication of a large folio edition, one might expect any appreciable interest in Shakespeare to be attended at least by the publication of inexpensive single-text quarto editions.

Had Norton or Smethwick lived past 1642, they might have continued to reprint Shakespeare quartos, or contemporary trends in the book market may have pushed them in other directions. We can never know if they died just as their publication strategy was losing ground, or if their deaths themselves changed the landscape of Shakespeare publication. What is clear, however, is that Norton and Smethwick's heirs were uninterested in maintaining their predecessors' publication habits. We've seen how quickly Francis Smethwick transferred his late father's titles to Flesher. Like Flesher, Francis Smethwick appears to have been more interested in non-dramatic publication. In 1642, the younger Smethwick published *Three Sermons* by the Church of England clergyman Henry Smith (c. 1560–91). Likewise, upon his death, Norton's titles were transferred to his widow Alice Law, and thereafter to Law's second husband, the printer Thomas Warren. Warren did not reprint the perennially popular *Richard II*, *1 Henry IV*, and *Richard III*, but he did print two significant publications for the prominent Interregnum stationer Humphrey Moseley: the Beaumont and Fletcher collected folio of 1647 and Shirley's *Six New Plays* (1653).

These editions demonstrate that, despite the turn towards political and religious publication in the Civil Wars and Interregnum, stationers did continue to print professional drama. But there was a discernible shift in the types of plays published, and here Warren's publications for Moseley are representative. The title page to the Beaumont and Fletcher folio collection touted that its contents (thirty-four plays and one masque) were

---

[35] Sonia Massai, *Shakespeare and the Rise of the Editor* (Cambridge: Cambridge University Press, 2007), pp. 119–21.

"never printed before," while Shirley's *Six New Plays* likewise highlights
the novelty of its contents. During the theatre ban, dramatic stationers
focused on previously unprinted plays (or "new") plays. In so doing, they
reversed the publication trends of the preceding decades.

New Old Plays

Old plays, as a class, were perennially popular while the playhouses were
open. The professional theatre at its core was a repertory system, and
roughly half of the professional playbook market between 1576 and 1641
was devoted to reprints or "second-plus" editions: out of 730 titles, 373 are
first editions (51 per cent) and 357 are second-plus (49 per cent).[36] In the
Caroline period (1625–41), reprints of professional drama overtook first
editions: with 167 second-plus editions (54 per cent) and 140 first editions
(46 per cent) out of a total of 307. Alan B. Farmer and Zachary Lesser
argue that "[i]n the 1630s, the market for printed drama from the
professional theatre underwent an unprecedented division in which new
[Caroline] plays were split from a group of 'classic' plays first published
decades earlier." This bifurcation in the market and the Caroline trend of
reprinting Elizabethan and Jacobean playbooks, they continue, "resulted
in the first canon of early modern drama," which, they argue, has many
affinities with our current canon of early modern drama.[37]

   But the theatre ban ended (or at least interrupted) the Caroline trend for
dramatic republication, by both arousing demand for and facilitating the
supply of previously unprinted plays. In the absence of an active professional theatre, audiences were starved for dramatic novelty. The theatre
ban eliminated any potential rivalry that might cause playing companies to
withhold texts from printing houses. Underemployed acting companies
may well have sold off their back catalogues in an effort to raise cash. This
freed up more manuscripts for publication, and as a result, the number of
first editions of pre-1642 professional plays soared in the 1640s and 1650s.
First editions outnumbered reprints at a rate of three to one: out of the
165 professional plays printed between 1642 and 1660, 126 are first
editions (76 per cent) and only 39 are second-plus (24 per cent).[38] In a

---

[36] My quantitative analysis here relies on *DEEP*. See also Farmer and Lesser, "The Popularity of
    Playbooks Revisited," 7–9.

[37] Farmer and Lesser, "Canons and Classics," pp. 17–18, 37.

[38] Some scholars, such as Farmer and Lesser, count collections as a single play text. But because
    Interregnum stationers draw attention to the number of individual plays within their collections –
    e.g., *Six New Plays* – it seems more appropriate to count each play in the collection separately.

moment when there was virtually no new professional drama being composed, and with a reliable roster of titles that had been printed and
reprinted in the decades prior, playbook stationers changed their publishing strategy to focus on first editions. Novelty became a potent marketing
device in a period with no active commercial theatre producing new
material on stage: stationers cannily advertised their "new plays," "never
printed before." Paradoxically, new professional playbooks dominated the
market at precisely the moment that the composition of new professional
plays ebbed.

Andrew Crooke's publication output exemplifies the interest in dramatic novelty during the theatrical prohibition. Crooke was one of Allot
and Chetwind's adversaries in the legal battle of 1637–61, and he in fact
published some of the contested Allot titles during the period in question,
including Bishop Lewis Bayly's *Practice of Piety,* one of the most frequently
reprinted devotional texts in the seventeenth century. Crooke clearly
wasn't averse to reprints, but when it came to plays, he reflected the
market's preference for novelty. He printed only one dramatic text in this
period, Richard Brome's *Five New Plays* (1659), an octavo collection of
five previously unprinted plays. This volume imitated Humphrey
Moseley's *New Plays* series, a series of dramatic octavo collections of
previously unprinted professional plays by James Shirley, Richard
Brome, Philip Massinger, Thomas Middleton, and Lodowick Carlell,
printed between 1653 and 1657. In terms of chronology, the novelty
claimed by some of these "new plays" was rather tenuous. Moseley's
edition of Middleton's *Two New Plays* (1657) included *More Dissemblers
Besides Women,* first performed forty-three years earlier in 1614. Prior to
1642, a first edition printed several decades after its first performance
would not be marketed as a "new play" but rather as a new edition of an
older play. For example, paratexts from the first known edition of *The Jew
of Malta* (1633), staged four decades prior, describe it as a play performed
in the "later age" that is "now newly brought to the press." Given its aged
theatrical history, the play's novel print history is not sufficient to charac-
terize it as a "new play."

The closure of the theatres, however, allowed stationers to redefine
dramatic novelty in a way that favoured their own medium. "New plays"
were now chiefly defined in terms of previous unavailability in print, rather
than recent dates of composition or performance. Given the market appeal
of novelty, combined with the actual age of the plays, Interregnum
stationers took great pains to advertise and justify the newness of their
wares. It is telling that a dramatic series titled *New Plays* emerged only once

new professional plays were no longer being written. In their stationers'
address to Richard Brome's *Five New Plays* (1659), Andrew Crooke and
Henry Brome draw attention to the improbability and rarity of their new
edition, and defend its title:

> We bring what in these dayes you scarce could hope for, Five new Playes.
> We call them new, because till now they never were printed. You must not
> think them posthumous Productions, though they come into the world
> after the Author's death: they were all begotten and born (and own'd by
> Him before a thousand witnesses) many years since; they then trod the
> Stage (their proper place) though they pass'd not the Press.[39]

Seventeen years after the theatres closed, with no active industry generating
new compositions, readers could "scarce hope for" new professional plays.
Seemingly against all odds, Crooke and Brome have produced not one, but
multiple "new plays." The stationers defensively acknowledge that while
Brome's plays are old in terms of their composition and performance
history, they are still novel because they "pass'd not the Press."
Paradoxically, amid this assertion of novelty, the stationers also take pains
to assert the plays' age. Perhaps anticipating scepticism from readers
presented with "new" professional plays from a dramatist who had been
dead for seven years, written for an industry long defunct, the stationers
note the plays' composition and commercial performance "many years
since." The new plays are suspended between past and present, interesting
for their novelty and for their ability to evoke a fading theatrical past. Plays
actually newly written during the theatrical prohibition could not have the
same appeal. Although deprived of their "proper place" onstage, old plays
could, at least, recall that tradition and be remade into new ones in print.

By the 1640s, however, there was at least one dramatist who was old in
every sense: Shakespeare. His plays were "begotten and born" and had
"trod the stage" many years since, and they had certainly "passed the
press." Shakespeare was the most-printed dramatist in his own lifetime.
Although there was a slight decline in Shakespearean publications in the
decades immediately following his death, he was still steadily published in
the 1620s and 1630s, outpacing his dramatic contemporaries.[40] Over
three-quarters of all of his quartos (sixteen of twenty-one plays) were

---

[39] Andrew Crooke and Henry Brome, "The Stationers to the Reader," in Richard Brome, *Five New
Plays of Richard Brome* (London: Andrew Crooke and Henry Brome, 1659), sig. a3v.
[40] See Erne, *Shakespeare and the Book Trade*, p. 18.

reprinted within twenty years of their first edition.[41] Shakespeare had more second-plus editions than any of his contemporaries by the time F1 appeared in 1623. The two folios of 1623 and 1632 did not stem the tide of Shakespearean single-text publication; as we've seen, a spate of single-text quartos was issued around the same time as F1 and F2. By 1639, the thirty-eight plays we now recognize as Shakespeare's had been printed in seventy single-text editions, one quarto collection, and two monumental folios. *1 Henry IV* had been printed eleven times; only *Mucedorus*, the most-printed play in the seventeenth century, was printed more often. Even if Shakespeare was not actively being printed, due to the endurance of dramatic quartos and folios, Interregnum England must have been awash with Shakespeare books.[42] Since frequent publication contributed to a play's apparent oldness, the consistently, repeatedly reprinted plays of Shakespeare must have seemed positively ancient to mid seventeenth-century readers. David Scott Kastan ascribes the mid-century slump in Shakespeare publication to the fact that "Old Shakespeare" seemed by then to be "distant and old-fashioned."[43] But, far from seeming "distant," Shakespeare appeared old by virtue of his ubiquity in print.

The emphasis on dramatic novelty during the theatre ban partly explains why the era's stationers largely neglected Shakespeare. It is unsurprising that stationers were in no hurry to reprint Shakespeare's historically less popular plays: the first quartos of *Much Ado About Nothing* (1600), *2 Henry IV* (1600), and *Troilus and Cressida* (1609) mark the first and last times these plays were printed in single-text editions.[44] But stationers were also largely uninterested in printing Shakespeare's historically more popular titles. A book catalogue from 1661 advertising the stock of Restoration stationer Henry Herringman lists "Loves labour lost," "*Hamlet* Prince of *Denmark*," and "*Romio and Juliet*" among its titles. The three plays had been popular in print into the Caroline period; John Smethwick printed Q2 of *Love's Labour's Lost* in 1631, and the fifth quartos of both *Hamlet* and *Romeo and Juliet* in 1637. Herringman did not reprint these titles, so he must have acquired Smethwick's stock of unsold copies of the three

---

[41] Ibid., pp. 25–55; See also Zachary Lesser, "Shakespeare's Flop: John Waterson and *The Two Noble Kinsmen*," in *Shakespeare's Stationers*, ed. Straznicky, pp. 177–96 (p. 177).

[42] Alan B. Farmer, "Playbooks and the Question of Ephemerality," in *The Book in History, The Book as History: New Intersections of the Material Text*, ed. Heidi Brayman, Jesse Lander, and Zachary Lesser (New Haven: Yale University Press, 2016), pp. 87–125.

[43] Kastan, *Shakespeare and the Book*, p. 84.

[44] *Much Ado* and *2H4* do not reappear in the Stationers' Register after they were entered to Andrew Wise and William Aspley in 1600, and neither did *T&C* after it was entered by Richard Bonian and Henry Walley in 1609.

plays; that he was still trying to offload these titles over twenty years later suggests that Interregnum readers were largely uninterested in them. George Bedell and Mercy Meighan did not reprint *The Merry Wives of Windsor* after acquiring it on 7 November 1646 from Mercy's late husband Richard Meighan, who was the last to reprint the play in a single-text edition (Q3 1630), and who printed no plays whatsoever after 1640. But Mercy Meighan and Bedell published thirteen dramatic editions in the Interregnum, eleven of them first editions.

Humphrey Moseley is largely responsible for the Interregnum playbook market's reorientation towards first editions. As the most prolific dramatic stationer of the Civil Wars and Interregnum, Moseley single-handedly shaped the era's field of printed drama; he also influenced other stationers. Moseley's activity in the playbook trade was frenetic and ambitious; Maureen Bell describes him as "buying up every 'old' play that came his way."[45] In fact, as his entries in the Stationers' Register indicate, Moseley was especially interested in acquiring "new" old plays, some of which he then set to printing. Moseley's edition of Beaumont and Fletcher's *Comedies and Tragedies* (1647) explicitly excluded those already in print. As Moseley notes in his stationer's epistle to the reader: "You have here a new book; I can speak it clearly, for all this large Volume of Comedies and Tragedies, not one, till now, was ever printed before. A collection of Plays is commonly but a new impression, the scattered pieces which were printed single, being then onely Republished together. Tis otherwise here."[46] Denigrating the supposedly recycled contents of other collections, Moseley stresses both the novelty and value of his collection, reassuring readers that they won't pay for texts they already own. Moseley could be referring to any number of collected works that reprinted material from single-text editions, including Ben Jonson's *Works* in folio (1616 and expanded in 1640). It seems most likely, however, that he is referring to Shakespeare's folios.

The Beaumont and Fletcher folio presents itself as a successor to Shakespeare's F1. The 1647 folio is dedicated to Philip Herbert, Earl of Pembroke and Montgomery. The King's Servants actors who signed the 1647 dedication explain that their choice of dedicatee was "directed by the example of some, who once steered in our qualitie," namely their

---

predecessors in the company, Heminge and Condell, who chose Philip and his late brother William as "Patrons to the flowing compositions of the then expired sweet Swan of Avon SHAKESPEARE." Yet the 1647 folio's prefatory matter also betrays an ambivalence about Shakespeare. The canonized poet of F1, the "sweet Swan of Avon," lends his authority seemingly in order to justify the prestige presentation of Beaumont and Fletcher. Meanwhile, collections like Shakespeare's F1 are denigrated as "but a new impression," surpassed by Moseley's "new book." This characterization is manifestly untrue: as Moseley would have known, half of the plays in Shakespeare's F1 had never been printed before. Yet beyond the obvious promotional value of Moseley's misrepresentation, his description hints at the ubiquity of Shakespeare in print by 1647, liberally "scattered" throughout the market despite a lack of recent publication.

Though Shakespeare did not align with Moseley's publication philosophy for the most part, Moseley did dabble in Shakespearean publication, largely when he could acquire new "Shakespeare" titles. On 9 September 1653, Moseley entered forty-two titles, including four he ascribed to "Shakespeare": "*The merry Devill of Edmonton*," by "Wm: Shakespeare," "*Henry ye. first, & Hen: ye 2d.*," by "Shakespeare, & Davenport," and "*The History of Cardenio. By Mr Fletcher. and Shakespeare.*"[47] Moseley's interest in one of these "Shakespeare" plays was short-lived: he did not reprint *The Merry Devil of Edmonton* in the nineteen months that he held its rights. In an unclear chain of transfer, on 4 April 1655 the rights to *Merry Devil* were acquired by William Gilbertson, who printed the sixth quarto of the play in 1655.

Although Moseley did not publish his other three "Shakespeare" titles acquired in 1653, he clearly maintained an interest, since on 29 June 1660 he registered three more plays "by Will: Shakespeare": "*The History of King Stephen*," "*Duke Humphrey*," and "*Iphis & Iantha, a marriage without a man.*" Moseley never printed any of these "Shakespeare" plays either, and all six plays, previously unprinted when Moseley acquired them, are now lost. Why didn't Moseley print them? David McInnis suggests that "the dubiousness of the authorial ascription may itself be the reason these manuscripts never made it to print: Moseley may have staked his hopes on unsupportable claims of Shakespearean authorship as his planned marketing strategy."[48] Moseley may also have had doubts

---

[47] Arber, *Registers of the Company of Stationers*, I, pp. 428–9.

[48] David McInnis, *Shakespeare and Lost Plays: Reimagining Drama in Early Modern England* (Cambridge: Cambridge University Press, 2021), p. 246. Thank you to David for sharing a copy of his manuscript with me prior to publication.

about Shakespeare's vendibility. He acquired the rights to *The Two Noble Kinsmen* from John Waterson on 31 October 1646; book advertisement catalogues from 1660 reveal that Moseley was still trying to unload the now twenty-six-year-old copies of the first edition (Q1 1634).[49] In these advertisements, Moseley does not even bother mentioning Shakespeare, attributing *Kinsmen* to Fletcher alone.

In attempting to recover Moseley's motivations, it seems significant that most of the "Shakespeare" plays he acquired had never been printed, and the only previously printed play, *Merry Devil*, was either quickly transferred to (or else was reclaimed without conflict by) another stationer who quickly reprinted it. Moseley was interested in new Shakespeare, or whatever he thought of as Shakespeare, or could potentially pass off as Shakespeare. When something he thought of as new Shakespeare turned out to be old, he either neglected it or let someone else publish it. Given his track record, one can imagine Moseley planning an edition of Shakespeare's *New Plays*. His inaction with the 1653 entries, and his acquisition of more Shakespeare titles in 1660, might reflect his desire to acquire more new titles before going to press, and to issue a volume of Shakespeare's *Six New Plays* instead of *Three New Plays*, but Moseley died in 1661, thwarting yet another potential Shakespeare publication.

During the theatre ban, stationers focused their attention on plays and playwrights who were previously unavailable or less prevalent in the book market. It did not seem particularly urgent to confirm Shakespeare's presence with yet another reprint, or even an edition of Shakespeare's *Three New Plays*. Jonson's record is even worse than Shakespeare's, as I note in the Introduction. Though he was frequently invoked as England's greatest dramatist, Jonson's publication numbers also declined steeply in the Interregnum. (As with Shakespeare, *The Wits Interpreter* depicts Jonson's likeness on its title page but does not reproduce any extracts from his plays or poems). The sole Interregnum "Jonson" publication is also a new play; Moseley printed the first edition of *The Widow* (1652), ascribing it to Jonson, Fletcher, and Middleton; modern criticism regards it as Middleton's alone. We can never know if Moseley was trying to deliberately deceive book buyers by misattributing a previously unprinted play to Jonson; what is clear is that his only interest in Jonson involved a new play.

Interregnum stationers' interest in previously unprinted pre-1642 plays was obviously commercial. Whatever their intentions, however, the renewed interest in dramatic novelty in the Interregnum had lasting effects

---

[49] Lesser, "Shakespeare's Flop," p. 178.

on the canon and corpus of English Renaissance drama. Before Moseley published the Beaumont and Fletcher folio in 1647, eighteen of their plays had been printed in forty editions. The folio collection, and Moseley's single-text folio edition of Fletcher's *The Wild Goose Chase* (1652, attributed to the duo) made thirty-six more Beaumont and/or Fletcher plays available for the first time, fully tripling the dramatists' authorial canon in print from eighteen to fifty-four titles. The authorial canon of Thomas Middleton would be far smaller without the publishing activity of the Interregnum: along with the first edition of *The Widow* (1652), other Middleton plays first printed in this period include *The Changeling* (1653), *The Spanish Gypsy* (1653), *The Old Law* (1656), *No Wit, No Help Like a Woman's* (1657), *More Dissemblers Besides Women* (1657), and *Women Beware Women* (1657). Several of these texts have been frequently reprinted in dramatic anthologies. C. W. Dilke's *Old Plays* (1814–15) and Thomas White's *Old English Drama* (1830) included *Women Beware Women,* a play still regularly featured in twentieth- and twenty-first-century anthologies.[50] *The Changeling* is nearly ubiquitous in anthologies printed since the turn of the twentieth century; Jeremy Lopez calls it "the touchstone of the modern anthology."[51] A response to *The Taming of the Shrew,* Fletcher's *The Woman's Prize, or The Tamer Tamed* (first printed in the folio of 1647) is often taught alongside Shakespeare's play; it appears in the current *Norton Anthology of Renaissance Drama.* Without the prohibition on playing and the subsequent turn towards dramatic novelty in the book market, *Women Beware Women, The Tamer Tamed,* and *The Changeling* might have been three more lost Jacobean plays, rather than mainstays of the modern canon of early modern drama.

Overall, however, the Interregnum was an era devoted not to the canonization of particular dramatists, but rather to the expansion of the textual field of professional drama. In other words, this era was less interested in establishing the English dramatic canon than in fleshing out the dramatic corpus. Rather than aesthetic criteria (finding the "best" plays) the dominant criterion is quantitative: *Three New Plays, Five New Plays.* Along with novelty, quantity is key. Moseley has always been characterized as a canon- and dramatic king-maker,[52] but his expansion and preservation of the English dramatic corpus is arguably more important. Moseley never published two editions from the same playwright in the *New Plays* series; after issuing a small sample of a dramatist's corpus, he moved on to another one; he invested in dramatic breadth over depth. Compared with the handsome folio editions of

[50] Lopez, *Constructing the Canon*, pp. 9–10.   [51] Ibid., pp. 49, 89.
[52] Kastan, "Humphrey Moseley"; Kewes, "Sociable Pocket-Books."

Shakespeare, Jonson, and Beaumont and Fletcher, the *New Plays* series is humbler in both form and content. The *New Plays* are printed in the "smaller and less dignified" octavo format,[53] and some editions include paratexts in which conventional prefatory modesty borders on insult. John Hall's commendatory poem, "To the surviving Honour and Ornament of the English Scene, Iames Shirley" printed before *The Cardinal* in *Six New Plays* (1653), reluctantly hoists James Shirley, a very popular dramatist in the mid seventeenth century, to the upper-middle ranks of the dramatic canon:

> Yet this I dare assert, when men have nam'd
> Johnson (the Nations Laureat,) the fam'd
> Beaumont, and Fletcher, he, that will not see
> Shirley, the fourth, must forfeit his best eye.[54]

Even in his own commendatory poem – a space that invites hyperbole – Shirley receives the faint praise of being the fourth-best dramatist. By the 1640s and 1650s, there was a clear dramatic hierarchy; while mid seventeenth-century commentators may have debated whether Jonson, Shakespeare, or Beaumont and Fletcher was the best English dramatist, Shirley was ranked below some combination of the three. Indeed, it was in mid seventeenth-century dramatic paratexts that Shakespeare, Jonson, and Fletcher were identified as the standard-bearers of dramatic excellence. Their sobriquet the "triumvirate of wit" comes from John Denham's commendatory poem in the Beaumont and Fletcher folio (1647).[55] Other dramatists were sometimes said to meet or outdo the triumvirate's standard: Aston Cockayne's commendatory poem for Richard Brome's *Five New Plays* (1653) equates Shakespeare and Beaumont and Fletcher's talents with those of their successors:

> Judicious Beaumont, and th' Ingenious Soule
> Of Fletcher too may move without controule.
> Shakespeare (most rich in Humours) entertaine
> The crowded Theatres with his happy veine
> Davenant and Massinger, and Sherley, then
> Shall be cry'd up againe for Famous men.[56]

Even if, as with "fourth-best" Shirley, later dramatists failed to live up to the triumvirate's earlier example, simply being mentioned in the same

---

[53] Kewes, "Sociable Pocket-Books," pp. 5–6.
[54] Hall, "To the Surviving Honour" in Shirley, *The Cardinal*, sig. A4v.
[55] John Denham, "On Mr. JOHN FLETCHER'S Workes," in Beaumont and Fletcher, *Comedies and Tragedies*, sig. b1v.
[56] Aston Cockayne, "A Praeludium to Mr. RICHARD BROME'S Playes," in Brome, *Five New Plays by Richard Brome*, (London: Humphrey Moseley, Richard Marriot, and Thomas Dring, 1653), sig. A3r.

breath as Shakespeare, Jonson, and Fletcher served to elevate them through association. Indeed, the notion that late-Stuart dramatists like Shirley, William Davenant, and Philip Massinger represent the "dramatic contemporaries" of early Jacobean dramatists – with all that phrase implies about literary periodization and cultural value – emerges partly from the listing of dramatists in Interregnum paratextual criticism. Yet for Jonson and Shakespeare, this reputation did not translate into actual print popularity. Of the "triumvirate of wit," only Fletcher had a significant number of his plays still unpublished by the 1640s; hence, he was the only one of the three for whom his esteemed reputation was complemented by robust full-length play publication, bringing up Fletcher's authorial canon to a size comparable to Jonson and Shakespeare's. Indeed, that Shakespeare, Jonson, and Fletcher were named the "triumvirate" partly means there are more plays available with those names attached to them: in some ways, quantity was indistinguishable from, or at least tied to, quality. This is why the Beaumont and Fletcher folio is so intriguing and important: the details of its publication and reception allow us to see the Interregnum expansion and preservation of the corpus of English professional drama happening in real time.

The Interregnum marks the last concentrated period of new publications of pre-1642 plays. The publication of previously unprinted pre-1642 plays continued in the first years of the 1660s, but greatly declined as Restoration drama gained momentum.[57] The ersatz dramatic novelty offered by previously unprinted pre-1642 plays simply could not compete with newly written Restoration plays. The declining interest in unprinted pre-1642 plays after 1660 made the remaining dramatic manuscripts increasingly vulnerable to loss. If a previously unprinted pre-1642 play was not printed in the Interregnum, the chances were that it never would be. Interregnum stationers, therefore, were among the last and most important agents to shape the textual field of Renaissance drama as we recognize it today. The focus on dramatic novelty during the Interregnum happened at the expense of Shakespeare and Jonson, but their loss was Renaissance drama's gain.

Shakespeare in Print, 1642–1660

Although he was mostly excluded from an Interregnum playbook market focused on novelty, Shakespeare did continue to circulate in this period. Shakespeare's textual ubiquity and cultural malleability made him

---

[57] See Chapter 4.

conducive to different forms of textual re-appropriation in the
Interregnum. The stationer William Leake's Interregnum Shakespeare
editions, *The Merchant of Venice* (Q3 1652, a reissue of Lawrence
Hayes's Q3 1637) and *Othello* (Q3 1655), look forward and backward.
The editions seem to offer commentary on recent events while highlight-
ing the plays' ties to the distant theatrical past. Leake acquired the rights to
Merchant sometime after Hayes's death in 1637 and before his reissue of
Q3 in 1652; Leake did not record the acquisition in the Stationers'
Register until 17 October 1657. In acquiring the rights, Leake would also
have obtained Hayes's unsold copies of the first issue of *Merchant* Q3.
There must have been a sufficient number of copies to bother reissuing
them with a new cancel title page; this suggests relatively poor sales of
Merchant in the late 1630s and 1640s, and that Leake envisioned renewed
interest in the play in the 1650s. Lukas Erne argues that Leake's *Merchant*
reissue was related to vigorous Parliamentary debates in the early 1650s
about the readmission of the Jews to England.[58]

   Contemporary political events may also have prompted Leake's belated
republication of *Othello*. Leake waited sixteen years to make use of his
rights to the play, having acquired the rights to "Orthello [*sic*] the more of
venice a Play" on 25 January 1639 from Robert Mead and Christopher
Meredith. Leake's relative indifference to *Othello* is highlighted by his keen
publication of Beaumont and Fletcher's plays. Acquiring *A King and No
King*, *Philaster*, and *The Maid's Tragedy* in the same transfer of 25 January
1639, Leake published them early and often, issuing two reprints each of
Philaster in 1639 and 1652, *A King and No King* in 1639 and 1655, and
The Maid's Tragedy in 1641 and 1650.[59] When Leake eventually came
around to printing *Othello* in 1655, the publication coincided with a
Protectorate naval victory over Barbary corsairs. In April 1655, the
Parliamentarian English admiral Robert Blake destroyed a fleet of
Barbary corsairs (also called Barbary pirates or Ottoman pirates) of the
Dey of Tunis at Porto Farina on the Tunisian Coast. The corsairs had been
a serious cause of commercial and maritime destabilization in England
since the mid sixteenth century and had worsened in recent years.
Ongoing conflicts with Morocco and the Ottoman regencies of Algeria,
Tunisia, and Tripoli in the 1620s, 1630s, and 1640s contributed to the

[58] Erne, *Shakespeare and the Book Trade*, pp. 130–4.
[59] Leake may have falsified some of his imprints: "Q1650" of *The Maid's Tragedy* might have been printed in 1660, "Q1652" of *Philaster* might have been printed in 1661. See Bourne, "High Designe," p. 276 n. 4.

outbreak of the Civil War in 1642. Among other foreign policy failures with the region, Charles I bungled a response related to the capture of hundreds of English, Scottish, Irish, and Welsh seamen by Barbary corsairs, a misstep Parliament seized on in the lead-up to the Civil Wars.[60] Admiral Blake's efforts marked a distinct victory for the Protectorate. Leake's publication of *Othello* could be interpreted as an attempt to capitalize on the widespread celebrations.[61] Barbary corsairs are invoked as a foreign menace in the play's first scene, in which Iago informs Brabantio that as a result of Desdemona's secret marriage to Othello, "you'll have your daughter covered with a Barbary horse, you'll have your nephews neigh to you, you'll have coursers for cousins and jennets for germans" (1.1.113–15), with "coursers" (war-horses) punning on "corsair." Blake's victory was accompanied by a spate of other Moor plays in the mid-1650s, including another belated publication attributed to a long-dead dramatist, *Lust's Dominion* (1657, first performed in 1600), attributed to Christopher Marlowe.[62]

But if Leake's *Othello* celebrates the Protectorate's naval victory, its politics would ostensibly be at odds with those expressed in *The Merchant of Venice*, which seems to critique Parliament's readmission of the Jews. Compounding the confusion, Leake's recently adopted printer's mark and bookshop sign – a crown – could indicate royalist leanings. Given that Commonwealth iconography consciously rejected symbols of royalty, Leake's mark seems like a deliberate provocation when one discovers he began working at the sign of the Crown around 1646, and only started using the mark in 1650, a year after the regicide.[63] Perhaps Leake's *Othello* edition reflects his jumping on the publication bandwagon or his participation in a bipartisan national celebration, rather than a betrayal of royalist politics. In any event, Shakespeare's all-purpose respectability allows Leake to comment on recent political events without abdicating any fundamental neutrality.

---

[60] Nabil Matar, "The Barbary Corsairs, King Charles I," *The Seventeenth Century*, 16 (2001), 239–58 (pp. 239–40).

[61] "The Journal of John Weale 1654–1656," ed. J. R. Powell, *The Naval Miscellany, Vol. IV* (Navy Records Society, 1952), p. 109; Adrian Tinniswood, *Pirates of Barbary: Conquests and Captivity in the Seventeenth-Century Mediterranean* (New York: Riverhead Books, 2010), pp. 225–6.

[62] Critics have offered other explanations for the belated publication of *Lust's Dominion*: see Charles Cathcart, "'You will crown him King that slew your King': *Lust's Dominion* and Oliver Cromwell," *Medieval and Renaissance Drama in England*, 11 (1999), 264–74; Hugh Mackay, "*Lust's Dominion* and the Readmission of the Jews," *Review of English Studies*, 59 (2008), 542–67.

[63] Leake's previous mark, an ornamented coat of arms, is visible on *Topicks in the Laws of England* (1646). Leake's crown first appears on *Man Become Guilty* (1650).

In the mid seventeenth century, Shakespeare's credibility depended partly on his venerability. Even as his texts seem to intervene in a recent event, it was important to simultaneously assert their ties to the past. Lukas Erne notes the orthographical updates of Leake's *Merchant of Venice* reissue: "Iewe" becomes "Jew," and the 1637 date of impression becomes 1652. He argues that "Leake may have counted on the updated title-page to convey the impression that his book – even though containing an old play by a dead dramatist – constituted a relevant intervention into a lively debate of the moment," and concludes that Leake's "objective was to pass off the remnants of an old edition as a new one."[64] But while Leake potentially tried to make his play*books* appear new in order to assert the play's topicality, he makes little effort to make the *plays* themselves seem new. The title pages of *Merchant* (1652) and *Othello* (1655) each feature a decades-old performance attribution, respectively claiming to be "As it hath beene divers times acted by the Lord Chamberlaine his Servants," and "As it hath beene divers times Acted at the Globe, and at the Black-Friers, by his Majesties SERVANTS." Of course, the practice of referring to old performances on title pages was common before the theatres closed. Leake's *Merchant* reissue replicates the performance attribution on Hayes's *Merchant* Q3 1637, which in turn replicates the attribution from *Merchant* Q1 1600. Hayes's deliberate emphasis on *Merchant*'s Elizabethan provenance was a common tactic in the 1630s. As Lesser and Farmer explain, far from attempting to conceal the ages of the "dramatic classics" they published, Caroline publishers of pre-1625 reprints emphasized the plays' age in their prefatory materials.[65] Thomas Berger similarly argues that Caroline reprints of Shakespeare plays strove to "recapture an earlier, simpler world."[66] Already an object of nostalgia by the Caroline period, Elizabethan and early Jacobean theatrical attributions took on different meanings after the theatres closed. In 1655, *Othello* Q3's title-page boast that the text appeared "As it hath beene divers times Acted at the Globe, and at the Black-Friers, by his Majesties SERVANTS" invoked the demolished Globe and Blackfriars playhouses, with both his Majesty and "his servants" now defunct.

With *Merchant* and *Othello*, Shakespeare is variously enlisted to intervene in contemporary Parliamentary debates and to mark a recent

[64] Erne, *Shakespeare and the Book Trade,* pp. 130–4.
[65] Farmer and Lesser, "Canons and Classics," pp. 32–3.
[66] Thomas L. Berger, "Looking for Shakespeare in Caroline England," *Viator,* 27 (1996), 323–59 (p. 337).

Protectorate naval victory. The Interregnum edition of *Lucrece* (1655), published with the Royalist John Quarles's continuation, *The Banishment of Tarquin*, explicitly enlists Shakespeare in royalist politics, with varying results. Since antiquity, the story of the rape of Lucretia has been interpreted as a warning about the dangers of tyrannical monarchy and an encomium to the triumphant start of the Roman republic. Although a range of readings of *Lucrece* are viable, it is difficult to read Shakespeare's poem as a straightforward endorsement of royalism, at least the kind of tyrannical royal government which Prince Tarquin brutally represents. Adam G. Hooks describes Quarles's Interregnum edition as an "audacious" and "not entirely successful" attempt to reshape *Lucrece* into a "royalist morality tale."[67] *The Banishment of Tarquin* narrates the rapist Tarquin's exile and concludes with his painful death by having his eyes pecked out by birds, a "punishment appropriate for those responsible for the overthrow of a monarchy"; the person responsible is Tarquin himself.[68] Tarquin is, in an indirect way, his own regicide, complicating the story's royalist message; the muddy politics of *The Banishment of Tarquin* speaks to the resistance mounted by *Lucrece* to becoming a royalist poem. But it is Shakespeare's prior associations, rather than *Lucrece*'s specific politics, which facilitate efforts towards a royalist reworking of the story. Hooks argues that Quarles's edition's front matter "evoked a familiar brand" of Shakespeare as a royalist poet laureate, also visible in John Benson's *Poems* (1640).[69] The royalist repackaging of a fundamentally republican myth suggests a fissure between Shakespeare's authorial persona and his text. So strong was Shakespeare's royalist image, it seems, Quarles thought it could override the ideological contents of the poem and its sources.

The Shakespeare "brand" of a royalist poet laureate may have attracted *Lucrece*'s publishers, John Stafford, a committed Royalist, and William Gilbertson, a publisher of "popular texts" such as ballads, plays, and sermons. Hooks notes, "If *The Rape of Lucrece* was an opportunity for Stafford and Quarles to forward a royalist agenda, for Gilbertson *The Banishment of Tarquin* may have been a way to add value to a newly acquired title."[70] Gilbertson's desire to "add value" to *Lucrece* betrays his doubts about the Shakespeare brand's saleability, as does his wider record

---

[67] Adam G. Hooks, "Royalist Shakespeare: Publishers, Politics, and the Appropriation of *The Rape of Lucrece* (1655)," in *Canonising Shakespeare: Stationers and the Book Trade, 1640–1740*, ed. Emma Depledge and Peter Kirwan (Cambridge: Cambridge University Press, 2017), pp. 26–37 (pp. 28, 30).
[68] Hooks, "Royalist Shakespeare," p. 30.   [69] Ibid.   [70] Ibid., p. 35.

of publishing Shakespeare. Zachary Lesser argues that, in general, William Gilbertson did not seek out "new and promising copy" but instead "sought out books that had already proved their worth."[71] In the case of Shakespeare, however, Gilbertson turned to a "new and promising text," and his investment in Shakespeare republication was tentative at best. In addition to his joint acquisition of *Lucrece* with Stafford in 1655, on 4 April 1655, Gilbertson acquired the sole rights to Thomas Dekker's *The Shoemaker's Holiday*, Christopher Marlowe's *Doctor Faustus*, and several texts associated with Shakespeare: *Venus & Adonis, King Leir* (a source for *King Lear*), *Mucedorus*, and *The Merry Devil of Edmonton* (both attributed to Shakespeare). Gilbertson reprinted *The Shoemaker's Holiday* (1657) and *Doctor Faustus* (1663),[72] but of the "Shakespeare" titles Gilbertson only reprinted *The Merry Devil of Edmonton* (1655) and *Lucrece*, with its new content. Even for stationers focused on Elizabethan bestsellers, Shakespeare was not a priority. One reason could be that Gilbertson's "newly acquired title" was unmistakably aged. One of Shakespeare's most popular works in the early seventeenth century, *Lucrece* was reprinted and frequently commonplaced; Gabriel Harvey mentioned it with *Hamlet* as a text for "the wiser sort."[73] The Interregnum *Lucrece* draws on this poetic reputation; the title page attributes the poem to "The Incomparable Master of our English Poetry, Will: Shakespeare, Gent." and includes a frontispiece portrait adapted from the Droeshout folio portrait – yet it does not rely on this long-standing poetic reputation to move copy. Shakespeare's image, however, could lend his considerable cachet to the new material readers apparently craved.

By the mid seventeenth century, Shakespeare was associated with various kinds of qualities, plays, and characters, while specific engagement with his works began to wane. This is exemplified by the mid-century allusions to Falstaff, by some measures Shakespeare's most popular character. In the 1640s and 1650s, although no full-length Shakespeare plays with the character were printed, Falstaff continued to be Shakespeare's most-invoked character. A 1640s play (printed in 1689) mentions him as the emblem of Shakespeare's entire dramatic corpus, exemplifying a talent

[71] Zachary Lesser, "Typographic Nostalgia: Playreading, Popularity and the Meanings of Black Letter," in *The Book of the Play: Playwrights, Readers and Stationers in Shakespeare's England*, ed. Marta Straznicky (Amherst: University of Massachusetts Press, 2006), pp. 99–126 (pp. 109–10).

[72] On Gilbertson's edition of *Doctor Faustus*, see Meghan C. Andrews, "The 1663 *Faustus* and the Royalist Marlowe," *Marlowe Studies: An Annual*, 1 (2011), 41–58.

[73] Lesser and Stallybrass, "The First Literary *Hamlet*," pp. 384, 394; Roberts, *Reading Shakespeare's Poems*, pp. 102–42.

that can never be reproduced: "Shakespeare's Invention / His Quill as quick as Feather from the Bow! / Oh who can such another Falstaff show?"[74] Another poem printed in 1658 mentions him as a standard of national literature, which later artists strive to exceed: "To thee compared our English poets all stop / And vail their bonnets, even Shakespeare's Falstop."[75] These allusions suggest Falstaff's status as Shakespeare's representative character, the emblem of his genius, one whose popularity even surpassed Shakespeare's. They do not, however, reveal any familiarity with Falstaff's specific exploits, say, or with the texts of *1* and *2 Henry IV*, or *The Merry Wives of Windsor*. The *Shakespeare Allusion Book*, which testifies to the wealth of references to Falstaff in the mid seventeenth century, notes that "a good many of these critical allusions are due to the acceptance of a tradition, rather than to adequate personal acquaintance with the poet's works," continuing that "the borrowings from his text, once so common a feature, decrease in number, while the mere references to Falstaff, etc. are much more common."[76]

Falstaff also seems to have been popular on the illegal Interregnum stage. In 1662, Henry Marsh published *The Wits, or Sport upon Sport, Part 1*, a collection of "drolls," short, usually comic playlets and extracts from longer plays by several dramatists.[77] The stationer Francis Kirkman reprinted Marsh's edition in 1672, and published a second part in 1673; in the follow-up volume, Kirkman states that drolls were staged during the theatrical prohibition: "When the publique theatres were shut up . . . then all we could divert ourselves with were these humours and pieces of plays, which . . . were only allowed us, and that but by the stealth too."[78] *The Wits Part 1* is dominated by drolls from plays by Beaumont and Fletcher (who provide the sources for fourteen of the collection's twenty-seven drolls, more than half), but also provides extracts from plays by James Shirley, William Cavendish, and two by Shakespeare: "The Bouncing Knight, or The Rob[b]ers Rob[b]ed" (from *1 Henry IV*) and "The Grave-makers"

---

[74] R[obert] W[ild], *The Benefice* (London: R. Janeway, 1689), p. 10.

[75] *Naps upon Parnassus* (London: Nathanial Brookes, 1658), sig. B4v.

[76] *The Shakespeare Allusion Book*, ed. Clement Mansfield Ingleby, Lucy Toulmin Smith, and F. J. Furnivall (London: Chatto & Windus, 1909), p. lxiii.

[77] *The Wits, or, Sport upon Sport, Part 1* (London: Henry Marsh, 1662).

[78] *The Wits, or, Sport upon Sport, Part 2* (London: Francis Kirkman, 1673), sig. A2v. See also *The Wits, or, Sport upon Sport, Part 1* (London: Francis Kirkman, 1672). There is some debate as to whether drolls were actually performed during the Interregnum. In "Dramatic Extracts in the Interregnum," John Astington argues *The Wits* represents a printed anthology without necessarily having a theatrical counterpart; Janet Clare, Laura Estill, and Emma Depledge share my view that professional drolls were indeed performed on the Interregnum stage. Janet Clare, "General Introduction," in *Drama of the English Republic*, pp. 21–2; Estill, *Dramatic Extracts*, pp. 78–9; Depledge, *Shakespeare's Rise*, pp. 16–23.

(from *Hamlet*). Peter Holland and Michael Dobson respectively argue that the Shakespearean drolls "resonantly echo the complete texts to which they witness" and "iconically … stand in for the play" from which they were taken.[79] Echo and icon are appropriate characterizations of drolls, as they indeed are distorted, partial, isolated reflections of the original play. That the drolls are able to stand in for the original – indeed, in some cases, that they are intelligible at all – depends on the viewer's familiarity with the source. For instance, *The Wits*' "The Bouncing Knight," an amalgam of Falstaff episodes from *1 Henry IV*, includes an Argument that explains the first scene, but leaves out the requisite background information for the "other scenes of mirth that follow." The four atomized, context-less episodes abruptly shift from one to the next, with little narrative continuity. In the second episode, Falstaff reacts to having his pocket picked, but there is no depiction or mention of Hal's role in the scheme, lessening the irony of Falstaff's criticism of the Hostess. In the third, Falstaff's entrance "as to the wars" is not prefaced by any information about the rebellion and ensuing wars. This scenelet concludes with Falstaff's honour speech and his exit, then abruptly shifts to "Jack in fight falls down as he were dead," and Hal's meditations over his body. The transition is effective insofar as Falstaff states his doubts about the value of honour, and immediately acts dishonourably to save his hide. Falstaff tells Hal that he is "afraid of this gunpowder Percy," and takes responsibility for his death, yet Percy never actually appears in the droll, nor is his role explained. The audience never learns who kills Hotspur, undercutting the joke about Falstaff claiming responsibility for his death. Overall, these episodes make little narrative sense. Discussing the amalgam of abbreviated scenes in "The Bouncing Knight," Janet Clare comments that "[s]uch a redaction obviously depends on a folkloric appreciation of the character, divorced from any narrative framework."[80] The compilers of "The Bouncing Knight" trusted either that the audience would be able to fill in the required information for themselves, or, more likely, that the pleasure of watching an uninterrupted pastiche of scenes centred on the beloved Falstaff would be enjoyable even devoid of context.

The frontispiece to *The Wits* (Figure 2.2) also marks the first visual rendering of Falstaff, and only the second pictorial representation of a

[79] Peter Holland, "Shakespeare Abbreviated," in *The Cambridge Companion to Shakespeare and Popular Culture*, ed. Robert Shaughnessy (Cambridge: Cambridge University Press, 2007), pp. 26–45 (p. 26); Michael Dobson, "The Grave-Makers," in *The Oxford Companion to Shakespeare*, ed. Michael Dobson, Stanley Wells, Will Sharpe, and Erin Sullivan (Oxford: Oxford University Press, 2015), p. 172.

[80] Clare, *Drama of the English Republic*, p. 23.

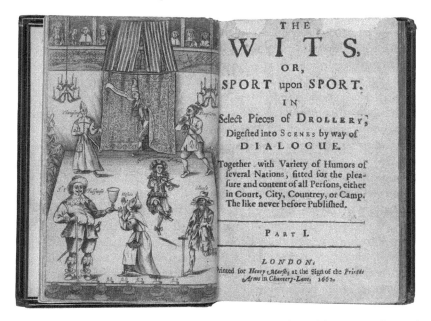

Figure 2.2   Frontispiece from *The Wits, or Sport upon Sport (Part 1)* (Henry Marsh, 1662).
Courtesy of the Folger Shakespeare Library.

Shakespeare character, after Henry Peacham's etching of characters from
Titus Andronicus (c. 1595).[81] But whereas Peacham depicted a scene from
one play, *The Wits'* frontispiece depicts characters from different plays by
different dramatists. Lifted out of the particular dramatic context of *1
Henry IV* and separated from other Shakespearean characters, Falstaff and
'Hostes' Quickly appear alongside "The Changeling," and with the protagonist from J. Cook's *Greene's Tu Quoque*, "Simpleton" from Robert
Cox's *Simpleton the Smith*, "French Dancing Master" from William
Cavendish's *The Variety*, and "Clause" from Fletcher's *Beggar's Bush*,
who are all shown performing before an audience in Puritan garb.[82]
Falstaff is no longer tethered to the specific Shakespeare plays in which
he appeared, but rather is incorporated into a wider dramatic corpus,
representing English drama more broadly.

[81] T. J. King, "The First Known Picture of Falstaff (1662): A Suggested Date for His Costume,"
Theatre Research International, 3.1 (1977), 20–2.
[82] S. P. Cerasano, "Must the Devil Appear?: Audiences, Actors, Stage Business," in *A Companion to
Renaissance Drama*, ed. Arthur F. Kinney (Oxford: Wiley, 2002), pp. 193–211 (p. 196).

In general, between 1642 and 1660, we see a relative increase in allusions to Shakespeare's name and play titles compared with specific quotations of his works.[83] Shakespeare and some select characters were representative symbols, clearly worthy of admiration but often detached from the actual contents of his texts. The mid seventeenth century inherited Shakespeare's earlier reputation and accepted it on faith, without necessarily reading him anew. The portraits of Shakespeare attached to the Interregnum editions of *Wits Interpreter* (1655) and *Lucrece* (1655) were deployed to legitimate non-Shakespearean texts, where those texts respectively omitted Shakespeare's own words, or went against the grain of conventional readings of Shakespeare's text and its sources. By contrast, in John Cotgrave's *English Treasury of Wit and Language* (1655), Shakespeare's texts are deployed apart from his authorial persona. As noted above, *The English Treasury* anonymizes its dramatic extracts, omitting the names of their source plays and dramatists, and often conceals contextual clues, replacing character names in speech prefixes and in the dialogue. A conversation between Gratiano and Salarino about Lorenzo's lust in *The Merchant of Venice* becomes in *The English Treasury* a generic conversation between "1." and "2.," on the topic "Of Desire," beginning "It is a marvel he outstays his hour / For Lovers ever run before the clock."[84] Elsewhere in the volume, proper names are replaced with "Man," "Sir," and "Lady." The lack of sources and identifying features has led to the relative critical neglect of *The English Treasury*, despite its significance as the first printed commonplace book composed exclusively of dramatic extracts.[85] Thanks partly to digital advances, more scholarly attention has recently been paid to *The English Treasury*, where Shakespeare is the most-extracted author. This appears to be powerful evidence for Shakespeare's ongoing popularity in the mid seventeenth century. In addition to its general anonymization of extracts, however, *The English Treasury*'s treatment of Falstaff also forces us to qualify this claim.

Despite being Shakespeare's most-alluded to character from his most-printed play, Falstaff is nowhere to be found in any of Cotgrave's 160 Shakespearean extracts. Falstaff's appeal resides beyond the reach of the commonplacing reader: though vital and verbose, and the most memorable part of *1 Henry IV*, the lying, thieving knight cannot be remade into an obvious moral exemplar. The commonplacing of Shakespeare has long

[83] See "Period III. 1642–1660," in *Shakespeare's Centurie of Prayse*, ed. Clement Mansfield Ingleby and Lucy Toulmin Smith, 2nd ed., 2 vols. (London: New Shakespeare Society, 1879), II, pp. 241–310.

[84] Cotgrave, *The English Treasury*, p. 76.

[85] Bentley, "Cotgrave's *English Treasury*," p. 188; Anne Isherwood, "'Cut out into little stars': Shakespeare in Anthologies" (doctoral dissertation, King's College London, 2014).

been offered as evidence of his "literariness," defined in the commonplace tradition in terms of a text's ability "to reproduce timeless and impersonal authority attributed to sententiae in classical texts."[86] But Falstaff is too famous, too distinctively "Shakespearean," for the practice of reading that favours the decontextualized fragment. *The English Treasury*'s exclusion of Falstaff forces us to finally dismiss it as a sign of Shakespeare's ongoing "popularity" in the Interregnum. Cotgrave did not want readers to connect the book to Shakespeare. Falstaff was "popular," but for Cotgrave, Shakespeare had other functions, suited for the commonplace genre's emphasis on conventional wisdom. Likewise, the perennial appeal of Falstaff indicates that commonplacing was far from the only or even main form of literary engagement in the early modern period.[87] Nevertheless, Shakespeare's disparate abilities as a writer – the creator of both the uncommonplaceable, unforgettable wag Falstaff and of a wealth of depersonalized didactic chestnuts – contributed to his broad circulation in the mid seventeenth century.

In some ways, the commonplacing of Shakespeare by Cotgrave and other mid seventeenth-century anthologists continues decades-old trends. Shakespeare was heavily featured in the Elizabethan commonplace books of the Bodenham circle, *Englands Parnassus* (1600), and *Belvedere* (1600), which cite Shakespeare more than any other English dramatist. The Bodenham circle also included commonplace markers in Shakespeare's first "literary drama," *Hamlet* Q1 (1600).[88] Along with *Hamlet*, *Richard II* and *Romeo and Juliet* were particular favourites of Elizabethan commonplacers. Ted Tregear argues that this is due to the presence of advice-giving elders in each play: "Anthologists looking out for sententious material know to save their attention for a particular type of character: John of Gaunt, Friar Lawrence, Polonius. Not only do sentences suit the characters of older men . . . but old men are often brought on stage specifically for the purpose of speaking sentences."[89] Frequently anthologized lines in print and manuscript include John of Gaunt's dying words in *Richard II* 2.1 and the speeches of Polonius (called Corambis in *Hamlet* Q1), including his famous advice to Laertes, marked with inverted commas in *Hamlet* Q1 and oft-quoted thereafter.[90]

[86] Lesser and Stallybrass, "The First Literary *Hamlet*," p. 417.
[87] On commonplacing and other kinds of early modern literary appreciation, see the Introduction.
[88] Lesser and Stallybrass, "The First Literary *Hamlet*," pp. 394, 40.
[89] Ted Tregear, "Music at the Close: *Richard II* in the Elizabethan Anthologies," *Studies in Philology*, 116.4 (2019), 696–727 (p. 708).
[90] Tregear, "Music at the Close," p. 697.

The commonplacing of Shakespeare continued in the mid seventeenth century, when this mode of reading took on new cultural and political dimensions. In the politically fraught moment of the 1650s, Adam Smyth explains, "nostalgia was often more than a consequence of the mechanics of verse circulation and miscellany compilation"; printed miscellanies from this period often "make a point to distance [themselves] from the present, and instead connect with a sense of the past."[91] As a genre which venerates the past, recirculates older texts, and reshapes them to highlight conventional wisdom, the printed commonplace book was exempt from the demands of novelty that drove the full-length playbook market. If old Shakespeare was excluded from the new playbook market, he was a perfect fit for the commonplace tradition. Moreover, although commonplacing was well-established as a practice, Cotgrave's all-drama *English Treasury* was an innovative dramatic form, one bolstered by the considerable inclusion of Shakespeare's reliable texts.

Mid-century commonplacing continued some older practices from the Elizabethan period, but also forged new modes. Cotgrave's *English Treasury* asserts drama's literary status, but not to the exclusion of its origins in the English vernacular theatre. Cotgrave's preface calls dramatists "able schollers, and linguists" who "have culled the choicest Flowers out of the great number of Greek, Latin, Italian, Spanish and French Authors (Poets especially), to embellish and enrich the *English scene* withal, besides almost a prodigious accruement of their own luxuriant fancies" (emphasis mine).[92] English dramatists are "scholars" who domesticate classical and continental wisdom, and who possess their "own luxuriant fancies" tied to a native "English scene."

Although, like the Bodenham circle, Cotgrave favours Shakespeare, he by and large neglects its preferred plays and characters. *Richard II*, "irresistibly anthologizable" for Elizabethan commonplacers[93] – extracted forty-nine times in *Belvedere* alone[94] – is cited only twice in *The English Treasury*: passages from secondary characters Thomas Mowbray and the Duchess. John of Gaunt, that paradigmatic old spouter of old saws, is omitted entirely. Cotgrave's single extraction from *Romeo and Juliet* duly quotes sentence-speaker Friar Lawrence, but this one entry represents a sharp decline from the play's respective fourteen and thirteen citations in

---

[91] Smyth, *Profit and Delight*, p. 148. See also Estill, *Dramatic Extracts*, pp. 77–114.
[92] Cotgrave, "To the Courteous Reader," in *The English Treasury*, sig. A3r.
[93] Tregear, "Music at the Close," p. 702.
[94] Lukas Erne and Devani Singh, eds. *Bel-vedére or The Garden of the Muses* (Cambridge: Cambridge University Press, 2020), p. 348.

Belvedere and *Englands Parnassus*. Cotgrave in general turns away from Shakespeare's Elizabethan bestsellers – *Richard III* is omitted entirely – and pays more attention to the late romances *Cymbeline*, *The Winter's Tale*, and *Pericles* (with five extracts apiece). In many ways, this later and wider selection of Shakespeare plays is unsurprising: Cotgrave generally cited more recent drama,[95] and in 1655 he had a far larger corpus of Shakespeare plays in print to work from than the Bodenham circle had in 1600.[96] In other ways, however, Cotgrave's textual appropriation of Shakespeare is surprising: Zachary Lesser and Peter Stallybrass argue that, after 1607, Shakespeare turned his back on sententious plays in favour of romances, which "were far less likely" "to be considered literary in the sense defined by the commonplace tradition."[97] Cotgrave modifies the commonplace tradition by drawing Shakespeare's late romances into it.

Hamlet was a favourite of both Cotgrave and Elizabethan commonpla-cers, but in *The English Treasury* it is Prince Hamlet, rather than Polonius, who emerges as the play's most-quotable character. Cotgrave cites Hamlet's statement, "For murder, though it have no tongue, will speak / With most miraculous organ," which recalls the English maxim "murder will out" made famous in "The Prioress's Tale" and "The Nun's Priest's Tale" from Chaucer's *Canterbury Tales*. The proverb's early modern currency is evidenced by Shakerly Marmion's *The Antiquary*, which includes a character who states, "Tis an old saying / Murder will out."[98] "Murder will out" is an English proverb, not a translated classical or classizing sentence, and exemplifies Cotgrave's interest in perpetuating a specifically English tradition.

Shakespeare was increasingly associated with Englishness in the Interregnum; this association could take many forms. While Cotgrave emphasizes Shakespeare and his dramatic contemporaries' status as able English "scholars," other contemporaneous appropriations of Shakespeare explicitly repatriated Shakespeare's characters while moving them down the socio-economic ladder. For example, a dialogue from the comic miscellany *Cupids Master* (1656) recasts *The Taming of the Shrew*'s elite

---

[95] Bentley, "Cotgrave's *English Treasury*," p. 199.
[96] Indeed, that most of Shakespeare's dramatic works were readily available in a single folio collection probably contributed to his anthologization; the second- and third-most cited authors in *The English Treasury* are the folio authors Jonson and Fletcher. Early "popularity" begets more popularity, or at least facilitates textual transmission.
[97] Lesser and Stallybrass, "The First Literary *Hamlet*," p. 417.
[98] *Oxford Dictionary of Proverbs*, 6th ed., ed. Jennifer Speake (Oxford: Oxford University Press, 2015), p. 363.

Italian characters Katherina and Petruchio as working English domestics "Kate of the Kitchin" and "Tom the Tailor." Their exchange is printed in blackletter, a typography associated with old-fashioned English texts.[99] In *Cupids Master*, Shakespeare becomes the writer of home-spun English jollities, a refraction of his image as a source of home-grown English wisdom in *The English Treasury*.

In a departure from the Elizabethan commonplace tradition, *The English Treasury* only cites Polonius twice and does not commonplace his marked sections in *Hamlet* Q1, neglecting his famous advice to Laertes, which seems to cry out for anthologization. Polonius's two entries match the number of extracts given to the Player King from *The Murder of Gonzago,* including this reflection, "On Inconstancy": "What to ourselves in passion we propose, / The passion ending, doth the purpose lose. / The violence of either grief or joy / Their own enactures with themselves destroy."[100] In *Hamlet*, the Player King's stilted, didactic, rhyming lines are not meant to represent the height of Shakespeare's art or wisdom. They are, in form and content, deliberately old-fashioned, of a piece with other dramatic antiquities in *The Murder of Gonzago*, and contrasted with *Hamlet*'s innovative high style.[101] But Cotgrave reproduces extracts from the deliberately antique *Murder of Gonzago*, and takes them as typical of Shakespeare. Cotgrave's *Hamlet* citations, then, continue and extend the commonplace tradition's appreciation of oldness. Commonplacers continued to look to old men as reliable sources of wisdom, but in *The English Treasury*, the Elizabethan favourites Friar Lawrence, John of Gaunt, and Polonius have been displaced by a different old man: Shakespeare himself.

The circulation of Shakespeare in print in the Interregnum, in the full-length plays and poems *The Merchant of Venice, Othello*, and *Lucrece*, as well as in the abbreviated commonplace tradition reveal his elastic cultural associations: he is appropriated for royalist and republican ends, the creator of both the indelible rascal Falstaff and anonymous didactic chestnuts, seen both as an "able scholar" and an author of down-market dialogues. His images and texts are frequently separated, revealing the acceptance of Shakespeare's long-standing cultural reputation without citing his works, or else the circulation of useful saws without authorial attribution. All capitalize on some facet of Shakespeare's oldness. Shakespeare's age also informs my final examples: the accidental publication of *King Lear* in

---

[99] Depledge, *Shakespeare's Rise*, p. 29; Lesser, "Typographic Nostalgia," p. 107.
[100] Cotgrave, *The English Treasury*, p. 142.
[101] On the "antique patina" of *The Murder of Gonzago*, see Munro, *Archaic Style*, pp. 161–3.

1655, and the misattribution of play titles to Shakespeare in the two comprehensive dramatic catalogues of 1656. These examples attest to "Shakespeare" as a clear dramatic category, its power and range suggested by the way it was sometimes mistakenly applied to different kinds of texts.

Accidental Publication, Misattribution, and the Category of "Shakespeare"

In 1655, the stationer Jane (Jean) Bell published the third quarto of Shakespeare's *King Lear*. In so doing, she unwittingly violated Miles Flesher's rights to the play. Bell had recently acquired the rights to *The True Chronicle History of King Leir*, the primary dramatic source for Shakespeare's *King Lear*, from Richard Oulton, but she printed Shakespeare's version instead. The source of the *Lear/Leir* confusion is partly related to the Stationers' Register's system of entrance on the basis of play title. On 22 April 1640, Oulton acquired the rights to "Lear and his 3 daughters" from "Mistris Aldee his mother in Law deceased."[102] This *Lear* was actually *Leir*; the change in spelling obliterated the sole distinction between *King Leir* and *King Lear* in the Stationers' Register.[103]

Bell's republication of an old play distinguished her from her fellow dramatic stationers who were focused on novelty. But Bell was not exclusively focused on publishing drama: she reprinted *King Lear* among a roster of generically diverse old titles she acquired from Richard Oulton, suggesting that her ownership of a title – any title – was the primary motivator behind her *King Lear* publication, rather than any particular interest in Shakespeare. Her edition of *King Lear* includes a book list advertising "Books Printed; and are to be Sold by Jane Bell at the Eastend of Christ-Church." This catalogue includes classic Elizabethan plays and poems (*Friar Bacon and Friar Bungay, Urania*), domestic manuals (*The Gardeners Laborinth, Grafting and Planting, A Book of Cookery*), and Gervase Markham's *The English Horseman*. The disparate collection of literary and non-literary texts is united by the fact that they were old texts and reprints. It is the book list advertisement from *King Lear* Q3 that provides the evidence for Bell's acquisition of texts from Richard Oulton.

---

[102] Arber, *Registers of the Company of Stationers*, IV, p. 481.
[103] Leo Kirschbaum, "How Jane Bell Came to Print the Third Quarto of Shakespeare's *King Lear*," *Philological Quarterly*, 17 (1938), 308–11 (p. 310); and David Scott Kastan, "In Plain Sight: Visible Women and Early Modern Plays," in *Women Making Shakespeare: Text, Reception and Performance*, ed. Gordon McMullan, Lena Cowen Orlin, and Virginia Mason Vaughan (London: Bloomsbury Arden Shakespeare, 2014), pp. 47–56 (pp. 51–3).

Although the Oulton–Bell transfer is not listed in the Stationers' Register, Bell's book list features the same titles in the Stationers' Register transfer of 22 April 1640 from "Mistress Aldee" to Richard Oulton: the titles are even listed in the same order.[104] Oulton's titles were transferred wholesale to Bell, and Bell set to reprinting most of them. Upon acquiring *Lear and his 3 daughters*, Bell succeeded in her aim to print an old text; she just printed the wrong one.

By the Interregnum, once vivid recollections of plays and playwrights had grown increasingly hazy. Playwrights could be famous, and known for certain types of plays, all while they were detached from the specific plays they wrote and precise knowledge of the plays' contents began to fade. Lois Potter observes the conceptual separation between Christopher Marlowe's authorial persona and his texts by the 1650s, which explains the misattribution of *Lust's Dominion* to him in 1657, as well as an Interregnum allusion to *The Jew of Malta* that confuses the plot even as it links the play to Marlowe.[105] The combination of Marlowe's cultural authority and his absence from the contemporary print market made him particularly susceptible to confusion. Likewise, the growing distance between Shakespeare's name and his texts led to errors about what he actually wrote. At the same time, in the 1650s there was an increased effort to list, classify, and catalogue printed texts and playbooks. All of the Interregnum full-length Shakespeare playbooks – Leake's *Merchant* and *Othello,* and Bell's *Lear* – include printed book list advertisements. Many of Leake's and Bell's non-Shakespearean publications also feature book list advertisements, in which editions of Shakespeare are listed mid-way through or at the end of the list, not given pride of place at the top. In those lists, Shakespeare is merely one textual commodity among many.

Some of these catalogues were primarily commercial, but still had cultural effects. Book lists and catalogues identify English plays' genres and authors, including texts that lack authorial ascriptions on their title pages. In these cases, the catalogues reveal mid seventeenth-century ideas about who was responsible for writing particular plays. In the two comprehensive "exact and perfect" dramatic catalogues of 1656 printed by Rogers and Ley and Archer (discussed in the Introduction), Shakespeare is by far the author to whom the most plays are misattributed, with

---

[104] See Arber, *Registers of the Company of Stationers*, IV, p. 120.
[105] Lois Potter, "Marlowe in the Civil War and Commonwealth: Some Allusions and Parodies," in *Poet and a Filthy-Playmaker: New Essays on Christopher Marlowe*, ed. Kenneth Friedenreich, Roma Gill, and Constance B. Kuriyama (New York: AMS Press, 1988), pp. 72–82.

seventeen titles. Beaumont and/or Fletcher are a distant second with five misattributions. One might guess that the compilers were attempting to capitalize on the selling power of Shakespeare's name, the same motive Lukas Erne ascribes to the stationers responsible for the Shakespearean misattributions on the title pages of ten editions printed between 1584 and 1633, making him the only dramatist to have plays misattributed to him in these years.[106]

Although it is tempting to interpret the catalogues' misattributions as a rare sign of Shakespeare's commercial dominance in the Interregnum, the misattributions must be traced to a different cause. To begin, as discussed in the Introduction, the "exact and perfect catalogues" present themselves as credible reference works. Their contents are informational in ways that compromise any commercial function, such as including older, out of print, and presumably less saleable plays, and organizing the titles in a non-hierarchical alphabetical order. And even if the misattributions derived from pecuniary motives, Shakespeare would not be the obvious choice. As we've seen, he was far from the best-selling dramatist in 1656; Humphrey Moseley did not even bother to mention him when advertising old copies of *The Two Noble Kinsmen* in his book catalogues, assigning it to Fletcher alone. Between 1642 and 1660, no title pages misattribute plays to Shakespeare, but over the same period, a dozen title pages misattribute playbooks to Fletcher, Beaumont, Chapman, Marlowe, Jonson, "T. G." (probably Thomas Goffe), and "S. R." (probably Samuel Rowley).

Critics have long complained about the two comprehensive catalogues' frequent errors, such as misattributions and misspellings.[107] In fact, the catalogues are mostly accurate, and sometimes surprisingly so. For example, Edward Archer's catalogue includes the first attribution of *The Tragedy of Mariam* to Elizabeth Cary. The errors deserve our attention precisely because the "exact and perfect" catalogues make explicit claims about their correctness, and because they get so much right. In the case of original misattributions (i.e. those not derived from early printed editions), some are due to simple mechanical errors, such as misalignment. Other errors are due to obvious confusions between plays and playwrights with similar sounding names. Rogers and Ley assign Massinger's *Bondman* to Fletcher

---

[106] Erne, *Shakespeare and the Book Trade*, pp. 56–81.
[107] W. W. Greg, *A List of Masques, Pageants, &c. Supplementary to A List of English Plays* (London: Bibliographical Society, 1969), p. li. See also Greg, "Authorship Attributions in the Early Play Lists, 1656–1671," *Edinburgh Bibliographical Society Transactions*, 2 (1946), 303–30; Hooks, "Booksellers' Catalogues," p. 459; MacDonald P. Jackson, *Determining the Shakespeare Canon* (Oxford: Oxford University Press, 2014), p. 14.

(who wrote *Bonduca*); Archer assigns *The Iron Age* to the wrong Thomas (Dekker instead of Heywood); the anonymous *Every Woman in her Humour* is assigned to Jonson. Many of the errors, in other words, do not come out of nowhere, but reveal the types of plays associated with particular playwrights. The associations simultaneously reveal real knowledge and real vagueness about who wrote what.

The comprehensive catalogues of 1656 misattribute texts to Shakespeare not to exploit his selling power but rather because those plays seemed "Shakespearean." Apart from mistakes derived from simple mechanical error (*The Roman Actor* and *A Trick to Catch the Old One* are misaligned with *Romeo and Juliet* and *The Taming of a Shrew*), other misattributions derive from two sources. The first is a specific earlier tradition that linked Shakespeare to the play, such as an early playbook attribution or a performance history with Shakespeare's company.[108] In this category we can place *The Puritan Widow*, *Thomas Lord Cromwell*, *King John of England, both parts* (where the catalogues replicate or expand early playbooks' attributions to "Shakespeare," "W.S.," or "W. Sh."), *Mucedorus*, and *The Merry Devil of Edmonton*.[109] The second category is rooted in Shakespeare's wider cultural associations in the period, much like the misattribution of a *Humour* play to Jonson. These include popular anonymous plays (*Mucedorus*, *The First Part of Jeronimo*, *The Spanish Tragedy*, *The Merry Devil of Edmonton*, and *Arden of Faversham*),[110] revenge tragedies involving fathers and sons (*The Spanish Tragedy*, *The Tragedy of Hoffman*), a play from a large folio collection (Beaumont and Fletcher's *Chances*), and serialized history plays (*Edward II*, *Edward III*, *Edward IV Parts 1 & 2*). Many of these plays have at various points been included in the Shakespeare canon;[111] *Edward III* appears in the current Norton and Arden 3 Shakespeares. All the misattributions potentially reflect the types of plays perceived as "Shakespearean" in the mid seventeenth century.

---

[108] As Peter Kirwan points out, because Shakespeare occupied a central position in the Chamberlain's/ King's Servants, it seems likely titles not strictly written by him would be assigned to him in virtue of being performed by his company. Peter Kirwan, *Shakespeare and the Idea of Apocrypha* (Cambridge: Cambridge University Press, 2015), pp. 72–3.

[109] For the Shakespearean attributions for *The Merry Devil of Edmonton* and *Mucedorus*, see Peter Kirwan, "The First Collected Shakespeare Apocrypha," *Shakespeare Quarterly*, 62 (2011), 594–601.

[110] In Archer's catalogue, Shakespeare's name is listed next to *The Arraignment of Paris*, but W. W. Greg demonstrated that Archer actually intended to attribute the following entry, *Arden of Faversham*, to Shakespeare, but accidentally misaligned the entries. W. W. Greg, "Shakespeare and *Arden of Feversham*," *Review of English Studies*, 21 (1945), 134–6.

[111] See Peter Kirwan, "Consolidating the Shakespeare Canon, 1640–1740," in *Canonising Shakespeare*, ed. Depledge and Kirwan, pp. 81–8 (p. 87).

"Shakespeare" had become a recognizable category of organization and collection, albeit a broad one.

If at least some of these plays were seen as Shakespeare's – at least by the compiler and the reader who took the "exact and perfect" catalogues at their word – this would change our impression of how historical readers experienced Shakespeare in mid seventeenth-century print culture. Shakespeare's *Mucedorus* attribution, for example, makes him responsible for the most-reprinted quarto in the seventeenth century, a play that by the 1610s was beloved, familiar, and paradigmatically old[112]: apt descriptions for Shakespeare's cultural reputation between 1642 and 1660. Decades of republication had made him into a well-known cultural figure, but also oversaturated the print market. The combination of Shakespeare's cultural authority and absence from the contemporary print market made him particularly susceptible to appropriation and misappropriation. The confusions in the Stationers' Register and misattributions in the catalogues indicate that even stationers couldn't recall if Shakespeare was responsible for *Lear* or *Leir*, and they were quick to ascribe popular old plays like *Mucedorus* and *The Spanish Tragedy* to popular old Shakespeare. In the Interregnum, Shakespeare's ubiquity transformed him into an accessible category of dramatic organization at the same time that it drove stationers to publish new plays by other dramatists and new dramatic forms, exalted through their association with old Shakespeare. Shakespeare's oldness, then, allowed English drama to be renewed; out of a Shakespearean dearth grew the lush field of early modern drama.

---

[112] Kirwan, *Shakespeare and the Idea of Apocrypha*, pp. 99–106.

CHAPTER 3

Canonizing Beaumont and Fletcher

Whether considered alone or in combination with his various collaborators, most memorably Francis Beaumont, John Fletcher was by many measures the most prominent professional dramatist in the Interregnum in terms of reputation, in print and on stage. The Beaumont and Fletcher folio of 1647 was the most important dramatic publication of the period. Several of their plays were illegally performed (or slated for performance) in London in the 1640s, and on the Continent in the 1650s; their plays were favoured for droll adaptation on the Interregnum stage. They were frequently invoked in contemporary dramatic paratexts as standards of dramatic value.

Many critics ascribe Fletcher and Beaumont's Interregnum popularity to their plays' political valences. This chapter adds nuance to that reading, arguing that while the *subject matter* of many Beaumont and Fletcher plays is unmistakably political, political ideology is often overshadowed by relentless formal experimentation, especially the exploration of paradoxes at the levels of plot, character, and language. *A King and No King* is the Platonic example of this phenomenon. Its title (and, to some extent the play text) ostensibly subverts the monarchy (or reveals the illogic of those who attempt to do so), and indeed the title was taken up as a slogan in the mid seventeenth century from the royalist and republican sides alike. But the logic-defying antithesis contained within the title and expressed by the paradoxical plot also resonated in the mid seventeenth century for reasons largely apolitical. Royalist dramatic producers and consumers were attracted to Beaumont and Fletcher for their ingenious aesthetic elements, a kind of literary appreciation that self-consciously attempted to distance itself from politics. Of course, this itself entails a paradox: the effort to designate an area of culture – Beaumont and Fletcher plays, but also the pre-Civil War drama more broadly, for which these dramatists were seen to stand – as apolitical is itself an invested political move in the period.

This chapter begins by briefly surveying received accounts of the popularity and significance of Beaumont and Fletcher plays in the seventeenth century. The various political dimensions ascribed to their plays – endorsing absolutist, anti-absolutist, or mixed government politics, in the context of Jacobean or Civil War England – tend to overlook the plays' thoroughgoing interest in formal paradox, an "apolitical" dimension that made the play highly appealing to one end of the political spectrum. The second section provides a close reading of *A King and No King* in which the subject of monarchy – in addition to being obviously relevant in a moment when the status of the monarchy was contested – also counter-intuitively becomes a mere vehicle to explore the play's primary concern with the self-contradictory nature of identity.[1] The play explores the tensions and intersections between kingship and kinship, undermining seemingly immutable identities and relationships. Arbaces wants to be the husband of his sister Panthea, conflating identities that are mutually exclusive, even self-negating, as he contemplates ending both of their lives to evade the category error. In the end, Beaumont and Fletcher's ingenious plot reconciles seemingly irreconcilable identities: Arbaces turns out to be simultaneously *king and no king* and also *kin and no kin* to his sister and mother, to use a pun that recurs throughout the play. Kingship in *A King and No King*, if not entirely a red herring, can be something of a distraction; it is especially important insofar as it adds another element, the public identity of a king, to the already overdetermined identities of brother and lover. If the play has a message about the monarchy, it is that the institution is wholly contingent, bestowed not by divine authority but by the careful plotting of a crafty court minister who alters monarchical succession with a good, old-fashioned baby-swap plot. This, however, is not only an ideological statement but also an opportunity for Beaumont and Fletcher to display their narrative and linguistic ingenuity by making the impossible possible. The play's formal genius stems largely from its negotiation of the contradiction "P and not P" making this impossible scenario true. While anything could stand in for "P," in this case, it happens to be a king: in addition to dramatizing a mercurial and tyrannical king, the play's instrumental treatment of the monarchy for the purposes of the plot further undermines the king's position. But ironically, this apoliticized reading was appealing for political reasons: *A King and No*

---

[1] This chapter relied on Lee Bliss's Revels Plays edition of Francis Beaumont and John Fletcher, *A King and No King* (Manchester: Manchester University Press, 2004).

King's aesthetic legerdemain at the expense of the monarchy appealed more to royalist audiences than outright royalist propaganda.

The chapter's final section considers the particular appeal of *A King and No King* in the Interregnum. The play's provocative title circulated as shorthand for the senselessness of undermining the English monarchy; "a king and no king" became a phrase independent from the play text. By contrast, the contents of Beaumont and Fletcher's paradoxical play spoke to a moment when the world "was turned upside down," when new plays were marketed in terms of old ones, when anodyne plays were more subversive than propaganda, when stage plays had no stages. Paradox, then, encapsulates both the contents and critical reception of *A King and No King*, and of Fletcherian drama more generally. To name Beaumont and Fletcher's plays "royalist" in their affiliations is not to name their content royalist; we might say that Beaumont and Fletcher's plays are political and not political.

A King and No King: Political Criticism of Beaumont and Fletcher

Ever since Samuel Taylor Coleridge's denunciation of Beaumont and Fletcher as "servile de jure Royalist[s]" in the early nineteenth century effectively cemented this characterization of their work,[2] critics have tried to insist that Beaumont and Fletcher's plays espouse overt political ideology of one kind or another. Many critics have followed Coleridge by positing the conservatism of tragicomedy in general and of Fletcherian tragicomedy in particular: Beaumont and Fletcher's plays have been described as "theatrical propaganda pieces for James I" and readily conscripted into a mid seventeenth-century royalist political agenda.[3] According to such readings, *A King and No King*, with an incest-pursuing monarch as its protagonist, appears to participate in "absolutism's rejection of morality as a criterion for sovereignty."[4] As other critics have argued, however, these sorts of readings overlook the frequent presence of "vile despots and contemptible favorites" in Beaumont and Fletcher's work,

---

[2] *Coleridge on the Seventeenth Century*, ed. Roberta Florence Brinkley (Durham: Duke University Press, 1955), p. 658.

[3] Bliss, *A King and No King*, p. 15; classic absolutist/royalist readings include Robert K. Turner, *John Fletcher's A King and No King* (Lincoln: University of Nebraska Press, 1963) and John F. Danby, *Elizabethan and Jacobean Poets* (London: Faber & Faber, 1952), who writes "there can be little doubt that Beaumont and Fletcher, broadly speaking, were 'royalist'" (p. 185).

[4] Rebecca W. Bushnell, *Tragedies of Tyrants: Political Thought and Theater in the English Renaissance* (Ithaca: Cornell University Press, 1990), p. 160

which reveals the authors' "distaste for the theory and practice of absolutism."[5] Beginning in the mid twentieth century, thanks to the nuance of
these latter analyses, the long-standing critical edifice of royalist readings of
Beaumont and Fletcher began to sway, with more critics providing evidence that ostensibly "royalist" plays seemed to sharply critique James I or
else espouse republican politics *avant la lettre*.[6]

Problems exist for both strains of interpretation: royalist readings give
outsized importance to the apparent "conciliatory endings" of Fletcherian
tragicomedy that see the king restored to the throne.[7] A focus on endings
overlooks the "winding plots" for which Beaumont and Fletcher were
famed, not to mention their penchant for undermining kingly authority
with buffoonish, sometimes illegitimate kings. In *A King and No King*, the
source of monarchical power is not consistent with absolutism: King
Arbaces's authority is bestowed not by God but by the human machina-
tions of the court minister Gobrius, who has positioned Arbaces on the
throne. This point leads Lee Bliss to observe that "the supposedly 'royalist'
ending has not reproduced the traditional social and political hierarchy:
rather, Gobrius has effected a quiet palace coup."[8] But such readings
merely reverse the valences of royalist readings. Zachary Lesser rejects the
binary absolutist/anti-absolutist or royalist/republican readings of *A King
and No King*, noting that "both focus exclusively on the monarchy, thereby
obscuring the importance of the other institution central to English
politics and to the play: Parliament."[9] Although he shifts his critical focus
from monarchy to Parliament, Lesser remains convinced of the centrality
of politics to the play, arguing that *A King and No King*'s "political project"
is "promoting mixed monarchy as a viable mode of governance,"[10] a
pressing political concern in the Jacobean court in the 1610s.

By focusing on the original context of the play's production, Lesser
rejects the anachronistic interpretations that dominate modern criticism of
the play, which "depend on a Whiggish literary history that reads the
conflicts and ideologies of the Civil War back into the early Jacobean

---

[5] Lawrence Bergmann Wallis, *Fletcher, Beaumont and Company, Entertainers to the Jacobean Gentry* (New York: King's Crown Press, 1947), p. 136.
[6] Philip J. Finkelpearl, *Court and Country Politics in the Plays of Beaumont and Fletcher* (Princeton: Princeton University Press, 1990), pp. 178–9; Judy H. Park, "The Tragicomic Moment: Republicanism in Beaumont and Fletcher's 'Philaster'," *Comparative Drama*, 49.1 (Spring 2015), 23–47.
[7] Park, "The Tragicomic Moment," p. 23.   [8] Bliss, *A King and No King*, p. 27.
[9] Zachary Lesser, "Mixed Government and Mixed Marriage in 'A King and No King': Sir Henry Neville Reads Beaumont and Fletcher," *English Literary History*, 69.4 (2002), 947–77 (p. 948).
[10] Lesser, *Politics of Publication*, p. 188.

court."[11] But, as Lesser himself notes, the tradition of reading Civil War politics into *A King and No King* first began in the 1640s and 1650s, a period which, not coincidentally, saw the emergence of the first critiques of the play. A politicized presentist (from perspective of the 1640s) critical approach was the characteristic way of engaging with Beaumont and Fletcher from the outset, establishing a critical trend in which Lesser himself participates. Interregnum readers co-opted Beaumont and Fletcher for their own contemporary political agendas, but not only, as others have argued, for the ideology of their plays' contents. They were also drawn to Beaumont and Fletcher for their plays' relentless exploration of paradox, which spoke to the paradoxical status of English drama and English politics at the time. That is, it is not necessarily the specific content of the plays that contemporaries (at least Royalist contemporaries) pointed to for political meaning, but the concepts of drama, style, plotting, and art. If *A King and No King* endorses a vision of "mixed monarchy," as important as monarchy is the element of *mixture*, which enables it to engage in pure aesthetic play, of the kind that appealed to belletrist Royalist readers.

A Kin and No Kin: Close Reading *A King and No King*'s Self-Contradictory Identities

The basic subject matter of *A King and No King* is manifestly "political." The Iberian King Arbaces returns home, victorious after a long war with the rival kingdom Armenia. In Iberia, Arbaces exchanges his warrior's sword for the sceptre of a king. Although his ministers complain about the unmistakably brave Arbaces's extremes of mood and action, his status as king is never seriously questioned: his "loving subjects" (2.2.81) recognize him as king, as do the counselors who think he should moderate his moods. The play doesn't lend itself to obvious royalist or republican readings: the king's relationship with his ministers is barely explored. The play is preoccupied with the limits of monarchical authority, but it is dramatized through a private struggle, a battle between Arbaces's incestuous lust for his newly adult sister Panthea and his conscience that restrains him. Critics have argued that Arbaces's contemplation of incest while retaining his kingly authority is consistent with a royalist reading,

---

[11] Lesser, "Mixed Government," p. 949. See also Lesser, "Tragical-Comical-Pastoral-Colonial: Economic Sovereignty, Globalization, and the Form of Tragicomedy," *English Literary History*, 74. 4 (2007), 881–908 (p. 882).

dramatizing the principle that no action, no matter how depraved or criminal, can divest the king of his God-given authority. In fact, Arbaces's loyal government ministers warn him that indulging in incest could invalidate his kingly authority, at least on a practical level, with Mardonius telling him, "If you do this crime, you ought to have no laws, for after this it will be great injustice in you to punish any offender for any crime" (3.3.99–101). Yet warnings from others are few, and mostly people in the play do not really seem to mind the prospect of Arbaces indulging in incest: Panthea reciprocates his desires, and the clown Bessus offers to act as pander between brother and sister. Arbaces feels the burden of external mores, human and divine, forbidding the act of incest, but in practice, it is his own conscience that limits him most. Arbaces clearly has the power and resources to protect himself from the consequences of any incestuous action. But he wants to have sex with Panthea legitimately, and realizes that even a king cannot suspend the moral laws contravening sex between siblings. The fact that other characters in the play do not have the same beliefs undermines the idea that there are objective moral laws with which kings need to comply. The limit of kingly authority is important to the play, however, insofar as Arbaces's nearly limitless power mocks his inability to obtain the one thing he wants: a sanctioned sexual relationship with Panthea. As he explores various scenarios to make incest licit, every time he is confronted by limits imposed less by morality than by logic. A king probably has the power to do something wrong and make it appear right (or at least get away with it), but even kings cannot turn something into its contrary.

In the end, Arbaces gets what he wants, but not through his own actions: his kingly authority is revealed to be the result of a baby-swap plot carried out decades earlier by the court minister Gobrius, his true father, who gave the infant Arbaces to the childless King of Iberia and Queen Arane; they later conceived Panthea, the true heir to the throne. Upon learning Panthea is not really his sister, Arbaces marries her, becoming her royal consort. Thus, Arbaces is revealed to be no king *and* king. While the play's simultaneous undermining and upholding of monarchy can (and should, and has) be interpreted in terms of politics, we can also productively see monarchy as a vehicle to explore the play's sustained interest in paradoxes related to identity. Arbaces's overlapping public and private identities of king, son, brother, and lover are in tension with each other: the play is interested in what happens when one facet of the self collides with another, threatening to undo the entire organism. The play explores the transformations, multiplications, and divisions that threaten to obliterate a seemingly coherent, continuous sense of self. The exploration of the fundamentally protean nature of personal identity is a defining feature of all of Beaumont and Fletcher's plays, to a much greater degree than the work of their contemporaries.[12] It was this feature, as much as any overt political messages, that made Beaumont and Fletcher the favourite dramatists of the Interregnum.

Obviously, the title of *A King and No King* would resonate strongly in the Interregnum, when the title aptly described the situation of the era's three most important public figures: the executed King Charles I, his son Prince Charles, kept from the throne, and Oliver Cromwell, a non-king accorded the powers of one. Critics are correct to dwell on the political significance of *A King and No King*'s title (and the play's contents) in the Interregnum; I will not rehash their arguments here. But, as I will show, the title's riddling syntax – not only its ideological implications – is equally paramount. Removing "king," one sees that the contradiction of the play's title, "P and not P" – by definition, one cannot be something and its negation – is investigated throughout the play via syntax, imagery, plotting, and characterization. The play puts consistent pressure on its own seemingly self-evident tautology, "Men are but men" (5.3.86), by showing how men can be "not men" by acting irrationally, beastly, or by not being at all, thus falsifying a logical triviality ("A is A"). By the play's end, Beaumont and Fletcher manage to make a logical contradiction – "P and not P" – true. Although the play might not offer a clear ideological message, its negotiation of paradox does have political implications. In classical logic, if something can simultaneously be itself and its opposite, anything is possible.[13] By belying tautologies and making contradictions true, Beaumont and Fletcher make the impossible actual and anything possible – a provocative idea in an age of fixed institutions.

Throughout *A King and No King*, Beaumont and Fletcher toy with various verbal, rhetorical, and ontological paradoxes. At every point of the play, something is not as it should be – opposites are reconciled, self-identical things diverge. Focusing on the Arbaces plot leads to politicized readings focused on the status of the monarchy, but shifting our focus

---

[12] Eugene Waith, *The Pattern of Tragicomedy in Beaumont and Fletcher* (New Haven and Oxford: Yale & Oxford University Presses, 1952), pp. 38–9.

[13] This is proved by the principle of *ex falso quodlibet*, or what logicians since the twelfth century have called an "explosion": a "true contradiction" entails the truth of all assertions, propositions, factual, counterfactual and impossible, and the acceptance of everything. Richard Cross, *Communicatio Idiomatum: Reformation Christological Debates* (Oxford: Oxford University Press, 2019), p. 80. Thank you to Nathan Howard for bringing this principle to my attention.

away from Arbaces can help us see the main plot in a new light – one with different political insights. The play's first lines concern an inanimate object assigned an opposite function: the wise Iberian counselor Mardonius, returning from the wars, muses to the clown Bessus that he would like to transform his sword and its basket hilt into a knife and vessel for eating and drinking wine (1.1.2–3). The transformation of instruments of war into tools for festivity during peacetime raises issues about the continuity of identity: if something takes on an opposing function, is it still the same thing? This image recurs when Bessus deploys it to prove his valour: "If I do not make my back biters eat [my sword] to a knife . . . say I am not valiant" (1.1.448–9). Here, Bessus expresses confidence in his identity (as valiant) through the utterance of an impossibility or at least an implausibility (he will make his detractors "eat his sword into a knife"). The *impossibilia* (or adynaton) device usually functions as hyperbolic exaggeration for effect, but in this case, in a roundabout way, Bessus pulls it off: his detractors bully him into giving them his sword and knife, but they return his knife because he is a pitiful coward (3.2.139–50). Because Bessus has (in a manner of speaking) transformed his sword into a knife, by his own lights he proves himself valiant, no matter that this outcome rests on his cowardice.

Following this sword-into-knife discussion, the rest of Act 1 Scene 1 is imbued with oxymoronic imagery, contradictory syntax, and antithetical phrases. Its key, oft-repeated word is "if," alongside its related term, "were," and modal verbs "ought" and "should"; the scene's primary mood is subjunctive. This language creates a series of hypotheticals, conditional formulations, counterfactuals, and irreality statements. Various lines deal with outright contradiction: Gobrius rebukes Arane with an illogical threat: "you will weep because you cannot weep" (2.1.22–5). Escorting the vanquished Armenian King Tigranes back to Iberia as his prisoner, Arbaces boasts, "I will not have him know what bondage is / Till he be free from me" (1.1.203–4). This entails another contradiction: Michael Neill observes, "Though formally a prisoner," Tigranes is actually freer than Arbaces, who is "enslaved to his passions."[14] Arbaces's conflicting desires are first dramatized to humorous effect: at several turns, he demands that his courtiers speak, then rebukes them to remain silent. He likewise demands that they leave and remain, leaving his confused courtiers suspended between going and staying on stage (1.1.307). Arbaces wants it

---

[14] Michael Neill, "The Defence of Contraries: Skeptical Paradox in *A King and No King*," *Studies in English Literature, 1500–1900*, 21.2 (1981), 319–32 (p. 324).

both ways – he is torn between mutually exclusive options. This creates an atmosphere of contingency and instability: his conflicted mundane actions anticipate his more weighty conflict between committing incest and following his conscience.

The play's characters make ample use of paraleipsis, apophasis, and occupatio, rhetorical devices which, by denying or pretending to pass over a topic, draw attention to it. The boastful Arbaces claims he does not brag, since he "could" relate even grander exploits (which he then proceeds to list) (1.1.125–32). Bessus is charged with escorting the chaste Armenian maid Spaconia to Iberia to serve as a lady-in-waiting to Panthea. Arriving in Iberia, Bessus assures everyone that Spaconia is *not* a prostitute, which has the unintended and opposite effect of making everyone think she is indeed a prostitute (2.1.176–95). Attempting to suppress something often only makes it more conspicuous; as noted in the Introduction, the irony of censorship is that people powerfully seek out what is denied to them.

The play's negotiation of verbal, rhetorical, and ontological paradoxes provides context for its central concern with self-contradictions related to personal identity: fundamental transformations of identity, divided and multiple identities, the "loss" of self, simultaneously being and not being. Characters variously picture themselves in each other's roles: both Mardonius and Tigranes respectively imagine themselves in King Arbaces's place (respectively as king or victor), uttering statements like "If I were king . . ." (1.1.73), "Were you not my king . . ." (1.1.324), and "Had Fortune thrown my name above Arbaces . . ." (1.1.115–16). Arbaces himself imagines others in his place: to Mardonius, Arbaces states, "were you my king, I would have . . ." (1.1.273); Mardonius later tells Arbaces what might happen "were you no king . . ." (1.1.373). This is not only a threat to Arbaces's monarchical identity, but also a broader exploration of counterfactuals: what it means to be someone else. The various hypothetical scenarios of Arbaces being unkinged anticipate the play's final resolution. But changing places with the king is also a special instance of the play's interest in shifting roles, both internally and externally. The play endorses a notion of identity that is not essential or fixed but unstable, tenuous, and fungible.

The play's first prolonged investigation of the self-contradictory nature of personal identity plays out in a comic key. The clown Bessus has unwittingly contributed to the victory against Armenia: attempting to flee the enemy, he retreats in the wrong direction, charging instead fiercely towards them. Bessus's cowardice has won the day, as Mardonius notes: "A hot charge thou gav'st, as, I'll do thee right, thou art furious in running away, and I think we owe thy fear for our victory" (1.1.71–3). Bessus, a well-known coward, achieves an opposite reputation as valiant, but does so by acting cowardly. Elsewhere in the play, his cowardice is expressed in terms of being non-existent: others call him "an airy, thin, unbodied coward" (5.1.47), an "empty name" (5.1.24), yet another paradox. Although Bessus acquires some measure of respect, his new reputation comes at a price. The scores of people Bessus wronged, who previously excused those wrongs as the antics of a coward, now turn up to settle scores with him (1.1.76–80; 3.2.232). Bessus wriggles out of this problem with a rhetorical truism: "Shall Bessus the valiant maintain what Bessus the coward did?" (3.2.118–20). Ultimately, Bessus enjoys the benefits of valour without incurring negative consequences by invoking a paradox.

Through Bessus, *A King and No King* interrogates the continuity and coherence of individual identity. If we fundamentally change, are we the same person? Should we be held responsible for the actions of our "former" selves? What responsibility do we have to our past selves, and those we impacted when we were different? Given that the "brave coward" Bessus retains both past and present identities, fusing them even when they appear to be mutually exclusive, the play hints at the endless possibility opened up for the individual by true contradiction. When Bessus's new-found valour is put on trial, he ends the proceedings by declaring: "We are valiant to ourselves, and there's an end" (5.3.107). Bessus claims an alternative identity for himself through the language of self-assertion, despite all evidence regarding his true nature to the contrary.

Contradictions related to the instability of identity and ironic self-defeat in the Bessus comic subplot recur in a darker key in the tragicomic major plot centred on King Arbaces, whose private identities as son and brother conflict with his public role as the king. Arbaces's worst enemy is himself (a close second is his own mother, who has plotted to kill him on various occasions). He lacks self-discipline and is given to extremes: Mardonius calls him "vainglorious and humble, and angry and patient, and merry and dull, and joyful and sorrowful, in extremities, in an hour" (1.1.84–6). Many of Arbaces's traits are admirable in isolation, but troublesome when consolidated into one person: Mardonius laments, "Thy valour and thy passion severed would have made two excellent fellows in their kinds. I know not whether I should be sorry thou art so valiant or so passionate, would one 'em were away" (1.1.172–6). Mardonius wishes that Arbaces's identity could be split in two; this, of course, is an impossibility. Arbaces's instability of moods prefigures the instability of his identity as king. *A King and No King* can be read as an allegory about kingship, but kingship is also a metaphor to explore personal identity.

After Arbaces falls in love with Panthea, he is further self-alienated, experiencing it as a crisis of identity. He describes the mysterious feeling as a hostile foreign agent taking residence in his body, an intruder which he cannot remove without harming himself:

> Am I what I was?
> What art thou that does creep into my breast?
> And dar'st not see my face?
> Show forth thyself . . .
> If thou beest love, be gone
> Or I will tear thee from my wounded flesh. (3.1.182–7)

Already a stranger to himself, Arbaces cannot understand what afflicts him: he cannot see the unknown agent (since one cannot "see [one's own] face"), and to do away with the intrusion would harm the whole organism. But the incursion is not a hated foreign power, but rather his love for someone too like himself. Arbaces, then, is not only tormented by his status as "king" but also by his position of "kin" to Arane and especially to Panthea, a homophone repeated throughout the play. The play's primary conflicts – the prospect of Arbaces and Panthea's incest; Queen Arane's desire to kill her son – are political, but also familial and psychological.[15] Arbaces's authority seems to be threatened by "treason" (1.1.475), but this is also a family squabble, because the perpetrator is his mother. Indeed, he thinks that his mother wants to kill him not for his flaws as a king, but rather for his excessive devotion to the "pomp or vanity of state," which made him "forget [his] natural offices" as a son (1.1.499–501). The political is continually displaced onto the personal, which readings primarily focused on Arbaces's kingship can miss. And yet, the private dimensions of Arbaces's struggles provide alternative political insights, focused less on individual rulers and more on the political implications of a personal identity that is largely untethered from fixed norms and rules.

Beaumont and Fletcher employ filicide and incest as formal figures to consider undesirable divergence and convergence, respectively, between family members. Arbaces is alienated from his mother but wants to get too close to his sister, and therefore threatens to overturn both the ostensibly

---

[15] On the politics of incest, see Bruce Thomas Boehrer, *Monarchy and Incest in Renaissance England: Literature, Culture, Kinship and Kingship* (Philadelphia: University of Pennsylvania Press, 2015).

fixed parent–child and sibling relationships and also the individual identities of parent, child, brother, and sister. These identities and relations are both internally and externally imposed, respectively by biology and by society's regulation of their meanings. Arane is called an "unnatural mother"; being a hateful, murderous mother seemingly obliterates the traditionally identity-forming categories of mother and son. (She turns out to be an "unnatural" mother for another reason, because she is not his biological mother.) Sex between brother and sister also destroys seemingly immutable familial relationships; Arbaces bemoans that he "loves his kindred better than any brother loves his sister" (3.3.58). Terry Eagleton notes that incest is "an enigma of affinity and otherness, identity and difference," in which "excessive intimacy results, ironically, in alienness"; by collapsing difference and coming too close to one's own self, "the incestuous one is an abomination who confounds essential distinctions."[16] Arbaces elsewhere wonders what would happen "were [Panthea] my father and my mother, too" (3.1.17), compounding the confusion by assigning multiple mutually exclusive familial identities to a single individual. That Panthea could be both sister and lover to Arbaces confounds their identities; that she could also be Arbaces's mother and father takes the identity-destroying scenario to a still further extreme.

For her part, Panthea is troubled by the same incestuous desire, loving Arbaces "as wives love husbands" (3.3.72). Caught between familial loyalties, Panthea laments that her fidelity to her murderous mother will destroy her brother, and vice versa. As a solution to this division, she imagines giving up her own life (1.2.27–40): the divided self is rendered coherent through obliteration. While internal strife tears coherent wholes apart, incest creates its own contradictions. Arbaces longs in vain to engage in oxymoronic "holy incest"; he notes that "doing" Panthea will "undo" them both (4.4.24–5). Arbaces imprisons Panthea to prevent incest, paradoxically conflating freedom and bondage (another recurring image) when he tells her "There is a way / To gain thy freedom, but 'tis such a one / As puts thee in worse bondage" (4.4.58–60). Characteristic of the play's swirling contrariety, Arbaces claims that both committing incest and not committing incest will ruin him: "I shall but languish for the want of that / The having which would kill me" (3.1.204–5). Self-realization results in self-negation, and vice versa.

---

[16] Terry Eagleton, *Sweet Violence: The Idea of the Tragic* (Hoboken: Wiley, 2009), pp. 162–3. See also James B. Twitchell, *Forbidden Partners: The Incest Taboo in Modern Culture* (New York: Columbia University Press, 1987).

At several points, Arbaces says that he is "not himself" or that he
has "lost himself"; Gobrius states that Arbaces "has been asunder from
himself, / A mere stranger to his golden temper" (4.1.19–21). This too
entails a contradiction. Aside from the fact that Arbaces's previously
"golden temper" is seriously suspect, how can one be split from, or a
stranger to oneself? We are by definition self-identical. This contradiction
is ironically compounded by Arbaces's desire to escape his identity: even
though he has "lost himself" by falling in love with his sister, he cannot
lose himself enough to actually enjoy morally and socially sanctioned sex
with her. Arbaces contemplates running away with Panthea to a place
where they are unknown, where they can hide both his status as king
and, more importantly, their sibling relationship (4.4.164). But even he
recognizes that, try as they might, no matter where they flee, Arbaces and
Panthea cannot escape themselves, their immutable, identical selves.

Arbaces contemplates drastic measures to evade human and divine
constraints against incest, which he deems to be an "ungodly sickness"
(3.1.199) and an "unmanly sin" (3.1.344). As Arbaces recognizes, this is
seemingly impossible:

> [H]e that undertakes my cure must first
> O'erthrow divinity, all moral laws
> And leave mankind as unconfined as beasts
> Allowing them to do all actions,
> As freely as they desire. (3.1.199–206)

Yet, like Bessus's *impossibilia*, Arbaces imagines conquering this impossible
situation by banishing various facets of his identity: undoing or concealing
his sibling identity or relationship, acting like a beast, killing himself. All of
these scenarios entail self-contradictions and a simultaneous doing and
undoing, which for Arbaces is an intractable paradox.

Early on in the play, Arbaces insists upon the divine source of his kingly
authority. He ascribes his victory in Armenia to the fact that his arm was
"propped by divinity" (1.1.128); he even claims to exceed this authority,
claiming to have "patience above a God" (1.1.235). Confident of his
divine authority, Arbaces hopes to draw on this power to unmake familial
relations by monarchical decree (again, note the homophone of kin and
king): "She is no kin to me, nor shall she be / If she were any, I create her
none" (3.1.168–9). But, try as he might to unmake sibling relationships,
Arbaces ultimately acknowledges that even an omnipotent king cannot
warp certain elements of reality: "I have lived / To conquer men and now
am overthrown / Only by words 'brother' and 'sister'. Where / Have those

words dwelling? I will find 'em out / And utterly destroy them; but they are / Not to be grasped" (4.4.116–21). Far from possessing unlimited power, in *A King and No King*, the monarch discovers that he is limited by the very thing that empowers the playwrights – language.

Unable to overcome consanguinity, Arbaces contemplates other ways he might legitimate incest, namely by becoming a "beast" or behaving irrationally, both of which involve relinquishing a defining human quality. Noting that "reason" is "the only difference betwixt man and beast" (4.4.64–6), Arbaces exclaims, "Accursed man / Thou boughtst thy reason at too dear a rate!" (4.4.131–3), for "Who ever saw the bull / Fearfully leave the heifer that he liked / Because they had one dam?" (4.4.136–8) This recalls Aristotle's dictum that "man is a rational animal"; by logical syllogism, then, an irrational animal is not a man. Arbaces therefore wants to abandon reason, undoing his humanity, and with it, his obligation to adhere to the human taboos against incest. But Arbaces cannot reason himself out of being rational.

Unable to become an irrational beast, Arbaces imagines yet another way of evading the taboo of incest, envisioning a scenario in which he kills Panthea, rapes her, and then kills himself:

> I must begin
> With murder of my friend, and so go on
> To an incestuous ravishing, and end
> My life and sin with a forbidden blow
> Upon myself. (5.4.8–11)

Arbaces's imagined murder-necrophilia-suicide spree entails its own paradox of self-destruction. Neill notes that "[i]t is no accident that suicide should be the death towards which Beaumont and Fletcher's characters are constantly driven, for suicide, as [Rosalie] Colie suggests, is a kind of enacted paradox – 'self-contradiction at its irrevocable extremity.'"[17] Necrophilia is yet another self-contradictory act: the "purpose" of sex (i.e., making life) is pre-empted by death; reproduction is warped into the destruction of the self and the other. Arbaces's extreme scenario does not even solve his problem; instead of being legitimized, his moral transgression is trebled, with incest replaced by the three other "forbidden blows" of murder, necrophilia, and suicide. Even incest will not be evaded by these wranglings: sibling relationships are so inescapable that after her death, sex with Panthea's corpse will still be an "incestuous ravishing."

---

[17] Neill, "The Defence of Contraries," p. 321.

As Arbaces contemplates how to go about incest, his storyline intersects with Bessus's. Their interaction reveals the contrast between Bessus's independent, intrinsic identity and Arbaces's extrinsic, imposed one. Arbaces asks Bessus to procure Panthea for him, a task Bessus is all too happy to fulfil. Bessus has no qualms about helping Arbaces "have a bout" with his own sister; Bessus even offers to fetch Arbaces's mother Arane for him to have sex with as well (3.3.150; 171–2). Arbaces, shocked by Bessus's willingness to facilitate an incestuous coupling (no matter that he requested it), calls him out for his wickedness: "Hast thou no greater sense of such a sin? Thou are too wicked for my company" (3.3.155–6). That Bessus is unfazed by the prospect of incest suggests that the taboo against it is at least partly a social construct (which some can then choose to ignore) rather than solely an objective truth. If so, Arbaces's own private conscience constrains him as much as objective moral laws, another aspect of the divided self. Throughout the play, Arbaces is largely passive, his identity imposed on him from without: at the play's end, he shouts "tell me who I am" (5.4.154), a counterpoint to Bessus's "we are valiant to ourselves."

One need not contemplate the extreme actions of incest, sororicide, necrophilia, and suicide to seriously question one's humanity: the moderate Armenian King Tigranes (a foil to Arbaces), critiques himself in the same terms for contemplating a rather run-of-the-mill infidelity. Engaged to the Armenian maid Spaconia, Tigranes falls in love with the Iberian Princess Panthea, but he cannot enjoy her because he has previously arranged for Spaconia to travel with him to Iberia. Having placed himself in this quandary, Tigranes exclaims, "I have undone myself" (4.2.1), recalling Arbaces's more literal expression of self-destruction, and describes himself as "unmanly, beastly" for his "sudden doting on a new face" (4.2.27–8). Again, although Tigranes is a king, his is not only a "kingly" problem: Tigranes has simply fallen in love with another woman. In all of its plot lines, *A King and No King* dramatizes the tensions emerging from constantly shifting identities and roles – public and private, external and internal.

Through the (nearly) "beastly, unmanly" figures of Arbaces and Tigranes, the play gives the lie to the seemingly trivial statement uttered late in the play that "men are but men" (5.3.86) by exploring the different ways a person can *not be* a person: one could become an irrational beast, or even cease to be altogether. Characters routinely conflate life and death: Panthea seems to evoke Christian resurrection when she claims she loves Arbaces "more than I could love / A man that died for me if he could live / Again" (3.1.24–5). Although Tigranes muses what would happen "if my father / Should rise again . . ." (3.1.216–17), he accepts that resurrection is the exclusive realm of the divine. As the play reveals, however, Gobrius can also raise the dead; Tigranes's idle musing foreshadows Arbaces's situation, in which his "dead" father is resurrected, insofar as he is revealed to be the living Gobrius, undoing Arbaces's identity along with Gobrius's own. Having interrogated the tautology that "men are but men," at the play's end, King Arbaces, who has shuttled between the extremes of quasi-divinity endowed by kinghood and subhuman beastliness, turns out to be "Plain Arbaces." He is simply a man, positioned between animals and angels.

Political implications have been read into the revelation that Arbaces is "no king." The fact that Arbaces is not a king seems to explain prior erratic, unkingly behaviour, in that "he was not born to rule."[18] Yet the legitimate ruler Panthea also lacks mettle: in 1678, Thomas Rymer argued that "one might swear she had a knock in the cradle; so soft she is at all points, and so silly."[19] True, the play suggests that a king is king only by the efforts of the wider government, since the minister Gobrius puts Arbaces on the throne – a message inimical to absolutist royalist politics. But the play is at best a rather tepid endorsement of mixed monarchy. Gobrius's work is a testament to the power of plotting to make the impossible possible. Of all early modern commercial playwrights, Claire M. L. Bourne notes, "Beaumont and Fletcher were the ones routinely singled out for their skillful plotting and surprise endings," observing that their reputation for clever plotting was cemented in the 1620s.[20] As I demonstrate in the next section, however, this critical praise of Beaumont and Fletcher's formal qualities was most widely expressed in the 1640s and 1650s, a time of unprecedented upheaval, when Beaumont and Fletcher's concern with the instability of identity and societal norms would reverberate especially strongly.

"A king and no king": Provocative Titles, Pithy Phrases, and Belle-lettrist Literary Appreciation in the Civil Wars and Interregnum

The Civil Wars and Interregnum provided fertile ground for the reception of Beaumont and Fletcher. These consummate writers of paradox and the inconstancy and fungibility of personal identity were embraced in a

---

[18] Christopher William Nelson, "Perception, Power, Plays, and Print: Charles II and the Restoration Theatre of Consensus" (doctoral dissertation, Louisiana State University, 2012), p. 115.

[19] Thomas Rymer, *The Tragedies of the Last Age* (London: Richard Tonson, 1678), p. 45.

[20] Claire M. L. Bourne, *Typographies of Performance in Early Modern England* (Oxford: Oxford University Press, 2020), pp. 186, 29, 196.

moment defined by political and social inversion, described as "the world turned upside down."[21] Their paradoxical plays would speak to the general political mode and aesthetic of the times. As David Armitage notes, the very term "civil war" is an oxymoron, as "every conception of civil war is paradoxical in its own way."[22] He continues that ancient Greeks considered civil war a "metaphysical impossibility, like 'being at war with oneself.'"[23] This metaphysical impossibility is the very plot of *A King and No King*, concerning Arbaces's "lawless war against [himself]" (5.4.15). With its exploration of the potentially limitless possibilities for the individual, rooted in no higher meaning, Fletcherian tragicomedy – the contradictory genre par excellence – can, in a positive light, be regarded as an endorsement of individual freedom or a capitulation to ethical nihilism, in a negative one. Rather than a specifically royalist or republican play *avant la lettre*, *A King and No King*'s dizzying sense of liberty verging into nihilism can be complexly mapped onto the political and social mindset of the Interregnum. It is no coincidence that the vertiginous moment of the Interregnum was the moment of canonization for the playwrights who seem most persistently, explicitly interested in pulling the rug out from under characters and audiences alike.

 Civil War and Interregnum discourse, both political and dramatic, frequently invoked *A King and No King*, but in very different ways. The former focused on the politics of the play's title (often divorced from the play's contents), the latter on the formal ingenuity of the play itself. About two months into the first English Civil War, six weeks after the theatres closed, the anonymous pamphlet *The Last News in London* (1642) invoked the play in a dialogue between a country gentleman and a citizen:

COUNT[RY GENTLEMAN]. Why, I thought that playes & play-houses had been put downe:
CIT[IZEN]. Yes so they were in the Suburbes, but they were set up in the City, and Guild-hall is made a Play-house.
COUNT. But I pray, what Play was it that was Acted? . . .
CIT. Some say it was called *a King or no King*, or *King Careo* ["I lack a king"] . . .

---

[21] This phrase recurred throughout the Interregnum and is the title of Christopher Hill's *The World Turned Upside Down* (1972). Leah Marcus notes "the association between topsy-turvydom and civil war goes back to Horace." Marcus, *The Politics of Mirth* (Chicago: University of Chicago Press, 1986), p. 303 n. 2.
[22] David Armitage, *Civil Wars: A History in Ideas* (New Haven: Yale University Press, 2017), pp. 44–6.
[23] Ibid., p. 46.

COUNT. Truly it was a strange play, did not they whisper Treason in it? on my word we Country folks dare not be so bold as to make sport at Kings.[24]

Zachary Lesser notes that the royalist interlocutors "read the play in the context of the Civil War ... as a subversive attack on monarchy," unlike most later critical accounts which tend to co-opt the play for royalism.[25] But crucially, the country gentleman notes the play's ability to generate divergent critical reactions; the play is read in different ways by "country folks" (who take its contents seriously) as opposed to those in the city and suburbs (who regard it as "sport"). The play's politics are not singular, but yield disparate interpretations from the audience.

Lesser juxtaposes this 1642 account with one from April 1654, in which the diplomat John Nicholas records a performance of *A King and No King* for English exiles in Holland before Mary, the princess royal[26]: "the gentlemen and maides of honour to the Princess Royal are preparing to act a play ... the very name of which seems to please many in her Court ... it being so judicious and discreetly chosen, viz. *A King and no King*; but all loyal persons are astonished when they hear it named."[27] Lesser notes that "Nicholas may have been the first, certainly not the last, to read a royalist politics into" *A King and No King*.[28] Like the account of 1642, Nicholas charts two diverging politicized receptions of *A King and No King*, noted for its ability to prompt diametrically opposed responses from those who thought the play "discreetly chosen" and those who were "astonished" by the selection. Moreover, as is typical of one major strand of *A King and No King*'s Interregnum reception, Nicholas is fixated not so much on the play as on its *title* – loyal persons are outraged when they hear the play "named," not when they actually watch it.

The provocative title of *A King and No King* was frequently invoked throughout the Civil Wars, Interregnum, and Restoration. The combination of political relevance and riddling syntax made the phrase irresistible. But it was often used in ways that had little to do with the play itself: the

[24] *The last Nevvs IN LONDON. OR, A DISCOVRSE Between A Citizen and a Country-Gentleman* (London: R. R., 1642), p. 2.
[25] Lesser, "Mixed Government," p. 947.
[26] Mary, Princess Royal (1631–60), was the eldest daughter of King Charles I and Queen Henrietta Maria (1609–69). Living in the Dutch Republic as the consort of William II, as the Princess of Orange she supported English royalist exiles in Holland. Marika Keblusek, "Mary, Princess Royal (1631–1660)," in the *ODNB*, http://doi.org/10.1093/ref:odnb/18252.
[27] *Calendar of the Clarendon State Papers Preserved in the Bodleian Library*, ed. W. H. Bliss, the Rev. W. Dunn Macray, the Rev. O. Ogle, and F. J. Routledge, 5 vols. (Oxford: Clarendon Press, 1869–1970), V, p. 229, catalogue 1845.
[28] Lesser, "Mixed Government," p. 947.

title took on a life of its own apart from the play proper. Indeed, the phrase was in circulation *before* the first performance of Beaumont and Fletcher's play in 1611. In *The Encounter Against M. Parsons* (1610), the Protestant cleric Thomas Morton deploys the phrase as part of his polemical exchanges with English Jesuit Robert Parsons following the failed Gunpowder Plot (1605), and subsequent controversy about the Jacobean Oath of Allegiance (1606), requiring English Catholics to swear allegiance to James I over the Pope.[29] Following the Gunpowder Plot, English Jesuits were particularly associated with equivocation, implying something untrue through ambiguous phrasing.[30] Morton singles out Parsons's wily evasions, noting his attempt to conflate the excommunication of princes with their deposition:

> Thus it fareth with Mr. *Parsons:* for the reason of this *Impossibilitie* was taken not onely from the *Excommunication of Princes:* but from the *Deposing* of them, and so the Reader might haue easily discerned, if Mr. *Parsons,* to inure his penne to deceitfulnesse, had not craftily concealed that point. This *deposing of Kings from their Kingdomes* inferred, as I then sayd, as much an *Impossibilitie* as *King,* and no *King.*[31]

Morton uses "king and no king" to convey the logical impossibility of deposing princes, but also to lay bare the sort of crafty equivocation with which the Jesuits deceive the (Protestant) English public. In the context of the aftermath of the Gunpowder Plot, "a king and no king" becomes both a way to express the unshakable stability of the monarchy, and a display of (potentially nefarious) verbal ingenuity. *A King and No King* was first staged in 1611, a year after the publication of Morton's *Encounter.* Beaumont and Fletcher potentially picked up on his phrase (perhaps in wider circulation after the Gunpowder plot) to explore not only the stability of the monarchy, but also to make use of the phrase's cleverness and inherent contradictoriness, deployed to test the limits of "impossibility" which it is used to express.

Royalist propaganda made use of the phrase, deploying its paradoxical syntax to convey the preposterousness of republican usurpation of kingly

---

[29] On the Morton-Parsons exchanges, see Michael L. Carrafiello, "St. Paul and the Polemicists: The Robert Parsons-Thomas Morton Exchanges, 1606–10," *The Catholic Historical Review,* 95.3 (2009), 474–90.

[30] For early modern drama scholars, this history is often filtered through *Macbeth*'s negotiation of equivocation. See Máté Vince, "The Porter and the Jesuits: Macbeth and the Forgotten History of Equivocation," *Renaissance Studies,* 35.5 (2021), 838–56.

[31] Thomas Morton, *The Encounter Against M. Parsons* (London: W. Stansby, 1610), p. 33.

authority.[32] Some examples, like *The Discovery of Mysteries* (1643), invoke the parent play, "for the Lords and Commons to make Orders and Ordinances without the King … is a meere usurpation of the Regall power … and a plaine making of our good King to be somewhat like him in the Comedy, a King and no King."[33] The regicide later literalized the phrase: there was no king (Charles I was dead), and a king (Prince Charles, in exile, but also the would-be commoner king Oliver Cromwell). After 1649, "a king and no king" was repurposed to describe the "real tragedy" of contemporary Interregnum politics, displacing the original tragicomedy of the play. (Some commentators may have even been thinking of Morton, since the unsuccessful Catholic plotters of 1605 were frequently aligned with the successful Puritan regicides of 1649.)[34] A report from November 1647 suggests that the King's Servants intended to perform a "wholy Tragicall" adaptation of the play by "H. Peters."[35] While, as I discuss below, the King's Servants did indeed illegally stage *A King and No King* in October 1647, this particular reference must be a macabre joke, rather than actual theatrical gossip. In 1647, the New Model Army was locked in a dispute with the Long Parliament over how to handle Charles I. The Army seized the King in June 1647, and was determined to bring him to trial. Hugh Peters (or Peter) was the Army's chaplain; he was reputed to have preached regicide and some accounts suggest he was the first to propose the trial and execution of Charles I. He is also said to have participated in Charles's beheading in 1649.[36] It is highly unlikely either that Peters adapted *A King and No King* or that the King's Servants would

---

[32] Although the phrase is ascribed to republican ideology, searching multiple instances of the phrase (seventy-two found instances on *EEBO*), I found no explicitly republican uses of the phrase (perhaps because *A King and No King* requires an acceptance of the initial premise "A king").

[33] Gryffith Williams, *The discovery of mysteries: or, The plots and practices of a prevalent faction in this present Parliament. To overthrow the established religion, and the well setled government of this glorious Church* (Oxford: [Henry Hall], 1643).

[34] Anne James, *Poets, Players, and Preachers: Remembering the Gunpowder Plot in Seventeenth-Century England* (Toronto: University of Toronto Press, 2016), p. 244.

[35] *Mercurius Vapulans*, 27 November 1647. See Hotson, *Commonwealth and Restoration Stage*, pp. 28–9; Wiggins and Richardson, *British Drama*, VI, p. 132.

[36] Peters' reputation as an early, determined, and voluble advocate of regicide was well established after the Restoration; his actual status during the late 1640s is more difficult to determine. Jordan S. Downs notes that, in 1660, "[w]hen charged with treason for his outspoken promotion of the king's execution more than a decade earlier, Hugh Peter claimed that he had done no more than other ministers at a time … It was, Peter professed, unreasonable that he should be singled out for his subversive actions when he had been 'force[d] upon' to join 'the best Ministers' who were taking their sermons 'into the field' to drum up fighting spirit. Unconvinced, his commissioners ordered that he suffer a traitor's death, and in mid-October he was sent to the block." Jordan S. Downs, "The Curse of Meroz and the English Civil War," *The Historical Journal*, 57.2 (2014), 343–68 (p. 365). Thank you to Isaac Stephens for discussing this historical detail with me.

perform any version he wrote. (Moreover, a tragic *King and No King* simply could not work: Arbaces and Panthea's deaths would obliterate the resolution of the play's central contradiction and its formal ingenuity). Rather, the report appears to make a darkly comic (and highly prescient) comment about the regicide as a real-life tragic version of *A King and No King*, "authored" by Peters and the other regicides, performed on the public stage of the scaffold.[37]

That the regicide represented the real-life tragic version of *A King and No King* seems to have been a pervasive idea: an anti-Cromwellian tract states that Cromwell, a king in all but name, "represented the real Tragedy of a King and no King; whose mouth water'd after that Title, but that he durst not assume it, having fought so long against it, and was sworn to the deposition of all Kingship for the future."[38] Another account notes that Charles I's opponents set up "a Paper ... near the Gates of Whitehall, importing that on the Morrow next there was to be Acted in the House of Peers a famous Tragie-Comedie, called, [A King and No King]." Of this reference, Tiffany Stern notes that "titles of popular plays became known and could themselves be used for political reasons."[39] A play's title is one of the many "documents of performance" that could circulate separately from its parent play. Indeed, the power of these references depend solely on the tragic potential of *A King and No King*'s title (the prospect that there could be "no king") and not any latent tragedy in the play's overall plot, which is mostly non-existent (Arbaces's life is never really threatened, apart from his own flirtation with suicide). With its potent combination of politics and paradox, the title of *A King and No King* seemed destined to become an indelible phrase, when there were various contenders for the title of king, and also potentially none at all. More broadly, the "impossibility" of the title was a distillation of the topsy-turvy political moment of the Civil Wars.

In the Interregnum, the phrase "a king and no king" could be invoked without alluding to the parent play or a dramatic context ("real" or fictional) at all, usually to refer to the impossibility of stripping a true king of his power. Thomas Fuller refers to "a king and no king, I meane a titular

[37] Thank you to Martin Wiggins for discussing this reference with me.
[38] *The English devil: or, Cromwel and his monstrous witch discover'd at White-Hall* (London: George Horton, 1660), p. 3.
[39] Tiffany Stern, *Documents of Performance in Early Modern England* (Cambridge: Cambridge University Press, 2009), pp. 56–7. Stern refers to *Observations on the historie of The reign of King Charles* (London: H. L. Esq, 1656), p. 244.

King without power."[40] A royalist tract titled *A Vindication of King Charles* (1648) posits the absurd hypothetical "if the *Sunne* were stripped of his abundant shining" analogizing it with Charles's current quandary, "so take from the *King,* his Royall Prerogative, let him be as a *King* and *no King.*"[41] Thomas Bayly uses the phrase to answer the question "Whither the People can make a King or not": "if they have not one already of Gods making, they may; such are Kings, and no King."[42] The syntax of "P and not P" was widely applicable, with different terms substituted into the phrase to describe the confusion of the times: "it's said we have had (for a great while) a King and no King, a Parliament & no Parliament, one party setting it selfe against another party."[43] Gryffith Williams, the author of a 1664 account on episcopal controversy, muses that "I conceived I should be *a Bishop and no Bishop:* or a Bishop without the *authority* and power of a Bishop . . . this puts me in mind of a *Play Book* that I saw on a Booksellers Stall, intituled, *A King and no King.*"[44] Again, it is the title, rather than the plot, which provides political fodder; notably, the speaker invokes the print context of *A King and No King,* when he observes it is the play's title page (visible at a bookseller's stall) that inspires his comments.

A King and No King's title and play text, then, could be appreciated separately. Some Royalist commentators deployed the play title or phrase in a political context, while extolling the formal ingenuity of the play's contents in other contexts. In 1647, Jasper Mayne observes the "*contradiction in Power,*" in cases where a king is "chosen, and created by the People": "Whereupon will either follow this That the same Person at the same Time may be a *King,* and no *King.*"[45] In 1648, Robert Herrick used the phrase to head a couplet about the instability of royal authority when it relies on public approval: "A king and no king: / That Prince, who may doe nothing but what's just, / Rules but by leave, and takes his Crowne on trust."[46] Mayne and Herrick were part of a royalist coterie of poets, expressed through and partly established in the prefatory criticism they provided for each other's publications. This royalist textual community is

[40] Thomas Fuller, *The History of Holy Warre* (Cambridge: Roger Daniel for John Williams, 1647), p. 73.
[41] Edward Symmons, *A Vindication of King Charles* (London: 1648).
[42] Thomas Bayly, *The royal charter granted unto kings, by God himself and collected out of his Holy Word* (London, 1649), p. 9; see also pp. 86–7.
[43] John Price, *Clerico-classicum* (London: M.S. for H. Cripps, 1649), p. 56.
[44] Gryffith Williams, *The persecution and oppression. . .of John Bale* (London: 1664), p. 42.
[45] Jasper Mayne, *Ochlo-machia. Or The peoples war, examined according to the principles of Scripture & reason* (Oxford: L. Lichfield, 1647), p. 10.
[46] Robert Herrick, *Hesperides* (London: John Williams, 1648), p. 393.

exemplified by and made legible in the copious front matter to the
Beaumont and Fletcher folio (1647) and William Cartwright's posthumous dramatic collection, *Comedies and Tragicomedies* (1651) (further
discussed in Chapter 5).[47] While in 1648 Herrick used the phrase "a king
and no king" to political effect, a year earlier in his commendatory poem to
the Beaumont and Fletcher folio, Herrick praises the play *A King and No
King*, noting its "high design" and "rare plot."[48] Writing when England
was embroiled in a conflict that challenged the institution of the monarchy, Herrick remains mute on the potential provocations of *A King and No
King*'s incendiary title. Clearly, Herrick is aware of the political valences of
the phrase in the current climate. But in the context of the folio, Herrick
celebrates the language and narrative structure of that play and of
Beaumont and Fletcher's dramatic corpus, where "words with lines, and
lines with Scenes consent, / To raise an Act to full astonishment."[49]
Herrick and Mayne exemplify Royalists' bifurcated appreciation of
"*A King and No King*": as a play title, or as a phrase deployed for political
readings, while the play itself was subject to bellelettrist readings.

The "royalist" appropriation of *A King and No King* has been consistently misinterpreted in two different but related ways. The first strain
detects overt royalist ideology in Beaumont and Fletcher's plays, exemplified by Samuel Taylor Coleridge's famous indictment of the dramatists'
"ultra-royalism."[50] The second argues that by claiming the plays, Royalists
warped Beaumont and Fletcher's plays' politics. Gordon McMullan
describes the 1647 folio as "a Royalist propaganda coup by the publisher
Humphrey Moseley that erased the plays' original politics and reshaped
them for quite different ideological purposes."[51] Moseley did frame the
plays with royalist paratexts, but those paratexts did not forcefully ascribe
royalist politics to the plays' contents. Royalists were belletristic: they saw
themselves as guardians of timeless high culture, as opposed to Puritans,
who produced and consumed topical political propaganda like newsbooks
and pamphlets. In Martin Butler's memorable formulation, as far as

[47] Gavin, *The Invention of English Criticism*, p. 29; See also Stella P. Revard, "Thomas Stanley and 'A
Register of Friends'," in *Literary Circles and Cultural Communities in Renaissance England*, ed.
Claude J. Summers and Ted-Larry Pebworth (Columbia: University of Missouri Press, 2000),
pp. 148–72.
[48] Robert Herrick, "Upon Master Fletcher's Incomparable Playes," in Beaumont and Fletcher,
Comedies and Tragedies, sig. d3r.
[49] Ibid.   [50] Brinkley, *Coleridge*, p. 658.
[51] Gordon McMullan, "The Lateness of *King Lear*: Alteration and Authenticity in Shakespeare and
Tate," in *The true blank of thine eye: approches critiques de King Lear*, ed. Pascale Drouin and Pierre
Iselin (Paris: Presses de l'université Paris-Sorbonne, 2009), pp. 83–101 (pp. 94–5).

Royalists were concerned, "[they] were sensitive to the arts, and Puritans were ignorant blockheads."[52] Michael Gavin argues that, compared with the "contentious discourse of animadversion" of ephemeral print media, royalist prefatory criticism was "comparatively sociable and commendatory," and "demonstratively belletristic": "Elevated above the tastes of 'common men' and the vulgar publications of the controversial press, royalist prefatory criticism was designed to mark an arena of literary discussion apart from political dispute as such."[53]

The key figure of bellelettrist publishing in the Interregnum is, once again, Humphrey Moseley. The "royalist" publisher Moseley, to use a frequent epithet, in fact published little straightforwardly royalist material.[54] As Kastan notes, Moseley published few "newsbooks, sermons or political pamphlets that provided steady income for most of his fellow stationers. His publications were mainly literary and historical."[55] His literary publications were not delimited by political affiliation: he had no qualms about publishing John Milton (in *Poems* [1645]), whose republicanism did not detract from his artistry. Royalist prefatory criticism generally remains above the fray of topical concerns; only "very occasionally did royalism become explicit," as N. W. Bawcutt notes.[56] Of course, Moseley and his coterie's purposefully belletristic literary appreciation was itself a political gesture. Lois Potter argues that the contributors cover their staunch royalist politics with "a veil of aesthetics" to offer "subversion for the polite reader."[57] Ann Baynes Coiro describes Moseley as "a guerrilla fighter on the front line of high culture."[58] Befitting the publisher of Beaumont and Fletcher, Moseley was a "royalist publisher," but not really a publisher of royalism.

Modern critics describe the prefatory matter in the Beaumont and Fletcher folio as "conscious acts of [royalist] propaganda"[59] and "unmistakably Royalist in sympathy."[60] The adjectives royalist contributors used to describe Beaumont and Fletcher's plays suggest a different focus: "neat," "rare," "subtle," "winding."[61] In his commendatory poem, the Cavalier poet William Cartwright focused on dramatic plot, noting that spectators

---

[52] Butler, *Theatre and Crisis*, p. 9.   [53] Gavin, *Invention of English Criticism*, p. 25.
[54] See for instance, Kewes, "Sociable Pocket-Books"; Lois Potter, *Secret Rites and Secret Writing: Royalist Literature, 1641–1660* (Cambridge: Cambridge University Press, 1989), p. 20; Ann Baynes Coiro, "Milton and Class Identity: The Publication of *Areopagitica* and the 1645 Poems," *Journal of Medieval and Renaissance Studies*, 22 (1992), 261–89.
[55] Kastan, "Humphrey Moseley," pp. 112–13.   [56] Bawcutt, "Puritanism," p. 195.
[57] Potter, *Secret Rites*, p. 38   [58] Coiro, "Milton and Class Identity," p. 277.
[59] Butler, *Theatre and Crisis*, pp. 9–10   [60] Kastan, "Performances and Playbooks," p. 180.
[61] Bourne, *Typographies*, pp. 197 n.37, 198

and readers of their plays were left "wondering how the thing will be until it is."[62] Thomas Peyton fantasizes that the collection will entertain royalist soldiers, who retain their artistic sensibilities even on the battlefield; addressing the text, Peyton states, "I'll send thee to the army, they that fight / Will read thy tragedies with some delight." Beaumont and Fletcher's plays are meant to "delight" soldiers, not work them up into a royalist froth.

During the Interregnum, Beaumont and Fletcher are consistently praised in formal terms, precisely when we might expect political commentary to be at its highest. Beaumont and Fletcher's extracts in John Cotgrave's *English Treasury of Wit and Language* (published by Moseley in 1655) exemplify their paradoxical status in the Interregnum. Laura Estill notes that many of Cotgrave's headings – "Of Warre," "Of Tyrannie, Tyrants," and "Of Rebellion and Sedition" – although long used in commonplace books, would be "particularly charged" in the 1650s.[63] But of the eighteen dramatic passages cited under the volume's politically pointed headings, only one is from a Beaumont and Fletcher play. A passage from *Rule a Wife and Have a Wife*, which speaks to youth's naive idealization of battle, is listed under "Of Warre": "The wars are dainty dreams to young hot spirits / Time and experience will allay those visions" – hardly an endorsement of jingoist royalism. The volume's five *A King and No King* extracts are listed under headings related to private, personal identity, not political, public (let alone royalist) values: "Of Adversity, Affliction"; "Of Bastardy"; "Of Inconstancy"; "Of Reason."[64] "Of Adversity, Affliction" cites Arbaces's complaint from 5.1, in which he wishes to "mangle" "the book of fate" with his sword, "That all the destinies should quite forget / Their fix'd decrees, and haste to make us new, / For other fortunes; mine could not be worse."[65] Arbaces here longs to unsettle what he sees to be the fixity of fate; little does he know that, like so many of Beaumont and Fletcher's characters, his is about to be totally overturned.

Royalists claimed Beaumont and Fletcher's plays as royalist artefacts because their artistry appealed to the Royalist self-conception as admirers of high culture. The royalist leader and military commander Sir George Lisle (c. 1610–28 August 1648) also provided a commendatory poem to

---

[62] William Cartwright, "Upon the Report of the Printing of the Dramaticall Poems of Master John Fletcher," in Beaumont and Fletcher, *Comedies and Tragedies*, sig. d2r.
[63] Estill, *Dramatic Extracts*, p. 90.
[64] Cotgrave, *The English Treasury*, pp. 5, 25, 141, 175, 246. See McEvilla, *Cotgrave Online*.
[65] Cotgrave, *The English Treasury*, p. 5.

the Beaumont and Fletcher folio. Lisle's "To the memory of my most honoured kinsman, Mr. Francis Beaumont" extols the emotive power of his distant cousin Beaumont's plays: "Thou strik'st our sense so deep, / At once thou mak'st us Blush, Rejoyce, and Weep."[66] Lisle's aesthetic appreciation in his commendatory poem is not meant to be idiosyncratic, but rather representative of a larger community of readers who are collectively moved (*"our* sense," "mak'st *us* blush, rejoice and weep") by Beaumont's artistry. Praising "Such pow'rfull Sceanes, as when they please, invade. / Your Plot, Sence, Language, All's so pure and fit, / Hee's Bold, not Valiant, dare dispute your Wit,"[67] Lisle's militaristic metaphor of the "invasion" of Beaumont's "powerful scenes" gestures at the ongoing political and military crises, but the dramatist's power is deployed for narrative and linguistic victories.

Lisle's poem exemplifies the sort of royalist prefatory criticism that seems wilfully to ignore the present political conflict. Lisle was a royalist commander in the Civil Wars; he was killed in 1648, a year after the publication of the Beaumont and Fletcher folio, at the Siege of Colchester, where the injustice of his execution without trial by order of Thomas Fairfax made Lisle into a royalist martyr. In 1647, Lisle could have leaned into royalist propaganda, yet this "marvelously gallant cavalier"[68] provided a poem to a dramatic collection in which he praises the plays' "sceanes," "plot," "Sence," and "Language." Notably, in his poem, Lisle praises not King Arbaces (or King Tigranes), but his wise counselor: "Were thy Mardonius arm'd ... My life on't Hee had been o'th' Better side."[69] Admittedly, Lisle arms and enlists Mardonius to fight "on the better side," doubtless the royalist side in the Civil Wars that claimed Lisle's life in the following year. Yet Mardonius is recruited for his wisdom, not his support of absolutism, which is not depicted in the play (Mardonius discourages Arbaces from indulging in the immoral desires which could threaten his authority). Lisle's poem speaks to the lasting appeal of Beaumont and Fletcher's dramatic characters, not their overt political leanings.

The royalist appreciation of Beaumont and Fletcher's plays in the 1647 folio offers another counterintuitive kind of dramatic reception:

[66] George Lisle, "To the Memory of My Most Honoured Kinsman, Mr. Francis Beaumont," in Beaumont and Fletcher, *Comedies and Tragedies*, sig. b1r.
[67] Ibid.
[68] Charles Mills Gayley, *Beaumont, the Dramatist: A Portrait with Some Account of His Circle, Elizabethan and Jacobean, and of His Association with John Fletcher* (New York: Russell & Russell, 1969), p. 204.
[69] Lisle, "To the Memory," sig. b1r.

Moseley's much touted "all-new" Beaumont and Fletcher folio explicitly excluded already-printed Beaumont and Fletcher plays, yet several of the commendatory poems invoke the excluded plays: *A King and No King, The Maid's Tragedy, The Scornful Lady* and *Philaster*, all of which had reached their fourth or fifth editions by the 1640s and 1650s. In his commendatory poem, Thomas Stanley describes Aspasia's moving plight in *The Maid's Tragedy* and the relief provided by the comedy *The Scornful Lady*: "And when Aspasia wept, not any eye, / But seemed to wear the same sad livery [. . .] / But then the Scornful Lady did beguile / Their easy grief, and teach them all to smile."[70] In "Upon Mr. John Fletcher's Plays," Edmund Waller refers to *The Scornful Lady* as evidence of the dramatists' virtuosity, which affronts his own talents: "when I venture at the Comick Stile / Thy Scornful Lady seems to mock my toile."[71] Paradoxically, in the Beaumont and Fletcher folio, the appeal of new plays is staked on old ones; the value of the present volume is derived chiefly from plays that are absent.

Although excluded from the folio due to their age, Beaumont and Fletcher's "old" plays were embraced on the illegal Interregnum stage. Critics interpret illegal theatrical performance as a form of royalist defiance, "a demonstration of solidarity with the lost court culture in the 1630s and a contribution to royalist morale."[72] The illegal performance of the ostensibly royalist Beaumont and Fletcher's plays, *A King and No King* in particular, seems to suit this interpretation.[73] *A King and No King* was slated for illegal performance in London on 5 or 6 October 1647; it was raided by the authorities. This was seemingly a royalist provocation: Dale Randall remarks that "the title itself might draw a crowd."[74] But if Royalists wanted to perform plays that endorsed their own views, other plays had clearer royalist associations. "The Players' Petition" (1643), a satirical poem that requests the authorities' permission to resume playing, promises that, should the theatres reopen, they will exclude any material that might incite opposition to Parliament, citing three plays in particular:

---

[70] Thomas Stanley, "On the Edition," sig. b4v.
[71] Edmund Waller, "Upon Mr. John Fletcher's Plays," in Beaumont and Fletcher, *Comedies and Tragedies*, sig. b2r.
[72] Ann Hughes and Julie Sanders, "Gender, Exile and The Hague Courts of Elizabeth, Queen of Bohemia and Mary, Princess of Orange in the 1650s," in *Monarchy and Exile: The Politics of Legitimacy from Marie de Médicis to Wilhelm II*, ed. Philip Mansel and Torsten Riotte (Basingstoke: Palgrave Macmillan, 2011), pp. 44–65 (p. 58); on illegal interregnum performance as royalist defiance, see also Randall, *Winter Fruit*, pp. 44, 140–56.
[73] Bliss, *A King and No King*, p. 33; Maguire, *Regicide and Restoration*, p. 36.
[74] Randall, *Winter Fruit*, p. 44.

"We vow / Not to Act anything you disallow. / Aspiring *Cataline* shall be forgot / Bloody *Sejanus*, or who ere could plot / Confusion to a State, the wars betwixt / The Parliament & just *Henry the sixt.*"[75] Ben Jonson was famously anti-Puritan, and his plays were politically hot; *Catiline* and *Sejanus* dramatize the failure of republican government. *Henry VI* dramatizes the last English Civil War, here provocatively described as a conflict between Parliament and a "just" monarchy. In contrast, Beaumont and Fletcher's plays seem to be relatively neutral. In one reference to an illegal performance of *The Scornful Lady*, the notion that the play could be politically provocative is played for laughs. In the satirical pamphlet *The Ladies, A Second Time, Assembled in Parliament* (1647), the all-female House of Commons is discussing the widespread revival of performance, "Whereupon was demanded what plaies they were, and the answer being given, that one of them was the the scornefull Lady, the house tooke it in high disdaine, as an absolute contempt of their power."[76] To be sure, the illicit performance of *A King and No King* was subversive, but *any* illegally performed play was subversive, since it subverted Parliamentary law.

Onstage, insofar as *A King and No King* had particular "royalist" associations, it was related chiefly to its stage history, not its contents. The Parliamentarian newsbook *Perfect Occurrences* recounts the raided illegal performance of *A King and No King* in October 1647, noting

> A Stage Play was to have been acted in Salisbury Court this day (and bills stuck up about it), called A King and No King, formerly acted in the Black-Fryars, by his Majesties servants, about 8 years since, written by Francis Beaumont and John Fletcher. The sheriffs of the City of London with their officers went thither and found a great number of people, some young lords and other eminent persons, and the men and women with the [money] boxes . . . The Sheriffes brought away Tim Reade the Foole, and the people cryed out for their monies, but slunke away like a company of drowned Mice without it.[77]

The report mentions neither the authors' nor the play's politics, nor does it exploit the seemingly obvious subversion implied by *A King and No King*'s title. But the newsbook is curiously specific about the play's last legal performance "at Blackfriars" "eight years since," that is, 1639. The reference consciously or unconsciously reproduces the formulaic language of

[75] MS Ashmole 47, fols. 132–3 and MS Rawlinson poet. 71, fols. 164–8, reproduced by Hyder E. Rollins in "A Contribution," p. 275 n.24.
[76] Henry Neville, *The Ladies, A Second Time, Assembled in Parliament* (London: 1647), p. 11.
[77] *Perfect Occurrences*, 8 October 1647.

title pages, suggestive perhaps of the broad cultural currency of early modern playbooks (and of bipartisan consumption of them), thereby establishing the conditions for a satisfying defeat of an entrenched cultural institution. The triumph of the raid derives from silencing a play associated with the Stuart court, as it was once performed by "his Majesties servants." The journal relishes the disparity between a moment eight years ago, when a monarch-backed troupe performed legitimately, and the present moment, when players and elite spectators slink away, cowed by the sheriffs of London.

The Royalist newsbook *Mercurius Pragmaticus*'s account of the October 1647 raid also emphasizes the storied stage history of the "old play," but says nothing about *A King and No King*'s ostensibly incendiary title or contents:

> Though the House hindred the Players this weeke from playing the old play, King and no King, at Salisbury Court, yet believe me,
>> He that does live, shall see another age,
>> Their follies stript and whipt upon the stage.[78]

The passage appears to allude to George Wither's *Abuses Stript and Whipt* (1613), a social satire for which Wither was imprisoned, which had the inadvertent effect of drawing more attention to the work: a fitting warning for those who attempt to suppress theatre that they will ultimately be exposed and ridiculed. The newsbook dwells on the oldness of *A King and No King* rather than make overt claims about its politics. By the 1640s, Beaumont and Fletcher had already been "old" for two decades. The first edition of *The Noble Gentleman* (F1 1647) appeared with a printed prologue written for the play's 1626 revival, which refers to its first performance around 1606: "we know / That what was worne some twenty yeare agoe, / Comes into grace againe, and we pursue / That custome, by presenting to your view / A play in fashion then." Beaumont and Fletcher's play is tied to a particular moment, "then" (i.e., around 1606, in the early days of the Jacobean court), which is partly revived through performance along with the play itself. The subversion of Beaumont and Fletcher's plays was partly due to their status as "old plays" that tied them to the Stuart performance tradition.

---

[78] *Mercurius Pragmaticus*, 5–12 October 1647. This prophecy seems to have struck a particular chord with at least one contemporary reader; the annotator "John ffowle" recopied the newsbook's final couplet in the margins of a copy of *Mercurius Pragmaticus*, 5–12 October 1647, now at the Folger (Folger Call Number M1768.49, no 4). My thanks to Marissa Nicosia for drawing this to my attention.

Parliament understood that nostalgia for the Stuart court and its cultural artefacts threatened its authority. Paradoxically, then, old plays written before present conflicts could be more subversive than new ones, and not only because old plays might assume unanticipated new meanings as the political context shifted. Relatively benign plays could be threatening precisely by virtue of their innocuousness. The "Address to the Reader" from William Peaps's *Love in Its Ecstasy* (composed c. 1634, printed 1649) reassures the reader (and the authorities) that even though the play is printed in tumultuous times, its anodyne contents reflect the peaceful moment in which it was composed:

> You may be confident there lyes no Treason in it nor State invective, (The common issues of this pregnant age). It is inoffensive all, soft as the milkie dayes it was written in, for although it appears now so late before you like a winter blossome in the middle of a boysterous and ill-boding season, yet this Interlude was long since the early recreation of a Gentleman not fully Seventeene, and those times admitted but of small distempers.[79]

This belated "winter blossom" evokes the "soft and milkie days" of the pre-war court when it was written, in contrast to the "ill-boding season" of the late 1640s. For this reason, the preface claims, the content is not treasonous. But apart from the risk that plays contained treason or state invective, the Parliamentarian authorities opposed performance precisely because it evoked what Royalists saw as the halcyon period before 1642.

Beaumont and Fletcher were obvious candidates for theatrical nostalgia tied to the Stuart court, due in part to their consistent association with the "final" events of English professional theatre: *The Scornful Lady* was the last play performed at court, before Prince Charles.[80] The 1 January 1649 performance of *Rollo, Duke of Normandy* at the Cockpit is characterized as "the last ever performance by the former King's Men company."[81] Evidence suggests Beaumont and Fletcher were popular on the droll stage: they are by far the best-represented dramatists in the droll collection *The Wits* (1662, printed in the Restoration but with its drolls staged in the Interregnum), with just over half (fourteen of twenty-seven) of the volume taken from Beaumont and/or Fletcher's plays. Dale Randall detects a range of topical political allusions in *The Wits*,[82] including the titles of *The Loyal*

---

[79] William Peaps, *Love in Its Ecstasy* (London: Mercy Meighen, Gabriell Bedell, and Thomas Collins, 1649), sig. A2r.
[80] Lucy Munro, *The King's Men* (London: Bloomsbury Arden Shakespeare, 2020), p. 177.
[81] *British Drama 1533–1642: A Catalogue, Vol. 7: 1617–1623*, ed. Martin Wiggins and Catherine Richardson (Oxford: Oxford University Press, 2020).
[82] Depledge also notes topical allusions in Shakespearean drolls. *Shakespeare's Rise*, pp. 19–20.

Citizens (from Beaumont and Fletcher's *Cupid's Revenge*) and *The Lame Commonwealth* (from their *Beggar's Bush*, yet another play ostensibly about kingship that depends on mistaken identity); the *Philaster* droll depicts the restoration of a dispossessed prince, ending with the crowd shouting, "Long may'st thou live brave prince, brave Prince, brave Prince."[83] By contrast, in 1932, John Elson argued that "no contemporary political allusions occur in the drolls ... the drolls were designed to entertain, not to propagandize."[84] I basically agree with Elson, with some modification. Judging from *The Wits,* while various political authorities appeared on the droll stage, kings never did. Like *A King and No King*, the titles of the drolls, but not necessarily their contents, are politically pointed, but it could be that the titles were not even uttered onstage, but were only available to the readers of the printed collection.

The drolls seize on Beaumont and Fletcher's signature motifs, namely overturning ostensibly stable identities, through dramatic devices of baby-swap plots and cases of mistaken identity, as well as dramatizing identity-defying actions like incest and cross-class marriages. For example, for the titular "Surprise" (a droll drawn from *The Maid in the Mill*), a lowly miller's daughter is revealed to be the long-lost daughter of an aristocrat, enabling a marriage of social equals between her and the Count. Finding out his sister is actually high born, the miller's son hopes for a similar revelation about his identity: "though I have been brought up in a Mill, yet I had ever a minde (methought) to be a greater man." He tells his mother, "Woman, tell the truth, my father shall forgive thee, whatsoever he was; were he Knight, Esquire, or Captain; less he could not be." Unfortunately for the son, this potential instance of mistaken identity is forestalled: his parents really are millers. Learning the truth about his sister's identity and his own, the son regrets missing the opportunity to marry her: "farewell Sister-foster. If I had known the Civil Law would have allowed it, thou hadst had another manner of husband then thou hast." "The Surprise" is a romp, but its concerns are reminiscent of *A King and No King*.[85]

Counterintuitively, then, belletrism and the Stuart stage history of these "old" plays made them more satisfying (for Royalists) and threatening (for Republicans) than new plays, irrespective of content. This is illuminated by a brief look at the new plays written by William Davenant in the 1650s. Davenant's plays were sanctioned for performance in that decade largely

---

[83] Randall, *Winter Fruit*, p. 155.
[84] *The Wits, or Sport upon Sport*, ed. John James Elson (Ithaca: Cornell University Press, 1932), p. 22.
[85] "The Surprise," in Elson, *The Wits*, pp. 237–51.

because they did not have the same fraught associations with pre-1642 culture. Critics have discussed the politics of Davenant's 1650s proto-operas, noting that the plays strive "to work within the cultural and aesthetic parameters of the newly modelled godly Commonwealth led by Oliver Cromwell" and flatter Cromwell's colonial ambitions.[86] This view has been reassessed by scholars who note that the plays do not simply kowtow to the cultural and political values of the Commonwealth.[87] If the authorization of Davenant's plays for performance cannot be explained by their promotion of Commonwealth values, why, then, were they allowed to be performed when pre-1642 stage plays were banned? Clare argues that the "indistinct generic identity" of Davenant's dramatic works – "part debate, part opera, part masque, and part play" – enabled Davenant to sidestep the theatrical prohibition.[88] Yet the quality emphasized by Davenant himself was his plays' novelty: the title of *The First Day's Entertainment* signalled the advent of a new theatrical tradition. On the title pages of *The Siege of Rhodes* (1656), *The Cruelty of the Spaniards in Peru* (1658), and *The History of Sir Francis Drake* (1659), Davenant calls them not "stage plays" but instead instances of the fresh genre of "recitative musique" performed with the novelties of moveable scenery and actresses. Their "indistinct generic identity" signals that they could not fit into existing categories. Davenant's plays were tolerated because they presented themselves as something totally new: not merely new compositions, but a new performance genre. Equally important as the specific plays' political contents, then, was the generic novelty of such works, which allowed the Commonwealth to claim them as their own cultural products, since symbols of the old order posed a threat to the nascent government.[89] Just as Royalists claimed the broad concept of pre-1642 English drama as their own cultural phenomenon, the opposing faction had to claim something other than that as theirs, and Davenant's proto-operas provided a convenient generic and chronological separation.

Broadening our view from *A King and No King* to the dramatists' wider corpus, Fletcherian tragicomedy spoke to the fraught political moment of

---

[86] Clare, *Drama of the English Republic*, p. 1. Janet Clare, "The Production and Reception of Davenant's *Cruelty of the Spaniards in Peru*," *The Modern Language Review*, 89.4 (1994), 832–41 (p. 832).

[87] Clare, "Davenant's *Cruelty of the Spaniards*"; Stephen Watkins, "The Protectorate Playhouse: William Davenant's Cockpit in the 1650s," *Shakespeare Bulletin*, 37.1 (2019), 89–109.

[88] Clare, "Davenant's *Cruelty of the Spaniards*," p. 832.

[89] For instance, recall that the Parliamentary newsbook *Perfect Occurrences* reporting a raid of *A King and No King* in October 1647 dwelled on the fact it was an "old play" with a Caroline performance history, not on the play's incendiary contents; see earlier in this Chapter.

the Civil Wars and Interregnum, but not because their plays amounted to royalist propaganda. The term "tragicomedy" is an oxymoron; the genre's paradoxical mixed mode reconciles the contrary demands of comedy and tragedy. "Paradox," Lesser notes, is the "characteristic figure" of tragicomedy as a genre, arguing that "the tragicomic form itself resists polarization almost by definition."[90] Critics have posited the genre's resonance with successive historical moments in the early modern period. In the Elizabethan period, John Lyly "sought to justify the tragicomic 'minglemangle' of *Midas* (1589–90) on the grounds that 'the whole world is become an hodge-podge.'"[91] The genre's development and success in Jacobean England "can be attributed to the adequation of its self-consciously mixed form to the pressing political questions of early Stuart society."[92] Tragicomedy is said to have appealed to the royalist ethos before the Civil Wars; the genre's obliqueness was useful to safely give voice to royalist political complaints during the Wars. Meanwhile, tragicomedy's narrative arc of loss and return also spoke to Royalists after the Restoration.[93] Tragicomedy, then, is a protean genre, speaking equally to cultural moments defined by confusion, revolution, and happy resolutions. But tragicomedy's seeming universal applicability entails a paradox: by being everything to everyone, it risks being nothing to no one. Or, put another way, the genre's lack of clear political investments makes it widely applicable for different political moments.

When the public theatres were still open, *A King and No King*'s title was reworked to describe the paradoxical relationship between printed drama and theatrical performance. Printed on the title page to Richard Hawkins's 1631 edition of *A King and No King* (Q3) was "A Play and No Play, who this Booke shall read / Will judge and weepe, as if 'twere done indeed."[94] Claire Bourne notes that Hawkins's "canny riddle" conflating performance and print "preemptively solves the either/or dilemma" in Stephen Orgel's oft-cited description of the relationship between stage and page: "a play is

[90] Lesser, "Tragical-Comical-Pastoral-Colonial," p. 882.

[91] Neill, "The Defence of Contraries," p. 320.

[92] Lesser, "Tragical-Comical-Pastoral-Colonial," p. 882

[93] Potter, *Secret Rites*, pp. 72–112; Maguire, *Regicide and Restoration*, p. 36; Randall, *Winter Fruit*, p. 367; Victor Holtcamp, "A Fear of 'Ould' Plays: How *Mucedorus* Brought down the House and Fought for Charles II in 1652," in *The Shakespeare Apocrypha*, ed. Douglas Brooks (Lewiston: Edwin Mellen Press, 2007), pp. 145–70 (p. 155).

[94] Francis Beaumont and John Fletcher, *A King and No King* (London: Richard Hawkins, 1631), sig. A2r.

not a book."[95] The already-complex relationship between stage and page was reconfigured after 1642: the paradox of "a play and no play" would take on new meanings when the theatres closed. Indeed, Orgel's tautological statement utterly collapses between 1642 and 1660 when plays were not played, and books were the only legitimate form that plays could take. This is echoed by the play itself: as we've seen, *A King and No King* falsifies "A is A" and makes "P and not P" true, fitting descriptors for the state of drama during the Interregnum, when Beaumont and Fletcher's plays were new and old, innocuous and subversive, political and not political, printed in a book that lamented the loss of the stage while illegal performance continued apace.

A King or No King: Beaumont and Fletcher after 1660

The 1640s and 1650s arguably represent the apex of Beaumont and Fletcher's critical estimation in the seventeenth century; indeed, perhaps, of their entire reception history. Speaking to an unsettled political and cultural moment, Beaumont and Fletcher's disorienting tragicomedies dramatize the contingency of identity and the instability of institutions, producing a dizzying sense of possibility. In tragedy, the unsettled boundary of being and not being expresses existential dread: Hieronymo's oft-quoted lines from *The Spanish Tragedy*, in which he introduces something only to immediately deny it ("O World, No World . . . O Life, No Life") and Hamlet's "to be or not to be" hint at the futility of existence. In the context of tragicomedy, however, the annihilation of identity and absence of reliable institutions is not destructive, but life-affirming – "the best news! I am found no King!" – presenting characters with an opportunity to chart new identities.

After the Restoration, *A King and No King* continued to appear on the stage and in print: It was performed by Thomas Killigrew's King's Company often in the early 1660s, and reprinted in 1661 and 1679.[96] As noted above, Gryffith Williams's Restoration sighting of "a *Play Book* [. . .] on a Booksellers Stall, intituled, *A King and no King*" prompted his

---

[95] Bourne, *Typographies*, p. 8. Hawkins's riddle appeared on the title page of subsequent *A King and No King* reprints, including Q4 1639, Q5 1655, and Q6 1661; it does not appear on Q7 1676, nor on Q8 1693; nor in F2 1679.

[96] On the performance history of *A King and No King*, see Bliss, *A King and No King*, pp. 31–40 and Arthur Colby Sprague, *Beaumont and Fletcher on the Restoration Stage* (Cambridge, MA: Harvard University Press, 1926).

reflection that "I should be *a Bishop and no Bishop*."⁹⁷ As this suggests, the play's title continued to resonate, both politically and aesthetically. Nahum Tate borrowed the play's title for his farce *A Duke and No Duke* (1693). Tate's plot is actually an adaptation of Sir Aston Cockayne's comedy *Trappolin Supposed a Prince*, yet another reminder of how the riddling, politically loaded syntax of *A King and No King*'s title had a life apart from the play.⁹⁸

Although the play continued to circulate, it was no longer the critical darling it once was. Lee Bliss notes that "because it was initially so popular and admired, *A King and No King* allows us to trace the seismic shift in aesthetic criteria that within fifty years had virtually forced it from the stage."⁹⁹ In *The Tragedies of the Last Age* (1678), the neoclassical critic Thomas Rymer critiqued *A King and No King* for its unwieldy narrative and surprise ending: "We blunder along without the least streak of light, till in the last act we stumble on the plot."¹⁰⁰ Rymer convinced John Dryden, who had previously celebrated the play, of its faults, leading Dryden to describe it as "that inferior sort of traged[y] which end[s] with a prosperous event."¹⁰¹ Claire Bourne observes that Rymer's main reason for calling *A King and No King* and other Beaumont and Fletcher plays "failures was essentially the same as other [earlier] critics' reasons for admiring them: they kept readers in the dark," and notes that Beaumont and Fletcher served as "flashpoints for debates about dramatic decorum that lasted well into the eighteenth century."¹⁰² Nevertheless, although Beaumont and Fletcher's eccentric plots may have fallen out of fashion, *A King and No King* continued to be staged. In 1691, Gerard Langbaine defended the play, observing that *A King and No King*, "notwithstanding its errors discovered by Mr. Rymer ... has always been acted with Applause, and has lately been reviv'd on our present Theatre with so great success."¹⁰³ After sporadic performances between 1700 and 1707, the play was staged only a handful of times in the eighteenth century, such that the headnote to George Colman's 1778 edition notes, "Notwithstanding its prodigious merit, it has not been performed for many years past; nor do we

---

⁹⁷ Williams, *The persecution and oppression...*, p. 42.   ⁹⁸ Bliss, *A King and No King*, pp. 37–8.
⁹⁹ Ibid., p. 36.   ¹⁰⁰ Rymer, *Tragedies*, sigs. E6r–v.
¹⁰¹ John Dryden, "Preface," in *Troilus and Cressida, or Truth Found Too Late* (London: Abel Swall and Jacob Tonson, 1679), sig. A3r.
¹⁰² Bourne, *Typographies*, pp. 218–20.
¹⁰³ Gerard Langbaine, *An Account of the English Dramatic Poets* (London: George West and Henry Clements, 1691), p. 210.

find that it ever received any alterations."[104] Like many early modern plays revived in the Restoration, some elements of Beaumont and Fletcher's plays were "clarified" but in general their plays were performed without major changes: their intricate plots yielded less readily to simplification than plays by other dramatists, notably Shakespeare's. *A King and No King* continued to be staged even when out of step with contemporary tastes; because the play could not easily be altered, when the play became truly intolerable, it largely disappeared from the stage.

A King and No King's title, however, could be altered: when the play was reprinted in *Fifty Comedies and Tragedies*, the second Beaumont and Fletcher folio of 1679, the title listed in the table of contents was *A King or No King*.[105] This title replaces the bold antithesis of *A King and No King* with a trivializing tautology – by definition, everything in the world is either "king" or "no king." This alteration, probably accidental (the head and running titles feature the original title), nevertheless speaks to the political and cultural shift after 1660, when the seemingly unprecedented possibility offered (to some) during the Interregnum – when immemorial institutions collapsed, and individuals could suddenly chart new identities – was foreclosed by the Restoration of the monarchy, and with it the institutions and mores of the period before the wars. When Charles II assumed the throne, the riddle of "a king and no king" that had characterized the prior two decades was replaced with the factual statement of "a king or no king" – Charles was king, and no one else. Of course, the Restoration offered new opportunities for those sidelined by the conflicts of the previous two decades: Royalists and theatre professionals, to name two obvious examples. But, as we shall see in the next chapter, the "fresh start" that many theatre professionals anticipated after the reopening of the public playhouses did not come to pass; for many, the restrictions that characterized Interregnum theatre continued even after the theatres were officially restored.

---

[104] Francis Beaumont and John Fletcher, *A King and No King*, in *The Dramatic Works of Beaumont and Fletcher*, ed. George Colman, 10 vols. (London: T. Evans and P. Elmsley, 1778), I, p. 71.
[105] "A CATALOGUE Of all the COMEDIES and TRAGEDIES Contained in this BOOK in the same Order as Printed," in Francis Beaumont and John Fletcher, *Fifty Comedies and Tragedies* (London: John Martyn, Henry Herringman, and Richard Marriot, 1679), sig. A4v.

CHAPTER 4

Chronic Conditions

The ordinance banning stage plays never fully succeeded in silencing performance. Illicit and clandestine performance was pervasive. Professionals performed in London playhouses throughout the 1640s and 1650s; plays were staged at provincial inns and fairs, and private homes; players also performed plays for the exiled court on the Continent.[1] In some cases, authorities turned a blind eye; in others, they carried out destructive raids. In March 1653, preparations for a performance of Thomas Killigrew's *Claracilla* at Gibbons's Tennis Court were interrupted by Parliamentary soldiers, who were apparently tipped off by another theatre professional. The royalist newsbook *Mercurius Democritus* reported that "an ill Beest, or rather Bird (because the rest denied him a share of their profits) beshit his own nest, causing the poor Actors to be routed by the Souldiery though he himself hath since the prohibition of Playes had divers Tragedies and Comedies acted in his own house."[2] Leslie Hotson argues the "ill Beest" is William Beeston, the experienced theatre manager who continued to carry out theatrical business during the Interregnum; the newsbook suggests that the actor Theophilus "Bird" was likewise involved.[3] Beeston apparently betrayed the performance because his company held the playing rights to *Claracilla*, but was denied his share of the profits.[4] During the theatrical prohibition, even as they struggled with governmental opposition, theatre professionals also

[1] Several scholars have written extensively on performance during the prohibition; Janet Clare provides a helpful survey of theatrical activity in her introduction to *Drama of the English Republic*, pp. 2–8. For an extensive examination, see Hotson, *Commonwealth and Restoration Stage*, pp. 3–120.
[2] *Mercurius Democritus*, 2–9 March 1653.
[3] Hotson, *Commonwealth and Restoration Stage*, pp. 49–50. Christopher Matusiak notes H. M. Beeston's opposition to Hotson's "singularly unjust" claim about her ancestor William's treachery. "The Beestons and the Art of Theatrical Management in Seventeenth-Century London" (doctoral dissertation, University of Toronto, 2009), p. 2. No matter the specific actors, however, the intra-actor rivalry is clear from the pamphlet.
[4] Hotson, *Commonwealth and Restoration Stage*, p. 50.

wrangled among themselves. As we shall see, competition and treachery between professionals attempting to scratch out a living in straitened theatrical circumstances continued even after the theatres reopened.

The restoration of the playhouses in 1660 is typically regarded as a fresh start in English theatre history. David Roberts argues that year "was a watershed for how plays looked, sounded, felt, and read" and describes several "revolutions" in Restoration theatre practice, including the performance of female roles by actresses, the use of a proscenium arch, elaborate moveable scenery, the elevation of theatrical taste, and the formation of a dramatic canon.[5] This narrative is an aesthetic counterpart of the Act of Oblivion, the official governmental policy of forgetting that effectively erased the years 1640 to 1660 from the historical record.[6] The story of the Restoration's cultural and political "fresh start" continues to inform modern historiography. Tim Harris notes that "very few histories work across the seventeenth century as a whole, which makes it very difficult to see continuities across the century."[7] Even scholars who resist treating 1660 as a political watershed continue to do so for theatrical contexts. Mihoko Suzuki argues that "the impact of the English Civil Wars continued to resonate well after 1660,"[8] but maintains that treating 1660 as a decisive period marker makes sense for English theatre, because it was indeed restored under drastically different conditions.[9] The "fresh start" theory of the Restoration has also affected ideas about the origins of dramatic criticism and theatre historiography, typically traced to the period after 1660.[10]

---

[5] David Roberts, *Restoration Plays and Players* (Cambridge: Cambridge University Press, 2014), p. 32.

[6] Janet Clare, "Acts of Oblivion: Reframing Drama, 1649–65," in *From Republic to Restoration*, ed. Janet Clare (Manchester: Manchester University Press, 2018), pp. 148–60 (p. 149). Jonathan Sawday, "Re-Writing a Revolution: History, Symbol and Text in the Restoration," *The Seventeenth Century*, 7 (1992), 171–99 (pp. 171, 173).

[7] Tim Harris, "Periodizing the Early Modern," p. 35. Exceptions include Tim Harris, "Introduction: Revising the Restoration," in *The Politics of Religion in Restoration England*, ed. Tim Harris, Paul Seward, and Mark Goldie (Oxford: Oxford University Press, 1990), pp. 1–28 (pp. 6–9); Jonathan Scott, *England's Troubles: Seventeenth-Century English Political Instability in European Context* (Cambridge: Cambridge University Press, 2000); Jonathan Scott, *Commonwealth Principles: Republican Writing of the English Revolution* (Cambridge: Cambridge University Press, 2004); Steven Pincus, *Protestantism and Patriotism: Ideologies and the Making of English Foreign Policy, 1650–1668* (Cambridge: Cambridge University Press, 1996); Keith Wrightson, "The Enclosure of English Social History," *Rural History*, 1.1 (1990), 73–82.

[8] Mihoko Suzuki, "Did the English Seventeenth Century Really End at 1660? Subaltern Perspectives on the Continuing Impact of the English Civil Wars," in *Early Modern Histories of Time*, ed. Williams and Poole, pp. 230–49 (pp. 230–1).

[9] Ibid., p. 240.   [10] I discuss this in more detail in Chapter 5.

It is true that the theatres were reopened in 1660, thus ending the theatrical prohibition at the heart of this study, but, in many ways, 1660 is also a false turning point. As this chapter demonstrates, the 1660s marked not simply a change but a continuation of several dramatic conditions of the 1640s and 1650s. Perhaps the most obvious rebuttal to the "fresh start" theory of Restoration theatre is that sanctioned theatrical activity resumed in England in 1656, when William Davenant received permission to stage *The Siege of Rhodes* at Rutland House in September of that year. This performance of *The Siege of Rhodes* is a landmark in English theatre, bearing many of the hallmarks of "new" Restoration theatre: Catherine Coleman performed the role of Ianthe, the production featured elaborate moveable scenery by John Webb, and the text consisted of recitative proto-opera, all of which signalled the advent of a new theatrical tradition.[11] *The Siege of Rhodes* was preceded by Davenant's smaller-scale *The First Day's Entertainment* (its very title signals a new beginning), sanctioned by the Council of State and also performed at Rutland House, on 23 May 1656.[12] Davenant followed *Siege* with *The Cruelty of the Spaniards in Peru* (summer 1658) and *The History of Sir Francis Drake* (late 1658/early 1659). Davenant's career reflects how the Interregnum continued to shape dramatic activities into the Restoration, especially in the early years. He revived an expanded version of *The Siege of Rhodes* in 1663, with additional scenes, characters, and speeches. Having received permission to stage plays from Cromwell's government while the theatres were officially closed, Davenant continued to enjoy special treatment after the theatres reopened in 1660; Charles II granted him and Thomas Killigrew the exclusive right to stage plays. But while the two patentees enjoyed power and success, for the vast majority of theatrical professionals, the duopoly largely foreclosed the new opportunities promised by the reopened theatres.

Killigrew and Davenant's theatrical duopoly continued to limit theatrical activity in ways that recall the Interregnum era, but mostly go unnoticed in scholarly discourse. This chapter extends earlier work by scholars such as Rachel Willie and Emma Depledge who push back against the tradition of treating 1660 as a sharp boundary in dramatic history.[13] Noting Charles II's exclusive theatrical patents, as well as the high

---

[11] Janet Clare notes that Flecknoe's operatic *Ariadne Deserted by Theseus* predates Davenant's operatic features; moreover, she points out that stylistic elements of *The Siege of Rhodes* harken back to the pre-1642 court masque. Clare, *Drama of the English Republic*, p. 186.

[12] Jackson I. Cope, "Rhetorical Genres in Davenant's *First Day's Entertainment* at Rutland House," *Quarterly Journal of Speech*, 45.2 (1959), 191–4 (p. 191).

[13] See Willie, *Staging the Revolution*.

admission prices to Restoration theatre, Depledge observes that the theatrical duopoly "excluded spectators, performers and theatre managers who were no longer legally allowed to ply their trade."[14] An "underground theatre movement" appears to have persisted as a result of the continued restrictions on theatre, with drolls and other "alternative entertainments" associated with the Interregnum still performed even after the theatres were officially restored.[15] A recent essay by Janet Clare also "challenge[s] conventional scholarly periodization of theatre in which 1660 is a point of departure," noting instead several continuities across the traditional boundary of 1660, such as the continued popularity in print and performance of Civil War and Interregnum pamphlet plays, closet drama, and sanctioned plays after the Restoration.[16] Building on this work, this chapter attends to the practitioners whose theatrical activities continued to be stymied by governmental opposition. It also considers the alternatives they sought; during the Interregnum, as we have seen, some theatrical professionals turned to publishing playbooks to revive their dramatic livelihoods in a new medium.[17] After the theatres were restored, erstwhile and would-be actors continued to involve themselves in dramatic textual culture. Dramatic publishing in the Restoration, much like theatrical performance, followed a pattern of feast or famine: while the ambitious stationer Francis Kirkman acquired an outlaw status for his playbook piracies, Henry Herringman inherited Humphrey Moseley's (d. 30 January 1661) position as the pre-eminent dramatic and literary publisher of his time, along with many of the rights to Moseley's plays.[18] In the contexts of Restoration theatre and dramatic publication, then, success continued to be out of reach for many. Those whose dramatic fortunes declined during the Interregnum did not necessarily see them rise once the theatres were restored. As Interregnum dramatic practices endured, so too did attitudes: many characteristic features of Interregnum dramatic discourse – regarding pre-1642 drama primarily as printed artefacts, and examining these "old plays" with clarifying critical hindsight – endured into the period after 1660, and came to be defined as Restoration dramatic criticism.

---

[14] Depledge, *Shakespeare's Rise*, pp. 31–2.   [15] Ibid., pp. 31–4.

[16] Clare, "Acts of Oblivion"; on Interregnum closet drama and pamphlets in the Restoration, see Marissa Nicosia, "Couplets, Commonplaces, and the Creation of History," in *From Republic to Restoration*, ed. Clare, pp. 69–84.

[17] See Chapter 1; see also Nicosia, "Printing as Revival."

[18] C. William Miller, "Henry Herringman, Restoration Bookseller-Publisher," *Papers of the Bibliographical Society of America*, 42 (1948), 292–306.

Professionals Excluded from the Restoration Theatre Industry

In August 1642, Henry Herbert wrote in his office book: "here ended my allowance of plays, for the war began in August 1642."[19] As the Master of the Revels between 1623 and 1642, Herbert "was the recognized superior of all actors and theatre people in London,"[20] with the power to licence plays, players and playmakers, and regulate the erection of playhouses. During the theatre closures, Herbert retired quietly from public life.[21] On 20 June 1660, Charles II reinstated Herbert to his Master of the Revels post; Herbert soon began granting theatrical permissions, and the companies reflexively submitted to his authority.[22] On 14 August 1660, players represented by Nicholas Burt issued a promise that they would duly pay Herbert's fees for reviewing plays. Around the same time, a disabled war veteran named John Rogers petitioned the Crown for "a tolleration to erect a playhouse or to haue a share out of them already tollerated." Rogers had lost his entire estate "at the beginning of the late Calametys," and "lost his limbs and the vse thereof" serving in the wars, "in consideracion whereof, and being soe much deacreapitt as not to act any more wars," he asked for a new career in the theatre industry, promising to suppress any "riots, tumults or molestations" that might occur at playhouses. The Crown forwarded the request to Herbert – at first, even Charles II deferred to Herbert on theatrical matters – who hired Rogers for theatre security, granting him a weekly allowance for "guarding [the King's] playhouses from all molestations and injuries."[23] In the wide-open moment of the Restoration, all kinds of imaginative futures seemed possible. Rogers's request suggests that the public expected the restored theatres to provide opportunities, not only for former actors but also for those whose lives had been overturned during the recent crises. At least initially, this expectation was fulfilled. But the early optimism about renewed theatrical opportunities was mostly not borne out.

Theatrical professionals who had been underemployed for the previous two decades clearly thought their luck was finally changing. As Charles II

[19] N. W. Bawcutt, ed., *The Control and Censorship of Caroline Drama: The Records of Sir Henry Herbert, Master of the Revels 1623–1673* (Oxford: Oxford University Press, 1996), p. 211, entry 435.
[20] G. E. Bentley, "The Salisbury Court Theater and Its Boy Players," *Huntington Library Quarterly*, 40.2 (1977), 129–49 (p. 143).
[21] Richard Dutton, "Herbert, Sir Henry," in the *ODNB*, http://doi.org/10.1093/ref:odnb/13029.
[22] John Freehafer, "The Formation of the London Patent Companies in 1660," *Theatre Notebook*, 20 (1965), 6–30 (p. 14). Christopher Matusiak, "Was Shakespeare 'not a company keeper'?: William Beeston and MS Aubrey 8, fol. 45v," *Shakespeare Quarterly* 68.4 (2017), 351–373, p. 364.
[23] Joseph Quincy Adams, ed., *The Dramatic Records of Sir Henry Herbert Master of the Revels 1623–1673* (New York: Benjamin Blom, 1964), pp. 83–4, Document IV.

was preparing to land at Dover in 1659, playing resumed on a large scale in open defiance of the prohibition, shortly before the official Restoration. Three companies were active on the scene: at the Cockpit, the bookseller and former King's Men wardrobe keeper John Rhodes managed a young company that featured future stars Thomas Betterton and Edward Kynaston.[24] At the Red Bull performed another troupe, composed mostly of veteran "Old Actors," and led by Michael Mohun, who had been a promising young actor when he debuted around 1634. During the Civil Wars, Mohun fought as a soldier on the royalist side, distinguishing himself and earning the rank of major, and he continued to be known as "Major Mohun" in the Restoration.[25] At Salisbury Court, William Beeston managed a troupe that included Theophilus Bird senior and junior, as well as Beeston's son George.[26] When Charles II was restored on 24 May 1660, the existing bans on performance presumably lost their force. But Rhodes, Mohun, and Beeston were still technically operating outside the law, having no official licence.[27] Following old habits, Beeston sought out Herbert's permission – the Beeston family had long operated in the theatre industry, and had extensive ties with Herbert. In June 1660, Herbert approved Beeston's request "to Sett, Lett or vse" Salisbury Court as a playhouse, "Prouided that noe persons be admitted to Act in the said Play house but such as shall be allowed by the Master of his Majesties Office of the Revels."[28] On 20 August 1660, Herbert issued a statement "To the Actors of the Playhouses called the Red Bull, the Cockpitt, and Theatre in Salesbury Court,"[29] seemingly confident that the other companies would also recognize his long-standing and restored authority.

But the theatrical ambitions of Rhodes, Mohun, Beeston, and Herbert, as well as many other lesser-known and would-be theatre professionals, were dashed by the theatrical duopoly that Charles II granted to Killigrew and Davenant on 21 August 1660. Killigrew and Davenant had petitioned the King for exclusive power to regulate their own companies and playhouses, falsely claiming that Herbert consented to the arrangement.[30] The King's patent gave them "full power & authority" to "Erect two companies

[24] See Paula R. Backscheider, "Behind City Walls: Restoration Actors in the Drapers' Company," *Theatre Survey*, 45.1 (2004), 75–87 (p. 76).

[25] John H. Astington, "Acting in the Field," *Theatre Notebook*, 60.3 (2006), 129–33; John H. Astington, "Mohun [Moone], Michael," in the *ODNB*, http://doi.org/10.1093/ref:odnb/18885.

[26] See Freehafer, "Formation," pp. 7–10; Matusiak, "Company Keeper," p. 364.

[27] Freehafer, "Formation," p. 13.   [28] Adams, *Sir Henry Herbert*, p. 81, Document I.

[29] Ibid., pp. 83–4, Document IV.

[30] Clare, "Davenant's *Cruelty of the Spaniards*," p. 833; Freehafer, "Formation," p. 15.

of players ... to purchase, build and erect, or hire at their charge ... two houses or theatres."[31] Killigrew was also empowered to "silence" players if they did not submit to his authority.[32] Such an arrangement was unprecedented, and Herbert protested, noting that the patents infringed upon the long-standing authority of his office as the Master of the Revels.[33] Previously having granted permission to Beeston to manage Salisbury Court in June 1660, Herbert on 5 November 1660 complained that Davenant "erected a company of Players at Salsbery Court ... by his owne pretended Authority, and Authorised them to playe Playes, and took the profits &c., in defiance of the authority of the master of the Reuells."[34]

Herbert strenuously insisted on his old authority for a decade after the Restoration. Killigrew and Davenant closely guarded their new privileges, and consistently undermined Herbert's traditional powers.[35] At first they agreed to pay Herbert fees for reviewing plays, but took care that he could not exploit this role. In a petition filed against Herbert, Davenant stated that while Herbert did not have the authority to "give Plaiers any license or authoritie to play," he "was allowed the correction of plays, and fees for so doing."[36] Davenant requested that the Crown limit Herbert's fees so that they did not amount to "extortion," and prescribe how long Herbert "shall keep plays in his hands, in pretence of correcting them."[37] Eventually, the patentees flouted even this curtailed role: in 1662, Herbert complained that Killigrew and Davenant's companies "doe refuse to pay the said fees and profitts formerly payd and due to the said office."[38]

In his initial protest against Killigrew and Davenant's proposed patents, Herbert presciently noted that their duopoly "is destructive to a hundred persons at least that depende upon the Quality and the Houses and Haue no other Livelyhood."[39] What would happen to people like John Rogers, the veteran turned theatre security guard? Herbert's objection recalls earlier complaints about the financial effects of the theatrical prohibition in the Interregnum, seen, for instance, in *The Actors Remonstrance* (1643), which evokes the players, tiremen, theatre vendors, and their families, tipped into poverty by theatrical restrictions. But Herbert was both victim and victimizer, as players were caught between the patentees and a Master of the Revels who insisted on his old authority. After Killigrew filed a monarchical warrant to sanction Rhodes's, Beeston's, and Mohun's

[31] Adams, *Sir Henry Herbert*, pp. 87–8, Document VII.   [32] Freehafer, "Formation," p. 14.
[33] Adams, *Sir Henry Herbert*, p. 86, Document VI.   [34] Ibid., pp. 105–6, Document XIX.
[35] Ibid., p. 113, Document XXIII; p. 119, Document XXVI.   [36] Ibid., p. 119, Document XXVI.
[37] Ibid., pp. 119–20, Document XXVI.   [38] Ibid., p. 123, Document XXIX.
[39] Ibid., p. 89, Document VIII.

companies for violating his patent, accusing them of performing "scandalous plays, raising the price, and acknowledging noe authority," Mohun struck a bargain with Herbert, agreeing to pay him a weekly fee in exchange for protection from Killigrew.[40] Herbert could not deliver on this promise, and in October 1660 a disgruntled Mohun stopped paying him, noting that "so farre Sir Henry Herbert hath bene from protecting us, that he has been a continual disturbance unto us."[41] Herbert's irrelevance became embarrassingly apparent. In 1662, the prominent actor Thomas Betterton and other Davenant actors assaulted a Master of the Revels messenger, in a clear sign of disrespect to the office.[42]

Between 1660 and 1670, Herbert filed a series of complaints, petitions, and lawsuits against Davenant, Killigrew and their players,[43] in which he repeatedly – and increasingly desperately – pressed for his own rights, gleaned from monarchical patents, precedent, and loyalty. Herbert's insistence on the "ancient" authority of his office became a common refrain. He noted that he had executed this office "for about 40 years, in the times of King James, and of King Charles, both of blessed memory, with excepcion only to the time of the late horrid rebellion."[44] Herbert, ignoring the Act of Oblivion, appealed to historical continuity, while Killigrew and Davenant enjoyed the advantages of the myth of discontinuity and ostensible fresh beginnings that characterized the Restoration. Another of Herbert's breviates against Davenant reached even further into the past, invoking the authority granted to the Master of the Revels by every English monarch since Henry VIII,[45] and noting the Elizabethan statute that "the King cannot grante away an incident to an office, though the office bee in the King's Gift."[46] Herbert raised the spectre of the dead Charles I to sway his son, noting that the theatrical duopoly was "destructive to the powers granted ... by the Late Kinge of Blessed Memory."[47] A related tactic was to remind Charles II of Davenant's apparent disloyalty

---

[40] See Freehafer, "Formation," pp. 15–19; Backscheider, "Behind City Walls," p. 82.

[41] Adams, *Sir Henry Herbert*, pp. 94–5, Document XIV.

[42] Betterton was eventually indicted for the assault. See Hotson, *Commonwealth and Restoration Stage*, pp. 210–13; David Roberts, *Thomas Betterton: The Greatest Actor of the Restoration Stage* (Cambridge: Cambridge University Press, 2010), pp. 74–5.

[43] See Adams, *Sir Henry Herbert*, p. 101, Document XVI; pp. 102–3, Document XVIII; pp. 104–6, Document XIX; pp. 108–10, Document XXI; pp. 110–13, Document XXII.

[44] Ibid., p. 85, Document VI; p. 92, Document XI. See also p. 93, Document XII, where Herbert invokes the "grant vnder the Great Seale of England," which gave him jurisdiction over "plays, players, and playmakers, and the permission for erecting of playhouses," an office held "by mee for almost fforty years, with Exception only to the late times."

[45] Adams, *Sir Henry Herbert*, p. 102, Document XVIII.   [46] Ibid., p. 104, Document XVIII.

[47] Ibid., p. 89, Document VIII.

during the Interregnum. Herbert attempted to discredit Davenant by noting that he "exercised the Office of Master of the Reuells to Oliuer the Tyrant," who tolerated the performance of his plays.[48] He claimed that Davenant's "The First and Second Parte of Peru" (i.e., *The Cruelty of the Spaniards in Peru* and *The History of Sir Francis Drake*) kowtowed to Cromwellian politics, foregrounding the cruelty of colonial Spain to make "Oliver's crueltyes appear mercys" in comparison.[49]

Herbert never regained his old authority. By 1669, he was still appealing to "his Majestie's commission, granted to the Master of the Revells, under the great seale, for the authorizing of all public shews."[50] Herbert finally faded from public view in 1670, and died in 1673, whereupon Killigrew assumed the office of the Master of the Revels. Joseph Quincy Adams observes that after the Restoration, Herbert "struggled hard to re-establish the Office in its former powers; but the times had changed, and he never fully succeeded."[51] Indeed, one might say that the times had not changed enough since the 1650s. In many ways, Herbert's post-1660 theatrical career had more in common with theatrical practitioners' lives during the prohibition, when their activities were curtailed by governmental pressures. For those shut out of the theatrical duopoly – the majority of former or would-be theatre professionals – the theatre continued to be a "dead" opportunity.

Other theatrical professionals hoping for theatrical success in the restored theatres also had their ambitions quashed. As we have seen, the actor and theatre manager Michael Mohun, lacking a monarchical patent, sought out Herbert's authority. Mohun also apparently sought playing rights from Humphrey Moseley, who held the publishing rights to many of the pre-1642 titles that provided the foundation of the early Restoration theatrical repertoire. This arrangement has a kind of symmetry, given that Moseley had acquired many of his dramatic manuscripts from theatre companies during the lean years of the Interregnum. In a letter of 30 August 1660 to Herbert, Moseley certifies that Mohun sought and received the rights to perform his plays, to the exclusion of other companies.[52]

---

[48] Ibid., p. 122, Document XXVIII.
[49] Ibid., p. 85, Document VI. This has some measure of truth, as Davenant revised the plays after the restoration. See Clare, "Davenant's *Cruelty of the Spaniards*" and Watkins, "Protectorate Playhouse."
[50] Adams, *Sir Henry Herbert*, p. 138, Document XLI.   [51] Ibid., p. 9.
[52] Ibid., p. 90, Document IX.

It is not surprising that in the transitional days of the Restoration theatre, practitioners relied on printed playbooks for scripts. But why turn to Moseley, whose rights were only those of a publisher? The early Restoration theatre lacked institutional memory; without a firm sense of which theatre companies owned what, the publication rights of the stationer offered some reassuring clarity. Julie Stone Peters notes that "Moseley seems to have assumed that, since there were no clear successors to the pre-Interregnum companies, and since he held the *publication* rights to many of the King's Men's plays, he had authority to designate acting rights as well."[53] This arrangement, if valid, clearly had some advantages: in addition to having exclusive performance rights to Moseley's popular titles, Mohun would have playing rights to the patentees' own works, including Killigrew's *Princess* and several of Davenant's plays and masques, to which Moseley held the rights.[54]

The unlicenced theatres vexed Killigrew and Davenant. On 20 August 1660, Davenant issued a warrant stating that the Cockpit, Salisbury Court, and the Red Bull were all in operation "without the least colour of authority" and requested that "all constables and other officers of the peace … suppress and disperse" the acting companies. Although the players had been previously licenced by Herbert, the royal patent issued on 21 August 1660 bolstered Davenant's complaint, and the companies for a time ceased their activities.[55] Killigrew exerted his right to "silence" the companies on three separate occasions, issuing fines and sanctions between the end of July and early October 1660 (before the royal patent of 21 August, Killigrew acted under the authority of a royal warrant of 9 July).[56] John Freehafer notes, however, that patentees underestimated "the toughness of a band of actors whose leaders had had almost unparalleled experience in defying authority of every sort, civil and military, Puritan and Royalist."[57] Playing continued, and Killigrew eventually resorted to imprisonment: a letter from Herbert to Mohun from 13 October 1660 notes the "late restraint" of Mohun's actors and their recent "restitution" to "liberty."[58] Imprisonment, of course, was also a tactic employed by Parliamentary soldiers against illegal players in the Interregnum.

The patentees wanted the extra-legal companies to come to terms with them, so that they could benefit from their human and material resources. Mohun, Beeston, and Rhodes were understandably reluctant to submit to

[53] Peters, *Theatre of the Book*, p. 343.   [54] Freehafer, "Formation," pp. 17–18.   [55] Ibid., p. 17.
[56] Ibid., pp. 14–19.   [57] Ibid., p. 15.   [58] Ibid., pp. 15, 19.

the disadvantageous terms that duopoly holders would invariably apply to their subordinates. But, after being repeatedly silenced and imprisoned, the companies finally yielded to the patentees. Mohun's Red Bull players provided the basis of Killigrew's King's Company; Davenant's Duke's Company drew from Rhodes's young Cockpit actors[59] and co-opted Beeston's newly renovated Salisbury Court theatre (Beeston's players apparently moving to the newly vacant Cockpit).[60] Being absorbed into the theatrical duopoly must have been humiliating for these well-connected and seasoned theatre professionals: Mohun's distinguished service in the wars, for instance, did not secure him special privileges, apart from evading Killigrew for a time. Rhodes was reduced mostly to provincial performances, a "bitter pill" for one who had planned to regularly stage performances in the London theatres.[61] By 1665, Rhodes had left the industry entirely, identifying himself only as a draper of Jewen Street, "aged sixty and upwards."[62]

Beeston's company was co-opted by George Jolly, another theatre manager whose experience exemplifies the trials of post-1660 theatrical professionals excluded from the duopoly.[63] An actor involved in illegal performance in England in the late 1640s, Jolly left for Germany in 1648 following tighter sanctions, where he staged plays for exiled royalist communities.[64] Jolly performed elaborate and flattering spectacles for Charles II on the Continent, and returned to England at the Restoration. Jolly appears on the English theatre scene by November 1660, when he petitioned Charles II for a licence to stage plays.[65] Charles, likely recalling Jolly's Continental performances, on 24 December 1660 granted Jolly a separate theatre patent, said to "be effectual notwithstanding any former grant made by us to our trusty and well beloved Servant Thomas Killegrew Esqre and Sir William Davenant."[66] Jolly staged plays at the Cockpit for part of 1661 to December 1662.[67]

---

[59] Ibid., pp. 6–8, 19–25. Milhous and Hume, "New Light," pp. 499–501, 509. Thomas Betterton was co-opted by Killigrew but then restored to Davenant's company. Freehafer, "Formation," p. 25.

[60] Leslie Hotson, "George Jolly, Actor-Manager," *Studies in Philology* 20.4 (1923), 422–43 (p. 431).

[61] Roberts, *Betterton*, p. 74.

[62] Rhodes, a wardrobe keeper before the wars, was a member of the Drapers' Company, and Backscheider notes that Rhodes may have started building his theatre company in the mid-1650s, partly by hiring actors as apprentice drapers. "Behind City Walls," pp. 78–9, 82–3.

[63] Freehafer, "Formation," p. 29.

[64] On performance on the Continent during the prohibition, see Jerzy Limon, *Gentlemen of a Company: English Players in Central and Eastern Europe, 1590–1660* (Cambridge: Cambridge University Press, 1985), pp. 14, 59–60; Milhous and Hume, "New Light," pp. 489–91.

[65] Hotson, "George Jolly," p. 431.   [66] Qtd. by ibid., p. 432.

[67] Ibid., p. 433; Freehafer, "Formation," p. 28.

Davenant and Killigrew recognized Jolly as a serious threat to their duopoly, and contrived to cheat him out of his patent. Hotson carefully traces the steps of Davenant and Killigrew's "chicanery" by consulting a series of primary documents.[68] Essentially, Davenant and Killigrew had previously agreed to rent the advantages associated with Jolly's patent (allowing them use of his theatrical space, for instance), paying him a weekly fee. In early 1663, Jolly left London to perform plays in Norwich, with a repertoire that included J. Cook's *Greene's Tu Quoque*, John Ford's *Tis Pity She's a Whore*, Fletcher's *The Little Thief*, and Philip Massinger's *A New Way to Pay Old Debts*.[69] When Jolly left town, Davenant and Killigrew approached the King, falsely claiming that Jolly had sold his patent to them outright, and asking that his licence be made over to their names. The King approved the request, drafted a new licence to Killigrew and Davenant, and revoked Jolly's patent.[70]

Jolly, hardened from his experience in the difficult performance conditions of Interregnum London and Germany, continued to stage plays illegally in London. He staged "Dr. Fostus" in 1663, and in 1665, the French visitor Chappuzeau commented on the theatrical season of "un troisième," presumably with Jolly as the third patent holder in addition to Killigrew and Davenant.[71] In March 1667, Killigrew ordered Jolly to cease his theatrical activities, about which he had been "several times commanded to the contrary." Jolly defied this command, too, and another of April 1667. In late 1667, Jolly reached an arrangement where he stopped independent playing activities in exchange for managing a theatre nursery, training junior actors for Killigrew's and Davenant's companies, a role he seems to have carried out until 1673. The Nursery could not rival the King's and Duke's Companies, which poached its best talents and took a portion of its profits.[72] The determined Jolly ended his career in straitened circumstances: he states that Killigrew "unjustly opposed George Jolly to the Ruine of himselfe his wife & Children."[73] The illegal playing, arrests, and financial ruin that had characterized Interregnum theatrical activity continued even after playing officially resumed.

Finally, the long career of William Beeston (c. 1610–82) also had a troubled end due to Killigrew and Davenant's rapaciousness. Describing

---

[68] Hotson, "George Jolly," pp. 434–7.
[69] Bernard M. Wagner, "George Jolly at Norwich," *The Review of English Studies*, 6.24 (1930), 449–52.
[70] Hotson, "George Jolly," p. 437.
[71] Wagner, "George Jolly at Norwich," p. 451; Hotson, "George Jolly," p. 440.
[72] Hotson, "George Jolly," p. 441, 443.   [73] Qtd. by ibid., p. 439.

himself as "bred up in the art of stage playing," Beeston had extensive familial and personal experience in the theatrical industry.[74] Christopher Matusiak has assiduously chronicled the Beeston family's theatrical exploits across the seventeenth century.[75] William's father Christopher Beeston was a major theatre impresario, governing the Cockpit Theatre from 1616 onward. William joined his father in managing the Cockpit in the 1636–7 season, installing the boy troupe which came to be known as Beeston's Boys. In the late 1630s and early 1640s, William seemed to be on the cusp of a brilliant theatrical career: he took over a thriving business following his father's death in 1638, receiving an annuity of 20 pounds and several valuable dramatic manuscripts. His widowed stepmother Elizabeth Beeston and her new husband Lewis Kirke took charge of the Cockpit, while William became its "Governour & Instructer" of the young actors Michael Mohun, Robert Shatterel, Nicholas Burt, and John Lacy.[76] Beeston faced some setbacks – in 1640, Davenant briefly displaced him as the governor of the Cockpit after its actors staged an unlicenced play critical of the King. In 1641, however, Davenant was imprisoned for his involvement in the Army Plot (an attempted military coup against Parliament), and Beeston was back as the Cockpit's governor.[77]

The closure of the theatres in 1642 obviously disrupted Beeston's career, but Beeston kept active in the industry. He staged illegal performances, unsuccessfully attempted to revive a group of boy players at the Cockpit in 1650, and, in 1652, purchased Salisbury Court theatre, where his Beeston's Boys performed between 1652 and 1656.[78] In a paratext appended to *Love's Dominion* (1654), Richard Flecknoe identified Beeston as the best person to manage "the REFORMED Stage," due to "his long Practice and Experience in this way, as also for having brought up most of the Actors extant."[79] But after the theatres reopened, the internal and external expectations that Beeston would be a prominent figure in the

[74] G. E. Bentley, *The Jacobean and Caroline Stage*, 7 vols. (Oxford: Clarendon Press, 1941–68), II, p. 370.
[75] See Christopher Matusiak, "Christopher Beeston and the Caroline Office of Theatrical 'Governor,'" *Early Theatre*, 11.2 (2008), 39–56.
[76] Matusiak, "Company Keeper," p. 358.
[77] Christopher Matusiak, "Beeston, Kirke, and the Cockpit's Management," p. 167; Matthew Steggle, *Richard Brome: Place and Politics on the Caroline Stage* (Manchester: Manchester University Press, 2004), pp. 11, 157.
[78] Schoch, *Writing the History of the British Stage*, p. 63; Helen Moore, "Admirable Inventions: Francis Kirkman and the Translation of Romance in the 1650s," in *Seventeenth-Century Fiction: Text and Transmission*, ed. Jacqueline Glomski and Isabelle Moreau (Oxford: Oxford University Press, 2016), pp. 143–58 (p. 147).
[79] Bentley, *The Jacobean and Caroline Stage*, II, pp. 373–4.

industry did not come to pass. The duopoly granted to Beeston's old rival Davenant effectively excluded Beeston from any significant role in the industry. Beeston obtained a grant from his old associate Henry Herbert, and briefly re-formed Beeston's Boys at Salisbury Court in summer 1660. But Davenant and Killigrew's patents entitled them to co-opt Beeston's talent and theatrical space, and, Matusiak notes, "the legitimacy of the license Herbert granted him evaporated."[80] Beeston continued to stage plays illegally, and was arrested in 1663 and 1664 "for acting stage playes without leave."[81] Evidently unable to compete with the duopoly, Beeston eventually joined it, becoming an actor with Killigrew's King's Company after 1666.[82] The Great Fire of 1666 destroyed Salisbury Court and with it Beeston's investment; another fire of 1672 that compromised the King's Company drove Beeston to performances at seasonal fairs to make a living, a far cry from the elite theatre to which he was accustomed.[83]

Despite the troubled ending to his storied theatrical career, Beeston's legacy included perpetuating the memory of pre-1642 theatre. Thanks to Beeston's transgenerational theatrical memory (which included his father Christopher's stories from the early seventeenth century), Dryden called him "the chronicle of the stage."[84] In the 1680s, the biographer John Aubrey called on the elderly Beeston, who provided him with anecdotes about Jonson, Fletcher, Shakespeare, and other dramatic figures; Aubrey's Beeston notes are now regarded as an important archive of evidence for Shakespeare's biography.[85] Those who had weathered the closure of the theatres provided key insights into dramatic history that were recorded in the later seventeenth century. As I will discuss below, by the 1650s Beeston had already acquired his reputation as one who preserved and embodied pre-1642 theatrical memory.

Along with the prominent theatre professionals Herbert, Mohun, Rhodes, Jolly, and Beeston, there must have been many lesser-known and would-be theatrical personnel who found the Restoration theatre almost as inhospitable to their participation as it had been during the Interregnum. In at least one case, an actor's career seems to have fared better during the theatrical prohibition than after the Restoration: in 1652, Nicholas Spencer was advertised as performing illegally at the Red Bull;[86] there is no evidence this performance was disrupted. In 1661, Herbert gave

[80] Matusiak, "Company Keeper," p. 365.
[81] TNA LC 5/185, fol. 70v; LC 5/186, fol. 13. Qtd. by Matusiak, "Company Keeper," p. 366.
[82] Andrew Gurr, "Beeston [Hutchinson], William," in the *ODNB*, http://doi.org/10.1093/ref:odnb/67810.
[83] Matusiak, "Company Keeper," p. 367.   [84] Qtd. by ibid., p. 353.   [85] Ibid., pp. 353, 351.
[86] *Mercurius Democritus*, 16–22 December 1652.

Spencer permission to act, but he was prevented by Davenant "from exercising his quality by threats and arrests, and by paying of five and twenty shillings in money."[87] Apart from a select few, then, for most, the hard theatrical conditions of the 1640s and 1650s continued even after the theatres were restored; as we shall see, partly as a result of this, so too did the ideas that characterized Interregnum dramatic discourse.

Francis Kirkman and the Pivot to Printed Drama

Francis Kirkman (1632–c. 1680), another figure who dabbled in illegal performance in the Interregnum, turned his attention towards printed drama in this period, continuing in this role after the theatres reopened. In 1652, the young Kirkman dedicated his self-published translation of *Loves and Adventures of Clerio and Lozia* (1652) to William Beeston; the dedication reveals both his appreciation for the pre-1642 dramatic past and his ambition to be involved in illegal performance. Between 1650 and 1652, Beeston was training boy players at the Cockpit; Kirkman's dedication inserts himself into the company's activities, bearing witness to Beeston's dramatic judgement: "Divers times (in my hearing) to the admiration of the whol Company," Kirkman writes, "you have most judiciously discoursed of poesie." Kirkman also suggests that Beeston should stage his translated romance: "you will find much newness in the Story, worthy an excellent Poet to insoul it for the Stage, where it wil receive ful perfection."[88] Clearly, the young Kirkman had caught the theatre bug; twenty years later in his autobiography *The Unlucky Citizen* (1673), Kirkman refers to his youthful "itch for performance" during the Interregnum, which he claims was satisfied by a few performances on the illicit stage. If this is true, it may have been under Beeston's management at Salisbury Court.[89]

Richard Schoch makes a case for Kirkman's consistent investment in theatricality from the Interregnum into the Restoration: "Kirkman's dedication of *Clerio and Lozia* imagined a life in performance that political circumstances would not permit for another eight years. Yet when the moment came he was ready. Soon after the return of the Cavaliers and the reopening of the theatres in 1660, and to meet the consequent heightened

---

[87] Adams, *Sir Henry Herbert*, p. 104, Document XVIII.
[88] Francis Kirkman, "Dedication," in Antoine Du Périer, *Loves and Adventures of Clerio and Lozia*, trans. Francis Kirkman (London: J.M. for William Ley, 1652), sig. A2r.
[89] Schoch, *Writing the History of the British Stage*, p. 64.

demand of dramatic works, Kirkman began publishing plays."[90] But why, given his early theatrical ambitions to "insoul" plays on stage, did Kirkman turn so decidedly to printed drama after the theatres actually reopened? In his edition of *The Thracian Wonder*, Kirkman explains his ambitions for a rapid and copious dramatic publishing agenda, furnished by his extensive collection of dramatic manuscripts: "I have several others that I intend for you suddenly ... I have several Manuscripts of this nature, written by worthy Authors, and I account it much pity they should now lye dormant, and buried in oblivion, since ingenuity is likely to be encouraged, by reason of the happy Restoration of our Liberties."[91] Kirkman obviously saw the Restoration as a moment where dramatic demand would be increased by the return of Cavaliers and Cavalier culture, but there is no indication he linked his publishing agenda with an intention to transmit playbooks into a "life in performance."[92] Nevertheless, Schoch argues that Kirkman "brought a *theatrical* outlook to the entire enterprise" of dramatic publication.[93] Even his comprehensive catalogues of printed drama, ostensibly staunch artefacts of print culture, appear to point back towards the theatre; the catalogue served as an "*envoi*, sending the reader on a new journey ... back to the scene of playhouse origins ... The overriding message of the catalogue," Schoch continues, "was that behind nearly every instance of printed drama ... stands a theatrical *a priori*."[94] But Schoch mischaracterizes Kirkman's enthusiasm for the theatre as persistent and unchanging. Paradoxically, the reopening of the theatres only encouraged Kirkman to produce more printed drama, not to act in plays, produce playbooks that would be performed by theatre companies, or even to go to the theatre.

In fact, Kirkman's youthful theatrical enthusiasm of 1652 did not endure intact into the Restoration. In *The Unlucky Citizen*, Kirkman indicates he does not think particularly highly of stage plays. He recalls that during the Interregnum, "I have had so great an *Itch* at *Stage-playing*, that I have been upon the Stage, not only in private to entertain Friends, but also on a *publique Theatre*, there I have Acted, but not much nor often, and that *Itch* is so well laid and over, that I can content my self with seeing

[90] Schoch, *Writing the History of the British Stage*, p. 64; see also R. C. Bald, "Francis Kirkman, Bookseller and Author," *Modern Philology*, 41.1 (1943), 17–32 (p. 23); Johan Gerritsen, "The Dramatic Piracies of 1661," *Studies in Bibliography*, 11 (1958), 117–31 (p. 117).

[91] Francis Kirkman, "The Stationer to the Reader," in *The Thracian Wonder* (London: Francis Kirkman, 1661), sig. A2r.

[92] Bald, "Francis Kirkman," p. 23; Gerritsen, "Dramatic Piracies," p. 117.

[93] Schoch, *Writing the History of the British Stage*, p. 57. Emphasis Schoch's.   [94] Ibid., p. 61

two or three Plays in a Year." Kirkman's theatrical "itch," related to both playing and playgoing, is satisfied and "over"; he is content to see only a couple of plays each year, and not bother with acting at all. Kirkman's desire to see no more than "two or three plays in a year" is dwarfed by the more than 800 printed playbooks he held in his personal collection, which he offered for lending and listed in his catalogues.

Kirkman did dabble in theatrical production after the Restoration; he wrote, staged, and published a one-act political play, *The Presbyterian Lash* (1661), at the Pye Tavern in Aldgate (another performance outside Davenant and Killigrew's duopoly).[95] For the most part, however, Kirkman was focused on printed drama that had no contemporary counterpart on stage. In 1661, he published several plays: Webster and Rowley's *A Cure for a Cuckold*, *Gammer Gurton's Needle*, *Tom Tyler his Wife*, *Band, Cuff and Ruff*, and J. C.'s *Two Merry Milkmaids*.[96] These works were old plays, their theatrical attributions referring to performance conditions before 1642. *Gammer Gurton's Needle* and *Tom Tyler* were pre-professional Tudor interludes, each of which alludes to its century-old performance tradition on its title page, respectively, "Played on the Stage near a hundred years ago" and "AN EXCELLENT OLD PLAY AS It was Printed and Acted about a hundred Years ago." The two plays were also printed in blackletter, further signalling their antiquity.[97] When published in 1661, the two plays would be of interest perhaps to a niche audience, but unlikely to be a large draw. Charles Whitworth, *Gammer Gurton's Needle*'s modern editor, describes the play's "unexpected appearance" in 1661, observing "it must have seemed quaint, to say the least"; he ascribes Kirkman's publication of *Gammer Gurton's Needle* to his "antiquarian enthusiasm."[98]

Kirkman also cast the more recent theatrical past as ancient history. He published the first edition of Webster and Rowley's *A Cure for a Cuckold* (Q1 1661, first performed c. 1624–5), with a vague theatrical attribution: "As it hath been several times Acted with great Applause." In his preface, Kirkman calls it "an excellent old play" (the same descriptor applied to the

---

[95] Isaac Stephens discusses the performance of the one-act *The Presbyterian Lash* at the Pye Tavern in Aldgate in "Memory's Lash: Staging Parochial Politics in Restoration London." Thanks are due to Isaac for sharing this article with me prior to publication.

[96] Bald, "Francis Kirkman," p. 23.   [97] See Lesser, "Typographical Nostalgia."

[98] Charles Whitworth, ed. *Gammer Gurton's Needle* (London: A&C Black, 1997), p. xxi. I discuss Kirkman's editions of *Gammer* and *Tom Tyler* in more detail in "A Century of Drama: Restoration Reprints of Tudor Drama," in *Reprints and Revivals*, ed. Eoin Price and Harry Newman (Cambridge: Cambridge University Press, forthcoming).

century-old *Tom Tyler*) and notes that "several persons remember the acting of it."[99] Kirkman clearly has no direct experience of *A Cure for a Cuckold*'s pre-1642 performance; as with *Tom Tyler*, his experience of the stage play is limited to theatrical memory accessible only by the text and second-hand reports. His interest in the theatre is primarily *historical*, nostalgic, and largely imaginary: he does not particularly want to actually stage plays or go to the theatre, but he does take pains to invoke the now-distant phenomena of pre-1642 theatre through his printed productions.

For many born in the late 1620s, 1630s, and 1640s, English drama was first and foremost textual. Indeed, textuality dominated dramatic consumption even after the theatres reopened in 1660: as Milhous and Hume have shown, unlike in the pre-1642 period, after 1660, it was cheaper to purchase a play quarto than it was to attend the expensive licenced theatres.[100] People born in these middle decades of the seventeenth century, accustomed to experiencing drama primarily as text, became important dramatic commentators, stationers, and playwrights of the Restoration. Born in 1631, John Dryden's ideas about drama seem to rely on forms of reading and attitudes fostered by the theatrical prohibition. In *An Essay of Dramatic Poesie* (1668), Dryden frames drama as poetry, directly borrowing from 1640s and 1650s dramatic discourse. As Ann Baynes Coiro notes, in the *Essay*, the character Neander (a fictional surrogate for Dryden himself) "deploys a key rhetorical switch that royalists had devised when the stage was dark: theatre becomes 'poesie.'"[101] Moreover, in his dedication to *The Spanish Friar* (1681), Dryden suggests that the text is the best way to encounter drama. "The lights, the scenes, the habits, and above all, the grace of action" of stage plays Dryden deems to be "false beauties" and "no more lasting than a rainbow," for, as he explains:

> when the actor ceases to shine upon them, when he guilds them no longer with his reflection, they vanish in a twinkling. I have sometimes wondered, in the reading, what was become of those glaring colours ... [thoughts and words] are but confusedly judged in the vehemence of action: all things are there beheld, as in a hasty motion, where the objects onely glide before the eye and disappear.[102]

---

[99] Francis Kirkman, "The Stationer, to the Judicious Reader," in John Webster and William Rowley, *A Cure for a Cuckold* (London: Francis Kirkman, 1661), sig. A2r.

[100] Judith Milhous and Robert D. Hume, *The Publication of Plays in London, 1660–1800: Playwrights, Publishers, and the Market* (London: British Library, 2015), p. 13.

[101] Coiro, "Reading," p. 552.

[102] John Dryden, "Dedication," in John Dryden, *The Spanish Friar* (London: Richard and Jacob Tonson, 1681), sig. A3v.

Dryden's sentiment recalls James Shirley's description of the stage from the Beaumont and Fletcher folio (1647) as a "conjuring glass," with the dramatic landscape "as suddenly removed as represented." In his dedication, Dryden charts for himself a permanent transition from stage to page as the proper medium of dramatic consumption: "As 'tis my interest to please my audience, so 'tis my ambition to be read."[103] Samuel Johnson called Dryden "the father of English criticism," and one can trace Dryden's advocacy of the benefits of dramatic reading forward to the print-centric dramatic views of Johnson and the Romantics.[104] But the origins of Dryden's sentiments can be traced backward to the era of the theatrical prohibition.

In *The Unlucky Citizen*, Kirkman (b. 1632) likewise describes the distractions of performance: he suggests that the benefits of playgoing are lost on the average spectator. While stage plays "are the fittest Divertisments for our *English Gentry*," Kirkman explains, "I know that all sorts of people, of all quallities go to *see* them, and *see* them I may well say, and that properly, for they do nothing else, not understanding them at all." Most spectators focus on laughter, dancing, music, "painting," the handsomeness of the actors, a clown's lines, other audience members – in short everything "except the cheifest Part, the end of the *Play*, the *Soul* and *Plot of it*" which "but few of the *Vulgar* understand."[105] Like Dryden, Kirkman's statement recalls Shirley's Interregnum-era warnings about the bewitching nature of performance, which offers diversion but not understanding. Yet, in his advocacy of dramatic reading over performance, Shirley was finding a silver lining of the theatrical prohibition. Kirkman and Dryden, both with access to and involvement with the theatre, still prefer and advocate for dramatic reading and publication over performance.

Jody Greene argues that Kirkman's career demonstrates his "obsession" "with the matter of print," evidenced across the genres of romance, drama, and autobiography, of which his *Unlucky Citizen* represents an early instance.[106] Kirkman stated that he was "desirous to appear in the World like somebody," acquiring external confirmation of his existence

[103] Ibid.
[104] Marta Straznicky, "Introduction," in *The Book of the Play*, ed. Straznicky, pp. 1–20 (p. 2).
[105] Francis Kirkman, *The Unlucky Citizen* (London: Francis Kirkman, 1673), p. 261.
[106] Jody Greene, "Francis Kirkman's Counterfeit Authority: Autobiography, Subjectivity, Print," *Papers of the Modern Language Association*, 121.1 (2006), 17–32 (p. 19).

through the material manifestation of print. As Greene explains, for Kirkman, "The state of not being published is … a transitory, developmental stage that needs to be surpassed if this aspiring author – and subject – is to avoid disappearing."[107] Kirkman's private literary ambitions translate into a notion of dramatic identity that relies on print publication. For a play, the state of not being published, only staged, is a transitory, developmental stage that needs to be surpassed if the play is to avoid disappearing: a play's existence fundamentally depends on print. Kirkman's catalogues only included printed drama, not only for practical economic reasons, but also because these are the only ones, for all intents and purposes, to properly "exist." This represents a key shift in dramatic thinking that emerged thanks to the theatrical prohibition, a shift that informed dramatic criticism in the Restoration and beyond, and continues to inform scholarly practice. Before the theatres closed, a play's existence was largely tied to performance; this recalls Stanley Wells and Gary Taylor's well-known pronouncement in *The Oxford Shakespeare*: "it is in performance that the plays lived and had their being."[108] Accordingly, relatively few commercial plays made it into print between 1567 and 1642; print publication wasn't absolutely necessary, since plays "were published by being acted."[109] Wells and Taylor's performance-centric view of drama aligns, perhaps, with the pre-1642 reception of plays, but this definition of plays no longer obtains. While performance usually precedes print, for us to study plays, they must have some textual instantiation, at the very least a fragment, allusion, or title in the historical record. These scholarly conditions were set in motion in 1642, and perpetuated by drama enthusiasts like Kirkman and Dryden who continued to describe dramatic encounters primarily in terms of dramatic reading and print publication, even when offered an alternative.

For Kirkman, while the Restoration seemed to present new opportunities for printed drama, the kind of dramatic printed matter he produced – catalogues, drolls, pirated editions of popular professional drama, and old plays by lesser-known authors – suggest that he was on the margins of dramatic print publication, much like he had been in the theatre industry. In 1661, Kirkman started working at the sign of John Fletcher's Head, advertising the shop sign in his imprints. The shop sign announces

---

[107] Ibid., p. 22.
[108] *The Oxford Shakespeare*, ed. Stanley Wells and Gary Taylor (Oxford: Oxford University Press, 1986), p. xxxix.
[109] Wells and Taylor, *The Oxford Shakespeare*, p. xxxiv.

Kirkman's investments in pre-1642 drama and Fletcher in particular, whom, with Shakespeare and Jonson, Kirkman prioritized in his 1671 play-book catalogue. But, as we have seen with Robert Pollard's shop at Ben Jonson's Head, a stationer advertising himself in relation to a playwright did not necessarily print many of his plays. In fact, Kirkman did print Fletcher, but all of these editions were pirated. Around 1661, Kirkman entered into a publication syndicate with Thomas Johnson, Nathanial Brookes, and Henry Marsh, "a partnership," R. C. Bald comments, "which Kirkman was later to repent."[110] With the syndicate, Kirkman in 1661 pirated several Fletcher plays, some with fake Interregnum imprints and some with conspicuously plain ones: *The Scornful Lady* (Q7 "1651" and Q8 "1651"); *Philaster* ("1652"); Fletcher and Massinger's *Elder Brother* ("1637" and 1661); *A King and No King* (1661); *The Maid's Tragedy* (1661); *The Beggar's Bush* (in folio, 1661); and potentially *The Humorous Lieutenant* (1661).[111] When his syndicate's piracies came to light, Kirkman was betrayed by his partners. By 1662, he was no longer working at Fletcher's Head, but rather selling books from Marsh's shop.[112] In his preface to *The Unlucky Citizen*, Kirkman claims, "By this means I recollecting all the remarkable passages of my life, found that in all conditions, and in all capacities, I had generally been *unlucky*."[113] Throughout his life, Kirkman was a victim of poor timing, a theatre lover born in a time without legal theatre, and prevented from legitimately publishing the plays of his favourite dramatists. Kirkman eventually worked at the sign of Robin Hood's Head, a fitting location for one who operated in the margins of legality.

Printing Pre-1642 Drama in the Restoration

In the preface to the second part of *The English Rogue*, Kirkman suggests he was an unwilling participant in his syndicate's piracies: "though the Copies were other mens, I thought this criminal, but they made a tush at it."[114] Nevertheless, it was Kirkman who attracted the ire of Humphrey Robinson and Anne Moseley, the rightful joint holders of the Fletcher

---

[110] Bald, "Francis Kirkman," p. 24.
[111] Gerritsen, "Dramatic Piracies," p. 122. See entries in W. W. Greg, *A Bibliography of the English Printed Drama to the Restoration*, 4 vols. (London: Bibliographical Society, 1939–59), II. They also pirated Thomas Heywood's *Love's Mistress* (Q3 "1640").
[112] Bald, "Francis Kirkman," p. 24.   [113] Kirkman, *The Unlucky Citizen*, sig. A3r.
[114] Kirkman, "The Preface to the Reader," in *The English Rogue Continued* (London: Francis Kirkman, 1671), sig. A7r.

copyrights, which they inherited from Humphrey Moseley, Robinson's partner and Anne's husband, who died in January 1661. Robinson and Anne Moseley issued their own edition of *Beggar's Bush* in 1661, on the title page of which they accuse Kirkman and his crew of peddling an illicit, overpriced edition: "You may speedily expect those other Playes, which *Kirkman*, and his Hawkers have deceived the buyers withall, selling them at treble the value, that this and the rest will be sold for, which are the onely Originall and corrected copies, as they were first purchased by us at no mean rate, and since printed by us."[115] Kirkman, for his part, had his revenge: in the preface to the first edition of *The Thracian Wonder*, he appears to mock Humphrey Moseley for his habit of entering titles into the Stationers' Register without actually printing them: "I shall not (as some others of my profession have done) promise more than I will perform in a year or two, or it may be never; but I will assure you that I shall never leave printing, as long as you shall continue buying."[116] Moseley's hoarding of plays in the Interregnum made it more difficult for other stationers to acquire publication rights. The legacy endured into the Restoration: Moseley's rights transferred to Robinson and Anne Moseley, and many thence to Henry Herringman.

Despite Anne Moseley and Robinson's promise that the reader "may speedily expect those other Playes" pirated by Kirkman and his syndicate, they did not print any other Fletcher plays. Anne Moseley did print other pre-1642 plays, and overall Fletcher's rate of publication between 1660 and 1670 is comparable to several other pre-1642 dramatists.[117] Anne and Humphrey's daughter, also named Anne Moseley, appears to have taken over her mother's business after 1664. The younger Anne demonstrated enthusiasm for publishing romance, advertising twenty-one "Excellent Romances" in a book list included at the end of *Cassandra* in 1667. James Grantham Turner notes the younger Anne's

---

[115] Francis Beaumont and John Fletcher [and Philip Massinger (?)], *Beggar's Bush* (London: Humphrey Robinson and Anne Moseley, 1661), sig. A1r.

[116] Kirkman, "Stationer's Address," in *Thracian Wonder*, sig. A2r.

[117] Anne Moseley printed Brome's *The Northern Lass*, Fanshawe's translation of *Il Pastor Fido*, and potentially a reprint of *The Changeling* (1668); Other Fletcher publications appearing between 1660 and 1670 include *Wit Without Money* and *The Night Walker* (both published by Andrew Crooke in 1661); *Monsieur Thomas* (Robert Crofts, c. 1661 and 1663); *The Faithful Shepherdess* (Bedell and Collins, 1665). Between 1670 and 1700, Fletcher was reprinted in twelve single-text editions, typically with contemporary theatrical attributions. Between 1660 and 1670, James Shirley, Thomas Middleton, William Rowley, and William Lower were each reprinted in four single-text playbooks; John Webster and Richard Brome were reprinted three times each; Christopher Marlowe, Robert Davenport, and William Hemmings were each identified as author on two editions, and *Mucedorus* was reprinted twice (1663 and 1668).

astuteness in exploiting the buyer's "desire for freshness and newness" by advertising the majority of items as "a new" or "excellent new" romance.[118] That Anne, with her nose for newness, chose not to publish Fletcher implies a reason why he did not maintain his impressive Interregnum publication record into the Restoration. After providing a burst of dramatic novelty in the Interregnum, he settled into a rate of print publication comparable to his contemporaries, while novelty was pursued elsewhere, including in other genres.

Still, Fletcher fared better in print than Jonson and Shakespeare in the Restoration. As we have seen, despite Jonson's clear cultural stature in the Interregnum, he was by and large not reprinted. This pattern continued into the Restoration: between 1660 and 1700, of the single-text plays, only *Catiline* was reprinted, twice, once in 1669, following its revival at the Theatre Royal on 18 and 19 December 1668 and 2 and 13 January 1669 (to which the title page alludes), and again in 1674, featuring the same attribution.[119] As this suggests, an important difference between the Interregnum and Restoration reception of pre-1642 dramatists is that plays could now be legally staged: the 1669 publication of *Catiline* was clearly tied to its recent theatrical revival, and many Restoration editions of pre-1642 plays were printed with contemporary theatrical attributions and cast lists featuring Restoration actors. When the Restoration theatre opened, it first turned to pre-1642 plays to furnish its theatrical repertoire while contemporary dramatists wrote new plays. Most of these pre-1642 plays had already been printed. James J. Marino has suggested that, after 1660, bookshops may have furnished the theatres with copies of plays, reversing the pre-1642 direction of dramatic transmission.[120] After 1660, the prior printed dominance of Fletcher, Shakespeare, and, to a lesser extent, Jonson, must have contributed to their revival on stage. Between 1660 and 1670, out of 911 total performances listed in *The London Stage Database*,[121] there were 121 performances of 28 different Fletcher

---

[118] James Grantham Turner, "'Romance' and the Novel in Restoration England," *Review of English Studies*, 63 (2012), 58–85 (pp. 61, 69).

[119] *Guy Earle of Warwick*, an apocryphal play attributed to "B. J." (presumably Jonson) published by Edward Vere and William Gilbertson (1661), with a pre-1642 performance attribution "by his late MAJESTIES Servants." *The Devil is an Ass* was apparently reissued in 1669 (Greg 457 bII), although as Greg notes, "the only recorded copy is found in a volume containing the title of the Second Volume." *Bibliography*, II, p. 606.

[120] James J. Marino, *Owning William Shakespeare: The King's Men and Their Intellectual Property* (Philadelphia: University of Pennsylvania Press, 2011), p. 147.

[121] *The London Stage* and its online counterpart, *The London Stage Database* provide peerless information about Restoration performances; nevertheless, as they acknowledge, the information is partial. *The London Stage Database* notes "our collective knowledge of theater in the period is

plays (alone or with collaborators) or adaptations;[122] 66 performances of 13 different Shakespeare plays or adaptations;[123] and 35 performances of 6 different Jonson plays or adaptations.[124] While some of these pre-1642 plays were reprinted following their revivals, the majority were not. This suggests, then, not only, or even chiefly, the dominance of Shakespeare, Fletcher, and Jonson on the Restoration stage, but also their convenience, their many printed plays offering a stop-gap supply source for the Restoration theatre while contemporaries developed their own dramatic works.[125]

Thus, while Shakespeare fared fairly well on the early Restoration stage, he lagged in print. After the dearth of Shakespearean publication in the Interregnum,[126] there was still apparently little demand for new Shakespeare playbooks in the Restoration until the late 1670s.[127] As noted above, a 1661 catalogue advertising plays sold by Henry Herringman lists "Loves labour lost," "*Hamlet* Prince of *Denmark*," and "*Romio and Juliet*"; Herringman did not reprint these titles, and so evidently acquired this unsold stock of copies from the 1630s from John Smethwick.[128] Other

hampered by gaps in the documentary record" and cites Robert Hume and Judith Milhous's calculation that "the information available for the years 1660–1700 – before newspapers began printing daily advertisements for the major theaters – represents perhaps 7% of the performances that actually took place in London." "About" in *The London Stage Database*, ed. Mattie Burkert et al., https://londonstagedatabase.uoregon.edu/about.php; Judith Milhous and Robert D. Hume, eds., *The London Stage, 1660–1800: A New Version of Part 2, 1700–1729...Draft of the Calendar for Volume 1, 1700–1711*, www.personal.psu.edu/hb1/London%20Stage%202001/preface.pdf.

[122] *The Tamer Tamed, The Loyal Subject, Wit Without Money, Beggar's Bush, Philaster, The Maid's Tragedy, The Scornful Lady, The Elder Brother, Chances, Humorous Lieutenant, A King and No King, Rollo, Duke of Normandy, The Maid in the Mill, The Mad Lover, The Spanish Curate, Rule a Wife and Have a Wife, The Little Thief (Night Walker); Monsieur Thomas (Father's Own Son), Faithful Shepherdess, Love's Pilgrimage, The Custom of the Country, The Sea Voyage (The Storm), The Wild Goose Chase, Love Despised (Cupid's Revenge), The Island Princess, Women Pleased, The Coxcomb,* and *The Little French Lawyer. The London Stage Database* counts *Knight of the Burning Pestle* as a Fletcher play; I have excluded it as a play solely attributed to Beaumont; similarly, I have excluded *The Coxcomb* and *Sir Salomon* from my Jonson counts.

[123] *Othello, 1 Henry IV, Merry Wives of Windsor, Hamlet, Twelfth Night, Law Against Lovers* (adaptation that combines *Measure for Measure* and *Much Ado About Nothing*); *Romeo and Juliet; Midsummer Night's Dream, Henry VIII, King Lear, Macbeth, Sauny the Scot* (adaptation of *Taming of the Shrew*), *Tempest.*

[124] *The Silent Woman/Epicene, Alchemist, Bartholomew Fair, Volpone, Catiline, Every Man in His Humour.*

[125] Paulina Kewes argues that the Restoration valorization of Shakespeare, Fletcher, and Jonson has been overstated, and that Restoration dramatists were more popular. Kewes, *Authorship and Appropriation*, p. 10.

[126] See Chapter 2.

[127] Don-John Dugas, *Marketing the Bard: Shakespeare in Performance and Print, 1660–1740* (St. Louis: University of Missouri Press, 2006), pp. 113–14; Depledge, *Shakespeare's Rise*, pp. 67–93.

[128] Francis X. Connor, "Henry Herringman, Richard Bentley and Shakespeare's Fourth Folio (1685)" in *Canonising Shakespeare*, ed. Depledge and Kirwan, pp. 38–55 (p. 46).

Shakespeare publications include the apocryphal *The Birth of Merlin* (co-attributed to William Rowley, printed by Kirkman's syndicate in 1662), and the Third Folio of 1663, reissued in 1664 with seven additional plays – *Pericles, The London Prodigal, Thomas Lord Cromwell, Sir John Oldcastle, The Puritan Widow, A Yorkshire Tragedy*, and *Locrine*, with all but *Pericles* now deemed to be apocryphal. The misattribution of these titles, along with the considerable investment in F3, has been interpreted as evidence of Shakespeare's growing marketability in the early Restoration, perhaps tied to Shakespeare's reintroduction to the stage.[129] Yet all of F3's added titles are misattributed to Shakespeare in Archer's comprehensive catalogue of 1656, which, as we have seen in Chapter 2, did not necessarily reflect Shakespeare's "popularity" but rather a sense of "Shakespeare" as a category. As discussed in Chapter 2, Chetwind and Mary Allot had been waiting twenty years to use their Shakespeare rights; the volume may therefore actually reflect the release of two decades of pent-up frustration, rather than any contemporary demand for Shakespeare, evidenced by the fact that, following F3 in 1664, Shakespeare was not reprinted for nearly a decade. William Cademan's edition of *Macbeth* (Q1673) and Herringman

---

[129] For instance, Peter Kirwan suggests that the return of Shakespeare to the stage, and consequently his marketability, after the Restoration may explain the misattribution of *The Birth of Merlin* and six of the added F3 titles to Shakespeare. Kirwan, "Consolidating the Shakespeare Canon," pp. 82, 84. See also Kirwan, *Shakespeare and the Idea of Apocrypha*. Robert F. Fleissner explains *The Birth of Merlin* was "misattributed to Shakespeare for publicity purposes through a curious misassociation with *King Lear*. In brief, my point is that the title page in effect proclaims the "'fulfillment' of the well-known 'Fool's Prophecy' in the tragedy" containing "a sonnet, sometimes called 'Merlin's Prophecy,' and the prophecy that Merlin will be born to prophesy it." Robert F. Fleissner, "The Misattribution of *The Birth of Merlin* to Shakespeare," *Papers of the Bibliographical Society of America*, 73.2 (1979), 248–52 (p. 248). In her modern critical edition, Joanna Udall summarizes the various theories about Shakespearean attribution and alternative authorship. *A Critical, Old-Spelling Edition of The Birth of Merlin*, ed. Joanna Udall (London: The Modern Humanities Research Association, 1991). See also Will Sharpe, "Authorship and Attribution," in *William Shakespeare and Others, Collaborative Plays*, ed. Jonathan Bate and Eric Rasmussen with Jan Sewell and Will Sharpe (Basingstoke: Palgrave, 2013), pp. 729–30; MacDonald P. Jackson and Gary Taylor, "Works Excluded from This Edition," in *Thomas Middleton and Early Modern Textual Culture: A Companion to the Printed Works*, ed. Gary Taylor and John Lavagnino (Oxford: Clarendon Press, 2007), pp. 444–8 (p. 444). Richard Finkelstein argues that the seven added F3 plays reflect Puritan politics that opposed the dominant Restoration culture. Richard Finkelstein, "The Politics of Gender, Puritanism, and Shakespeare's Third Folio," *Philological Quarterly*, 79.3 (2000), 315–41. John Jowett notes that the printer Ellen Cotes (widow of Richard Cotes, one of the printers and publishers of F2) actively retained the titles to *Oldcastle, Pericles*, and *Yorkshire Tragedy*, as well as possessing Isaac Jaggard's share of sixteen plays printed in F1 and F2, as well as five or six titles from Thomas Pavier inherited from her late husband. Philip Chetwind, publisher of F3, must have reached an arrangement with Ellen Cotes to print the titles she held, and this arrangement may have required him to include *Oldcastle, Pericles*, and *Yorkshire Tragedy* in F3's reissue. John Jowett, "Shakespeare Supplemented," in *The Shakespeare Apocrypha*, ed. Brooks, pp. 39–73 (pp. 47–50). See also Dugas, "Philip Chetwind and the Shakespeare Third Folio."

and John Martyn's edition of *Hamlet* (Q1676) represent the only two Shakespeare quartos published in the 1670s, with only the latter attributing the play to Shakespeare. Emma Depledge argues that *Hamlet* Q1676 represented Herringman and Martyn's attempt to test the market's appetite for Shakespeare; they entered twenty-five Shakespeare titles (some now apocryphal) in the Stationers' Register on 6 August 1674 (acquiring the rights from the late Ellen Cotes via her executor Andrew Clark). Depledge notes that while Herringman and Martyn were likely convinced of Shakespeare's cultural value, they seem to have doubted the financial soundness of publishing an expensive folio edition, given that few of Shakespeare's plays had been published in the last decade.[130] *Hamlet* Q1676 sold poorly, and no further Shakespeare editions appeared for five years. (Around this period, Herringman did print two Shakespeare adaptations, Dryden and Davenant's *The Tempest* (1674), revised by Thomas Shadwell, and Shadwell's *Timon of Athens* (1678); this speaks to Herringman's interest in publishing contemporary stage plays, discussed in more detail below.) Herringman did not follow through with publishing Shakespeare's Fourth Folio until 1685; Martyn having died in 1680, Herringman's partners in the venture were Richard Bentley, Edward Brewster, and Robert Chiswell. By the time F4 appeared, Depledge persuasively argues, the Exclusion Crisis (1678–82) motivated a considerable resurgence of Shakespeare on stage and page.[131]

In addition to Shakespeare F4, Herringman was also responsible for printing the Restoration folio collections of Beaumont and Fletcher and Jonson, publishing *Fifty Comedies and Tragedies of Beaumont and Fletcher* (with John Martyn and Richard Marriot) in 1679, as well as Jonson's *Works* (with Brewster, Chiswell, Thomas Bassett, Matthew Wotton, and George Conyers) in 1692. Working at the sign of the Blue Anchor in the fashionable New Exchange, a centre of Restoration literary life, Herringman succeeded Moseley as the pre-eminent publisher of drama, and he followed some Moseley-like publication habits, acquiring copyrights of popular pre-1642 drama but not printing them, at least not immediately. On 30 January 1673, the estate of Moseley's partner Humphrey Robinson transferred thirty-five "Beaument and Fletcher" plays to Herringman and Martyn, granting them each one half.[132] The new Beaumont and Fletcher folio followed six years later in 1679 – on other occasions Herringman made use of his pre-1642 acquisitions within

---

[130] Depledge, *Shakespeare's Rise*, p. 47.   [131] Ibid., pp. 67–93.
[132] Greg, *Bibliography*, III, p. 1018.

a month. Herringman had acquired printing rights to several Jonson plays in 1665 and 1667, from Anne Moseley, and only published the Jonson folio twenty-five years later, more than fifty years after the previous Jonson folio.[133] But while Herringman in many ways was continuing Moseley's publication strategies after the Restoration, other details of his career speak to changes in the production of printed drama after 1660.

Critics have described three distinct phases in Herringman's career: the first from the end of his apprenticeship in 1653 to about 1664, a middle phase from 1664 to 1678, and the last phase after 1678.[134] In the first phase, C. William Miller notes, Herringman published "almost anything which he thought the better-educated Londoners frequenting the Strand would buy . . . political pamphlets, sermons, plays, verse, romances, histories, philosophical discourses, and even a treatise on chess."[135] Between 1653 and 1656, plays occupied a relatively small part of Herringman's output; the first and second parts of James Howell's *Nuptials of Peleus and Thetis* (1654) represent his only dramatic publication. Herringman's relative lack of interest in drama seems to have been tied to the closure of the theatres, an inference bolstered by the fact that Herringman's next dramatic publications were the first plays sanctioned for performance during the Interregnum, Davenant's *The Siege of Rhodes* (1656), *The First Day's Entertainment at Rutland House* (1657), *The Cruelty of the Spaniards in Peru* (1658), and *The History of Sir Francis Drake* (1659). Herringman had already demonstrated interest in Davenant; he acquired the lucrative rights to *Gondibert* from the late John Holden (along with other stock and copyrights) in the spring of 1652.[136] Herringman's interest in dramatic publication, then, coincides with the resumption of sanctioned drama; as Miller notes, "as soon as the dramatists and poets resumed their writing, Herringman, shrewdly gauging his market, began to publish their works."[137] Indeed, Herringman printed *The Siege of Rhodes* and *The Cruelty of the Spaniards of Peru* in *advance* of the plays' premieres, suggestive of his acquaintance with Davenant and his attentiveness to the reopened theatres.[138] Herringman reprinted *The Siege of Rhodes* (and its newly written second part) in 1663 and 1670, and included those two plays and the other Commonwealth Davenant titles in his folio edition of Davenant's collected *Works* in 1673.

---

[133] Miller, "Henry Herringman," p. 300.
[134] Miller's first phase ends in 1666, Connor's in 1663. Miller, "Henry Herringman," p. 296; Connor, "Henry Herringman," pp. 42–8.
[135] Miller, "Henry Herringman," p. 297.   [136] Ibid., pp. 296–7.   [137] Ibid., p. 298.
[138] Bourne, *Typographies*, p. 240.

Herringman also published a folio collection of plays by the other theatrical patentee, Killigrew's *Comedies and Tragedies* (1664). Francis X. Connor notes that the edition, with a frontispiece portrait of Killigrew sitting beneath an inset portrait of Charles I, and a preface that refers to Killigrew's "twenty years banishment" during the Interregnum, suggests the stationer's "royalist bias," but argues that as the 1660s progressed, "Herringman, perhaps recognising the inevitable end of the enthusiasm for celebrations of the Restoration, appears to have stopped overtly referring to the past in his dramatic publications in order to focus instead on the fashionable audiences attending plays in the newly reopened theatres."[139] He printed new stage plays including Thomas Porter's *Villain* (1663) and Samuel Tuke's *The Adventures of Five Hours* (1663); his edition of George Etheredge's *Love in a Tub* (1664) was the first to mention a Restoration playhouse (Lincoln's Inn Fields) on the title page; and in 1664, Herringman published Dryden's first play in print, *The Rival Ladies*. He would become Dryden's primary publisher, and published other leading playwrights of the era, Robert Howard and Thomas Shadwell.[140] Herringman appears to have known many of these authors personally.[141] In his edition of Davenant's 1673 *Works*, Herringman refers to the late Davenant as "my worthy friend," and he describes their conversations about Davenant's hopes for his literary legacy. Herringman also employed the young Dryden to write his prefaces just before and after the Restoration.[142]

Herringman's dramatic publications between 1663 and 1678, then, largely focused on new Restoration drama: contemporary stage plays by living authors, many of whom he knew personally. Herringman's output in this period speaks to both the continuities and discontinuities in dramatic publication across 1660. As Chapter 2 argues, Interregnum dramatic stationers turned away from frequently reprinted Shakespeare and Jonson to publish "new plays," that is, plays written prior to 1642 that had not yet been printed. This exact strategy did not continue in the Restoration: only twenty-four first editions of pre-1642 plays appeared between 1660 and 1700, a number that represents a sliver of the entire Restoration playbook market.[143] Like Interregnum stationers, Restoration stationers were

[139] Connor, "Henry Herringman," p. 43.
[140] Ibid., p. 43, Michael Gavin, "Writing Print Cultures Past: Literary Criticism and Book History," *Book History*, 15 (2012), 26–47 (p. 38).
[141] Miller, "Henry Herringman," p. 294.
[142] Paul Hammond, *Dryden: A Literary Life* (Houndmills: Macmillan, 1991), p. 21.
[143] Tasso (trans. John Dancer), *Aminta* (London: John Starkey, 1660); J. S. [James Shirley?], *Andromana* (London: John Bellinger, 1660); William Lower, *The Amorous Fantasm* (London: John Ramzey, 1660); Thomas Middleton, *The Mayor of Queenborough* (London: Henry Herringman, 1661); Robert Davenport, *The City Night-Cap* (London: Samuel Speed, 1661);

interested in dramatic novelty, but this was redefined once the theatres reopened: "new plays" were those newly written and staged in the Restoration. (This redefinition was actually a reversion to the status of new plays when the theatres were open before 1642.) After 1660, "old plays" staged before 1642 continued to appear in print: in some cases, pre-1642 plays were revived and reprinted with contemporary theatrical attributions; others, such as Brome's *A Jovial Crew* (1661), said to be "Presented in a COMEDIE AT The Cock-pit in Drury-Lane in the year 1641 And Since acted by His MAJESTIES Servants at the New Theatre in Vere Street," alluded to both old and current performances, laying out continuities across the pre-1642 and post-1660 theatrical traditions. Kirkman's first edition of *A Cure for a Cuckold* (1661) was identified as "an excellent old play" on its title page, even as it drew attention to its first appearance in print. In 1665, Herringman printed Howard and Dryden's *The Indian Queen* in his edition of Howard's *Four New Plays* (1665). The collection's title recalls Moseley's innovative Interregnum serial publications. But, unlike Moseley's *New Plays*, which, as we have seen, bestowed (sometimes defensively) this title on decades-old plays that were heretofore unprinted, *The Indian Queen* was a "new play" in every way: it was the first edition of a play

John Webster and William Rowley, *A Cure for a Cuckold* (London: Francis Kirkman, 1661), B. J., *Guy Earl of Warwick* (London: Thomas Vere and William Gilbertson, 1661); John Webster, *The Thracian Wonder* (London: Francis Kirkman, 1661); *Tom Tyler and his Wife* (London: Francis Kirkman, 1661); Thomas Middleton, *Anything for a Quiet Life* (London: Francis Kirkman and Henry Marsh, 1662); "William Shakespeare" (?) and William Rowley, *The Birth of Merlin* (London: Francis Kirkman and Henry Marsh, 1662); William Hemings, *The Jews' Tragedy* (London: Matthew Inman, 1662); T. W. *Thorney Abbey, or the London Maid* (printed in collection, *Gratiae Theatrales* [London: R. D., 1662]); M. W. *The Marriage Broker* (printed in collection, *Gratiae Theatrales* [London: R. D., 1662]); I. T., *The Grim Collier of Croydon* (printed in collection, *Gratiae Theatrales* [London: R. D., 1662]); Thomas Killigrew, *The Princess* (printed in collection, Thomas Killigrew, *Comedies and Tragedies* [London: Henry Herringman, 1664]); Thomas Killigrew, *The Parson's Wedding* (printed in collection, Thomas Killigrew, *Comedies and Tragedies* [London: Henry Herringman, 1664]); Thomas Jordan, *Money is an Ass* (London: Francis Kirkman, 1668); William Davenant, *News from Plymouth* (printed in collection, William Davenant, *Works* [London: Henry Herringman, 1673]); William Davenant, *The Distresses* (printed in collection, William Davenant, *Works* [London: Henry Herringman, 1673]); William Davenant, *The Siege* (printed in collection, William Davenant, *Works* [London: Henry Herringman, 1673]); William Davenant, *The Fair Favourite* (printed in collection, William Davenant, *Works* [London: Henry Herringman, 1673]); *Gesta Grayorum* (London: W. Canning, 1688); R[obert] W[ild], *The Benefice* (London: R. Janeway, 1689). These twenty-four titles represent first editions printed between 1660 and 1700 of the plays W. W. Greg includes in his *Bibliography of the English Printed Drama to the Restoration*, namely, "all dramatic compositions which were either written before the *end* of 1642 (the year of the closing of the theatres on 2 September) or printed before the *beginning* of 1660 (the year of the Restoration on 8 May). Those works which were written during the seventeen years 1643 to 1659 inclusive but not printed till 1660 or later may reasonably, it seems to me, be held to fall within the domain of the Restoration drama." *A Bibliography of the English Printed Drama to the Restoration*, I, p. xiii.

published within a year of its premiere in January 1664 at the new Theatre Royal at Bridges Street, which had opened in May 1663. Furthermore, it was a richly scenic play that took full advantage of Restoration theatre's new moveable scenery,[144] and was explicitly presented as "new" Restoration drama in contrast to older dramatic offerings, as its epilogue indicates: "You have seen all that this old world coul'd do, / We therefore try the fortune of the new."[145] When compared with new Restoration plays, then, neither revived pre-1642 plays nor "new old plays" could compete with the unmistakable novelty of Restoration drama. The staging of new Restoration plays caused interest in older unprinted plays to ebb; after a spasm of first editions in the 1660s (driven largely by Francis Kirkman), the only newly printed pre-1642 plays in the 1670s were those included in Davenant's collected *Works* (1673), and only two more first editions of pre-1642 plays appeared for the rest of the century, printed in the 1680s. As noted in Chapter 2, this has had lasting effects on our impression of what we now call "early modern drama": of the estimated 3,000 plays that were composed for the professional theatres c. 1567–1642 in England, only 543 have survived in print or manuscript;[146] with a few exceptions, the corpus of early modern printed drama was by and large established by 1660.

Herringman's edition of Davenant's *Works* underscores his affinities with and differences from Moseley's Interregnum publication strategies. Having already acquired the titles to ten Davenant plays and masques from Anne Moseley on 19 August 1667,[147] Herringman on 14 October 1672 acquired from the Moseley estate rights to four previously unprinted Davenant plays staged before 1642: *The News from Plymouth, The Distresses, The Siege*, and *The Fair Favorite*. Humphrey Moseley (with Robinson) had previously entered three of these titles on 4 September 1646 (entering *The Siege* on 9 September 1653). We have already encountered Moseley and Robinson's large 4 September 1646 entry, which included dozens of play titles, including twenty-seven by Beaumont and Fletcher, which Moseley quickly published as part of the Beaumont and Fletcher folio in 1647. Moseley evidently had plans to eventually publish the four unprinted Davenant plays, which are among the long list of titles Moseley advertised between 1656 and 1660

[144] Bourne, *Typographies*, p. 246.

[145] John Dryden and Robert Howard, *The Indian-Queen*, in Robert Howard, *Four New Plays* (London: Henry Herringman, 1665), sig. Z4r. See Bourne, *Typographies*, pp. 246–7.

[146] David McInnis and Matthew Steggle, "Introduction: Nothing will Come from Nothing: Or, What Can We Learn from Plays That Don't Exist?," in *Lost Plays in Shakespeare's England*, ed. McInnis and Steggle, pp. 1–14 (pp. 1, 12 n. 2).

[147] See Greg, *Bibliography*, III, p. 1056.

as "Books I do purpose to print very speedtly [*sic*]."[148] Despite the public declaration, by the time of his death in 1661, Moseley had still not published those four Davenant titles acquired fourteen years earlier.

Herringman, by contrast, published these four Davenant plays very "speedily" indeed. A month after acquiring their rights from Anne Moseley's estate, on 18 November 1672, he advertised in the *London Gazette* "The Works of Sir William D'avenant, kt ... sixteen plays, whereof six were never before printed. Sold by Henry Herringman."[149] *The Works* appeared the next year, and included plays staged before 1642, during the Commonwealth, and after 1660.[150] Like Moseley's Beaumont and Fletcher folio, Herringman touts the fact that his edition includes "never before printed" plays, but unlike Moseley, he also included recently staged plays and already-printed plays: the first edition of *The Law Against Lovers*, staged in 1662, and *The Man's the Master* (Davenant's last play, as he died in April 1668), first staged on 26 March 1668, and printed singly by Herringman in 1669. As this suggests, unlike Moseley, Herringman was not fixated on print novelty: only six of sixteen Davenant plays are "never before printed," as Herringman himself advertises, both in the *London Gazette* and in the edition itself (note that he does not attempt to call them "new"). As a productive printer of Restoration drama, Herringman could both find and offer novelty elsewhere.

Davenant's *Works* anticipates the last phase of Herringman's career. Herringman acquired few new copyrights after 1678, and instead focused on publishing the titles he already owned,[151] including expensive folio publications of Beaumont and Fletcher, Shakespeare, and Jonson. While it could be that he detected new markets for these dramatists after 1678, it could also be that in the late stage of his career, Herringman did not care as much about economics. Connor argues that Herringman was motivated by his literary ambitions, rather than potential financial gain.[152] By the early 1680s, Herringman was wealthy, owing to his success as Dryden's

---

[148] Ibid., II, pp. 925–7.   [149] Ibid., III, p. 1056.

[150] The plays staged before the closure of the theatres are *Albovine, The Just Italian, Temple of Love, The Wits, The Platonic Lovers, The Unfortunate Lovers,* and *Love and Honour,* as well as the masques *Coelum Britannicum, The Temple of Love, The Triumphs of the Prince D'Amour;* the Commonwealth-era stage plays are *The First Day's Entertainment* and *The Siege of Rhodes Part 1;* and the Restoration-era plays are the theatrical anthology *The Playhouse to Be Let* (which includes portions of *The Cruelty of the Spaniards in Peru* and *Sir Francis Drake*) as well as *The Law Against Lovers* and *The Man's the Master.*

[151] Miller, "Henry Herringman," p. 301. He also printed Dryden: as Miller notes, "From 1678 to 1699, when he finally sold his Dryden holdings to Tonson, Herringman brought out more than forty Dryden publications" (p. 302).

[152] Connor, "Henry Herringman," p. 39.

primary stationer and his good fortune during the Great Fire of London, which decimated the shops and stock of his competitors but spared his own shop in the New Exchange.[153]

While Moseley's Beaumont and Fletcher folio collection comprised only unprinted plays, offered to the reader as a "new book," Herringman's contained all of their plays, including those that had been frequently reprinted in single-text editions: in the Restoration, completeness replaced novelty as the primary virtue of pre-1642 drama. Herringman revelled in the old plays' history: several of the plays featured newly added actor lists populated with pre-1642 actors, from the early actors Richard Burbage and Nathan Field to later King's Servants John Lowin and Joseph Taylor.[154] While the provenance and accuracy of these actor lists are unclear,[155] they represent a clear attempt to conjure the pre-1642 theatrical past through printed paratexts. Herringman's folio editions of Shakespeare and Jonson likewise reproduce the original actor lists and theatrical attributions from F1 1623 and F 1616, respectively.[156] In the 1679 Beaumont and Fletcher folio, Herringman declares his intention to "bring Ben Jonson's two volumes [of the 1640 works] into one ... and also to reprint Old Shakespeare."[157] While Moseley attempted to present Beaumont and Fletcher's decades-old plays as "new" in 1647, by 1679, Herringman had no qualms about his intention to print "Old Shakespeare," clearly a term of respect. While pre-1642 drama was prematurely aged by the theatre closures, then comparatively wizened still further after the development of new Restoration drama, we can reframe the oldness of pre-1642 plays after 1660. Instead of seeing them as stripped of the ability to appear new, pre-1642 plays were also relieved of the burden of parading as "new plays," because that role was filled by new Restoration drama. After the Restoration, pre-1642 playbooks could simply be old.[158] This is especially true for folio collections: while single-text Restoration editions of pre-1642 theatrical revivals featured contemporary theatrical attributions and cast

---

[153] Miller, "Henry Herringman," pp. 294–5, 298, 300. Jacob Tonson took over as Dryden's publisher in 1679.

[154] Burbage appears in *The Captain*, sig. 3Y4v; Field in *The Coxcomb*, sig. 22R3v; Lowin and Taylor in *The Laws of Candy*, sig. 2Q2; and Beaumont and Fletcher, *Fifty Comedies and Tragedies*, passim.

[155] Bentley, *The Profession of Player in Shakespeare's Time*, p. 217.

[156] See Heidi Craig, "The King's Servants in Printed Paratexts, 1594–1695," *Huntington Library Quarterly*, 85.1 (2022), 151–169 (pp. 167–8). Also Bentley, *The Profession of Player in Shakespeare's Time*, pp. 212–18.

[157] Henry Herringman, "The Booksellers to the Reader," in Beaumont and Fletcher, *Fifty Comedies and Tragedies*, sig. A1r.

[158] Stage plays of pre-1642 drama are different, because they were updated.

lists, the monumental printed editions of Shakespeare, Beaumont and Fletcher, and Jonson revelled in their venerability.

***

In many ways, Herringman's editions look ahead to the eighteenth century. His folio collections reinforced Beaumont and Fletcher's, Shakespeare's, and Jonson's Restoration reputations as the most important pre-1642 playwrights, to the near-exclusion of their contemporaries. After Herringman's death, many of his titles were sold to Jacob Tonson, elder and younger.[159] Tonson published collected editions of Beaumont and Fletcher (1711)[160] and Jonson (1716),[161] and of course the Tonson cartel was responsible for the burgeoning eighteenth-century tradition of Shakespeare editions with named editors, starting with Nicholas Rowe's 1709 edition, which used Herringman's F4 as a copy text.[162] Michael Gavin also notes that the extensive paratextual criticism in Herringman's editions, which "comprise a surprisingly large segment of Restoration critical writing and almost all of the formal essays traditionally understood as 'English criticism' between the years 1664 and 1680," helped pave the way for English literary criticism in the eighteenth century.[163]

But Herringman's editions also look backward, perpetuating trends from the Interregnum period in which he began his career. Herringman conceived of Beaumont and Fletcher, Shakespeare, and Jonson as a coherent group: in his Beaumont and Fletcher folio, he promised to issue folio editions of Shakespeare and Jonson, and he printed his Jonson folio in double columns, like Shakespeare's and Beaumont and Fletcher's folios had been, unifying the texts' appearance.[164] This union reflects Fletcher, Shakespeare, and Jonson's status as the "triumvirate of wit," a phrase with wide currency in the Restoration,[165] but which originated in John Denham's commendatory poem for the 1647 Beaumont and Fletcher folio, which Herringman reprinted in Denham's *Poems and Translations*

---

[159] Miller, "Henry Herringman," p. 305.   [160] See Bourne, *Typographies*, pp. 222–8.
[161] See Tessa Grant, "Tonson's Jonson: Making the 'Vernacular Canon' in the Early Eighteenth Century," in *The Oxford Handbook of Ben Jonson*, ed. Eugene Giddens (Oxford: Oxford University Press, 2013).
[162] See Murphy, *Shakespeare in Print*. On Tonson and Herringman, see Massai, *Shakespeare and the Rise of the Editor*.
[163] Gavin, "Writing Print Cultures Past," p. 38; Gavin, *The Invention of English Criticism*.
[164] Francis X. Connor, *Literary Folios and Ideas of the Book in Early Modern England* (New York: Palgrave Macmillan, 2014), p. 177.
[165] See Kewes, *Authorship and Appropriation*, pp. 149–51.

(1668).[166] Herringman's critical dramatic paratexts, moreover, are anticipated by the extensive Interregnum dramatic paratexts in editions by
Moseley and others. The actor lists Herringman included in the
Beaumont and Fletcher F2 1679 conjure the ghosts of pre-1642 actors,
but this effort had roots in Interregnum paratextual theatre history, as
evidenced in *The Wild Goose Chase* cast list of 1652.[167] Gavin distinguishes
between Moseley's retrospective publishing agenda and Herringman's
more contemporary one, arguing that, "whereas Moseley specialized in
publishing dead or exiled Royalists, Herringman's authors were alive and
present and contributed to an ongoing field of literary debate."[168]
Nevertheless, although they were by necessity fixated on the dramatic past,
Moseley and the authors who supplied paratexts for his editions were
likewise contributing to a field of dramatic criticism. Indeed, as I discuss
in the next chapter, the fact that they focused on old plays by dead
dramatists from a tradition perceived to be over fundamentally shaped
their criticism, in ways that continue to inflect modern critical practice.

Henry Herringman dominated both new and old dramatic publication
in the Restoration: he was responsible for printing the major folio collections of the two men placed in charge of the Restoration theatre, Killigrew
and Davenant; he was the primary stationer for the period's most successful dramatist, Dryden, whom he happened to employ as a young man, and
he published the folio editions of the three most important dramatists of
the pre-1642 stage. In effect, he was the unofficial print counterpart to
Killigrew and Davenant's theatrical duopoly. Herringman does not seem
to have been as ruthless as Davenant and Killigrew; he was well-liked and
regarded as honest, and his friendships with Davenant, Dryden and others
doubtless contributed to his success.[169] No matter their motives, however,
Davenant, Killigrew, and Herringman were clearly the winners of post-
Restoration theatrical and dramatic culture, while theatre professionals and
stationers like Herbert, Mohun, Rhodes, Beeston, Jolly, and Kirkman
struggled to make a living. For these latter practitioners, the "fresh start"
promised by the Restoration maintained the familiar stale stench of
Interregnum dramatic culture, mouldering over two decades of decline.

---

[166] Connor, "Henry Herringman," p. 46.   [167] See Chapter 1.
[168] Gavin, "Writing Print Cultures Past," p. 47 n. 58.   [169] Miller, "Henry Herringman," p. 294.

CHAPTER 5

Morbid Symptoms

> The crisis consists precisely in the fact that the old is dying and the
> new cannot be born; in this interregnum a great variety of morbid
> symptoms appear.
>
> —Antonio Gramsci

In November 1643, a royalist antiquarian's encounter with graffiti on the
wall of a London inn evoked carousing Jacobean playwrights and actors:
"The Tabard I find to have been the resort of Mastere Will Shakspear Sir
Sander Duncombe Lawrence Fletcher Richard Burbage Ben Jonson and
the rest of their roystering associates in King Jameses time as in the large
room they have cut their names on the Pannels." The anecdote appears in
"Some Notes for my Perambulation in and round the Citye of London for
six miles and Remnants of divers worthie things and men," a twenty-
seven-page manuscript discovered by Martha Carlin at the Edinburgh
University Library in 2014.[1] The anecdote is the closest thing we have
to a contemporary account of Shakespeare (d. 1616) fraternizing with his
fellow King's Servants, Richard Burbage (d. 1619), the company's lead
tragic actor, and the actor-sharer Lawrence Fletcher (d. 1608), as well as
Ben Jonson (d. 1637). James Shapiro argues that the Tabard anecdote
represents "the only act of literary fellowship on Shakespeare's part that we
know of during the Jacobean period."[2] But the story is not an eyewitness
account of Jacobean festivities, but rather a belated recreation of events,
based on textual remnants. These records are subject to misinterpretation:
while the Royalist places Sir Sander Duncombe at the scene with
Shakespeare and company, Duncombe, a physician and entrepreneur
active in the Caroline period, probably wasn't actually present, and

---

[1] "Some Notes for my Perambulations in and round the Citye of London," ed. Martha Carlin, *Shakespeare Documented*, https://shakespearedocumented.folger.edu/resource/document/shakespeare-roisterer-tabard-inn. Martha Carlin, "The Bard at the Tabard," *Times Literary Supplement* (24 September 2014), p. 15.
[2] James Shapiro, *The Year of Lear* (New York: Simon & Schuster, 2015), p. 6.

perhaps carved his name into the wall later on. The antiquarian's misreading of the inscription suggests the gap of time between the event and its record. As Juliet Fleming notes, graffiti can function as "a potent record" of the past but can also culpably obscure it.[3] The anecdote speaks both to the desire to accurately reconstruct history after the fact and the difficulty of doing so. Several months into the first English Civil War, an antiquarian relies on material artefacts to conjure an impression of Jacobean theatrical celebrities, mostly long since dead.

The "Perambulation" belongs to the tradition of peripatetic antiquarianism, the survey of monuments and the physical landscape into which narratives about the past are embedded,[4] and imitates John Stow's *The Survey of London* (1598), a nostalgic account of changes to London's landscape and activities following the English Reformation.[5] For peripatetic antiquarians, Angus Vine observes, "a material encounter often evoked a literary remembrance."[6] Stow likewise describes the Tabard in *The Survey of London*, and quotes *The Canterbury Tales'* description of the inn, the location where Chaucer's pilgrims gather in the Prologue. By incorporating literary figures and texts into their histories, Megan Cook explains, antiquarians "played a key role not only in the construction and dissemination of broad narratives about the English past, but also in some of the earliest articulations of what we might term literary history."[7] Cook argues that antiquarians helped canonize medieval vernacular authors, particularly Chaucer, casting him as paradigmatically English, temporally distant from the reader, and hence venerable.[8]

Like his antiquarian predecessors, the "Perambulation" author draws attention to pre-Reformation landmarks connected to medieval literary history, reproducing Stow's quotation of Chaucer's description of the Tabard Inn (adding another five lines), a place in which the "Perambulation" author now locates Shakespeare's revels, creating a trans-generational literary community that stretches across three centuries and

---

[3] Juliet Fleming, "Wounded Walls: Graffiti, Grammatology, and the Age of Shakespeare," *Criticism*, 39.1 (1997), 1–30 (p. 2).
[4] Daniel Woolf, *The Social Circulation of the Past: English Historical Culture, 1500–1730* (Oxford: Oxford University Press, 2003), pp. 142–5.
[5] Ian Archer, "The Nostalgia of John Stow," in *The Theatrical City: Culture, Theatre, and Politics in London, 1576–1649*, ed. David L. Smith, Richard Strier, and David Bevington (Cambridge: Cambridge University Press, 1995), pp. 17–34 (pp. 21–3).
[6] Vine, *In Defiance of Time*, p. 20.
[7] Megan Cook, *The Poet and the Antiquaries: Chaucerian Scholarship and the Rise of Literary History, 1532–1635* (Philadelphia: University of Pennsylvania Press, 2019), p. 2.
[8] Ibid., pp. 2–8.

traverses fiction and quasi-historical fact. The "Perambulation" also points out John Gower's "old House," and offers a brief biographical sketch of him as "a famous Poet and Citizen" and noting his "Worthiness as a Man."[9] Yet, even as he recapitulates earlier antiquarians' interests, the "Perambulation" author also seeks to distinguish himself, declaring that "it is intended by me only to notice those places and things that have been passed by or little mentiond by those great Antiquaries that have written of this noble Citye and ye which places are fast ruining . . . and may be useful to searchers of Antiquitye in time to come."[10] Among the fast ruining and previously unmentioned landmarks, the antiquarian includes "those Stews so long a source of profitt to ye Maiers of London and Bishopps of Winchester, the Bear Gardens and Playes." A sense of decline spurs an urge to preserve not only that which is being lost,[11] but especially that which has previously been overlooked.

The "Perambulation" author appears to have specialized knowledge of English theatre. His Tabard anecdote echoes the language from the theatrical patent of 19 May 1603, which incorporated Shakespeare, Burbage, Lawrence Fletcher, and "the rest of their associates" as King's Servants under James I's royal patronage.[12] The "Perambulation" author's interpolation into the patent's language – "the rest of their *roystering* associates" – suggests his impression of theatrical activity in James's time from the first years of the Civil War. *Pace* Shapiro, the image is not of "literary" fellowship, but is distinctly theatrical and rather rowdy, described with the words of the theatre patent and evoking the collaborative bonhomie of prominent Jacobean playwrights and actors.

The writer of 1643 treats spaces and men of the Jacobean theatre much in the same way that his antiquarian predecessors treated the greats of medieval English literature: venerable, paradigmatically English, and temporally distant from the reader. Unlike sixteenth-century antiquarians writing about the medieval Chaucer, however, it was decades, not centuries, that separated the "Perambulation" author from Shakespeare and his associates. The cultural distance the "Perambulation" author perceives

---

[9] Martha Carlin, "Gower's Southwark," in *The Routledge Research Companion to John Gower*, ed. Ana Saez-Hidalgo, Brian Gastle, and R. F. Yeager (New York: Routledge, 2021), pp. 132–49 (p. 144).

[10] "Some Notes for my Perambulations," fol. 3.

[11] On the relationship between historiography and destruction, see the Introduction.

[12] "Warrant under the privy seal for the issue of letters patent authorizing Shakespeare and his companions to perform plays throughout the realm under royal patronage," 18 May 1603, in *Records of the Lord Chancellor*, The National Archives, Kew, UK, Call number and opening: C 82/1690, no. 78. Accessed on *Shakespeare Documented*, https://shakespearedocumented.folger.edu/resource/document/king-james-establishes-kings-men-warrant-under-privy-seal.

speaks to the historical gulf opened by the cultural upheaval of the early 1640s, described earlier in this book; by 1643, both medieval monuments and Jacobean playhouses belonged to the same inaccessible past. But, in contrast to the representation of the "worthy citizen" Gower, in the "Perambulation," boisterous Jacobean theatre professionals are idealized without being sanitized. The author appears to yearn equally for the "drink and disorder"[13] and theatrical activity of the Stuart period, both of which were targeted by Parliamentary reforms. The "Perambulation" author embraces the English theatre in all its seedy, intoxicated glory – precisely the type of story usually "passed by" in public histories which the antiquarian wants to preserve for "the searchers of Antiquitye in time to come." The "Perambulation" of 1643 commemorates the "stews" of the Jacobean playhouses and bear gardens whose status as a "source of profit" became more obvious once they disappeared.

Several critics have noted that English theatre historiography, namely the deliberate study of theatrical practices and individuals, did not exist when early modern playhouses were active.[14] Richard Schoch explains this omission by arguing that, before the Restoration, "it was conceptually inconceivable that a post-classical account of the stage was a fit subject for historians," who were concerned only with the "great and grave."[15] Schoch ascribes the origins of theatre history as a field of study to two changes: "the establishment of theatre as an identifiable commercial activity in its own right" and "the weakening of the humanist paradigm that restricted history to public affairs." The first condition was met in the Elizabethan period; the second "would have to wait until the Restoration."[16] English theatre history is usually said to begin with Richard Flecknoe's *A Short Discourse of the English Stage* (1664).[17] Other strands of dramatic study are similarly traced to the period after 1660, when, as Claire M. L. Bourne argues, "for the first time in England, attempts were made to formulate a comprehensive, coherent, and prescriptive theory of drama."[18] Flecknoe, John Dryden,

---

[13] See Capp, *England's Culture Wars*, pp. 152–71.

[14] Holland, "A History of Histories," pp. 8–29.

[15] See also Jesse Lander, "the great deed model of history is uncomplicated: heroes perform feats of courage (*res gestae*) and scribes chronicle their accomplishments (*historia rerum gestarum*)." Jesse Lander, "Historiography," in *Cultural Reformations*, ed. Simpson and Cummings, pp. 56–74 (p. 57).

[16] Schoch, *Writing the History of the British Stage*, pp. 24, 47.

[17] Holland, "A History of Histories," pp. 8–29; Ellen MacKay, *Persecution, Plague and Fire*, pp. 3–4; Schoch, *Writing the History of the British Stage*, pp. 76–7.

[18] Bourne, *Typographies*, p. 219. See also John O'Brien, *Harlequin Britain: Pantomime and Entertainment, 1690–1760* (Baltimore: Johns Hopkins University Press, 2004), p. 33.

and Gerard Langbaine are regarded as pioneering figures in theatre history, dramatic criticism, and bibliography, respectively; while Thomas Rymer's *The Tragedies of the Last Age* (1678), Jeremy Collier's *A Short View of the Immortality and Profaneness of the English Stage* (1698), James Wright's *Historia Histrionica* (1699), and John Downes's *Roscius Anglicanus* (1708) are other founding texts of English dramatic criticism and theatre history.

If, as Schoch suggests, the birth of English theatre historiography required historians to pay attention to matters previously deemed to be trivial, then the "Perambulation" reveals that this occurred as early as 1643, as the author attends to the English playhouses and other spaces that were previously "passed by or little mentiond by those great Antiquaries." But it is not only that historiography lowered its standards to include theatre; the cultural and political upheaval of the 1640s and 1650s elevated theatre to the level of public affairs. While the theatres were open, there were isolated instances of the authorities targeting drama, but after 1642 this persecution attacked the whole industry. The Parliamentary prohibition that outlawed theatre immediately politicized English drama, bringing it into the scope of public history.[19]

Another reason that historiographical attention to the theatre began after the playhouses closed is that the formerly reliable institutions of theatre and drama were suddenly threatened with oblivion. When the playhouses were active, individual theatrical performances were transient, but the entire theatrical tradition was relatively enduring, even habitual. There was no pressing need to record the theatre's past, because some version of it was reliably present. But the prohibition enacted a shift in the ordinary course of affairs; the quotidian is accorded new attention after it disappears.[20] Schoch recognizes this, arguing that "people began to think historically about the stage in the Restoration because that was when historical events in the theatre demanded an explanation. The history of the stage was not written until the course of human events turned the past into a *problem:* a wound to be healed, a gap to be closed, a division to be overcome."[21] But, as this book has demonstrated, the wound/gap/division that punctured English theatrical life both occurred, and was recognized, in the 1640s and 1650s. The "Perambulation" suggests how the trauma of the English Civil Wars and the closure of the theatres spurred a theatrically

---

[19] On the politicization of drama, see Straznicky, *Privacy*, p. 15; Wiseman, *Drama and Politics*; Katrin Beushausen, *Theater and the English Public from the Reformation to the Revolution* (Cambridge: Cambridge University Press, 2018).

[20] Lander, "Historiography," p. 51.

[21] Schoch, *Writing the History of the British Stage*, p. 104: see also Paul Menzer, *Anecdotal Shakespeare: A New Performance History* (London: Bloomsbury Arden Shakespeare, 2015), pp. 10–11.

inflected documentary impulse as early as 1643. Those who trace the origins of theatre historiography to the Restoration, then, are starting too late; the same is true of other strands of sustained dramatic study said to originate after 1660. Indeed, the intertwined and reciprocally influential practices of theatre history, dramatic criticism, dramatic bibliography, and so forth,[22] all stem from the same historiographical drive, motivated by a sense of the drama's importance and a preoccupation with its vulnerability, both of which were established during the theatrical prohibition. While dramatic study flourished after the Restoration and took on forms – stand-alone critical essays and books, discrete bibliographies, self-conscious theatre histories – recognizable to modern scholars, it was founded on theatre historiographical impulses that surged during the theatrical prohibition as a reaction to widespread loss. The cultural crises of the 1640s and 1650s established the necessary conditions for better-known critical interventions after 1660.

While less recognizable to modern scholars as artefacts of dramatic study, several influential modes and documents emerged in the 1640s and 1650s in response to the closure of the theatres. As the Introduction demonstrates, Richard Flecknoe's "Whimzey" (1653), another work of peripatetic antiquarianism, anticipates his *Short Discourse of the English Stage* (1664) that is said to be the first theatre history proper, as it deliberately memorializes parts of the theatrical landscape and past performances. Because the "Whimzey" is a walking tour that describes the loss of theatre amid the broader destruction of the English Revolution, it is not recognized as a stand-alone theatre history. But the memorial impulse necessary for theatre historiography is unmistakable. Likewise, Langbaine's bibliographies can be traced back to the first comprehensive catalogues of drama published in 1656, also discussed in the Introduction; typically studied as commercial advertisements, the catalogues' documentary function has been overlooked. Other chapters in this book have considered several key moments in English dramatic study that occurred as a direct or indirect result of the theatrical prohibition: the first dramatic anthology; the canonization of English drama as a literary genre; the publication of previously unprinted plays to establish a corpus of early modern drama; the consolidation of pre-1642 drama into a coherent group from a newly established period, "old plays" from the "last age." This concluding chapter considers how historiography's embrace of English theatre and drama

---

[22] As Schoch notes, it is anachronistic to subject theatre history to "intellectual quarantine," separate from dramatic criticism, bibliography, and broader historiography. *Writing the History of the British Stage*, p. 23.

during the mid seventeenth century shaped the interrelated practices of theatre history and dramatic criticism. Both can be interpreted as responses to the loss of theatre: theatre history sought to *recollect* elements of the absent theatre, while dramatic criticism sought to *recreate* in print the kinds of communities and conversations that previously occupied the physical spaces of the theatre industry.

The "Perambulation" represents a broad response to the general assault on England's political and cultural traditions mounted in the early 1640s, but also reflects its author's particular interest in English theatre. Thanks to the author's innovative attention to the disreputable "stews" of English entertainment, the text he produced offers one of the earliest biographical sketches of Shakespeare and his theatrical associates. This pattern of historiographical recovery is visible throughout this period, with many people not strictly considered "theatre historians" or "drama critics" nevertheless generating early artefacts of dramatic study. For instance, the prolific artist Wenceslaus Hollar created an important record of the early modern playhouses as part of his commemoration of monuments threatened with decline in the mid seventeenth century. Hollar produced engravings for William Dugdale's *The History of St. Paul's Cathedral* (1658), which was motivated by depredations on English cathedrals during the English Revolution. As Dugdale explains, he was moved to create textual records of "what Monuments I could, especially in the principal Churches of this Realme; to the end, that by Inke and paper, the Shadows of them, with their inscriptions might be preserved for posterity, forasmuch as the things themselves were so neer unto ruine."[23] Hollar's engravings in Dugdale's *History of St. Paul's* depict the cathedral's statues of James I and Charles I, as well as an architrave inscription acknowledging Charles I's contribution to efforts to restore St Paul's; these had respectively been broken and defaced following an order from the Council of State in 1650. As Stuart Mottram notes, "Hollar's decision to include the statues is more likely a reflection of his and Dugdale's royalist agenda than it is a record of the portico's actual appearance in commonwealth and protectorate England."[24] In the face of ruin, Hollar and Dugdale resort to "ink and paper" to preserve England's cultural patrimony for posterity.

But, like the "Perambulation" author, Hollar did not limit himself to grand monuments. A decade before his print reconstruction of St Paul's, Hollar created a panorama, *The Long View of London* (Cornelis Danckerts, 1647) (Figure 5.1), which depicts the City of London from the perspective

---

[23] Qtd. in Mottram, *Ruin and Reformation*, pp. 132–3.   [24] Ibid., p. 149.

Figure 5.1   Wenceslaus Hollar, [*The Long View of London*] *Ad Londinum epitomen & ocellum* (Cornelis Danckerts, 1647).
Courtesy of the Folger Shakespeare Library.

of the Church of St Saviour, called St Mary Overie before the Reformation (the name was also used after it), and now called Southwark Cathedral.[25] Located near the Globe and Rose Theatres, St Saviour's was frequented by theatre professionals: theatre impresario Philip Henslowe and actor Edward Alleyn were vestrymen there; Henslowe, Fletcher, Massinger, and the actor Edmund Shakespeare, William's younger brother, were all buried there. (The "Perambulation" author likewise records "the Priory of St Mary Overye" as one of "many ancient places yet to be seen and fast falling in ruine and not noticed by others.") Hollar's *Long View* offers one of the most reliable sketches of the exterior of the Globe and the Hope Theatres, although he reverses their names.[26] As many scholars have noted, however, the Globe was already demolished (probably around 1644 or 1645) at the time Hollar completed his engraving. Scholars have chalked up this seeming inaccuracy to Hollar working in exile in Holland, using out-of-date sketches of the city.[27] But we might instead interpret Hollar's representation of the Globe in the same light as his representation of St Paul's statues for Dugdale's text – a wistful Royalist's preservation in ink and paper of monuments targeted by the political opposition. *The Long View* is among the most-reproduced images in early modern dramatic scholarship, especially common in introductory or foundational accounts of the field. For instance, a portion of the image appears on the flyleaf of the most recent edition of the Pelican Shakespeare. Hollar's *Long View* of 1647 is one of many artefacts of English theatre history produced after the theatres themselves closed which speak to the recuperative impulses of early modern historiography and the increasing inclusion of English drama within that broader scholarly practice.

Dramatic paratexts of the mid seventeenth century offer many prominent examples of a rising historiographical impulse that retrospectively documented early modern theatre and drama. Already in this book, for instance, we have seen the elaborate actor list from *The Wild Goose Chase* (1652), which praises the "incomparable" and "natural" performances of individual King's Servant actors, and therefore offers rare insight into the company's theatrical personnel and casting decisions in the 1630s.

---

[25] Arthur Mayger Hind, *Wenceslaus Hollar and His Views of London and Windsor in the Seventeenth Century* (Miami: HardPress, 2012); Richard Pennington, *A Descriptive Catalog of the Etched Work of Wenceslaus Hollar 1607–77* (Cambridge: Cambridge University Press, 1982).

[26] See I. A. Shapiro, "Bankside Theatres: Early Engravings," in *Shakespeare Survey*, vol. 1, ed. Allardyce Nicoll (Cambridge: Cambridge University Press 1948), pp. 25–37 (p. 33).

[27] See Richard Dutton, *Shakespeare's Theatre: A History* (New York: Wiley-Blackwell, 2018), p. 236; Graham Parry, "Wenceslas Hollar, the Antiquarians Illustrator," *Ariel*, 3.2 (1972), 42–52.

Dramatic paratexts deliberately shape our picture of early modern drama; sometimes quite literally, as with the frontispiece portraits of Thomas Middleton, Philip Massinger, and James Shirley produced for Humphrey Moseley's *New Plays* editions in the 1650s. These became the representative portraits of their respective authors; Middleton's frontispiece portrait from *Two New Plays* (1657) (Figure 5.2), for example, is prominently featured at the beginning of the Oxford edition of Middleton's *Collected Works* (2007); the title page of Barbara Ravelhofer's collection *James Shirley and Early Modern Theatre: New Critical Perspectives* (2016) reproduces Shirley's *New Plays* portrait (Figure I.2, p. 21). The frequently reproduced frontispiece to the droll collection *The Wits or Sport Upon Sport, Part 1* (1662) (Figure 2.2, p. 107), printed by Henry Marsh and later reprinted by Francis Kirkman, offers the first visual depiction of Falstaff and interior views of an early modern playhouse.[28] S. P. Cerasano notes that the depicted theatre is of a style "used much earlier than the Restoration," and appears to be a "structure very like the private, indoor playhouse, the Cockpit-in-Court used in the 1630s," and also observes that the spectators in the gallery above the stage and surrounding it are dressed in what appears to be attire from the late 1640s.[29] In *The Wits*, nostalgia operates on multiple levels: it is a backwards-facing anthology of drolls performed on the illegal Interregnum stage, while its elaborate frontispiece visualizes theatrical spaces of the past. The volume's very existence speaks to nostalgia's generative quality, creating for posterity printed records of traditions no longer extant.

Long a familiar feature of commercial drama, dramatic paratexts' function and frequency shifted in the Interregnum. Lukas Erne argues that during the late sixteenth and early seventeenth centuries, "commercial drama was increasingly endowed with literary respectability" through the rising inclusion of a wide range of paratexts, including dedications, prefatory epistles, commendatory poems, Latin title page mottos, cast and actor lists, arguments, commonplace markers, and act and scene divisions.[30] Play publication after 1642 continued this trend, reflecting, in part, the continued rise of English drama's cultural status after the theatres closed. But the 1640s and 1650s also marked a new moment in dramatic paratexts.[31] During this

---

[28] King, "The First Known Picture of Falstaff."   [29] Cerasano, "Must the Devil Appear," p. 196.
[30] Erne, *Shakespeare and the Book*, p. 99.
[31] See Sonia Massai and Heidi Craig, "Rethinking Prologues and Epilogues on Page and Stage," in *Rethinking Theatrical Documents in Shakespeare's England*, ed. Tiffany Stern (London: The Arden Shakespeare, 2020), pp. 91–110; Tamara Atkin and Emma Smith, "The Form and Function of Character Lists in Plays Printed before the Closing of the Theatres," *Review of English Studies*, 65.271 (2014), 647–72.

Figure 5.2   Authorial frontispiece portrait from Thomas Middleton, *Two New Plays*
(Humphrey Moseley, 1657).
Courtesy of the Huntington Library.

period, we see a rise in both the historiographical paratexts discussed elsewhere in this book (such as cast lists), and, relatedly, an uptick in dedications, epistles, and commendatory poems – that is, the types of paratexts that express social networks and critical opinions.

With the closure of the theatres and the exile and dispersal of communities during the early 1640s, overlapping networks of authors, patrons, and stationers attempted to recreate in print the sociable, political, and evaluative functions previously carried out in the theatre, the court, and manuscript coterie circulation.[32] Previously, much discussion happened in person; as Douglas Lane Patey has pointed out, in the early seventeenth century, "references to the act of criticism suggest not written but oral communication, whether in pit, coffeehouse, or polite social gathering."[33] But the closure of the playhouses and the surrounding political upheaval made such gatherings less frequent; discourse moved into textual spaces. As Michael Gavin argues, individuals of the 1640s and 1650s "used critical discourse in printed books – prefaces, dedications, and commendatory verse – to simulate an elite coterie of literary judgment."[34] The theatrical prohibition drove not only drama, but also dramatic criticism into print.

Crucially, textual communities in print did not require first-hand acquaintance (or, as I discuss below, even for its members to be alive). Michelle O'Callaghan cites Harold Love's exploration of "scribal communities" where the "exchange of texts in manuscript functions to give figurative, social, and sometimes political representation to a community." As O'Callaghan explains, the medium of print made these links public and "offered readers access to and means of participating in a coterie sociability that did not require personal knowledge."[35] Printed dramatic paratexts, then, established and expressed visible textual communities – composed of the authors who wrote the paratexts, the readers who consumed the paratexts, and individuals named in the paratexts – and functioned as spaces for literary criticism. Together, the communities and paratexts represent an incipient authoritative institution of dramatic criticism.

---

[32] Gavin, *The Invention of English Criticism*, pp. 24, 29; Sauer, *Paper-Contestations*, p. 6; Beushausen, *Theater and the English Public*.

[33] Douglas Lane Patey, "The Institution of Criticism in the Eighteenth Century," in *The Cambridge History of Literary Criticism, Vol. IV: The Eighteenth Century*, ed. H. B. Nisbet and Claude Rawson (Cambridge: Cambridge University Press, 1997), pp. 1–31 (p. 12).

[34] Gavin, *The Invention of English Criticism*, pp. 24, 8.

[35] Michelle O'Callaghan, *The English Wits: Literature and Sociability in Early Modern England* (Cambridge: Cambridge University Press, 2007), p. 177.

Dramatic paratexts became more prevalent after 1642: more playbooks included paratexts, and individual volumes had, on average, more prefatory material. The rise in commendatory verse was especially conspicuous: Heidi Brayman notes that "so extensive had preliminaries become by 1651 that one writer complained 'this fault [of excessive praise] is epidemical.'"[36] The Beaumont and Fletcher folio (1647) had thirty-seven commendatory poems, a record smashed by William Cartwright's *Tragedies and Comedies* (1651) with fifty-three commendatory poems. These paratexts create literary and political communities both actual and abstract. As Kevin Sharpe and Steven N. Zwicker explain, "While a verse or two from a friend or intimate might commend and domesticate the author and book, sometimes a panoply of eulogies and commendations formed a virtual academy of association and mapped a community of literary and political validation."[37] There was strength in numbers, whether to declare political affiliation, to display social power, or to perpetuate aesthetic judgements. Moseley defends the fifty-odd poems in the Cartwright volume on those last grounds:

> 'T hath past the Court, and University,
> (Th' old standing Judges of good Poetry:)
> Besides, as many Hands attest it here,
> As there are Shires in England, Weekes I' th' Yeere.[38]

The manifold paratext authors displace "the old standing judges of good poetry," the university and the court. Dramatic criticism is the purview of any engaged reader, not simply those associated with established institutions. Michael Gavin explains that "Moseley refers outward to the institutional stalwarts of critical judgement, the courts and the universities, but he places most of his emphasis on the testimony accumulated in the book itself."[39] The materialization of a large community of readers guarantees the book's merit; critical judgement is strengthened by aggregation, "the many hands" numbering "the weeks in the year." Moseley capitalizes on this embarrassment of riches to attract potential buyers and to address those sceptical of such effusive praise for a minor poet. In his commendatory poem to the Cartwright volume, he suggests any doubters should buy

---

[36] Heidi Brayman Hackel, *Reading Material in Early Modern England: Print, Gender and Literacy* (Cambridge: Cambridge University Press, 2005), p. 101.
[37] Kevin Sharpe and Steven N. Zwicker, "Introduction: Discovering the Renaissance Reader," in *Reading, Society and Politics in Early Modern England*, ed. Sharpe and Zwicker, pp. 1–37 (pp. 6).
[38] Humphrey Moseley, "The Stationer," in William Cartwright, *Comedies and Tragedies* (London: Humphrey Moseley, 1651), sig. ***11r.
[39] Gavin, *The Invention of English Criticism*, p. 26.

the book and see for themselves: "Six hundred Pages of good Wit? Read, try it: / Would all that cannot mend this book would buy it."[40]

While the Cartwright volume suggests that the proliferation and dispersal of aesthetic authority is ultimately more reliable than elite institutionalized opinions, others objected that paratexts could falsely establish cultural status through sheer force of numbers. There was backlash against Cartwright's volume.[41] The problem wasn't each individual poem's hyperbolic praise for a relatively minor playwright (like the poem which praised "rare CARTVVRIGHT; to whom all must bow, / That was best Preacher and best Poet too"); the generic conventions of the commendatory poem permitted such excess. Rather, it was the number of poems that rankled critics. Several commendatory poems for Richard Brome's *A Jovial Crew* (printed in 1652 by James Young for Edward Dod and Nathaniel Ekins) took aim at Moseley's transparent tactics to overhype the volume. James Shirley, in "To his worthy Friend Master RICHARD BROME, upon his Comedie, called, A Ioviall Crew," writes snidely that, although lacking excessive paratextual praise like Cartwright's volume, *A Jovial Crew* would nevertheless stand the test of time: "thy Play, although Not elevated unto Fifty two. / It may grow old as Time or Wit." As the Cartwright volume and *A Jovial Crew*'s commendatory verses indicate, paratextual spaces provided a key forum for dramatic criticism. Public conversations about drama occurred across, as well as within paratexts. The mockery of the Cartwright prefatory matter in *A Jovial Crew*'s own prefatory matter reveals paratextual dramatic criticism's reflexivity and meta-critical quality: such paratexts not only examined plays and dramatists, but also consider the paratext itself as a medium for dramatic criticism.

J. B. (likely Sir John Berkenhead)[42] also ridicules Moseley's edition of Cartwright in "To Master RICHARD BROME, on his Comedie of A Iovial Crew or The Merrie Beggars," stating that

---

[40] Moseley, "The Stationer," in Cartwright, *Comedies and Tragedies*, sig. ***11r.
[41] Cartwright's actual value is further belied by the volume itself; printed in octavo, he wasn't granted publication in the prestigious folio format like Beaumont and Fletcher.
[42] Tiffany Stern identifies Berkenhead through his social ties, as well as his habit of writing commendatory poems. As she explains, "Though Keith Whitlock (561) suggests that J. B. was John Benson, the printer of Jonson's 1640 *Poems*, there is no evidence that Benson was in the habit of writing commendatory verses, nor is it clear that he knew Brome or the other writers gathered together here. Given that all these encomiums share themes, J. B. is much more likely to have been Sir John Berkenhead (1617–79), journalist and poet, friend of Stanley and Shirley, who often signed his published verses and prefaces only with initials, and who had previously appeared alongside Richard Brome, Alexander Brome, Herrick and Sir John Denham in the commendatory poems to Francis Beaumont and John Fletcher's *Comedies and Tragedies* of

there comes
A Shole, with Regiments of Encomiums,
On all occasions, whose Astronomy
Can calculate a Praise to Fifty three [. . .]
Those will prove Wit by Power, and make a Trade,
To force by number when they can't persuade.
Here's no such need: For Books, like Children, be
Well Christ'ned, when their Sureties are but three.
And those, which to twelve Godfathers do come,
Signify former Guilt, or speedy Doom.
Nor need the Stationer, when all th'
Wits are past, Bring his own Periwig Poetry at last.[43]

J. B. flatly contradicts Moseley's claim that "many hands" are "judges of good poetry": instead, too many "godfathers" (a jocular colloquial term for members of a jury)[44] "signifie former Guilt, or speedy Doom," raising the reader's suspicions. Plays are "well Christ'ned" (by literal godfathers) "when their Sureties are but three." (In fact, *A Jovial Crew* has five commendatory poems.) J. B. lampoons Moseley's own overblown "periwig poetry" that attempts to conceal the volume's shortcomings. The periwig of the bourgeois stationer also hints at the commercial motivations of textual coteries, while the military metaphor of "Regiments of Encomiums" gestures to the apparently royalist underpinnings of para-textual dramatic criticism, which therefore likewise has ulterior motives apart from straightforward aesthetic judgements.

Instead of praise motivated by economics or politics, J. B. suggests that the reader draw their own conclusions, apart from the critics' (i.e., the authors of commendatory poems) opinions: "For, when their Labour's done, / The Reader's rul'd, not by their tastes, but's own." J. B. claims that the commendatory poem only reveals the poet's allegiances and the critic's idiosyncratic dramatic tastes. A poem demonstrates, "Onely that we're his Friends, and do suppose / 'Tis good: And that is all, that I shall say. / In truth I love him well, and like his Play."[45] Despite himself, however, J. B. here indicates how dramatic paratexts express social networks in print. Functioning both as a symbol of collective identification and a broadcaster of dramatic taste, the paratext invariably influenced readers. Indeed, J. B.

1647." Richard Brome, *A Jovial Crew*, ed. Tiffany Stern (London: Bloomsbury Arden Shakespeare, 2014), p. 77 n. 33.
[43] J. B., "To Master RICHARD BROME, on his Comedie of A Iovial Crew or The Merrie Beggars," in Brome, *A Jovial Crew* (1652), sig. A3r.
[44] Stern, "Introduction," in *A Jovial Crew* (2014), p. 78 n. 19.
[45] J. B., "To Master RICHARD BROME," in *A Jovial Crew* (1652), sig. A3r.

undermines the authority of his own assessment: large groups of commendatory poems by authors with weak social ties – because they were acquainted only in printed spaces, or belonged to different generations, or they were no longer living – were perhaps more credible as guarantors of literary value than friends' individual opinions, whose credibility was compromised by personal considerations.

Decades after Beaumont and Fletcher died, Moseley published their collected works in folio with an impressive thirty-seven commendatory poems by well-known poets and political figures. Ann Baynes Coiro argues that it is "remarkable that the royalists chose the plays of Beaumont and Fletcher as the cultural monument on which to stake their claims," so long after they lived.[46] But the retrospective nature of the volume is precisely the point; dissatisfied with the present, the Royalists take refuge in the cultural past when they were dominant. This past is populated by ghosts: the folio resurrects Jonson to reiterate his encomium to Beaumont, printing his poem "To Mr Francis Beaumont (then living)," written before Beaumont's 1616 death (and obviously before Jonson's own death in 1639).[47] Thomas Moisan observes that the point of one dead poet praising another "is to forge a moment of poetic continuity, less important for any praise meted out to Beaumont and Fletcher than for its pretensions to transgenerational reach."[48] We see this strategy throughout Interregnum paratextual discourse: Katherine Philips is given pride of place in William Cartwright's collection, as the first poem in the volume; she refers to Cartwright as her "friend," although she was only twelve years old when Cartwright died in 1643.[49]

The transgenerational literary community established in Interregnum paratexts could extend beyond living Interregnum authors to include figures from the Caroline, Jacobean, and Elizabethan periods. This occurred not only through a panoply of different paratexts in single volumes: individual paratexts also created textual communities by compiling long lists of well-known poets, dramatists, and other public figures, both alive and dead. John Finch's commendatory poem to Cartwright's

---

[46] Coiro, "Reading," p. 543.
[47] Other poems are by dead authors. Immediately preceding Jonson's poem is Richard Corbet's "On Mr Francis Beaumont (then newly dead)," written around 1625; Corbet himself died in 1635.
[48] Thomas Moisan, "The King's Second Coming," in *In the Company of Shakespeare: Essays on the English Renaissance in Honor of G. Blakemore Evans*, ed. Thomas Moisan and Douglas Bruster (Vancouver: Fairleigh Dickinson University Press, 2002), pp. 270–91 (p. 275).
[49] Carol Barash, *English Women's Poetry, 1649–1714: Politics, Community, and Literary Authority* (Oxford: Clarendon Press, 1996), p. 63.

collection of 1651, titled "To my dear Mother the University of Oxford," positions the late Cartwright within a lengthy roll call of well-known dramatic and literary figures: Suckling, Carew, Waller, Beaumont and Fletcher, Denham, Newcastle, Davenant, Stapleton, Fanshaw, Stanley, Cranshaw, Shirley, Quarles, Mayne, Cleveland, Birkenhead, Cowley, Vincent, and Brown.[50] Most of these poets were active in the mid seventeenth century; Beaumont and Fletcher stand out as dramatists who died decades earlier. The transgenerational textual community created in dramatic paratexts transcends temporal and corporeal limits. By joining poets living and dead, Royalists real and probable (i.e., individuals that Royalists felt confident *would* be royalist had they lived through the period), paratexts created a feeling of continuity, both aesthetic and political. Interregnum paratexts forge a symbiotic relationship between Royalists and dead dramatists: the former ensured the continued relevance of pre-1642 dramatists by superimposing contemporary politics onto them, while reputable dramatists like Beaumont and Fletcher lent their well-established cultural value to royalist writers.

As we have seen, Royalists' co-option of pre-1642 drama is well-established, thanks in large part to Moseley's extensive paratextual apparatuses. But Royalists did not have a monopoly on dramatic criticism. *Tragicomedia* (1653), by the Puritan preacher John Rowe, is an anti-theatrical tract that also represents an early instance of theatre history and politically inflected dramatic criticism. The tract describes a disaster that occurred during a provincial performance of *Mucedorus* in February 1653 in the Oxfordshire town of Witney.[51] Rowe claims not to have been present at the disaster; nevertheless, he relates the events in exacting journalistic detail. He describes how throngs of spectators were summoned by drums and trumpet, which had once been the familiar call to the playhouse.[52] Three to four hundred people crammed into the White Hart Inn; some of those who did not fit into the venue gathered in the yard and "pressed sorely to get in."[53] After a decade of official theatrical sanctions, audiences were eager for entertainment, yet the performance itself was almost beside the point. Rowe recounts that the "merry and

[50] Ross, *The Making of the English Literary Canon*, pp. 133–4. See also Sauer, *Paper-Contestations*, p. 141.
[51] Between September 1652 and February 1653, a touring group of provincial players staged *Mucedorus* across southeast England.
[52] Tiffany Stern, "On each Wall and Corner Poast': Playbills, Title-Pages, Advertising in Early Modern London," *English Literary Renaissance*, 36 (2006), 57–85.
[53] Rowe, *Tragicomoedia*, sig. *1r.

frolick" spectators were so "exceeding jovial [. . . that] the Players could hardly get Liberty that they themselves might Act."[54] The festive scene of villagers going to watch *Mucedorus* matches the play's contents: popular, nostalgic, cheerful. *Mucedorus* had long represented an ongoing delight in the fantasies and devices made available and used by "old plays." Since the 1610s, *Mucedorus* had simply been called "the play," standing in for an entire tradition of early modern theatre.[55]

The cheer in Witney soon turned grim. During *Mucedorus*'s fourth act, the floor of the overcrowded makeshift playhouse collapsed, injuring at least sixty spectators and actors and killing six people.[56] Rowe describes the event as an act of divine retribution against theatrical performance, and pinpoints the moment of collapse as a scene particularly offensive to God, explained through a detailed reading (including direct quotation) of the play and attention to theatrical performance:

> It pleased God to put a stop to their mirth, and by an immediate hand of his owne, in causing the chamber to sink, and fall under them, to put an end to this ungodly Play before it was thought, or intended by them. The Actors who were now in action were Bremo a wild man courting, and solliciting his Lady, and among other things, begging a Kisse in this verse:

Come kisse me (Sweet) for all my favours past.[57]

God purposefully destroyed the stage, Rowe declares, "in the middest of these amorous passages between Bremo, and his Lady . . . yea, immediately before they expected the greatest pleasure, and contentment." Rowe unpacks the scene's particular immorality: the "Lady" Amandine is "in truth a young man attired in a woman's Habit." Cross-dressing was a well-worn anti-theatrical hobbyhorse; throughout *Tragicomedia*, Rowe voices the typical anti-theatrical complaints associated with fundamental Puritanism so thoroughly that Janet Clare describes the tract as "a parody of old anti-theatrical polemic."[58] Rowe's account appears to be sincere, but it is distinctly retrograde: *Tragicomedia* essentially reproduces an Elizabethan tract against theatre. Rowe's account reveals how nostalgia imbued both theatrical activity and anti-theatrical responses during the Interregnum. With his energetic denunciation of the "wicked and ungodly

---

[54] Ibid.
[55] Richard Priess, "A Play Finally Anonymous," in *The Shakespeare Apocrypha*, ed. Brooks, pp. 117–39 (p. 118).
[56] Victor Holtcamp provides a full discussion of this incident in "A Fear of 'Ould' Plays."
[57] Rowe, *Tragicomoedia*, sig. 2*v.   [58] Clare, *Drama of the English Republic*, p. 8.

Play," Rowe betrays a longing for an earlier moment when anti-theatricalism was a site of moral authority. Just as the theatrical prohibition deprived spectators of entertainment, it diminished the urgency of anti-theatrical complaints. The Witney performance provided Rowe a rare opportunity to trot out old anti-theatrical grievances, as gleefully as the spectators trotted out to see an old play.

In addition to its debt to its Elizabethan anti-theatrical forebears in general, *Tragicomedia* has a specific antecedent, namely, the anti-theatrical pamphlet *A Godly Exhortation* (1583), which the Puritan John Field (father of the actor Nathan Field) wrote in response to the collapse of the Paris Garden on 13 January 1583 during a Sunday bear-baiting. Rowe cites the events, "Upon the 13 of January, Anno 1583" as an "instance so neere a kin to that of Witny, that it may not be omitted," and borrows many of Field's locutions and arguments in his account of the Witney catastrophe. For example, Rowe's description of those who "were carried in and led betwixt their friends, and so brought home to their houses with sorrowfull heavy hearts" is reminiscent of Field's description of the Paris Garden collapse in which spectators' bruised bodies "ledde betwixte theyr friendes, and so brought home wyth sorrowfull and heauy hartes."[59] Both writers see the playhouse's collapse as divine retribution for immoral pastimes – Field interprets the Paris Garden events as a "judgment of God," and relates them "to all estates for their instruction concerning the keeping of the Sabbath day holy." Both poignantly relate the spectators' confusion and horror amid their respective disasters. Rowe echoes and amplifies the pathos of Field's narrative: where the earlier writer reports the "woefull screekes & cries, wch did even pierce the skies: children there bewailing the death and hurts of their parents, Parents of their children: wives of their Husbands, and Husbands of their Wives," Rowe directly quotes the outpouring of familial grief, relating how there was "the Most lamentable cry, some crying one thing, some another, some crying aid for the Lords sake, others crying Lord have mercy on us, Christ have mercy on us, others cryed oh my Husband! a second, oh my Wife! a third, Oh my child! and another said, No body loves me so well as to see where my child is."

Rowe closely read and built on Field's earlier anti-theatrical tract for his account and critique of the theatrical event in 1653. Anti-theatrical tracts provide crucial insights into early modern theatrical practice: in their

---

[59] Rowe, *Tragicomoedia*, p. 44; John Field, *A Godly Exhortation* (London: Robert Waldegrave and Henry Carre, 1583), p. ciii.

denunciations, anti-theatricalists often reveal specific details about early modern staging and audience response.[60] For instance, Field and Rowe both indicate that early modern spectatorship was a family affair, with events attended by men, women, and children. Moreover, as his direct quotation of *"Come kisse me (Sweet) for all my favours past"* at the moment of collapse indicates, Rowe also possesses intimate knowledge of the text of *Mucedorus*. Throughout *Tragicomedia*, he quotes verbatim from a play text derived from the third quarto, even reproducing its typography. He must have owned or had access to a copy of *Mucedorus* – one of the sixteen quartos printed by the mid-1650s, perhaps the same edition the performers used for their play.[61] Ironically, despite his antipathy towards drama, Rowe embodies a new kind of dramatic criticism, which combines a review of a theatrical performance, discussion of contemporary stage practices, citation of an earlier theatre historian (i.e. Field), direct quotation and analysis of the text, politicized literary criticism, and dramatic critique based largely on textual encounters, since Rowe supposedly did not attend *Mucedorus*'s performance and relied on the printed text. Rowe's *Tragicomedia* anticipates later works of criticism such as Thomas Rymer's *Tragedies of the Last Age* (1678) and Jeremy Collier's *A Short View of the Immorality and Profaneness of the English Stage* (1698), which respectively critiqued early modern plays and denounced the immorality of Restoration comedy through attentive readings of the plays themselves.

Coda: Speaking with the Dead

John Rowe's *Tragicomedia* illuminates facets of Interregnum theatre history, informing us about the play selected for performance, the players' touring schedule, the summoning of the spectators and their behaviour once they arrive, the casting of roles, and so forth. Rowe's account speaks to how both opposition and disaster elicit commentary which, intentionally or not, establishes the historical record. As a result of the lack of a theatre historiographical impulse while the playhouses were active, contemporary documentation surrounding early modern theatre is scant.

---

[60] Tanya Pollard, "Introduction: Debating the Theatre in Shakespeare's England," in *Shakespeare's Theatre: A Source Book*, ed. Tanya Pollard (New York: Wiley, 2008), pp. x–xxiv (p. xi).

[61] Holtcamp, "'Ould' Plays," p. 146. Gilchrist notes, "Ascertaining the edition Rowe quotes is challenging. Vagaries of spelling and punctuation between Rowe and the various texts of *Mucedorus* do not point to a single edition, although the repetition of the word 'stay' in Envie's opening line (sig. A3r) points to an edition of 1618 or later." Kim Gilchrist, "*Mucedorus*: The Last Ludic Playbook, the First Stage *Arcadia*," *Shakespeare*, 15 (2019), 1–20 (p. 17 n. 38).

Ellen MacKay notes that "for theatre historians, early modern England is an awkward subject: a golden age fettered to a shadowy past ... an illustrious drama that happened off the record."[62] We cling to the few contemporary records of theatre history, like Philip Henslowe's peerless diary, or the rare description of Edward Alleyn's acting style, "stalking" across the stage.[63] But these accounts were produced for commercial or promotional reasons; instances of history set down for history's sake are rare. Theatrical disasters and noteworthy deaths merit notice because of their departure from the ordinary, and accounts of them provide isolated instances of theatre historiography before 1642. MacKay calls the Globe fire of 1613 "the best-remembered proceeding" of the early modern stage, and her monograph studies "those evocations of the theatrical past that 'flash up at a moment of danger,'" focusing on incidents of persecution, plague, and fire.[64] The collapse of the Paris Bear Garden in 1583 encouraged John Field to write an extensive account of bear-baiting, which provides us with key information about that form of entertainment. Burbage's funeral elegy and Shakespeare's memorial First Folio of 1623 offer insights into theatrical practice, theatrical social networks, and individual biography. After death or loss, the desire to remember spurs textual commemoration.

A process of posthumous recovery occurred on a grand scale after 1642, driven by the steadily accumulating theatrical disasters (and other out-of-the-ordinary events) and the perception that an entire tradition was in the process of being lost. In his "Account book and Diary," Sir Henry Mildmay describes his outing "To a play of warre" on 16 November 1643, at which, he laconically and ominously remarks, "there was a disaster."[65] When John Evelyn attended a tragicomedy in Drury Lane in February 1648, he noted it as a rare pleasure "after there had been none of these diversions for many Yeares during the Warr."[66] Most of our knowledge of Interregnum performance comes from accounts of governmental raids; clandestine performances remained secret when all went as planned. As theatrical losses and disasters accumulated – raids, demolished venues, actors abandoning the profession without clear successors – so too did the need to record the theatre's former glories. The shift in many theatrical attributions printed

---

[62] MacKay, *Persecution, Plague and Fire*, p. 1.
[63] On scholars latching onto the description of Alleyn's acting, see Lopez, "Alleyn Resurrected."
[64] MacKay, *Persecution, Plague and Fire*, pp. 5–7.
[65] Qtd. in Hotson, *Commonwealth and Restoration Stage*, p. 17.
[66] John Evelyn, *Diary and Correspondence of John Evelyn*, ed. William Bray, 4 vols. (London: Henry Colburn, 1850), I, p. 246.

on professional playbooks' title pages after 1649 – presenting the play performed by "his *Late* Majesties Servants," subtly but powerfully invokes a receding cultural and political moment. After the theatres closed, dramatic commentators examining pre-1642 drama perceived that they were engaging not with contemporary culture, but with the ghosts of the past.

Modern studies of the early modern period have been shaped by the critical aspiration to "speak with the dead," to cite the famous opening phrase of Stephen Greenblatt's *Shakespearean Negotiations* (1988). Greenblatt's landmark work of New Historicism addressed many intersecting discursive fields in the sixteenth and seventeenth centuries, incorporating literary study into a wider account of politics, economics, and history in an attempt to better understand modernity.[67] Greenblatt's desire to commune with ghosts depends not only on the deaths of his individual interlocutors, but on the impression that the entire socio-political-cultural period in question is dead and gone, severed from the present and therefore available for and in need of recovery by the literary historian. The New Historicists helped popularize the "early modern" as a critical term, while the traditional critical moniker of the "Renaissance" fell from relative favour due to its ostensibly more limiting associations with high culture, elite communities, and classical antecedents. But, of course, communion with the dead is also key to understanding the "Renaissance" as a critical concept: etymologically, "renaissance" implies rebirth and resuscitation. The German art historian Erwin Panofsky famously literalized the Renaissance as a kind of seance: "The Middle Ages had left antiquity unburied and alternately galvanized and exorcised its corpse. The Renaissance stood weeping at its grave and tried to resurrect its soul."[68] In *The Light in Troy: Imitation and Discovery in Renaissance Poetry*, Thomas Greene defines Renaissance culture through the metaphor of disinterment, resuscitation, and rebirth. But, Greene notes, the desire to resurrect the dead is present not only in sixteenth- and seventeenth-century attitudes towards classical antiquity, but also in modern approaches to the sixteenth and seventeenth centuries.

When did study-as-seance of sixteenth- and seventeenth-century drama begin? The Beaumont and Fletcher folio, as we have seen, was a

---

[67] Stephen Greenblatt, *Shakespearean Negotiations: The Circulation of Social Energy in Renaissance England* (Berkeley: University of California Press, 1988), p. 1. See also Wiles, "Medieval, Renaissance and Early Modern Theatre," p. 64. "Early modern" as a period description was in fact first coined in the Victorian period (Harris, "Periodizing the Early Modern," p. 23).

[68] Erwin Panofsky, *Renaissance and Renascences in Western Art* (Stockholm: Almquist & Wiksell, 1960), p. 113.

posthumous dramatic collection with commendatory poems written by
the dead, in which the dead Ben Jonson was resurrected to praise the dead
Beaumont while surrounded by living royalist paratextual authors. Jonson
died in the late 1630s, but already by the 1640s he was no longer
"contemporary": Royalists regarded him as a kind of revenant-prophet,
predicting mid-century strife from beyond the grave. After Jonson's death,
Ian Donaldson explains, "his presence was invoked and revived, time and
again, in the form of a ghost ... posthumously weighing in on current
troubles of the mid-century, just as his Jacobean works were viewed to
prophetically predict civil war."[69] This was not actually accompanied by
any widespread printing of Jonson's plays, but even as his print numbers
waned, the late Jonson's Head peered out from Robert Pollard's shop sign,
a Jacobean icon warning later ages about the crises to come.

Taken as individual instances, the Interregnum invocations of and
tributes to Jonson and Beaumont might be considered in similar terms
to Burbage's funeral elegy and Shakespeare's folio – posthumous engagement at the level of the specific actor or playwright. But taken all together,
the scale and significance of these latter engagements far exceed those
discrete tributes. The "Perambulation" of 1643 offers an early example
of using Shakespeare, Jonson, Burbage, and their theatrical collaborators as
a potent synecdoche for an absent political, social, and cultural period that,
both temporally and metaphorically, goes far beyond any personal lifespan
and corpus. Jonson died in 1639, but by the 1640s he belonged to another
time. By contrast, the "Age of Shakespeare" as modern scholars conceive it
extends to 1642, twenty-six years after his biological death, as evidenced by
the titles of foundational works like Andrew Gurr's *The Shakespearean
Stage, 1574–1642*, G. K. Hunter's *English Drama 1568–1642: The Age of
Shakespeare*, and G. E. Bentley's *The Profession of Actor in Shakespeare's
Time to 1642*, to name only a few. For early modern drama and theatre
scholars, the terminus of the "Age of Shakespeare" is not his actual death
but the closure of the theatres. Shakespeare is meant to metonymically
represent a broad period of cultural, political, and dramatic activity in the
sixteenth and seventeenth centuries, which reliably concludes with the
closure of the theatres. As the "Perambulation" of 1643 evidences, the
notion of an "Age of Shakespeare" that ended in 1642 can be traced to the
early 1640s itself. (Or rather, the "Age of Shakespeare, Burbage, and
Jonson" – the tract predates Shakespeare's meteoric ascendancy, and he

---

[69] Ian Donaldson, "Talking with Ghosts: Ben Jonson and the English Civil War," *Ben Jonson Journal*,
17 (2010), 1–18 (p. 13).

is still grouped with his theatrical fellows.) The "Perambulation" reflects on dead theatrical and dramatic communities that lived on the other side of an historical chasm; these individuals are emblems of the absent London theatre world, of the drama of an age which was gone, and of the pre-1642 period itself. The conception of a discrete period, corresponding to a dramatic style, was key to the birth of a dramatic field that involved critical study and disciplinary analysis. Only when a period is seen to be well and truly dead can necromantic critical engagements begin.

Dramatic commentators after 1642 focused on texts as their primary objects of dramatic study and medium of communication: English drama lived on in the printed playbooks, and dramatic discourse moved into dramatic paratexts and other printed texts. For modern scholars, too, plays have to have some textual component for them to be the object of study. As Zachary Lesser explains, "Although print publication of early modern plays from the professional theatre was almost always chronologically posterior to performance, for modern critics print must be logically prior to performance, since our historical evidence for the details of the performance of a given play exists almost entirely in the printed playbook itself."[70] Other scholars have discounted the relationship between drama on the stage and on the page: Stephen Orgel famously writes that "if the play is a book, it's not a play"; David Scott Kastan expands upon this to argue that "reading a play is not reading performance (the printed play as textualized drama) or even reading for performance (the printed play as potential drama); it is reading in the absence of performance."[71] But there are different kinds of performative absences, and these affect one's experience of play-reading. When "reading in the absence of performance" is voluntary and temporary, speaking to an individual's personal choice of reading instead of playgoing (at least for that particular engagement), it differs from play-reading enforced by the systemic absence of performance, and which represents the only legitimate means to access drama. That is, "reading in the absence of performance" is not a homogenous experience: as this book has shown, it was fundamentally different in 1600 and 1650 – or indeed in 2020, when the world's theatres were shuttered by a different kind of crisis, producing comparable shifts in dramatic production and consumption, innovations in dramatic media, and think pieces about the nature of drama without live theatre. Then and now, in the absence of in-

---

[70] Lesser, *Renaissance Drama and Politics of Publication*, p. 19.
[71] Stephen Orgel, "What Is an Editor?" *Shakespeare Studies*, 24 (1996), 23–9 (p. 23); Kastan, *Shakespeare and the Book*, p. 8.

person theatrical performance, we resort to our memories, imaginations, and alternative dramatic modes. Even as we hope for theatre to resume, we realize that the theatre as we knew it will never be fully recovered – in the wake of such a rupture, change is inevitable.

After the theatres closed in 1642, with each passing year, encounters with early modern theatre were increasingly textual, memorial, and imaginary, as those with first-hand experience of the pre-1642 stage successively shuffled off their mortal coils. At a given point, probably in the late seventeenth or early eighteenth century, the last person to see a pre-1642 performance died, marking a decisive shift in collective cultural memory. From then on, pre-1642 drama would only be accessible through one's imagination, second-hand reports, and textual records, each successively more distant from pre-1642 performance. These are the conditions in which we as modern scholars of early modern English drama work; these conditions were set in motion by the closure of the theatres in 1642. After the theatres died, the dramatic texts, methods, and attitudes created during the theatrical prohibition were bequeathed to us as our critical inheritance.

Bibliography

Early Modern Texts

The Actors Remonstrance or Complaint, for the silencing of their profession, and banishment from their severall Play houses (London: Edward Nickson, 1643)

B. J., *Guy Earle of Warwick* (London: Edward Vere and William Gilbertson, 1661)

Bayly, Thomas, *The royal charter granted unto kings, by God himself and collected out of his Holy Word* (London, 1649)

[Beaumont, Francis], *The Knight of the Burning Pestle* (London: Walter Burre, 1613)

Beaumont, Francis, and John Fletcher, *Comedies and Tragedies* (London: Humphrey Moseley and Humphrey Robinson, 1647)

   Fifty Comedies and Tragedies (London: John Martyn, Henry Herringman, and Richard Marriot, 1679)

   A King and No King (London: Richard Hawkins, 1631)

Beaumont, Francis, and [John Fletcher], *The Wild-Goose Chase* (London: Humphrey Moseley, 1652)

Beaumont, Francis, and John Fletcher, [and Philip Massinger(?)], *Beggar's Bush* (London: Humphrey Robinson and Anne Moseley, 1661)

Brome, Richard, *Five New Plays* (London: Humphrey Moseley, Richard Marriot, and Thomas Dring, 1653).

Brome, Richard, Hall, "To the Surviving Honour" in Shirley, *The Cardinal*, sig. A4v.

   Five New Plays of Richard Brome (London: Andrew Crooke and Henry Brome, 1659)

   A Jovial Crew: Or The Merry Beggars (London: J. Y. for Edward Dod and Nathaniel Ekins, 1652)

Cartwright, William, *Comedies and Tragedies* (London: Humphrey Moseley, 1651)

Cockayne, Aston, *Small Poems of Diverse Sorts* (London: William Godbid, 1658)

Congreve, William, *The Double Dealer* (London: Jacob Tonson, 1694)

Cotgrave, John, *The English Treasury of Wit and Language* (London: Humphrey Moseley, 1655)

C[ragge, J[ohn], *The Wits Interpreter* (London: Nathanial Brookes, 1655)

Downes, John, *Roscius Anglicanus* (London: H. Playford, 1708)

Dryden, John, *The Spanish Friar* (London: Richard and Jacob Tonson, 1681)

Dryden, John, and Robert Howard, *The Indian-Queen*, in Robert Howard, *Four New Plays* (London: Henry Herringman, 1665)

Du Périer, Antoine, *Loves and Adventures of Clerio and Lozia*, trans. Francis Kirkman (London: J. M. for William Ley, 1652)

The English devil: Or, Cromwel and his monstrous witch discover'd at White-Hall (London: George Horton, 1660)

The English Rogue Continued (London: Francis Kirkman, 1671)

"AN exact and perfect List of their Majesties Royal Fleet, now actually at Sea … Printed for John Amery … to be sold by Randal Taylor, near Stationers-Hall," in Joseph Bennet, *A true and Impartial account of the most material passages in Ireland since December, 1688* (London: John Amery, 1689)

The Famous Tragedie of King Charles I, Basely Butchered (1649)

Field, John, *A Godly Exhortation* (London: Robert Walde-Graut and Henry Carre, 1583)

Flecknoe, Richard, *Miscellania* (London: Thomas Roycroft for J. Martin and J. Allestrye, 1653)

"A Short Discourse on the English Stage," in *Love's Kingdom* (London: R. Wood, 1664)

Ford, John, and Thomas Dekker, *The Sun's Darling* (London: Andrew Pennycuicke, 1656)

Fuller, Thomas, *The History of Holy Warre* (Cambridge: Roger Daniel for John Williams, 1647)

Fulman, William, and Richard Perrinchief, *Basilika the Workes of King Charles the martyr* (London: Miles Flesher, 1662)

Gayton, Edmund, *Pleasant Notes upon Don Quixot* (London: William Hunt, 1654)

Goffe, Thomas, *The Careless Shepherdess* (London: William Ley and Richard Rogers, 1656)

Goughe, Alexander, *The Queen* (London: Thomas Heath, 1653)

Herrick, Robert, *Hesperides* (London: John Williams, 1648)

Heywood, Thomas, *The English Traveller* (London: Robert Raworth, 1633)

Jonson, Ben, *Catiline* (London: Walter Burre, 1611)

Killigrew, Thomas, *The Parson's Wedding*, in *Comedies and Tragedies Written by Thomas Killigrew* (London: Henry Herringman, 1664)

The Kingdom's Weekly Intelligencer, London, 2–9 January 1648/9

Kirkman, Francis, *The Unlucky Citizen* (London: Francis Kirkman, 1673)

Langbaine, Gerard, *An Account of the English Dramatic Poets* (London: George West and Henry Clements, 1691)

The last Nevvs IN LONDON. OR, A DISCOVRSE Between A Citizen and a Country-Gentleman (London: R. R., 1642)

The Man in the Moon, London, 23–31 January 1650

Massinger, Philip, Thomas Middleton, and William Rowley, *The Old Law* (London: Edward Archer, 1656)

Maunsell, Andrew, *Catalogue of English Printed Books* (London: Andrew Maunsell, 1595)

Mayne, Jasper, *Ochlo-machia. Or The peoples war, examined according to the principles of Scripture & reason* (Oxford: L. Lichfield, 1647)

Mercurius Democritus, London, 6–22 December 1652

Mercurius Democritus, London, 2–9 March 1653

Mercurius Pragmaticus, London, 5–12 October 1647, Folger M1768.49, no. 4

Mercurius Vapulans, London, 27 November 1647

The Moderate, London, 29 May–5 June 1649

Morton, Thomas, *The Encounter Against M. Parsons* (London: W. Stansby, 1610)

Naps upon Parnassus (London: Nathanial Brookes, 1658)

Neville, Henry, *The Ladies, A Second Time, Assembled in Parliament* (London: 1647)

Observations on the historie of The reign of King Charles (London: H.L. Esq, 1656)

Peaps, William, *Love in Its Ecstasy* (London: Mercy Meighen, Gabriell Bedell, and Thomas Collins, 1649)

A Perfect Account of the Daily Intelligence, London, 27 December–3 January 1654/5

A Perfect Diurnal, London, 17–24 December 1649

Perfect Occurrences, London, 8 October 1647

Perfect Occurrences, London, 8 June 1649

Price, John, *Clerico-classicum* (London: M.S. for H. Cripps, 1649)

Rowe, John, *Tragicomoedia, or a Relation of the wonderful Hand of God at Witney* (Oxford: Henry Cripps, 1653)

Rymer, Thomas, *The Tragedies of the Last Age* (London: Richard Tonson, 1678)

Shakespeare, William, *Comedies, Histories, and Tragedies* (London: Robert Allott, 1632)

 Troilus and Cressida (London: Richard Bonian and Henry Walley, 1609)

 Troilus and Cressida, or Truth Found Too Late (London: Abel Swall and Jacob Tonson, 1679)

Shirley, James, *The Cardinal* (London: Humphrey Moseley and Humphrey Robinson, 1652)

 The Court Secret (London: Humphrey Moseley and Humphrey Robinson, 1653)

 The Gentleman of Venice (London: Humphrey Moseley, 1655)

 Poems &c. (London: Humphrey Moseley, 1646)

The Stage Players Complaint (London: Thomas Bates, 1641)

"Some Notes for my Perambulations in and around the Citye of London." c. 1643 in Edinburgh University Library, Call number MS La. 11 422/211. Accessed on *Shakespeare Documented*: https://shakespearedocumented.folger.edu/resource/document/shakespeare-roisterer-tabard-inn

Stow, John, *Annales, or a generall chronicle of England* (London: Richard Meighen, 1631), Folger MS V.b.275

Suckling, John, *The Goblins* (London: Humphrey Moseley, 1646)

Symmons, Edward, *A Vindication of King Charles* (London, 1648)

The Thracian Wonder (London: Francis Kirkman, 1661)

"Warrant under the privy seal for the issue of letters patent authorizing Shakespeare and his companions to perform plays throughout the realm under royal patronage," 18 May 1603, in *Records of the Lord Chancellor*, The National Archives, Kew, UK, Call number and opening: C 82/1690, no. 78. Accessed on *Shakespeare Documented*, https://shakespearedocumented.folger

.edu/resource/document/king-james-establishes-kings-men-warrant-under-privy-seal.

Webster, John, and William Rowley, *A Cure for a Cuckold* (London: Francis Kirkman, 1661)

The Weekly Account, London, 4 October 1643

Weekly Intelligencer, London, 26 December 1654/5

The Weekly Intelligencer, London, 11–18 September 1655

W[ild], R[obert], *The Benefice* (London: R. Janeway, 1689)

The Wits, or, Sport upon Sport, Part 1 (London: Henry Marsh, 1662)

The Wits, or, Sport upon Sport, Part 1 (London: Francis Kirkman, 1672)

The Wits, or, Sport upon Sport, Part 2 (London: Francis Kirkman, 1673)

Wit's Recreation (London: Humphry Blunden, 1640)

Williams, Gryffith, *The discovery of mysteries: or, The plots and practices of a prevalent faction in this present Parliament. To overthrow the established religion, and the well setled government of this glorious Church* (Oxford: [Henry Hall], 1643)

The persecution and oppression. . .of John Bale (London: 1664)

Wright, James, *Historia Histrionica: An historical account of the English stage, shewing the ancient use, improvement and perfection of dramatick representations in this nation in a dialogue of plays and players* (London: William Haws, 1699)

Zouche, Richard, *The Sophister* (London: Humphrey Moseley, 1639).

Criticism and Modern Editions

Adams, Joseph Quincy, ed., *The Dramatic Records of Sir Henry Herbert Master of the Revels 1623–1673* (New York: Benjamin Blom, 1964)

Andrews, Meghan C., "The 1663 Faustus and the Royalist Marlowe," *Marlowe Studies: An Annual*, 1 (2011), 41–58

Arber, Edward, ed., *A Transcript of the Registers of the Company of Stationers of London, 1554–1640 A.D.*, 5 vols. (London: privately printed, 1875–94)

Archer, Ian, "The Nostalgia of John Stow," in *The Theatrical City: Culture, Theatre, and Politics in London, 1576–1649*, ed. David L. Smith, Richard Strier, and David Bevington (Cambridge: Cambridge University Press, 1995), pp. 17–34

Armitage, David, *Civil Wars: A History in Ideas* (New Haven: Yale University Press, 2017)

Astington, John H., "Acting in the Field," *Theatre Notebook*, 60.3 (2006), 129–33

Actors and Acting in Shakespeare's Time: The Art of Stage Playing (Cambridge: Cambridge University Press, 2010)

"Dramatic Extracts in the Interregnum," *Review of English Studies*, 54 (2003), 601–14

"Mohun [Moone], Michael," in *Oxford Dictionary of National Biography* (Oxford: Oxford University Press, 2004), doi.org/10.1093/ref:odnb/18885

Aston, Margaret, "English Ruins and English History: The Dissolution and the Sense of the Past," *Journal of the Warburg and Courtauld Institutes*, 36 (1973), 231–55

Atkin, Tamara, and Emma Smith, "The Form and Function of Character Lists in Plays Printed before the Closing of the Theatres," *Review of English Studies*, 65.271 (2014), 647–72

Backscheider, Paula R., "Behind City Walls: Restoration Actors in the Drapers' Company," *Theatre Survey*, 45.1 (2004), 75–87

Bald, R. C., "Francis Kirkman, Bookseller and Author," *Modern Philology*, 41.1 (1943), 17–32

Barash, Carol, *English Women's Poetry, 1649–1714: Politics, Community, and Literary Authority* (Oxford: Clarendon Press, 1996)

Barish, Jonas, *The Antitheatrical Prejudice* (Berkeley: University of California Press, 1981)

Barnard, John, "London Publishing, 1640–1660: Crisis, Continuity, and Innovation," *Book History*, 4 (2001), 1–16

Barroll, Leeds, *Politics, Plague and Shakespeare's Theatre: The Stuart Years* (Ithaca: Cornell University Press, 1991)

Bawcutt, N. W., "Puritanism and the Closing of the Theaters in 1642," *Medieval and Renaissance Drama in England*, 22 (2009), 179–200

   ed., *The Control and Censorship of Caroline Drama: The Records of Sir Henry Herbert, Master of the Revels 1623–1673* (Oxford: Oxford University Press, 1996)

Beaumont, Francis, and John Fletcher, *A King and No King*, ed. Lee Bliss (Manchester: Manchester University Press, 2004)

   A King and No King, in *The Dramatic Works of Beaumont and Fletcher*, ed. George Colman, 10 vols. (London: T. Evans and P. Elmsley, 1778), I

   The Wild Goose Chase, ed. Sophie Tomlinson, in *Three Seventeenth-Century Plays on Women and Performance*, ed. Hero Chalmers, Julie Sanders, and Sophie Tomlinson (Manchester: Manchester University Press, 2006)

Beecher, Douglas, "Nostalgia and the Renaissance Romance," *Philosophy and Literature*, 34.2 (2010), 281–301

Bell, Maureen, "Booksellers without an Author, 1627–1685," in *Thomas Middleton and Early Modern Textual Culture: A Companion to the Printed Works*, ed. Gary Taylor and John Lavagnino (Oxford: Oxford University Press, 2007), pp. 260–85

Bentley, G. E., *The Jacobean and Caroline Stage*, 7 vols. (Oxford: Clarendon Press, 1941–68)

   "John Cotgrave's *English Treasury of Wit and Language* and the Elizabethan Drama," *Studies in Philology*, 40 (April 1943), 186–203

   The Professional Player of Shakespeare's Time, 1590–1642 (Princeton: Princeton University Press, 1984)

   "The Salisbury Court Theater and Its Boy Players," *Huntington Library Quarterly*, 40.2 (1977), 129–49

Berger, Thomas L., "Looking for Shakespeare in Caroline England," *Viator*, 27 (1996), 323–59

Berry, Herbert, "Folger MS V.b.275 and the Deaths of Shakespearean Playhouses," *Medieval and Renaissance Drama in England*, 10 (1998), 262–93

Beushausen, Katrin, *Theater and the English Public from the Reformation to the Revolution* (Cambridge: Cambridge University Press, 2018)

Blagden, Cyprian, *The Stationers' Company: A History, 1403–1959* (Stanford: Stanford University Press, 1977)

Blayney, Peter W. M., "The Alleged Popularity of Playbooks," *Shakespeare Quarterly*, 56.1 (2005), 33–50

"The Publication of Playbooks," in *A New History of Early Modern English Drama*, ed. John D. Cox and David Scott Kastan (New York: Columbia University Press, 1997), pp. 382–422

Bliss, W. H., the Rev. W. Dunn Macray, the Rev. O. Ogle, and F. J. Routledge, eds., *Calendar of the Clarendon State Papers Preserved in the Bodleian Library*, 5 vols. (Oxford: Clarendon Press, 1869–1970), II

Boehrer, Bruce Thomas, *Monarchy and Incest in Renaissance England: Literature, Culture, Kinship and Kingship* (Philadelphia: University of Pennsylvania Press, 2015)

Boothby, Richard, *Death and Desire (RLE: Lacan): Psychoanalytic Theory in Lacan's Return to Freud* (New York: Routledge, 1991)

Bourdieu, Pierre, *Sociology in Question* (London: Sage, 1993)

Bourne, Claire M. L., "'High Designe': Beaumont and Fletcher Illustrated," *English Literary Renaissance*, 44.2 (2014), 275–327

Typographies of Performance in Early Modern England (Oxford: Oxford University Press, 2020)

Boym, Svetlana, *The Future of Nostalgia* (New York: Basic Books, 2002)

Brayman Hackel, Heidi, *Reading Material in Early Modern England: Print, Gender and Literacy* (Cambridge: Cambridge University Press, 2005)

Brinkley, Roberta Florence, ed., *Coleridge on the Seventeenth Century* (Durham: Duke University Press, 1955)

Brome, Richard, *A Jovial Crew*, ed. Tiffany Stern (London: Bloomsbury Arden Shakespeare, 2014)

Burckhardt, Jakob, *The Civilization of the Renaissance in Italy*, trans. S. G. C. Middlemore (New York: The Modern Library, 2002)

Burkert, Mattie, et al., *The London Stage Database*, https://londonstagedatabase.uoregon.edu

Bushnell, Rebecca W., *Tragedies of Tyrants: Political Thought and Theater in the English Renaissance* (Ithaca: Cornell University Press, 1990)

Butler, Martin, "Brome, Richard," in *Oxford Dictionary of National Biography* (Oxford: Oxford University Press, 2004), doi.org/10.1093/ref:odnb/3503

Theatre and Crisis, 1632–1642 (Cambridge: Cambridge University Press, 1984)

Capp, Bernard, *England's Culture Wars* (Oxford: Oxford University Press, 2012)

Carlin, Martha, "The Bard at the Tabard," *Times Literary Supplement* (24 September 2014), p. 15

"Gower's Southwark," in *The Routledge Research Companion to John Gower*, ed. Ana Saez-Hidalgo, Brian Gastle, and R. F. Yeager (New York: Routledge, 2021), pp. 132–49

Carlton, Charles, *Going to the Wars: The Experience of the British Civil Wars, 1638–1651* (New York: Routledge, 1994)

Carrafiello, Michael L., "St. Paul and the Polemicists: The Robert Parsons-Thomas Morton Exchanges, 1606–10," *The Catholic Historical Review*, 95.3 (2009), 474–90

Cathcart, Charles, "'You will crown him King that slew your King': *Lust's Dominion* and Oliver Cromwell," *Medieval and Renaissance Drama in England*, 11 (1999), 264–74

Cavarero, Adriana, *Relating Narratives: Storytelling and Selfhood* (New York: Routledge, 2000)

Cerasano, S. P., "Must the Devil Appear?: Audiences, Actors, Stage Business," in *A Companion to Renaissance Drama*, ed. Arthur F. Kinney (Oxford: Wiley, 2002), pp. 193–211

Cervone, Thea, "The Corpse as Text: The Polemics of Memory and the Deaths of Charles I and Oliver Cromwell," *Preternature: Critical and Historical Studies on the Preternatural*, 2.1 (2013), 47–72

Clare, Janet, "Acts of Oblivion: Reframing Drama, 1649–65," in *From Republic to Restoration*, ed. Janet Clare (Manchester: Manchester University Press, 2018), pp. 148–60

    Drama of the English Republic, 1649–60 (Manchester: Manchester University Press, 2002)

    "The Production and Reception of Davenant's *Cruelty of the Spaniards in Peru*," *The Modern Language Review*, 89.4 (1994), 832–41

Cockayne, Aston, *The Obstinate Lady*, ed. Catherine Shaw (New York: Garland Publishing, 1986)

Coiro, Ann Baynes, "Milton and Class Identity: The Publication of *Areopagitica* and the 1645 Poems," *Journal of Medieval and Renaissance Studies*, 22 (1992), 261–89

    "Reading," in *Early Modern Theatricality*, ed. Henry Turner (Oxford: Oxford University Press, 2015), pp. 534–55

Collinson, Patrick, "Ben Johnson's *Bartholomew Fair*: The Theatre Constructs Puritanism," in *The Theatrical City: Culture, Theatre and Politics in London, 1576–1649*, ed. David L. Smith, Richard Strier, and David Bevington (Cambridge: Cambridge University Press, 1995), pp. 157–69

    "Ecclesiastical Vitriol: Religious Satire in the 1590s and the Invention of Puritanism," in *The Reign of Elizabeth I: Court and Culture in the Last Decade*, ed. John Guy (Cambridge: Cambridge University Press, 1995), pp. 150–70

    The Puritan Character: Polemics and Polarities in Early Seventeenth-Century English Culture (Los Angeles: William Andrews Clark Memorial Library, University of California, 1989)

Como, David R., "Print, Censorship, and Ideological Escalation in the English Civil War," *Journal of British Studies*, 51.4 (2012), 820–57

Connor, Francis X., "Henry Herringman, Richard Bentley and Shakespeare's Fourth Folio (1685)," in *Canonising Shakespeare: Stationers and the Book*

Trade, 1640–1740, ed. Emma Depledge and Peter Kirwan (Cambridge: Cambridge University Press, 2017), pp. 38–55

Literary Folios and Ideas of the Book in Early Modern England (New York: Palgrave Macmillan, 2014)

Cook, Megan, *The Poet and the Antiquaries: Chaucerian Scholarship and the Rise of Literary History, 1532–1635* (Philadelphia: University of Pennsylvania Press, 2019)

Cope, Jackson I., "Rhetorical Genres in Davenant's *First Day's Entertainment at Rutland House*," *Quarterly Journal of Speech*, 45.2 (1959), 191–4

Craig, Heidi, "A Century of Drama: Restoration Reprints of Tudor Drama," in *Reprints and Revivals*, ed. Eoin Price and Harry Newman (Cambridge: Cambridge University Press, forthcoming)

"The King's Servants in Printed Paratexts, 1594–1695," *Huntington Library Quarterly*, 85.1 (2022), 151–169

"Missing Shakespeare, 1642–1660," *English Literary Renaissance*, 49.1 (2019), 116–44

Cross, Richard, *Communicatio Idiomatum: Reformation Christological Debates* (Oxford: Oxford University Press, 2019)

Cummings, Brian, and James Simpson, eds., *Cultural Reformations: Medieval and Renaissance in Literary History* (Oxford: Oxford University Press, 2010)

Danby, John F., *Elizabethan and Jacobean Poets* (London: Faber & Faber, 1952)

De Grazia, Margreta, "The Modern Divide: From Either Side," *Journal of Medieval and Early Modern Studies*, 37.7 (2007), 453–67

Depledge, Emma, *Shakespeare's Rise to Cultural Prominence* (Cambridge: Cambridge University Press, 2018)

Dobson, Michael, "The Grave-Makers," in *The Oxford Companion to Shakespeare*, ed. Michael Dobson, Stanley Wells, Will Sharpe, and Erin Sullivan (Oxford: Oxford University Press, 2015), p. 172

The Making of the National Poet: Shakespeare, Adaptation and Authorship, 1660–1769 (Cambridge: Cambridge University Press, 1992)

Dollimore, Jonathan, *Death, Desire and Loss in Western Culture* (London: Taylor & Francis, 1998)

Donaldson, Ian, "Talking with Ghosts: Ben Jonson and the English Civil War," *Ben Jonson Journal*, 17 (2010), 1–18

Downs, Jordan S., "The Curse of Meroz and the English Civil War," *The Historical Journal*, 57.2 (2014), 343–68

Dugas, Don-John, *Marketing the Bard: Shakespeare in Performance and Print, 1660–1740* (St. Louis: University of Missouri Press, 2006)

"Philip Chetwind and the Shakespeare Third Folio," *Harvard Library Bulletin*, 14.1 (2003), 29–46

Dugan, Holly, "'As Dirty as Smithfield and Stinking Every Whit': The Smell of the Hope Theatre," in *Shakespeare's Theatres and the Effects of Performance*, ed. Farah Karim-Cooper and Tiffany Stern (London: Bloomsbury, 2013), pp. 195–213

Dutton, Richard, "Herbert, Sir Henry," in *Oxford Dictionary of National Bibliography* (Oxford: Oxford University Press, 2004), doi.org/10.1093/ref: odnb/13029

Shakespeare's Theatre: A History (New York: Wiley-Blackwell, 2018)

Eagleton, Terry, *Sweet Violence: The Idea of the Tragic* (Hoboken: Wiley, 2009)

Elson, John James, ed., *The Wits, or Sport upon Sport* (Ithaca: Cornell University Press, 1932)

English Short Title Catalogue, http://estc.bl.uk

Erne, Lukas, *Shakespeare and the Book Trade* (Cambridge: Cambridge University Press, 2013)

Erne, Lukas, and Devani Singh, eds., *Bel-vedére or The Garden of the Muses* (Cambridge: Cambridge University Press, 2020)

Estill, Laura, *Dramatic Extracts in Seventeenth-Century English Manuscripts: Watching, Reading, Changing Plays* (Lanham: University of Delaware Press, 2015)

"The Urge to Organize Early Modern Miscellanies," *Papers of the Bibliographical Society of America*, 11.2 (2018), 27–73

Evelyn, John, *Diary and Correspondence of John Evelyn*, ed. William Bray, 4 vols. (London: Henry Colburn, 1850), I

The Diary of John Evelyn, ed. E. S. de Beer, 6 vols. (Oxford: Clarendon Press, 1955), III

Ezell, Margaret J. M., *The Oxford English Literary History, Volume V: 1645–1714: The Later Seventeenth Century* (Oxford: Oxford University Press, 2017)

Farmer, Alan B., "John Norton and the Politics of Shakespeare's History Plays in Caroline England," in *Shakespeare's Stationers: Studies in Cultural Bibliography*, ed. Marta Straznicky (Philadelphia: University of Pennsylvania Press, 2013), pp. 147–76

"Playbooks and the Question of Ephemerality," in *The Book in History, The Book as History: New Intersections of the Material Text*, ed. Heidi Brayman, Jesse Lander, and Zachary Lesser (New Haven: Yale University Press, 2016), pp. 87–125

Farmer, Alan B., and Zachary Lesser, "Canons and Classics," in *Localizing Caroline Drama: Politics and Economics of the Early Modern English Stage, 1625–1642*, ed. Alan B. Farmer and Adam Zucker (Basingstoke: Palgrave Macmillan, 2006), pp. 17–41

"The Popularity of Playbooks Revisited," *Shakespeare Quarterly*, 56.1 (2005), 1–32

"Structures of Popularity in the Early Modern Book Trade," *Shakespeare Quarterly*, 56.2 (2005), 206–13

"Vile Arts: The Marketing of English Printed Drama, 1512–1660," *Research Opportunities in Renaissance Drama*, 39 (2000), 77–165

eds., *DEEP: Database of Early English Playbooks*, http://deep.sas.upen.edu

Farr, Henry, "Philip Chetwind and the Allott Copyrights," *The Library*, 15 (1934), 129–60

Febvre, Lucien, *Le Problem de l'incroyance au XVIe siècle: La religion de Rabelais* (Paris: Editions Alain Michel, 1948)

Fincham, Kenneth, and Nicholas Tyacke, *Altars Restored: The Changing Face of English Religious Worship, 1547–c.1700* (Oxford: Oxford University Press, 2007)

Finkelpearl, Philip J., *Court and Country Politics in the Plays of Beaumont and Fletcher* (Princeton: Princeton University Press, 1990)

Finkelstein, Richard, "The Politics of Gender, Puritanism, and Shakespeare's Third Folio," *Philological Quarterly*, 79.3 (2000), 315–41

Firth, C. H., and R. S. Rait, eds., *Acts and Ordinances of the Interregnum, 1642–1660* (London: His Majesty's Stationery Office, 1911)

Fleissner, Robert F., "The Misattribution of *The Birth of Merlin* to Shakespeare," *Papers of the Bibliographical Society of America*, 73.2 (1979), 248–52

Fleming, Juliet, "Wounded Walls: Graffiti, Grammatology, and the Age of Shakespeare," *Criticism*, 39.1 (1997), 1–30

Fletcher, John, *A Critical Edition of John Fletcher's Comedy, The Wild-Goose Chase*, ed. Rota Herzberg Lister (New York: Garland Publishing, 1980)

Foucault, Michel, *Les mots et les choses* (Paris: Editions Gallimard, 1966)

Freehafer, John, "The Formation of the London Patent Companies in 1660," *Theatre Notebook*, 20 (1965), 6–30

Gavin, Michael, *The Invention of English Criticism: 1650–1760* (Cambridge: Cambridge University Press, 2015)

"Writing Print Cultures Past: Literary Criticism and Book History," *Book History*, 15 (2012), 26–47

Gayley, Charles Mills, *Beaumont, the Dramatist: A Portrait with Some Account of His Circle, Elizabethan and Jacobean, and of His Association with John Fletcher* (New York: Russell & Russell, 1969)

Gerritsen, Johan, "The Dramatic Piracies of 1661," *Studies in Bibliography*, 11 (1958), 117–31

Gilchrist, Kim, "*Mucedorus*: The Last Ludic Playbook, the First Stage Arcadia," *Shakespeare*, 15 (2019), 1–20

Grant, Tessa, "Tonson's Jonson: Making the 'Vernacular Canon' in the Early Eighteenth Century," in *The Oxford Handbook of Ben Jonson*, ed. Eugene Giddens (Oxford: Oxford University Press, 2013)

Greenblatt, Stephen, *Shakespearean Negotiations: The Circulation of Social Energy in Renaissance England* (Berkeley: University of California Press, 1988)

Greene, Jody, "Francis Kirkman's Counterfeit Authority: Autobiography, Subjectivity, Print," *Papers of the Modern Language Association*, 121.1 (2006), 17–32

Greg, W. W., "Authorship Attributions in the Early Play Lists, 1656–1671," *Edinburgh Bibliographical Society Transactions*, 2 (1946), 303–30

A Bibliography of the English Printed Drama to the Restoration, 4 vols. (London: Bibliographical Society, 1939–59), vol. II

A List of Masques, Pageants, &c. Supplementary to A List of English Plays (London: Bibliographical Society, 1969)

"Shakespeare and *Arden of Feversham*," *Review of English Studies*, 21 (1945), 134–6

Griffin, Andrew, *Untimely Deaths in Renaissance Drama: Biography, History, Catastrophe* (Toronto: University of Toronto Press, 2019)

Gurr, Andrew, "Beeston [Hutchinson], William," in *Oxford Dictionary of National Biography* (Oxford: Oxford University Press, 2004), doi.org/10.1093/ref:odnb/67810

Hagen, Tanya, "Thinking Outside the Bard: REED, Repertory Canons, and Editing Early English Drama," in *REED in Review: Essays in Celebration of the First Twenty-Five Years*, ed. Audrey W. Douglas and Sally-Beth MacLean (Toronto: University of Toronto, 2006), pp. 216–34

Haley, David, *Dryden and the Problem of Freedom: The Republican Aftermath, 1649–1680* (New Haven: Yale University Press, 1997)

Hammond, Paul, *Dryden: A Literary Life* (Houndmills: Macmillan, 1991)

"The Restoration Poetic and Dramatic Canon," in *The Cambridge History of the Book in Britain: Volume IV, 1557–1695*, ed. John Barnard and D. F. McKenzie with Maureen Bell (Cambridge: Cambridge University Press, 2002), pp. 388–409

Harris, Tim, "Introduction: Revising the Restoration," in *The Politics of Religion in Restoration England*, ed. Tim Harris, Paul Seward, and Mark Goldie (Oxford: Oxford University Press, 1990), pp. 1–28

"Periodizing the Early Modern: The Historian's View," in *Early Modern Histories of Time*, ed. Owen Williams and Kristen Poole (Philadelphia: University of Pennsylvania Press, 2019), pp. 21–35

Helgerson, Richard, "Milton Reads the King's Book: Print, Performance, and the Making of a Bourgeois Idol," *Criticism*, 29 (1987), 1–25

Heinemann, Margot, *Puritanism and Theatre* (Cambridge: Cambridge University Press, 1980)

Hind, Arthur Mayger, *Wenceslaus Hollar and His Views of London and Windsor in the Seventeenth Century* (Miami: HardPress, 2012)

Holderness, Graham, "'I Covet your Skull': Death and Desire in *Hamlet*," *Shakespeare Survey*, vol. 60, ed. Peter Holland (Cambridge: Cambridge University Press, 2017), pp. 224–37

Holland, Peter, "A History of Histories, from Flecknoe to Nicoll," in *Theorizing Practice: Redefining Theatre History*, ed. W. B. Worthen with Peter Holland (Basingstoke: Palgrave Macmillan, 2003), pp. 8–29

"Shakespeare Abbreviated," in *The Cambridge Companion to Shakespeare and Popular Culture*, ed. Robert Shaughnessy (Cambridge: Cambridge University Press, 2007), pp. 26–45

Holquist, Michael, "Corrupt Originals: The Paradox of Censorship," *Papers of the Modern Language Association*, 109.1 (1994), 14–25

Holtcamp, Victor, "A Fear of 'Ould' Plays: How *Mucedorus* Brought down the House and Fought for Charles II in 1652," in *The Shakespeare Apocrypha*, ed. Douglas Brooks (Lewiston: Edwin Mellen Press, 2007), pp. 145–70

Hooks, Adam G., "Booksellers' Catalogues and the Classification of Printed Drama in Seventeenth-Century England," *Papers of the Bibliographical Society of America*, 102.4 (2008), 445–64

"Royalist Shakespeare: Publishers, Politics, and the Appropriation of *The Rape of Lucrece* (1655)," in *Canonising Shakespeare: Stationers and the Book Trade, 1640–1740*, ed. Emma Depledge and Peter Kirwan (Cambridge: Cambridge University Press, 2017), pp. 26–37

Selling Shakespeare: Biography, Bibliography, and the Book Trade (Cambridge: Cambridge University Press, 2016)

Hotson, Leslie, *Commonwealth and Restoration Stage* (Cambridge, MA: Harvard University Press, 1928)

"George Jolly, Actor-Manager," *Studies in Philology*, 20.4 (1923), 422–43

Hughes, Ann, "The Scots, the Parliament and the People: The Rise of the New Model Army Revisited," in *Revolutionising Politics: Culture and Conflict in England, 1620–60*, ed. Paul D. Halliday, Eleanor Hubbard, and Scott Sowerby (Manchester: Manchester University Press, 2021), pp. 180–99

Hughes, Ann, and Julie Sanders, "Gender, Exile and The Hague Courts of Elizabeth, Queen of Bohemia and Mary, Princess of Orange in the 1650s," in *Monarchy and Exile: The Politics of Legitimacy from Marie de Médicis to Wilhelm II*, ed. Philip Mansel and Torsten Riotte (Basingstoke: Palgrave Macmillan, 2011), pp. 44–65

Ingleby, Clement Mansfield and Lucy Toulmin Smith, eds., *Shakespeare's Century of Prayse*, 2nd ed., 2 vols. (London: New Shakespeare Society, 1879)

Ingleby, Clement Mansfield, Lucy Toulmin Smith, and F. J. Furnivall, eds., *The Shakespeare Allusion Book* (London: Chatto & Windus, 1909)

Ingram, Randall, "First Words and Second Thoughts: Margaret Cavendish, Humphrey Moseley, and 'the Book'," *Journal of Medieval and Early Modern Studies*, 30.1 (Winter 2000), 101–24

Ioppolo, Grace, *Dramatists and Their Manuscripts in the Age of Shakespeare* (London: Routledge, 2013)

Isherwood, Anne, "'Cut out into little stars': Shakespeare in Anthologies" (doctoral dissertation, King's College London, 2014)

Jackson, MacDonald P., *Determining the Shakespeare Canon* (Oxford: Oxford University Press, 2014)

Jackson, MacDonald P., and Gary Taylor, "Works Excluded from This Edition," in *Thomas Middleton and Early Modern Textual Culture: A Companion to the Printed Works*, ed. Gary Taylor and John Lavagnino (Oxford: Clarendon Press, 2007), pp. 444–8

James, Anne, *Poets, Players, and Preachers: Remembering the Gunpowder Plot in Seventeenth-Century England* (Toronto: University of Toronto Press, 2016)

Jowett, John, "Shakespeare Supplemented," in *The Shakespeare Apocrypha*, ed. Douglas Brooks (Lewiston: Edwin Mellen Press, 2007), pp. 39–73

Karim-Cooper, Farah, and Tiffany Stern, eds., *Shakespeare's Theatres and the Effects of Performance* (London: Bloomsbury, 2013)

Kastan, David Scott, "Humphrey Moseley and the Invention of English Literature," in *Agent of Change: Print Culture Studies after Elizabeth*

L. Eisenstein, ed. Sabrina Alcorn Baron, Eric N. Lindquist, and Eleanor F. Shevlin (Boston: University of Massachusetts Press, 2007), pp. 105–24

"Performances and Playbooks: The Closing of the Theatres and the Politics of Drama," in *Reading, Society and Politics in Early Modern England*, ed. Kevin Sharpe and Steven N. Zwicker (Cambridge: Cambridge University Press, 2003), pp. 167–84

"In Plain Sight: Visible Women and Early Modern Plays," in *Women Making Shakespeare: Text, Reception and Performance*, ed. Gordon McMullan, Lena Cowen Orlin, and Virginia Mason Vaughan (London: Bloomsbury Arden Shakespeare, 2014), pp. 47–56

Shakespeare and the Book (Cambridge: Cambridge University Press, 2002)

Keblusek, Marika, "Mary, Princess Royal (1631–1660)," in *Oxford Dictionary of National Biography* (Oxford: Oxford University Press, 2004), doi.org/10.1093/ref:odnb/18252

Kelsey, Sean, "Politics and Procedure in the Trial of Charles I," *Law and History Review*, 22.1 (2004), 1–25

Kermode, Frank, *The Classic: Literary Images of Permanence and Change* (Cambridge, MA: Harvard University Press, 1975)

Forms of Attention (Chicago: University of Chicago Press, 1985)

Sense of an Ending: Studies in Theory of Fiction (Oxford: Oxford University Press, 1967)

Kewes, Paulina, *Authorship and Appropriation: Writing for the Stage in England, 1660–1710* (Cambridge: Cambridge University Press, 1998)

"'Give Me the Sociable Pocket-Books...': Humphrey Moseley's Serial Publication of Octavo Collections," *Publishing History*, 38 (1995), 5–21

King, T. J., "The First Known Picture of Falstaff (1662): A Suggested Date for His Costume," *Theatre Research International*, 3.1 (1977), 20–2

Kirschbaum, Leo, "How Jane Bell Came to Print the Third Quarto of Shakespeare's *King Lear*," *Philological Quarterly*, 17 (1938), 308–11

Kirwan, Peter, "Consolidating the Shakespeare Canon, 1640–1740," in *Canonising Shakespeare: Stationers and the Book Trade, 1640–1740*, ed. Emma Depledge and Peter Kirwan (Cambridge: Cambridge University Press, 2017), pp. 81–8

"The First Collected Shakespeare Apocrypha," *Shakespeare Quarterly*, 62 (2011), 594–601

Shakespeare and the Idea of Apocrypha (Cambridge: Cambridge University Press, 2015)

Kishlansky, Mark, "Mission Impossible: Charles I, Oliver Cromwell and the Regicide," *The English Historical Review*, 125.515 (2010), 844–74

Korda, Natasha, *Labour's Lost: Women's Work and the Early Modern English Stage* (Philadelphia: University of Pennsylvania Press, 2011)

Kramnick, Jonathan Brody, *Making the English Canon: Print-Capitalism and the Cultural Past* (Cambridge: Cambridge University Press, 1998)

Lacan, Jacques, "La Direction de la Cure," in *Ecrits* (Paris: Editions du Seuil, 1966)

Lacey, Andrew, *The Cult of King Charles the Martyr* (Woodbridge: Boydell and Brewer, 2003)

Lander, Jesse, "Historiography," in *Cultural Reformations: Medieval and Renaissance in Literary History*, ed. Brian Cummings and James Simpson (Oxford: Oxford University Press, 2010), pp. 56–74

Lerer, Seth, "Literary Histories," in *Cultural Reformations: Medieval and Renaissance in Literary History*, ed. Brian Cummings and James Simpson (Oxford: Oxford University Press, 2010), pp. 75–94

Lesser, Zachary, "Mixed Government and Mixed Marriage in 'A King and No King': Sir Henry Neville Reads Beaumont and Fletcher," *English Literary History*, 69.4 (2002), 947–77

"Playbooks," in *The Oxford History of Popular Print Culture*, vol. 1, ed. Joad Raymond (Oxford: Oxford University Press, 2011), pp. 521–35

Renaissance Drama and the Politics of Publication (Cambridge: Cambridge University Press, 2004)

"Shakespeare's Flop: John Waterson and *The Two Noble Kinsmen*," in *Shakespeare's Stationers: Studies in Cultural Bibliography*, ed. Marta Straznicky (Philadelphia: University of Pennsylvania Press, 2013), pp. 177–96

"Tragical-Comical-Pastoral-Colonial: Economic Sovereignty, Globalization, and the Form of Tragicomedy," *English Literary History*, 74.4 (2007), 881–908

"Typographic Nostalgia: Playreading, Popularity and the Meanings of Black Letter," in *The Book of the Play: Playwrights, Readers and Stationers in Shakespeare's England*, ed. Marta Straznicky (Amherst: University of Massachusetts Press, 2006), pp. 99–126

Lesser, Zachary, and Peter Stallybrass, "The First Literary *Hamlet* and the Commonplacing of Professional Plays," *Shakespeare Quarterly*, 59.4 (2008), 371–420

Limon, Jerzy, *Gentlemen of a Company: English Players in Central and Eastern Europe, 1590–1660* (Cambridge: Cambridge University Press, 1985)

Lopez, Jeremy, "Alleyn Resurrected," *Marlowe Studies*, 1 (2011), 167–80

Constructing the Canon of Early Modern Drama (Cambridge: Cambridge University Press, 2014)

Lynch, Jack, *The Age of Elizabeth in the Age of Johnson* (Cambridge: Cambridge University Press, 2003)

MacDonald, Helen, "In Search of Post-Brexit England, and Swans," *New York Times Magazine*, 5 January 2017

MacKay, Ellen, *Persecution, Plague and Fire: Fugitive Histories of the Stage in Early Modern England* (Chicago: University of Chicago Press, 2011)

Mackay, Hugh, "*Lust's Dominion* and the Readmission of the Jews," *Review of English Studies*, 59 (2008), 542–67

Maguire, Nancy Klein, *Regicide and Restoration: English Tragicomedy, 1660–1671* (Cambridge: Cambridge University Press, 1992)

"The Theatrical Mask / Masque of Politics: The Case of Charles I," *Journal of British Studies*, 28 (1989), 1–22

Marcus, Leah, *The Politics of Mirth* (Chicago: University of Chicago Press, 1986)

Marino, James J., *Owning William Shakespeare: The King's Men and Their Intellectual Property* (Philadelphia: University of Pennsylvania Press, 2011)

Marotti, Arthur, *Manuscript, Print and the English Renaissance Lyric* (Ithaca: Cornell University Press, 1995)

Marvell, Andrew, *Andrew Marvell: The Complete Poems*, ed. Elizabeth Story Donno (New York: Penguin, 2005)

Massai, Sonia, *Shakespeare and the Rise of the Editor* (Cambridge: Cambridge University Press, 2007)

Massai, Sonia, and Heidi Craig, "Rethinking Prologues and Epilogues on Page and Stage," in *Rethinking Theatrical Documents in Shakespeare's England*, ed. Tiffany Stern (London: The Arden Shakespeare, 2020), pp. 91–110

Masten, Jeffrey, "Ben Jonson's Head," *Shakespeare Studies*, 28 (2000), 160–8

Matar, Nabil, "The Barbary Corsairs, King Charles I," *The Seventeenth Century*, 16 (2001), 239–58

Matusiak, Christopher, "The Beestons and the Art of Theatrical Management in Seventeenth-Century London" (doctoral dissertation, University of Toronto, 2009)

"Christopher Beeston and the Caroline Office of Theatrical 'Governor'," *Early Theatre*, 11.2 (2008), 39–56

"Elizabeth Beeston, Sir Lewis Kirke, and the Cockpit's Management during the English Civil Wars," *Medieval and Renaissance Drama in England*, 27 (2014), 161–91

"Was Shakespeare 'not a company keeper'?: William Beeston and MS Aubrey 8, fol. 45v," *Shakespeare Quarterly*, 68.4 (2017), 351–373

McElligott, Jason, *Royalism, Print and Censorship in Revolutionary England* (Woodbridge: Boydell, 2007)

McEvilla, Joshua J., with contributions from Sean M. Winslow, *Cotgrave Online*, created 2014, revised Aug. 2020, *The Shakespeare Authorship Page*, ed. Terry Ross and David Kathman, https://shakespeareauthorship.com/cotgrave/ [Facet Search]

"John Cragge's *The Wits Interpreter*," *The Library*, 8.3 (2017), 337–44

McInnis, David, *Shakespeare and Lost Plays: Reimagining Drama in Early Modern England* (Cambridge: Cambridge University Press, 2021)

McInnis, David, and Matthew Steggle, "Introduction: Nothing will Come from Nothing: Or, What Can We Learn from Plays That Don't Exist?" in *Lost Plays in Shakespeare's England*, ed. David McInnis and Matthew Steggle (Basingstoke: Palgrave Macmillan, 2014), pp. 1–14

McKenzie, D. F., "The London Book Trade in 1644," in *Bibliographia*, ed. John Horden (Oxford: Leopard Head Press, 1992), pp. 131–52

"The London Book Trade in the Later Seventeenth Century," Sandars Lectures 1976, mimeographed copies deposited in British Library, Bodleian Library, Brotherton Library (University of Leeds), pp. 12–13.

McMahon, Sister Mary Catherine, "Aesthetics and Art in the *Astrée* of Honoré D'Urfé" (PhD dissertation, Catholic University of America, 1925)

McMullan, Gordon, "The Lateness of *King Lear*: Alteration and Authenticity in Shakespeare and Tate," in *The true blank of thine eye: approches critiques de King Lear*, ed. Pascale Drouin and Pierre Iselin (Paris: Presses de l'université Paris-Sorbonne, 2009), pp. 83–101

Menzer, Paul, *Anecdotal Shakespeare: A New Performance History* (London: Bloomsbury Arden Shakespeare, 2015)

Milhous, Judith, and Robert D. Hume, eds., *The London Stage, 1660–1800: A New Version of Part 2, 1700–1729...Draft of the Calendar for Volume 1, 1700–1711*, www.personal.psu.edu/hb1/London%20Stage%202001/preface.pdf

Milhous, Judith, and Robert D. Hume, "New Light on English Acting Companies in 1646, 1648, and 1660," *Review of English Studies*, 42 (1991), 487–509

  The Publication of Plays in London, 1660–1800: Playwrights, Publishers, and the Market (London: British Library, 2015)

Miller, C. William, "Henry Herringman, Restoration Bookseller-Publisher," *Papers of the Bibliographical Society of America*, 42 (1948), 292–306

Moisan, Thomas, "The King's Second Coming," in *In the Company of Shakespeare: Essays on the English Renaissance in Honor of G. Blakemore Evans*, ed. Thomas Moisan and Douglas Bruster (Vancouver: Fairleigh Dickinson University Press, 2002), pp. 270–91

Mottram, Stuart, *Ruin and Reformation in Spenser, Shakespeare and Marvell* (Cambridge: Cambridge University Press, 2019)

Moore, Helen, "Admirable Inventions: Francis Kirkman and the Translation of Romance in the 1650s," in *Seventeenth-Century Fiction: Text and Transmission*, ed. Jacqueline Glomski and Isabelle Moreau (Oxford: Oxford University Press, 2016), pp. 143–58

Munro, Lucy, *Archaic Style in English Literature, 1590–1674* (Cambridge: Cambridge University Press, 2013)

  The King's Men (London: Bloomsbury Arden Shakespeare, 2020)

  "Marlowe on the Caroline Stage," *Shakespeare Bulletin*, 27 (2009), 39–50

Murphy, Andrew, *Shakespeare in Print: A History and Chronology of Shakespeare Publishing* (Cambridge: Cambridge University Press, 2003)

Neill, Michael, "The Defence of Contraries: Skeptical Paradox in *A King and No King*," *Studies in English Literature, 1500–1900*, 21.2 (1981), 319–32

  Issues of Death: Mortality and Identity in English Renaissance Tragedy (Oxford: Oxford University Press, 1997)

Nelson, Christopher William, "Perception, Power, Plays, and Print: Charles II and the Restoration Theatre of Consensus" (doctoral dissertation, Louisiana State University, 2012)

Nicosia, Marissa, "Couplets, Commonplaces, and the Creation of History," in *From Republic to Restoration*, ed. Janet Clare (Manchester: Manchester University Press, 2018), pp. 69–84

"Printing as Revival: Making Playbooks in the 1650s," *Papers of the Bibliographical Society of America*, 111.4 (2017), 469–89

Northway, Kara J., "'I haue lost it': Apologies, Appeals, and Justifications for Misplacing *The Wild-Goose Chase* and Other Plays," in *Loss and the Literary Culture of Shakespeare's Time*, ed. Roslyn L. Knutson, David McInnis, and Matthew Steggle (Basingstoke: Palgrave Macmillan, 2020), pp. 75–93

O'Brien, John, *Harlequin Britain: Pantomime and Entertainment. 1690–1760* (Baltimore: Johns Hopkins University Press, 2004)

O'Callaghan, Michelle, *The English Wits: Literature and Sociability in Early Modern England* (Cambridge: Cambridge University Press, 2007)

Orgel, Stephen, "What Is an Editor?" *Shakespeare Studies*, 24 (1996), 23–9

Panofsky, Erwin, *Renaissance and Renascences in Western Art* (Stockholm: Almquist & Wiksell, 1960)

Park, Judy H., "The Tragicomic Moment: Republicanism in Beaumont and Fletcher's 'Philaster'," *Comparative Drama*, 49.1 (2015), 23–47

Parry, Graham, "Wenceslas Hollar, the Antiquarians Illustrator," *Ariel*, 3.2 (1972), 42–52

Patey, Douglas Lane, "The Institution of Criticism in the Eighteenth Century," in *The Cambridge History of Literary Criticism, Vol. IV: The Eighteenth Century*, ed. H. B. Nisbet and Claude Rawson (Cambridge: Cambridge University Press, 1997), pp. 1–31

Pennington, Richard, *A Descriptive Catalog of the Etched Work of Wenceslaus Hollar 1607–77* (Cambridge: Cambridge University Press, 1982)

Peters, Julie Stone, *Theatre of the Book, 1480–1880: Print, Text, and Performance in Europe* (Oxford: Oxford University Press, 2000)

Philips, Harriet, *Nostalgia in Print and Performance, 1510–1613* (Cambridge: Cambridge University Press, 2019)

Phillips, Mark Salber, *On Historical Distance* (New Haven: Yale University Press, 2013)

Pincus, Steven, *Protestantism and Patriotism: Ideologies and the Making of English Foreign Policy, 1650–1668* (Cambridge: Cambridge University Press, 1996)

Plomer, Henry Robert, *A Dictionary of the Booksellers and Printers Who Were at Work in England, Scotland and Ireland from 1641 to 1667* (London: Printed for the Bibliographical Society, 1907)

Pollard, A. W. and G. R. Redgrave, eds., *A Short-Title Catalogue of Books Printed Scotland, & Ireland and of English Books Printed Abroad, 1475–1640*, 2nd ed., 3 vols., rev. W. A Ferguson, and Katharine F. Pantzer (London: Bibliographical Society, 1976–9).

Pollard, Tanya, "Introduction: Debating the Theatre in Shakespeare's England," in *Shakespeare's Theatre: A Source Book*, ed. Tanya Pollard (New York: Wiley, 2008), pp. x–xxiv

Potter, Lois, "Marlowe in the Civil War and Commonwealth: Some Allusions and Parodies," in *Poet and a Filthy-Playmaker: New Essays on Christopher*

Marlowe, ed. Kenneth Friedenreich, Roma Gill, and Constance B. Kuriyama (New York: AMS Press, 1988), pp. 72–82

Secret Rites and Secret Writing: Royalist Literature, 1641–1660 (Cambridge: Cambridge University Press, 1989)

Powell, J. R., ed., "The Journal of John Weale 1654–1656," in *The Naval Miscellany*, vol. IV (London: Navy Records Society, 1952)

Priess, Richard, "A Play Finally Anonymous," in *The Shakespeare Apocrypha*, ed. Douglas A. Brooks (Lewiston: Edwin Mellen Press, 2007), pp. 117–39

Randall, Dale, *Winter Fruit: English Drama, 1642–1660* (Lexington: University Press of Kentucky, 1995)

Raymond, Joad, "Popular Representations of Charles I," in *The Royal Image: Representations of Charles I*, ed. Thomas Corns (Cambridge: Cambridge University Press, 1999), pp. 47–73

Reed, John Curtis, "Humphrey Moseley, Publisher," in *Oxford Bibliographical Society: Proceedings and Papers*, vol. 2 (Oxford: Oxford University Press, 1930), pp. 57–144

Revard, Stella P., "Thomas Stanley and 'A Register of Friends'," in *Literary Circles and Cultural Communities in Renaissance England*, ed. Claude J. Summers and Ted-Larry Pebworth (Columbia: University of Missouri Press, 2000), pp. 148–72

Roberts, David, *Restoration Plays and Players* (Cambridge: Cambridge University Press, 2014)

Thomas Betterton: The Greatest Actor of the Restoration Stage (Cambridge: Cambridge University Press, 2010)

Roberts, Sasha, *Reading Shakespeare's Poems in Early Modern England* (Basingstoke: Palgrave Macmillan, 2002)

Robinson, Benedict Scott, "Thomas Heywood and the Cultural Politics of the Play Collections," *Studies in English Literature, 1500–1900*, 42.9 (2002), 361–80

Rollins, Hyder E., "The Commonwealth Drama: Miscellaneous Notes," *Studies in Philology*, 20.1 (1923), 52–69

"A Contribution to the History of the English Commonwealth Drama," *Studies in Philology*, XVIII (1921), 267–333

Ross, Trevor, *The Making of the English Literary Canon: From the Middle Ages to the Late Eighteenth Century* (Montreal and Kingston: McGill-Queen's University Press, 1998)

Sanders, Julie, *Ben Jonson in Context* (Cambridge: Cambridge University Press, 2010)

Sauer, Elizabeth, *"Paper-Contestations" and Textual Communities in England, 1640–1675* (Toronto: University of Toronto Press, 2005)

Sawday, Jonathan, "Re-Writing a Revolution: History, Symbol and Text in the Restoration," *The Seventeenth Century*, 7 (1992), 171–99

Schoch, Richard, *Writing the History of the British Stage: 1660–1900* (Cambridge: Cambridge University Press, 2016)

Scott, Jonathan, *Commonwealth Principles: Republican Writing of the English Revolution* (Cambridge: Cambridge University Press, 2004)
   England's Troubles: Seventeenth-Century English Political Instability in European Context (Cambridge: Cambridge University Press, 2000)
Shapiro, I. A., "Bankside Theatres: Early Engravings," in *Shakespeare Survey*, vol. 1 ed. Allardyce Nicoll (Cambridge: Cambridge University Press, 1948), pp. 25–37
Shapiro, James, *The Year of Lear* (New York: Simon & Schuster, 2015)
Sharpe, Kevin, and Steven N. Zwicker, "Introduction: Discovering the Renaissance Reader," in *Reading, Society and Politics in Early Modern England*, ed. Kevin Sharpe and Steven N. Zwicker (Cambridge: Cambridge University Press, 2003), pp. 1–37
Sharpe, Will, "Authorship and Attribution," in *William Shakespeare and Others: Collaborative Plays*, ed. Jonathan Bate and Eric Rasmussen with Jan Sewell and Will Sharpe (Basingstoke: Palgrave, 2013), pp. 729–30
Simpson, James, "Ageism: Leland, Bale and the Laborious Start of English Literary History, 1350–1550," *New Medieval Literatures*, 1 (1997), 213–35.
Skerpan-Wheeler, Elizabeth, "The First 'Royal': Charles I as Celebrity," *Papers of the Modern Language Association*, 126.4 (2011), 912–34
Smith, Nigel, "Time Boundaries and Time Shifts in Early Modern Literary Studies," in *Early Modern Histories of Time*, ed. Owen Williams and Kristen Poole (Philadelphia: University of Pennsylvania Press, 2019), pp. 36–53
Smyth, Adam, *"Profit and Delight": Printed Miscellanies in England, 1640–1682* (Detroit: Wayne State University Press, 2004)
"Some Notes for My Perambulations in and round the Citye of London," ed. Martha Carlin, *Shakespeare Documented*, https://shakespearedocumented .folger.edu/resource/document/shakespeare-roisterer-tabard-inn
Sorelius, Gunnar, *'The Giant Race before the Flood': Pre-Restoration Drama on the Stage and in the Criticism of the Restoration* (Uppsala: Almquist & Wiksell, 1966)
Speake, Jennifer, ed., *Oxford Dictionary of Proverbs*, 6th ed. (Oxford: Oxford University Press, 2015)
Spires, Derrick R., "On Liberation Bibliography: The 2021 BSA Annual Meeting Keynote," *Papers of the Bibliographical Society of America*, 116.1 (2022), 1–20
Sprague, Arthur Colby, *Beaumont and Fletcher on the Restoration Stage* (Cambridge, MA: Harvard University Press, 1926)
Steggle, Matthew, *Richard Brome: Place and Politics on the Caroline Stage* (Manchester: Manchester University Press, 2004)
Stephens, Isaac, "Memory's Lash: Staging Parochial Politics in Restoration London"
Stern, Tiffany, *Documents of Performance in Early Modern England* (Cambridge: Cambridge University Press, 2009)
   "'On each Wall and Corner Poast': Playbills, Title-Pages, Advertising in Early Modern London," *English Literary Renaissance*, 36 (2006), 57–85
   "'A Ruinous Monastery': The Second Blackfriars Playhouse as a Place of Nostalgia," in *Moving Shakespeare Indoors*, ed. Andrew Gurr and Farah Karim-Cooper (Cambridge: Cambridge University Press, 2014), pp. 97–114

Stewart, Susan, *On Longing: Narratives of the Miniature, the Gigantic, the Souvenir, the Collection* (Durham: Duke University Press, 1992)

Štollová, Jitka, "'This Silence of the Stage': The Play of Format and Paratext in the Beaumont and Fletcher Folio," *Review of English Studies*, 68.1 (2017), 507–23

Straznicky, Marta, "Introduction," in *The Book of the Play: Playwrights, Stationers, and Readers in Early Modern England*, ed. Marta Straznicky (Amherst: University of Massachusetts Press, 2006), pp. 1–20

　Privacy, Playreading, and Women's Closet Drama, 1550–1700 (Cambridge: Cambridge University Press, 2004)

Suzuki, Mihoko, "Did the English Seventeenth Century Really End at 1660? Subaltern Perspectives on the Continuing Impact of the English Civil Wars," in *Early Modern Histories of Time*, ed. Owen Williams and Kristen Poole (Philadelphia: University of Pennsylvania Press, 2019), pp. 230–49

Taylor, Gary, *Reinventing Shakespeare: A Cultural History from the Restoration to the Present* (London: Hogarth Press, 1990)

Tinniswood, Adrian, *Pirates of Barbary: Conquests and Captivity in the Seventeenth-Century Mediterranean* (New York: Riverhead Books, 2010)

Tregear, Ted, "Music at the Close: *Richard II* in the Elizabethan Anthologies," *Studies in Philology*, 116.4 (2019), 696–727

Tubb, Amos, "Independent Presses: The Politics of Print in England during the Late 1640s," *The Seventeenth Century*, 27 (2012), 287–312

Turner, James Grantham, "'Romance' and the Novel in Restoration England," *Review of English Studies*, 63 (2012), 58–85

Turner, Robert K., *John Fletcher's A King and No King* (Lincoln: University of Nebraska Press, 1963)

Twitchell, James B., *Forbidden Partners: The Incest Taboo in Modern Culture* (New York: Columbia University Press, 1987)

Udall, Joanna, ed., *A Critical, Old-Spelling Edition of The Birth of Merlin* (London: The Modern Humanities Research Association, 1991).

Underwood, Ted, *Why Literary Periods Mattered: Historical Contrast and the Prestige of English Studies* (Stanford: Stanford University Press, 2013)

Vince, Máté, "The Porter and the Jesuits: *Macbeth* and the Forgotten History of Equivocation," *Renaissance Studies*, 35.5 (2021), 838–56

Vine, Angus, *In Defiance of Time: Antiquarian Writing in Early Modern England* (Oxford: Oxford University Press, 2013)

Vitale, Kyle, "A Reverence for Books" (doctoral dissertation, University of Delaware, 2016)

Wagner, Bernard M., "George Jolly at Norwich," *Review of English Studies*, 6.24 (1930), 449–52

Waith, Eugene, *The Pattern of Tragicomedy in Beaumont and Fletcher* (New Haven and Oxford: Yale & Oxford University Presses, 1952)

Wallis, Lawrence Bergmann, *Fletcher, Beaumont and Company, Entertainers to the Jacobean Gentry* (New York: King's Crown Press, 1947)

Walsham, Alexandra, "History, Memory, and the English Reformation," *The Historical Journal*, 55.4 (2012), 899–938

　"Introduction: Relics and Remains," *Past & Present*, 206 (2010), 9–36

Watkins, Stephen, "The Protectorate Playhouse: William Davenant's Cockpit in the 1650s," *Shakespeare Bulletin*, 37.1 (2019), 89–109

Wells, Stanley, and Gary Taylor, eds., *The Oxford Shakespeare* (Oxford: Oxford University Press, 1986)

Wharton, Annabel Jane, *Selling Jerusalem: Relics, Replicas, Theme Parks* (Chicago: University of Chicago Press, 2006)

Whitworth, Charles, ed., *Gammer Gurton's Needle* (London: A&C Black, 1997)

Wickham, Glynne, Herbert Berry, and William Ingram, eds., *English Professional Theatre, 1530–1660, Theatre in Europe: A Documentary History* (Cambridge: Cambridge University Press, 2000)

Wiggins, Martin, "Where to Find Lost Plays," in *Lost Plays in Shakespeare's England*, ed. David McInnis and Matthew Steggle (Basingstoke: Palgrave Macmillan, 2014), pp. 255–78

Wiggins, Martin, and Catherine Richardson, eds., *British Drama 1533–1642: A Catalogue, Vol. 6: 1609–1616* (Oxford: Oxford University Press, 2015)

Wiggins, Martin, and Catherine Richardson, *British Drama 1533–1642: A Catalogue, Vol. 7: 1617–1623* (Oxford: Oxford University Press, 2020)

Wiles, David, "Medieval, Renaissance and Early Modern Theatre," in *The Cambridge Companion to Theatre History*, ed. David Wiles and Christine Dymkowski (Cambridge: Cambridge University Press, 2012), pp. 55–72

Williams, William Proctor, "What's a Lost Play?: Toward a Taxonomy of Lost Plays," in *Lost Plays in Shakespeare's England*, ed. David McInnis and Matthew Steggle (Basingstoke: Palgrave Macmillan, 2014), pp. 17–30

Willie, Rachel, "Sacrificial Kings and Martyred Rebeles: Charles and Rainborowe beatified," *Etudes Episteme (Special Issue on Regicide)*, 20 (2011), https://doi.org/10.4000/episteme.428

Staging the Revolution: Drama, Reinvention and History, 1647–72 (Manchester: Manchester University Press, 2015)

Wiseman, Susan, *Drama and Politics in the English Civil War* (Cambridge: Cambridge University Press, 1998)

Wooding, Barbara, *John Lowin and the English Theatre, 1603–1647: Acting and Cultural Politics on the Jacobean and Caroline Stage* (Surrey: Ashgate, 2013)

Woolf, Daniel, *The Social Circulation of the Past: English Historical Culture, 1500–1730* (Oxford: Oxford University Press, 2003)

Wright, Louis B., "The Reading of Plays during the Puritan Revolution," *The Huntington Library Bulletin*, 6 (1934), 73–108

Wrightson, Keith, "The Enclosure of English Social History," *Rural History*, 1.1 (1990), 73–82

Zimmerman, Susan, *The Early Modern Corpse and Shakespeare's Theatre* (Edinburgh: Edinburgh University Press, 2005)

Zerubavel, Eviator, *Time Maps* (Chicago: University of Chicago Press, 2003)

Zwicker, Steven N., *Lines of Authority: Politics and English Literary Culture, 1649–1689* (Ithaca: Cornell University Press, 1993)

Index

Any dates supplied in parentheses next to titles refer to date of publication, unless otherwise specified. Although most publications are listed under their authors' names (if known), for cases in which the identity of an edition's publisher is significant to the discussion, that stationer's name is noted. Anonymous works and plays or editions discussed at length in the book are indexed under their titles.

All people from the early modern period are given an identifier in parentheses (e.g., "stationer"). This not only provides additional information, but also distinguishes the names of historical figures from those of modern critics, who are given no such descriptor.

In all subheadings, the Beaumont and Fletcher 1647 folio, *Comedies and Tragedies*, is referred to as "B&F folio (1647)."

234